Recovered Memories

and

False Memories

D0221818

DEBATES IN PSYCHOLOGY

Martin Conway (ed.) Recovered Memories and False Memories

Recovered Memories
and
False Memories

Edited by

MARTIN A. CONWAY

Department of Psychology
University of Bristol

WARNER MEMORIAL LIBRARY
EASTERN COLLEGE
ST. DAVIDS, PA. 19087

Oxford   New York   Tokyo
OXFORD UNIVERSITY PRESS
1997

9-29-98

Oxford University Press, Great Clarendon Street, Oxford OX2 6DP
Oxford New York
Athens Auckland Bangkok Bogota Bombay Buenos Aires
Calcutta Cape Town Dar es Salaam Delhi Florence Hong Kong
Istanbul Karachi Kuala Lumpur Madras Madrid Melbourne
Mexico City Nairobi Paris Singapore Taipei Tokyo Toronto
and associated companies in
Berlin Ibadan

Oxford is a trade mark of Oxford University Press

Published in the United States
by Oxford University Press Inc., New York

© Oxford University Press, 1997

All rights reserved. No part of this publication may be reproduced, stored in a retrieval
system, or transmitted, in any form or by any means, without the prior permission in writing
of Oxford University Press. Within the UK, exceptions are allowed in respect of any fair
dealing for the purpose of research or private study, or criticism or review, as permitted under
the Copyright, Designs and Patents Act, 1988, or in the case of reprographic reproduction in
accordance with the terms of licences issued by the Copyright Licensing Agency. Enquiries
concerning reproduction outside those terms and in other countries should be sent to the Rights
Department, Oxford University Press, at the address above.

This book is sold subject to the condition that it shall not, by way of trade or otherwise, be
lent, re-sold, hired out, or otherwise circulated without the publisher's prior consent in any form
of binding or cover other than that in which it is published and without a similar condition
including this condition being imposed on the subsequent purchaser.

A catalogue record for this book is available from the British Library

Library of Congress Cataloging in Publication Data
(Data available)

ISBN 0 19 852387 4 (Hbk)
0 19 852386 6 (Pbk)

Typeset by Hewer Text Composition Services, Edinburgh

Printed in Great Britain by
Biddles Ltd, Guildford & King's Lynn

RC 455.2 .F35 R426 1997

Recovered memories and false
memories

Acknowledgement

The original idea for the present volume came from Professor Larry Weiskrantz of the Department of Psychology, University of Oxford. The editor and authors thank Professor Weiskrantz for providing them with the opportunity to present papers on this important area.

Contents

Contributors

Zara Ambadar 635 L.R.D.C., 3939 O'Hara Street, University of Pittsburgh, Pittsburgh, PA 15260, USA.

Bernice Andrews Department of Psychology, Royal Holloway, University of London, Egham, Surrey TW20 0EX, UK.

Miriam Bendiksen 635 L.R.D.C., 3939 O'Hara Street, University of Pittsburgh, Pittsburgh, PA 15260, USA.

Chris R. Brewin Department of Psychology, Royal Holloway, University of London, Egham, Surrey TW20 0EX, UK.

Sven-Åke Christianson
Department of Psychology, University of Stockholm, S-106 91, Stockholm, Sweden.

Martin A. Conway
Department of Psychology, University of Bristol, 8 Woodland Road, Bristol BS8 1TN, UK.

Christine A. Courtois
Independent Practice, Three Washington Circle, Suite 206, Washington, DC 20037, USA.

Elisabeth Engelberg
Department of Psychology, University of Stockholm, S-106 91, Stockholm, Sweden.

Robyn Fivush Department of Psychology, Emory University, Atlanta, GA 30322, USA.

Lyn M. Goff
Department of Psychology, Box 1125, Washington University, One Brookings Drive, St Louis, MO 63130-4899, USA.

John F. Kihlstrom
Department of Psychology, Yale University, PO Box 208205, New Haven, CT 06520-8205, USA.

Wilma Koutstaal
Department of Psychology, Harvard University, William James Hall, 33 Kirkland Street, Cambridge, MA 02138, USA.

Kathleen B. McDermott
Washington University School of Medicine, Division of Radiological Sciences, 4525 Scott Avenue, Campus Box 8225, St Louis, MO 63110, USA.

Tamar Murachver
Department of Psychology, University of Otago, POB 56, Dunedin, New Zealand.

Kenneth A. Norman
Department of Psychology, Harvard University, William James Hall, 33 Kirkland Street, Cambridge, MA 02138, USA.

Margaret-Ellen Pipe
Department of Psychology, University of Otago, POB 56, Dunedin, New Zealand.

Elaine Reese
Department of Psychology, University of Otago, POB 56, Dunedin, New Zealand.

Henry L. Roediger, III
Department of Psychology, Box 1125, Washington University, One Brookings Drive, St Louis, MO 63130-4899, USA.

Daniel L. Schacter
Department of Psychology, Harvard University, William James Hall, 33 Kirkland Street, Cambridge, MA 02138, USA.

Jonathan W. Schooler
635 L.R.D.C., 3939 O'Hara Street, University of Pittsburgh, Pittsburgh, PA 15260, USA.

Michael Yapko
The Milton H. Erickson Institute of San Diego, 462 Stevens Ave., Ste. 309, Solana Beach, CA 92075-2066, USA.

ONE

Introduction: what are memories?

MARTIN A. CONWAY

From birth . . . the human being is concerned with the problem
of the relationship between what is objectively perceived and
what is subjectively conceived of . . . (Winnicott 1953, p. 11)

At the centre of the *recovered memory debate* is a dialogue between
psychotherapists and memory researchers concerning the veridicality of human
memory. When treating psychological illnesses psychotherapists often have to
explore a patient's past, sometimes confronting memories of troublesome or
traumatic experiences that date from earlier in the patient's life and frequently
from childhood. Such memories may not initially present as memories of difficult
experiences; as the therapy proceeds the patient may recall other long-forgotten
but related memories and, in what appears to be a very small proportion of
patients, memories of physical, emotional, psychological, and sexual abuse may
be suddenly and surprisingly remembered. But the techniques used by some
psychotherapists, hypnosis, imagery, and other memory 'recovery' practices,
coupled with a belief that the causes of current psychological distress lie in
a patient's past, put in place a context that promotes memory fabrication. A
vast body of research from the psychological laboratory and, increasingly, from
more real-world studies demonstrates that human memories are inaccurate,
incomplete, open to distortion, and wholesale fabrication (see Schacter *et al.*,
Chapter 4 this volume for a comprehensive critical appraisal of this work).
Indeed, experimentally inducing false memories in healthy young adults
appears almost trivially easy (cf. Hyman and Billings 1996; Hyman *et al.*
1996; Roediger *et al.*, Chapter 6 this volume), the implication being that in
the context of therapy, with a patient who is psychologically dysfunctional and
actively seeking help, the probability of memory distortion and fabrication is
multiplied many times over.

The hard edge of this debate and the point at which it intersects with society
generally is in the recall of memories of abuse, particularly childhood sexual
abuse. When such memories are recovered, either prior to or during therapy,
then a series of ethical and legal questions necessarily follow. The significance
of these questions rests on whether the memories are true or not and, if true,
whether they are accurate. Given that we know that memories can be inaccurate
and wholly false there is cause for real concern: concern that victims of abuse
may not be heard, because their memories are incorrectly judged false or,
on the other hand, concern that memory fabrication may lead to innocent

citizens being falsely labelled abusers. Thus, knowing that memories can be false, although obviously useful, does not get us very far in identifying and treating the abused and the abusers. As Michael Yapko comments in his excellent review of the problems in this area: 'To hold *any* position that fully excludes other possibilities simply seems unreasonable at this point in time' (Yapko, Chapter 2 this volume). How are we to advance? It seems to me that the only sure way forward is by research. We need more data, of a high quality, some sharp theoretical thinking, and explicit professional guidelines. To achieve these goals psychotherapists and memory researchers will have to collaborate (cf. Engelberg and Christianson, Chapter 10, and Schooler *et al.*, Chapter 11 this volume). A central aim of the present volume is to initiate this collaboration and, accordingly, contributors were asked to make strong but non-adversarial theoretical statements, describe new research directions, and make recommendations for improved clinical practice. One issue that the whole enterprise turns upon is our understanding of just what sorts of entities human memories are. Of course we already have extensive knowledge about memories, but the question of exactly what memories are is, surprisingly, only rarely asked by memory researchers and even less frequently considered by psychotherapists (but see Freud 1990, 1924; Kris 1956). As this question lies behind all the chapters in this volume I shall take it as a starting point to this introductory overview and first examine several general properties of memories.

WHAT ARE MEMORIES?

A memory metaphor of many centuries standing is the *spatial metaphor* (Roediger 1980; Roediger *et al.*, Chapter 6 this volume). In one of its most popular forms the spatial metaphor likens memory to a library: individual memories are the volumes on the shelves and an index helps a user (a rememberer) locate sought-for volumes (memories). When a book (memory) is located then it can be taken down from its shelf and read (remembering). The library metaphor, simple as it is, can be used to 'explain' (actually, 'recast' would be a better term) various aspects of memory. For example, from time to time volumes may be misplaced on the shelves, parts of the index corrupted, or a new volume incorrectly indexed. All of which would render specific volumes inaccessible or forgotten. Similarly, as the collection grows it becomes more effortful to search the increasingly lengthy index and to wearily inspect the many rows of shelved volumes. And it is always easier to locate the volumes most recently entered, perhaps the ink has yet to dry and fade in the index for these most recent additions: which could explain difficulties in retrieving remote memories compared with the ease of recollection of recent experience. We could take the library metaphor one step further and imagine that the librarian also acts as censor. She believes that there are some works that are simply too strong for the user of the library and although she puts the volumes on the shelves she does not enter their identifiers in the index. In order to find these volumes/memories the user/rememberer has to be lucky or be given assistance by an external agency: an agency that specializes in the ways of librarians and which knows where librarians typically put those volumes they have censored.

It often comes as a surprise to learn that the library metaphor and indeed the spatial metaphor itself is a hopelessly inadequate account of human memory. But inadequate it is, and, what is worse, it leads its adherents into mistaken assumptions about memories and remembering. Let us consider a brief selection of aspects of memory that are problematic for the memories-as-objects-in-a-store view. Take the case of patients who, following brain injury to the frontal lobes, confabulate memories (see Stuss and Benson 1986 for a review). Such patients sometimes describe at length and in detail experiences that are totally false. Interestingly, however, confabulations often feature actors, actions, and locations, which could plausibly have occurred and which are in fact from the patient's past. When confronted with their confabulated memories patients may deny that they ever recalled such memories (Baddeley and Wilson 1986) or they may stick to their story even in the face of strong contradictory evidence (cf. Moscovitch 1995). For such memories to occur it is clear that knowledge must be retrieved from long-term memory and then *constructed* into a representation which is the memory in that particular processing task. There are no books (memories) that can be taken down from the shelves (accessed) that could provide such false stories (rememberings). Instead, an account of confabulated memories requires some conception of how central control processes coordinate output from long-term memory and construct this into a memory (Burgess and Shallice 1996; Conway 1996a; Conway and Tacchi 1996; Moscovitch 1989, 1995).

Next consider a normal healthy person asked to retrieve a memory to a cue word – a popular procedure in autobiographical memory research (Conway and Bekerian 1987; Crovitz and Schiffman 1974; Robinson 1976; see Conway 1990 for a review). The individual is presented with the word *ship* and immediately responds with 'Oh yes, we took a cross-channel ferry last year when we went to France'. Another participant in the same experiment responds 'This was from a holiday I had in Greece when I was student. I remember lying on the top deck of a ferry going from the port of X to the Island of Y. I remember how warm the sun felt'. Yet another individual comments 'I remember I used to be fascinated by the big ships in the port of "X" when I was a child'. (These are actual responses by individuals taking part in autobiographical memory experiments in our laboratory.) What are we to make of the variable levels of specificity in each of these memory reports? It seems clear that the first respondent is not recalling a detailed memory but instead has something more general in mind. Which is not to deny that this respondent could not have developed her memory further and produced something much more detailed that we might have been willing to accept as a specific memory; it might be noted here that some (organic) amnesic patients have problems going beyond this stage (Conway 1993, 1996b) as do patients suffering from clinical levels of depression (cf. Williams 1996 for a review). The second respondent clearly has something approximating a specific memory; however, it is interesting to note that his memory includes more abstract information (when he was a student, a holiday in Greece) alongside specific details (the Greek ferry, the name of the port and island, the warmth of the sunshine). The response of the third participant seems altogether different, hardly a specific memory at all. Instead this person appears to be recalling a schematized set of experiences, a type of factual autobiographical knowledge (cf. Conway 1987), rather than a unique experience.

These levels of specificity in autobiographical memory recall provide us with a glimpse of the underlying organization of autobiographical knowledge. Many experiments have explored this further and concluded that autobiographical knowledge is represented in hierarchical knowledge structures organized around personal themes and goals that characterize various periods of a person's life. The knowledge structures represent knowledge from the most abstract or inclusive, for example *when I was at school*, to the most specific and least inclusive, for example an image of a classroom. Knowledge held at different levels can be used to access knowledge held at other levels. The whole system is exquisitely sensitive to incoming information, and patterns of activation constantly arise and dissipate within the knowledge structures – in a sense we are constantly reminded (Conway 1996a). But in order for a memory to be constructed, central control processes most coordinate and modulate the patterns of activation arising in the knowledge base. A basic function of such processes is to ensure that the endogenously arising patterns of activation in long-term memory do not *automatically* enter control processing sequences where they would disrupt performance. Indeed, when a memory does 'pop' into to mind the rememberer usually has to devote scarce cognitive resources to interpreting and understanding the spontaneously constructed memory.

Recent work in progress in our laboratory suggests that memory construction can be impaired in interesting ways when retrieval is accompanied by a demand to perform a secondary task. For instance, when a secondary task entails visual processing then memories are dominated by the retrieval of more abstract information. In contrast, if memory retrieval runs concurrently with a secondary task that takes up central control processing capacity then retrieval is dramatically slowed. Other current work that also implicates control processes focuses on how easily a memory can be held in mind. Our initial findings indicate that this is difficult and effortful. When a memory is fully recalled and then held in mind parts of it quickly begin to fade and must be recalled again, attention wavers and must be consciously refocused, and participants soon abandon the task. Finally our work in progress has also found that when the same memory is recalled on subsequent occasions the content of the memory varies. Only about 60 per cent of content is the same from one recall to the next, demonstrating an instability in the content of memories. This latter finding further suggests that memory construction is mediated by control processes which vary from one recall to the next and use different cues to probe autobiographical knowledge on different occasions of retrieval.

These types of findings, and there are many more from many different areas of memory research, the selective sample here is merely for illustrative purposes, definitively show us that memories are not like objects in a store nor is there anything approximating to a simple index. Instead, memories are dynamic mental constructions created by central processes modulating the activation of knowledge in long-term memory. A memory is 'retrieved' once a stable pattern of activation has been established across the indices of long-term autobiographical memory knowledge structures and a memory consists of this pattern *and* the particular set of control processes that guided construction (see Conway 1996*a*, and this volume). Despite the dynamic, transitory, and centrally modulated nature of memories once a memory has been constructed it exists, albeit for a short period of time, as a mental state or mental object. A rememberer can make judgments of this object, have attitudes and feelings toward it, in short the rememberer can relate to the memory. What sort of relations might a rememberer have with a memory? Here I want to briefly consider two potential relations between memories and rememberer (aware that there are undoubtedly many others).

The first is that *a constructed memory grounds the self*. By this I mean that once a memory is constructed it constrains the range of possible selves (Markus and Nurius 1986) and self-discrepancies (Higgins 1987) that can be plausibly held by the current self. For instance, a patient who recalls an episode or episodes of abuse cannot maintain a possible self in which they were not a victim. Such a grounding has many psychological entailments including a constriction of the range of possible selves a person might have been or could become. The discrepancies that emerge from such a grounding, for example between the self one should have been and self one is, further proscribe the range of plans and goals available to the individual. A final interesting, but speculative, point arising out of this line of reasoning is that because memories limit the self of the rememberer they might be likened to other objects that also influence the self, i.e. significant others such as parents, spouse, children, etc. Perhaps, just as people interact with others in their lives so they can interact in at least partly similar ways with their memories, i.e. by accepting the implications of some memories while rejecting the imperatives of others (cf. Barclay 1996).

The second is that *a memory must be known (to the rememberer) as a memory*. This is a source monitoring issue (cf. Johnson *et al.* 1993) which highlights the types of judgments a rememberer has to make of a memory. Essentially the rememberer has somehow to be able to categorize their own mental state or mental construction as being a construction of a particular type. How we distinguish between, for instance, wishes, dreams, thoughts, lies, images, and memories is currently unknown, although Johnson and her colleagues have made some progress on this problem (Johnson *et al.* 1993; see too Conway and Tacchi 1996). It is nevertheless now clear that this is a complex processes that can be prone to error, involving assessment of the content of activated knowledge, assessment of the type of knowledge, and metamemory judgments based, amongst other things, on the phenomenal experience that accompanies any given mental state (Conway *et al.* 1996). Mental constructions are then states that have to be classified. A pattern of activated long-term knowledge might be a memory, or it could be something from several other varieties of mental constructions, wishes, dreams, etc. Thus, a major task for the rememberer is to appropriately identify a mental state as a memory. This can be problematic when there is little in the mental construction to distinguish it from other types of constructions (cf. Conway *et al.* 1996), when the modulating influence of control processes are disrupted as occurs in frontal lobe pathology, and perhaps in other situations where, for instance, construction of a memory might help to explain current psychological distress (Conway and Tacchi 1996).

RECOVERED MEMORIES AND FALSE MEMORIES

Developing more articulate models of what memories might be is crucial to the resolution of the recovered memory debate. There are, however, other phenomena revealed by the debate that are arguably of equal importance and which will also require our attention if we are to gain a fuller understanding of what takes place in therapy. Michael Yapko conceives the debate revolving around three issues: memory, trauma, and suggestibility. Yapko argues that there is growing evidence that memories for trauma are different from memories for other types of experience. I think there is little doubt that he is correct on this point (cf. Christianson 1992; Conway 1995; McGaugh 1995). But Yapko is equally correct in questioning how much we currently know about memories for traumatic experiences other than they appear highly durable and may be unusually detailed. For example, what are the forgetting rates for memories of trauma? Do these reflect the operation of defensive processes or do they reflect the operation of general forgetting processes? Another assumption is that during the experience of trauma the individual may 'dissociate', so that although the event may be encoded it is encoded in such a way as to render it inaccessible to conscious awareness. But do all individuals do this? Each to the same extent? Does dissociation occur during the experience or is the repression imposed shorty after? In the case of repeated abuse if dissociative processes are operative at encoding are they equally operative in all episodes? Why do many trauma victims actually have intrusive flashbacks rather then repressed dissociated memories? Is what is repressed in childhood traumas not just the memories but the whole post-traumatic stress disorder (PTSD) response such that memory recovery would then allow the PTSD process to take place? We simply do not have good answers to these questions. Individual differences in response to trauma have not yet been studied and so, as Yapko concludes, we can do little but keep open minds and search for disambiguating evidence.

Yapko's emphasis on suggestibility is, in my judgment, particularly timely and perspicacious. Suggestibility in psychotherapy has not been a topic much discussed, nor have memory researchers investigated how suggestibility might influence the processes of memory construction. There can be little doubt that some patients in psychotherapy are in a highly suggestible state and eventually come to have 'memories' which are false, often implausibly and fantastically false (cf. Ofshe and Watters 1994, for a much remarked on case). It is also possible that suggestibility may play an important role in inducing false memories in certain recent memory experiments. It is instructive to note that averaging across studies (e.g. Ceci 1995; Hyman *et al.* 1996) about one-third of all participants develop fabricated memories. One is reminded here of the seminal investigations of Asch (1940, 1956) and his colleagues into the effects of group conformity on perceptual judgments. Asch (1952) found that when individuals were asked to judge the relative lengths of lines in a display, their judgment could be forced to diverge from the actual length of the lines if other individuals in the group in which they participated all judged a particular line to be the longest or shortest (even though it quite clearly was not). Up to one-third of all participants in the original studies conformed to the group judgment rather than reality on over 50 per cent of trials. Interestingly this powerful effect of conformity shows large individual variation and can be dramatically diminished if the group shows anything less than unanimity or if the conforming participant is provided with a non-conforming partner who responds accurately to the stimuli. The conclusions that emerged from the extensive series of investigations of conformity in this type of laboratory task were that conformity increase as: (a) a judgment is difficult or ambiguous, (b) an individual feels attracted to the group which is itself perceived as tightly cohesive, (c) members of the group are perceived as competent or experts and the individual is incompetent or a novice, and (d) the individual's responses are made public to other group members. It should also be noted that further work established that there may be a conforming personality who is particularly responsive and who readily conforms to these types of group pressures (Crutchfield 1955). The parallel between group conformity effects with patients in psychotherapy and in certain types of memory experiments is clear and demands our attention. From the point of view of laboratory-based investigation the relation between conformity and memory performance appears readily tractable. Similarly, extremely useful information might be gained by viewing group therapy sessions in the light of the conformity findings, even the dyadic group of therapist (expert) and patient (novice) might benefit from such a perspective.

Yapko's summary of what is know and unknown in the three areas of memory, trauma, and suggestibility, is both salutary and refreshing. His recommendation that given the current ambiguities and lack of knowledge further research should proceed on a case-by-case basis is wholly appropriate. Indeed, researchers concerned with recovered memories and the nature of memory in trauma and psychotherapy more widely, might well take their cue from the now rapidly advancing area of neuropsychology. In neuropsychology the case study has played a major role in opening up the area and in bringing to light memory phenomena (as well as other cognitive phenomena) that have led to important insights into memory functions, particularly functions to do with the nature of memory systems and the relationship between conscious awareness and memory. These issues are appraised in considerable detail in Chapter 4 by Schacter *et al.*, but before considering their perspective, we must address a further 'troublesome unknown': memory in childhood. Fivush *et al.* review in Chapter 2 the substantial body of evidence that currently shows that children and infants have far better developed long-term memories than previously thought. For example, Rovee-Collier and her colleagues have shown that an infant only a few days old is selectively responsive to its mother's voice (cf. Rovee-Collier and Shyi 1992 for a review) demonstrating that the infant must have *in utero* memory for the mother's voice. Other work reviewed by Fivush and her coauthors shows that infants have memories during their preverbal period which are expressed behaviourally. Later when a child enters the verbal period, from about 18 months of age, the verbal child shows strong evidence of remembering events that occurred in the preverbal period, although these are not expressible in language. Once children enter the period when they are aged two to five years they have many verbally reportable memories. Fivush and her colleagues provide evidence that one important basis for this emerging ability lies in verbal interchanges, particularly with adults, that help provide a structure for memories. Indeed, they propose that adult narration gives the child an organizing scheme that can later be used by the child to process many different types of events. In relation to this they describe the work of Goodman and her colleagues (for example Goodman *et al.* 1994) demonstrating that the accuracy and detail of children's memories for a painful medical procedure is determined by the child's understanding of the procedure and by parental willingness to talk about the experience. Fivush *et al.* are also somewhat sceptical about the suggestibility of children's memories. They point out that children below five years of age are not particularly prone to the effects of post-event information and that they recall everyday events accurately in some considerable detail. Nevertheless, the recall of preschool children does benefit noticeably when a cue is presented and this suggests that young children, who are after all novice rememberers, have yet to develop fluency in self-generating their own cues. Finally, it seems clear that there must be large individual differences in the development of memory dependent upon the quality of parent–child (verbal) interactions concerning past experiences. Children who do not have elaborated conversation with their parents or with other adults about shared experiences will develop detailed and cohesive memories less quickly than children who do talk with adults about the past. Children deprived in this way will take longer to develop the organizing long-term memory structures in which to encode experience and so will have impoverished childhood memories.

These recent findings of active and responsive memories in neonates, infants, and children below the age of five years are of particular relevance to the recovered memory debate as they show that young children have memories for the earliest of ages and that behaviour can be influenced by memories from the preverbal period. They also demonstrate that language and comprehension play important roles in the development of something like a fully articulated autobiographical memory. The view that children have detailed and durable memories is a comparatively new development and one which has arisen only in the last 15 years or so. Prior to this it seems that interest in the nature of an early emerging memory system was at least partly occluded by the phenomenon of infantile or childhood amnesia (see Pillemer and White 1989 for a review). The term childhood amnesia refers to the fact that very few adults can recall more than a handful of events from when they were aged below about five years (cf. Rubin *et al.* 1986; Wetzler and Nebes 1986). Thus, the older child and the adult cannot rememberer what they were able to remember when they were aged five years and younger. If we assume that this is not because these memories have been forgotten but rather because they have become inaccessible, i.e. the older child and adult can no longer generate cues effective in accessing this knowledge, then it follows that there may well be a quite substantial pool of memories that could potentially be retrieved if the appropriate cues could be located. Related to this is an intriguing (informal) observation that by no means all detailed knowledge relating to the period when a rememberer was aged nought to five years becomes inaccessible with age. In our own (unpublished) studies of recall from childhood we have found that although adults typically can recall very few memories of specific events with certainty they can none the less recall in very specific detail various locations, people, and activities that occurred during the period covered by childhood amnesia. For instance, the recall of details of houses lived in, houses of relations, nursery schools, places visited on holidays, images of parents, siblings, grandparents and other relations, various play activities, Christmas presents, and parks frequently visited, all experienced below the age of five years appear to be recalled in considerable details by adults. This discrepancy between good recall of many areas of preschool experience with poor recall of specific events is not one that has been formally investigated. Given that we now know that preschool children must have had plenty of memories in the preschool period it is doubly curious that as adults they should retain what appears to be good access to non-event information but only impoverished access to memories of specific events: memories that that were once fully accessible. This is clearly a conundrum which will require further research. But what we now know of preschooler's memories, elegantly reviewed and evaluated by Fivush *et al.*, is that they exist, they are closely related to conceptual schemes provided by adults in verbal interactions, and that they endure certainly through the preschool period and probably into later years. The exact point of age-of-onset of childhood amnesia, which is a phenomenon shown only by adults, is unknown although a recent longitudinal study (Fivush 1994) and other recent findings discussed by Fivush *et al.* suggest that this may be far later than previously suspected.

So far we have been mainly concerned with the conscious recollection of memories of specific events, but there are other types of knowledge and other types of remembering. In Chapter 4 Schacter *et al.* give a comprehensive and authoritative review of current findings that includes very valuable coverage of data and theory from neuropsychological and neurobiological investigations of memory. They focus on the three core issues of forgetting, distortion, and accuracy, and they raise a number of issues of especial relevance to the recovered memory debate. For instance, when comparing organic and psychogenic amnesia they note that the daily lives of neurologically injured patients with functional retrograde amnesia are completely disrupted. But such disruption is not present in patients who later recover memories of childhood sexual abuse (CSA) or even satanic ritual abuse. Outside the context of therapy these patients are often able to conduct their daily affairs. Quite clearly, then, psychogenic amnesia associated with memory recovery must differ from functional amnesia arising from brain injury. Moreover, for memory recovery of a small number of events, for example one or two, there is little reason to postulate any special memory mechanisms. Our current understanding of human memory can provide good accounts of how this may occur. Amnesia for many experiences and whole time periods cannot, however, be easily accounted for by current models of memory and it may be that new research and new theory will be required here (for two interesting recent case studies see Treadway *et al.*, (1992); Conway (1993, 1996*b*) reviews a range of case studies of neurological impairments of autobiographical memory).

Schacter *et al.*'s review of the neurochemical and neuroanatomical bases of traumatic memories is appropriately cautious. Their conclusion from the literature that the amygdala may be the site that modulates emotional influences upon the formation of memories is of some interest. The amygdala is in the limbic system and is closely associated with the hippocampus, an area now generally acknowledged to mediate the formation of the framework or outline of memories (Squire 1992). One possibility is that the processes supported by the amygdala influence the operation of the hippocampus or associated neorcortical areas in the formation of vivid memories of emotional experience (cf. Conway 1995). In their treatment of implicit memory, an area of some current interest to recovered memory theorists, Schacter *et al.* acknowledge that certain types of behaviour certainly could arise from autobiographical knowledge currently in long-term memory but not directly available to conscious recollection. Again, however, they recommend caution in interpreting behaviour in terms of implicit memory, i.e. inferring from a symptom that a certain type of experience must have occurred and that there must be some sort of memory for this experience. Implicit memory is not the panacea it may at first seem, and there is considerable debate amongst memory researchers over the theoretical basis of implicit memory findings. Some researchers have held to the view that implicit memory may reflect the operation of a *pre-semantic* system (Schacter and Tulving 1994). If this view is correct then it is unlikely that inaccessible 'memories' (in the sense of memories for discrete events) underlie implicit memory effects.

Schacter *et al.* also examine the now many studies of *source monitoring* (Johnson *et al.* 1993), which is one of the areas to which recovered memory researchers should be paying considerable attention. Source monitoring refers to a person's ability to accurately remember the source of an experience. Consider for example an experience we perhaps have all had: one recalls a very early memory from childhood, but cannot decide whether it is memory of an actual experience, a story often told by one's family, or some mixture of both. Such source monitoring questions are a fairly frequent part of everyday experience. An individual may leave her office, home, or car only to wonder whether she locked the door. This person may have an image in mind of the door locked, they know they would have intended to lock the door, at the time of departure they may have briefly, barely consciously, had an anticipatory image of locking the door. But after departing cannot accurately discriminate between their previous intention and action. Discriminating between different mental states is far more fallible and less accurate than one might think. Schacter *et al.* describe the relatively simple experiment of Roediger and McDermott (1995) (this is expanded upon in detail in Chapter 6) in which people were shown sets of words that implied another word which was not shown, for example petrol, steering-wheel, transport, road, drive, and not shown, car (referred to as the 'critical non-studied item'). Later when asked to recognize the words studied previously but now presented in the context of some new words plus the critical non-studied item, people reliably falsely recognize the critical non-studied item and often claimed that they consciously remembered its presentation in the previous lists. Undoubtedly when the original lists of words were studied each person would have thought, maybe even consciously, of the critical non-presented word. Later when taking the recognition test people are unable to accurately judge the source of the memory, i.e. whether they thought or read the word, but as they know they did something with the word they infer that it must have been presented. The power of source monitoring errors in the generation of false memories, especially in a context such as therapy, cannot be underestimated. As Schacter *et al.* conclude, memories can be accurate, in the sense that they refer at an abstract level to an experience, yet can at the same time contain many details that arise from source monitoring errors rather than actual experience. This must be especially true for an abused child who dissociates during the experience of abuse, is prevented from talking about the experiences, and who may not in any case have comprehension of what is occurring other then negative emotions. One implication of this is that errors in a memory, perhaps arising from failures of source monitoring, by no means indicate that the rememberer did not experience the event recalled. There is a difference between an event recalled and an event recalled *as* (cf. Wittgenstein

1953) or, put another way, between recalling that one has experienced something and recalling the details.

Kihlstrom too (Chapter 5) makes extensive use of the concept of implicit memory and how this may be conceived of as a modern counterpart to Freud's (1915) notion of the *return of the repressed*. By Freud's view when psychological defences failed then repressed materials could once again be activated. These mental contents cannot, however, be allowed to enter conscious awareness (to be constructed into, perhaps, memories) because of the threat that they would impose to the integrity of the whole system and are, consequently, repressed again. A result of this repression is the emergence of what Freud called substitutive formations and symptoms. Freud's views here may seem relatively straightforward but, as is often the case in his theorizing, there are complexities not immediately apparent. To begin with what Freud meant by the term 'memories', although initially corresponding to something like the library metaphor discussed earlier, rapidly developed into a more dynamic model which shares at least some features with the view of memories stated in the preceding section of this introduction. In Chapter 7 of the *Interpretations of dreams* (1900) Freud developed a complex model of memories and their interactions with perception and control processes. Thus, what Freud meant by the return of the repressed does *not* correspond to any simple idea of the reactivation of long-dormant memories. As Kihlstrom correctly points out, it is this simple memory-as-library view that informs the modern version of the return of the repressed. Moreover, for Freud after 1900 the issue of whether memories were accurate or inaccurate, although still of interest, was secondary to the work they could support in analysis.

One of Kihlstrom's main points is that in the modern version of the return of the repressed there is the potential for the fatal reasoning error of *affirming the consequent*. For instance, if a patient presents with a certain symptom and the therapist believes that symptom to be associated with, say, CSA, and then infers that the patient has in fact suffered CSA and as part of the treatment must recover the inaccessible memories of abuse, that therapist has made the logical error of affirming the consequent. In this case the consequent being the assertion that symptom 'X' is a feature of CSA psychopathology. Interestingly Freud himself was well aware of this potential error and in his study *The psychogenesis of a case of homosexuality in a woman* (1920) he poses the question: if all we knew were the infantile and childhood experiences of this patient could we predict her adult pathology? Freud's answer to this question was 'No'. The return of the repressed occurs in the context of an individual personal history and can only be studied in that context. Which is not to deny the validity of abstract theoretical propositions drawn from case studies but rather to emphasize the individual and personal context in which the effects of a personal and unique past manifest themselves. Kihlstrom's emphasis on treating cases individually and in searching for external corroborative evidence for abuse is, then, well judged. Also his aliasing of the return of the repressed with implicit memory is both useful and, in this treatment, retains the view that memories are constructed from many different sorts of knowledge. Of course, this requires a development of our understanding of the term 'implicit' memory if it is to be used to encompass declarative, pre-semantic, and procedural knowledge. But perhaps here is the point where the study of recovered memory can help shape our understanding of memory more generally. If repressed memories can influence cognition and behaviour then this is clearly an implicit effect which requires us to revise our current conceptualization of implicit memory, as Kihlstrom's chapter implies.

Amnesia, source monitoring, and implicit memory are all areas that can help in significant ways to develop our conceptualizations of memory recovery and accuracy. There are, however, other equally significant lines of laboratory research that are especially relevant to the issue of memory recovery and Roediger *et al.* in Chapter 6 provide a particularly important perspective on the phenomenon of *reminiscence*. All rememberers have experienced reminiscence in everyday conversations, perhaps around the dinner table, in discussions with family members, or in other social interactions. Reminiscence may also occur when an individual dwells or ruminates on their past and even the special case of suddenly and surprisingly being reminded of some long 'forgotten' event by a specific cue might be classed as reminiscence. In the laboratory, reminiscence is operationally measured by the additional information recalled on successive occasions of retrieval. Roediger *et al.* describe the fascinating findings from their group and others demonstrating that reminiscence occurs across a wide range of different experimental manipulations. Their conclusion is that across repeated episodes of remembering reminiscence is ubiquitous. In some respects this is good news for those therapeutic interventions that rely upon uncovering materials from the past that are not currently available to a patient. The knowledge that emerges in naturally occurring episodes of reminiscence in therapy may be useful in providing cues to access yet other areas of autobiographical knowledge and so by repeated reminiscence materials can be uncovered that may help a patient gain insight into their current predicament. Despite the robustness of reminiscence phenomena in the laboratory Roediger *et al.* are cautious, even pessimistic, about the generalization of these to very long retention intervals. The jump from laboratory demonstration to application in, for example, psychotherapy is not one that should be made lightly. Consider, for example, a rather less favourable finding of Roediger and his group. Repeated recall as well as promoting reminiscence also enhances recall of accurate information and *at the same time* recall of inaccurate information. Indeed, when an item erroneously recalled as having been previously studied is later recalled again, then confidence in the accuracy of the erroneously recalled item *increases*. No leap of the imagination is required to see how this process could, potentially, operate in the creation of inaccurate and even wholly false memories. Moreover, instructions to guess have an additional detrimental effect on memory accuracy. Guessing does not improve accuracy but does increase confusion on the part of the rememberer as to which of the correctly recalled materials are or are not accurate. These are salutary findings that suggest extreme caution should be exercised in eliciting both specific memories and details from memories. Roediger *et al.* conclude their chapter with a particularly illuminating discussion of the spatial metaphor of memory and make a telling point: when the spatial metaphor is assumed, either explicitly or implicitly, by a researcher and/or rememberer then it becomes increasingly difficult to evaluate the veracity of memories. This is because the spatial metaphor cannot encompass the notion of a false memory and so, in effect, all memories are assumed by default to be true (for a highly related proposal see Gilbert's (1991) outstanding discussion of the generation of true and false beliefs; Conway *et al.*, (1996) also discuss this at length).

Knowing about the dynamic nature of memories, about disruptions of remembering following brain injury, a growing understanding of the non-conscious effects of memory, and the positive and negative effects of repeatedly remembering, are all important advances. Yet these are largely *mechanistic* explanations which in a sense provide us with some idea of the mechanisms and processes that could support the type of memory phenomena observed in psychotherapy, i.e. the fabrication as well as the recovery of memories, the recovery of memories with fabricated details, and so on. But although they describe or foreshadow cognitive mechanisms of memory they imply little about when or why such mechanisms are used. As Brewin and Andrews argue in Chapter 8 these are at least in the main part non-intentional accounts. They are like explanations in physics or chemistry rather than explanations in biology. The former typically do not need to postulate goals of the systems they seek to explain whereas the latter do. Brewin and Andrews comments are well-taken and a lacuna in modern memory research is that explanations are typically not intentional (Conway 1991). Of course having some understanding of the mechanisms of memory places us in a very good position to develop intentional theories of remembering, but this enterprise is in its earliest stages. Nevertheless, a further feature of the recovered memory debate is that ultimately an intentional account is called for and to the extent that the debate spurs on theoretical efforts to create such an account, then this must be viewed as a positive outcome of the interchange between memory researchers and psychotherapists.

While taking the broader perspective early in their chapter Brewin and Andrews focus in on various specific issues in later sections. One issue is that of the ecological validity of laboratory based studies of memory (Neisser 1976). The low ecological validity of any single experiment is quite clearly a cause for concern, and generalizing from a single study or handful of such studies to memory phenomena in everyday life should only be done with great caution (as Roediger *et al.* emphasized in their chapter). In general, however, where many experiments using many different procedures converge on a general principle or mechanism, as for example in implicit memory, then generalization can be valid as well as fruitful and illuminating. There are, however, certain phenomena which can *only* be studied outside the rigour of the laboratory. This has been known for some time by memory researchers who over the past decade have extended the range of their investigations to many everyday memory phenomena, from memories for such naturally occurring events as a vacation (Bruce and Van Pelt 1989) to the very long term retention of knowledge acquired in high school and university (Bahrick 1984; for a review see Conway *et al.* 1992; for reviews of the everyday memory literature see Cohen 1996; Searleman and Herrmann 1994). Perhaps, the recovery of memories during psychotherapy is also an area that can only be studied outside the laboratory *in situ* (although the psychotherapeutic interchange is also a type of laboratory as Freud recognized). To the extent that this is the case then laboratory attempts to experimentally investigate postulates of psychotherapy seem certain to fail. Indeed, one major problem in exploring Freudian concepts in the laboratory has been the very low ecological validity of the laboratory setting in which psychodynamically meaningful situations can rarely (if ever) be created and controlled in a way acceptable to an experimenter. In this respect the much cited paper of Holmes (1990) reviewing experimental attempts to induce repression is seriously misguided in failing to acknowledge the *extremely low* ecological validity of the experimental work into repression. Brewin and Andrews are right to point this out and Holmes's conclusion, that there is no convincing evidence for repression, should be placed in context: if a set of studies are of such poor sensitivity that they are highly unlikely to detect the phenomenon they are intended to detect, as in the case of experimental studies of repression, then it should be concluded that the experiments have failed as experiments. It should never be concluded that the phenomenon in question, repression in this case, does not exist. That cannot be known on the basis of the experiments considered by Holmes. It does not follow, however, that better laboratory studies with greater sensitivity might not have something useful to contribute to our understanding of psychoanalytic concepts like repression. Personally, I find it ironic that at the time of writing there can be a debate over Holmes's conclusion that there is no such phenomenon as repression while at the same time some of the most exciting laboratory work currently being performed describes and evaluates a whole range of inhibitory memory mechanisms (see Anderson *et al.* 1994; Anderson and Bjork 1996); inhibitory mechanisms that Freud would have been fascinated by and which tend to favour central control processes as the main source of inhibition. The cognitive mechanisms which mediate repression are currently being delineated in the laboratory by Bjork and his colleagues, and at some point it is inevitable that these investigations meet up with psychoanalytic theory and practice. In order to promote this synthesis of motivational theories and accounts of cognitive mechanisms it is time, as Brewin and Andrews conclude, that memory researchers and clinicians collaborated: perhaps then the intentional part of the story could be written and the way meanings and motives utilize inhibitory memory mechanisms understood.

Courtois in Chapter 9 gives a very clear review of the recovered memory debate as it currently stands and makes a number of points based on clinical experience which raise issues of wide interest. One of Courtois' main points, a point which memory researchers were most probably unaware of, is that only a very small minority of patients have total amnesia. Instead most have some knowledge, of an abstract rather then detailed nature, that they were victims of CSA. Much the more common observation by therapists is that of variable access coupled with motivated forgetting as opposed to total amnesia. Rather like PTSD patients, CSA patients seem to manage their memories. Occasionally they come to mind but are quickly inhibited and the individual maintains access to only general autobiographical knowledge of the period of their abuse. As we will see shortly, even access to general knowledge can be variable too. One is reminded here of Freud's (1915) claims that repression is a constant rather than a one-off processes. If constant episodes of repression are successful then the individual will have no memory of having accessed the repressed materials. Phenomenally this must be rather similar to the classic anterograde amnesic (cf. Parkin and Leng 1993 for a review) who can retain information for a few minutes but who can no longer form accessible long-term memories. Interestingly such amnesics show impressive implicit learning even though they are never able to recall any learning episodes. Just as Freud suggested, and as Kihlstrom argues in his chapter, the CSA victim with variable access to their traumatic memories may mainly express these implicitly: by repetition, symptoms, and/or dysfunctional emotion. Courtois' observation is particularly relevant to those concerned with understanding how memory works in these cases. The implication, that central control processes apply constant inhibition to the conscious retrieval of disturbing long-term knowledge with variable success, is consonant with the emerging views of inhibitory memory mechanisms discussed above. It might also be noted that this inhibition may not in any sense be unusual or specific to the disorder under consideration. If as I suggested earlier long-term autobiographical knowledge is exquisitely sensitive to cues, and patterns of activation continually arise and dissipate in the knowledge base, then a general 'house-keeping' function of control processes might be to only allow activated knowledge into consciousness under certain specific conditions, i.e. when it might, at least potentially, be useful because of its strong association with the content and goals of current control processing sequences (Conway 1996a, and this volume). In short, a major and everyday function of control processes might be to inhibit the incorporation of endogenously arising patterns of activation in long-term memory into current task-specific processing sequences. Courtois' observation is then of especial interest to memory researchers and one which needs to be investigated in further detail. Finally, like Brewin and Andrews who are fellow clinicians, Courtois goes on to make a series of recommendations for professional practice. These recommendation have arisen out of the recovered memory debate and psychotherapists will find them useful and illuminating.

The final two chapters bring together memory researchers and clinicians in collaborative research projects. These two chapters report findings of wide significance and indicate the potential fruitfulness of this type of collaborative venture. One general point pertaining to both chapters is that they report series of carefully researched case studies, often with corroborated evidence, and it is this which, in part, gives them their strength. Engelberg and Christianson (Chapter 10) pose a functional question about memories for emotional experiences: what is their evolutionary value? Their answer is in one respect straightforward. Clearly it conveys a significant evolutionary advantage if an individual can remember traumatic experiences and how they survived those experiences. Memories of the experiences can be later recalled in a situation of safety, examined, dwelt upon, and plans generated for the early identification of potential future similar situations, alternate plans for action can be formulated, and the experience can be communicated to others. The complication is that a memory system which maintained preferential access to memories of negative experiences would distort emotional life, engender high levels of anxiety and preparedness for flight or fight, depression and behavioural inactivity, lack of responsiveness, and so forth. Engelberg and Christianson postulate then that there are two opposing mechanisms working against each other, one to preserve and prioritize memories of threatening negative experiences and the other to forget, repress, or otherwise make unavailable the very same memories.

In this context active strategies for the management of remembering reflect the operation of the two putative mechanisms. In one example they describe how a sexually abused child reported attempting to think about pleasant events until memories of the abuse were no longer in mind. In another case a serial killer when reminded of the murders he had committed would quickly pick up any written materials, for example labelled household goods, and read these repetitively until the dysphasic memories had passed. Once again these memory management tactics are reminiscent of the coping strategies adopted by PTSD patients and they represent the conflict between the need to remember and the need to forget. In their cases studies Engelberg and Christianson describe how more extreme forms of motivated forgetting may arise following the experience of trauma. A typical pattern is that the victim will remember little of the actual event. Sometimes a few fragmentary details are retained and sometimes the period of amnesia extends to large periods of the person's past as in the case of CM, a rape victim, who could not recall who she was, her address, of what had happened to her. Nevertheless, CM showed behavioural signs of fear and distress when taken back to the site of the rape. As no explicit memories were recovered at this time then this clearly is an effect of implicit memory. Some months later CM was to recover her memory of the rape incident when she encountered a highly specific cue. The cue was a pattern of brickwork in a path upon which she was jogging, at another location distant from the scene of the rape. During her period of amnesia one of the few details she had been able to recall related to a path and a pattern of brickwork. She had not known that this was to do with the rape, although she was distressed when she of thought of it. The recovery of memories to specific cues is of especial interest as highly specific cues may be able to override the inhibitory effects of control processes (see Conway, Chapter 7 this volume). Engelberg and Christianson suggest that retention of one or two fragmentary details from an experience of trauma may relate to a process known as cue-utilization (Easterbrook 1959). As emotional intensity increases then the range of potential cues attended to decreases, leading to a memory that is difficult to access as there are few cues than can be used to activate long-term knowledge of the event. Active attempts at forgetting and distorted encoding may all give rise to forms of defensive psychogenic amnesia in which the need to forget surmounts the need to vividly recall. Engelberg and Christianson provide other cases studies that illustrate this.

Schooler *et al.* in Chapter 11 take a different starting point from that of Engelberg and Christianson. They consider the views that(a) memory research is not ecologically valid, and(b) case study data are not scientific. Refreshingly they conclude that neither view is of much utility in gaining an understanding of recovered and false memories. Instead, argue Schooler *et al.*, what is required is some credible and informative data. In the case studies which follow, all of which feature recovered memories, they attempt at all points to corroborate the reports of their patients. A very promising advance is that Schooler *et al.* attempt to identify the pattern of phenomenal experience of the patients who recover memories. One observation to emerge from these case studies is that memories are frequently recovered to specific cues and the rememberer is aware of the effect of the cue. Another point is that the patient may not have forgotten the event in the way we normally think of forgetting, i.e. as an object lost in a store. Schooler *et al.*'s patients remember their traumas but in a non-emotional abstract fashion. One patient who recovered memories of abuse commented on her prior awareness of these memories that she had *repressed their meaning*. She knew the events had occurred but she did not/could not access details of them nor did her knowledge of occurrence carry with it emotional experience. She commented that her memory prior to recovery was like a memory of a childhood birthday: she knew the event had occurred but that was all. Another patient who recovered memories of CSA for which she had been totally amnesic was astonished to learn that she had spoken to her ex-husband about her childhood abuse, apparently in a non-emotional and disengaged way. As Freud (1915) implied, if repression is constant and repressed materials return only to be repressed again, there may be occasions when some repressed material becomes available – perhaps in the abstract and non-emotional way observed in Schooler *et al.*'s case studies. Presumably, the effects of constant repression censor both the return of the repressed materials and memories of recalling aspects of the repressed materials such that the rememberer does not remember that they have accessed the threatening knowledge. A counterpart to this, pointed out by Schooler *et al.*, is that once access to the repressed materials has been fully reestablished then it is very difficult for the patient to recall the nature of their previous amnesia for the memories. Schooler *et al.* call this the 'knew-it-all-along' phenomenon, and if it is characteristic of memory recovery then an implication is that we may have strikingly underestimated the rate of amnesia for childhood traumas.

FROM RECOVERED MEMORY DEBATE TO RECOVERED MEMORY RESEARCH

For scientific psychology the individual is a fundamental problem. We know that in certain situations particular types of individuals will fabricate memories. What we do not know, and what we cannot currently predict, is which specific individuals will do this. We also now know that memories can become unavailable to conscious recollection. This may be total or it may take the form of a type of defensive organization of autobiographical memory. Again although we know this must occur in some proportion of individuals we cannot identify who specifically these people are. Indeed, it seems that even if we knew the initial conditions we could not predict who would repress and who would not. Repression and defensive organization are contingent on other factors and outcomes that are currently unknown: although we can speculate that these may be related to personality characteristics, the exact nature of the trauma, the support available both at the time and later in a person's life, and other influences yet to be identified. When psychology turns its attention from patterns of behaviour in groups of people, or the population at large, to the individual in their specific life context then a different approach is called for. In neuropsychology the reporting of case studies has proved to be of considerable worth and I suggest that this is one way in which the study of recovered memories can progress. There are, of course, problems with the case study technique, not the least of which is selectivity of cases that are made public. In the study of recovered memories an additional problem is the corroboration of the experiences recalled. Frequently this is difficult, if not impossible, to obtain, although as Schacter *et al.* point out there may be indirect ways in which confidence in recovered memories can be justifiably raised or lowered. Nevertheless, corroboration is essential, for without it neither researcher not therapist can know whether they are studying fabrications or memories. One possibility is that as we come to understand more about fabricated and recovered memories we will be able to identify these with some accuracy simply on the basis of what is retrieved and how. A number of the chapters in this volume converge on the view that memories retrieved to highly specific cues, suddenly and surprisingly, have a higher probability of being memories of actual experiences (it does not follow that such memories are accurate, that is a separate question). Again, however, a recovery pattern like this requires corroboration itself and a person's claim that this is how they came to retrieve a memory cannot be taken at face value (indeed it is on these grounds that Loftus and Ketcham (1994) convincingly object to the Lipsker case). The corroborated case study approach recommended by Kihlstrom and Schooler *et al.*, and exemplified in Engelberg and Christianson's and Schooler *et al.*'s chapters, in which memory researchers and psychotherapists collaborate, seems a positive way forward. As more cases accumulate so patterns of remembering and of fabrication, and their associated variables, will become more visible.

REFERENCES

Anderson, M.C. and Bjork, R.A. (1996). Mechanisms of inhibition in long-term memory: a new taxonomy. In *Inhibition in attention, memory, and language* (ed. D. Dagenbach and T. Carr). Academic, New York.

Anderson, M.C., Bjork, R.A., and Bjork, E.L. (1994). Remembering can cause forgetting: retrieval dynamics in long-term memory. *Journal of Experimental Psychology: Learning, Memory, and Cognition.* **20**, 1063–87.

Asch, S.E. (1940). Studies in the principles of judgments and attitudes: I1. Determination of judgments by group and ego standards. *Journal of Social Psychology* **12**, 433–65.

Asch, S.E. (1956). Studies of independence and conformity: a minority of one against a unanimous majority. *Psychological Monographs.* **70**, (9, Whole No. 416).

Asch, S.E. (1952). *Social psychology.* Prentice-Hall, Englewood Cliffs, NJ.

Baddeley, A.D. and Wilson, B. (1986). Amnesia, autobiographical memory, confabulation. In *Autobiographical memory*, (ed. D.C. Rubin), pp. 225–52. Cambridge University Press.

Bahrick, H.P. (1984). Semantic memory content in permastore: fifty years of memory for Spanish learned in school. *Journal of Experimental Psychology: General*, **13**, 1–29.

Barclay, C.R. (1996). Autobiographical remembering: narrative constraints on objectified selves. In *Remembering our past. Studies in autobiographical memory*, (ed. D.C. Rubin) pp. 94–128. Cambridge University Press.

Bruce, D. and Van Pelt, M. (1989). Memories of a bicycle tour. *Applied Cognitive Psychology*, **3**, 137–56.

Burgess, P.W. and Shallice, T. (1996). Confabulation and the control of normal memory. *Memory* (In press.)

Ceci, S.J. (1995). False beliefs: Some developmental and clinical considerations. In *Memory disortion. how minds, brains, and societies reconstruct the past* (ed. D.L. Schacter), pp. 91–128. Harvard University Press, Cambridge, MA.

Christianson, S.-A. (1992). Emotional stress and eyewitness memory: a critical review. *Psychological Bulletin*, **112**, 284–309.

Cohen, G. (1996). *Memory in the real world.* Psychological Press, Hove, East Sussex.

Conway, M.A. (1987). Verifying autobiographical facts. *Cognition.* **25**, 39–58.

Conway, M.A. (1990). *Autobiographical memory: an introduction.* Open University Press, Buckingham.

Conway, M.A. (1991). In defense of everyday memory. *American Psychologist*, **46**, 19–26.

Conway, M.A. (1993). Impairments of autobiographical memory. In *Handbook of neuropsychology*, Vol 8, (ed. F. Boller and J. Grafman), pp. 175–91. Elsevier, Amoterdam.

Conway, M.A. (1995). *Flashbulb memories.* Erlbaum, Hove, East Sussex.

Conway, M.A. (1996*a*). Autobiographical memories and autobiographical knowledge. In *Remembering our past: studies in autobiographical memory*, (ed. D.C. Rubin), pp. 67–93. Cambridge University Press.

Conway, M.A. (1996*b*). Failures of autobiographical remembering *Basic and applied memory: theory in context*, (ed. D. Herrmann, M. Johnson, C.McEvoy, C. Hertzog, and P. Herte), pp. 295–315. Erlbaum, Hillsdale, NJ.

Conway, M.A. and Bekerian, D.A. (1987). Organization in autobiographical memory. *Memory & Cognition*. **15**, 119–32.

Conway, M.A. and Tacchi, P.C. (1996). Motivated confabulation. *Neurocase*. (in press.)

Conway, M.A., Cohen, G., and Stanhope, N. (1992). Very long-term memory for knowledge acquired at school and university. *Applied Cognitive Psychology*, **6(6)**, 169–89.

Conway, M.A., Collins, A.F., Gathercole, S.E., and Anderson, S.J. (1996). Recollections of true and false autobiographical memories. *Journal of Experimental Psychology: General.*, **125**, 69–95.

Crovitz, H.F. and Schiffman, H. (1974). Frequency of episodic memories as a function of their age. *Bulletin of the Psychonomic Society*, **4**, 517–18.

Crutchfield, R.A. (1955). Conformity and character. *American Psychologist*, **10**, 191–8.

Easterbrook, J.A. (1959). The effect of emotion on cue utilization and the organization of behaviour. *Psychological Review*, **66**, 183–201.

Fivush, R. (1994). Long-term retention of infant memories. *Memory*, **4**, 337–475.

Freud, S. (1900). *The interpretation of dreams*. In *The standard edition of the complete psychological works of Sigmund Freud*, Vols. 4–5 (ed. J. Strachey). Hogarth Press, London.

Freud, S. (1915). *Repression*. In *The standard edition of the complete psychological works of Sigmund Freud*, Vol. 14 (ed. J. Strachey) pp. 7–66. Hogarth Press, London.

Freud, S. (1920). The psychologenesis of a case of Homosexuality in a Woman. In *The standard edition of the complete psychological works of Sigmund Freud*, Vol. 2, (ed. J. strachey). Hogarth Press, London.

Freud, S. (1924). The loss of reality in neurosis and psychosis. In *The standard edition of the complete psychological works of Sigmund Freud*, Vol. 19, pp. 183–7, (ed. J. Strachey). Hogarth Press, London.

Gilbert, D.T. (1991). How mental systems believe. *American Psychologist*, **46**, 107–19.

Goodman, G.S., Quas, J.A., Batterman-Faunce, J.M., Riddlesberger, M.M., and Kuhn, J. (1994). Predictors of accurate and inaccurate memories of traumatic events experienced in childhood. *Consciousness and Cognition*. **3**, 269–95.

Higgins, E.T. (1987). Self-discrepancy: a theory relating self and affect. *Psychological Review*, **94**, 319–40.

Holmes, D. (1990). The evidence for repression: an examination of sixty years of research. In *Repression and dissociation: implications for personality, theory, psychopathology, and health* (ed. J. Singer), pp. 85–102. University of Chicago Press.

Hyman, I.E., Jr and Billings, J.F. (1996). Individual differences and the creation of false childhood memories. *Memory*. (In press.)

Hyman, I.E., Jr., Husband, T.H., and Billings, J.F. (1996). False memories of childhood experiences. *Applied Cognitive Psychology*. (In press.)

Johnson, M.K., Hashtroudi, S., and Lindsay, D.S. (1993). Source monitoring. *Psychological Bulletin*, **114**, 3–28.

Kris, E. (1956). The personal myth: a problem in psychoanalytic technique. In *The selected papers of Ernst Kris*. Yale University Press, New Haven, CT. (Collection published 1975.)

Loftus, E.F. and Ketcham, K. (1994). *The myth of repressed memory*. St Martin's Press, New York.

McGaugh, J. L. (1995). Emotional activation, neuromodulatory systems, and memory. In *Memory distortion. How minds, brains, and societies reconstruct the past* (ed. D. L. Schacter), pp. 255–73. Harvard University Press, Cambridge, MA.

Markus, H. and Nurius, P. (1986). Possible selves. *American Psychologist*, **41**, 954–69.

Moscovitch, M. (1989). Confabulation and the frontal systems: strategic versus associative retrieval in neuropsychological theories of memory. In *Varieties of memory and consciousness: essays in honour of Endel Tulving* (ed. H.L. Roediger III and F.I.M. Craik), pp. 135–60. Erlbaum, Hillsdals, NJ.

Moscovitch, M. (1995). Confabulation. In *Memory distortion. How minds, brains and societies reconstruct the past*, (ed. D.L. Schacter), pp. 226–54. Harvard University Press, Cambridge, MA.

Neisser, U. (1976). *Cognition and reality*. Freeman, New York.

Ofshe, R. and Watters, E. (1994). *Making monsters: false memories, psychotherapy, and sexual hysteria*. Scribner, New York.

Parkin, A.J. and Leng, N.R.C. (1993). *Neuropsychology of the amnesic syndrome*. Erlbaum, Hove, East Sussex.

Pillemer, D.B. and White, S.H. (1989). Childhood events recalled by children and adults. *Advances in Child Development and Behaviour*. **21**, 297–340.

Robinson, J.A. (1976). Sampling autobiographical memory. *Cognitive Psychology*, **8**, 578–95.

Roediger, H.L. III (1980). Memory metaphors in cognitive psychology. *Memory and Cognition*, **8**, 231–46.

Roediger, H.L. III and McDermott, K.B. (1995). Creating false memories: remembering words not presented in lists. *Journal of Experimental Psychology: Learning, Memory, and Cognition*, **803–14**.

Rovee-Collier, C.K and Shyi, G.C.W. (1992). A functional and cognitive analysis of infant long-term retention. In *The development of long-term retention* (ed. C.J. Brainerd, M.L. Howe, and V.F. Reyna), pp. 3–55. Springer, New York.

Rubin, D.C., Wetzler, S.E., and Nebes, R.D. (1986). Autobiographical memory across the adult lifespan. In *Autobiographical memory* (ed. D.C. Rubin), pp. 202–21. Cambridge University Press.

Schacter, D.L. and Tulving, E. (ed.) (1994). *Memory systems*. MIT Press, Cambridge, MA.

Searleman, A. and Herrmann, D. (1994). *Memory from a broader perspective*. McGraw-Hill, New York.

Squire, L.R. (1992). Memory and the hippocampus: a synthesis from findings with rats, monkeys, and humans. *Psychological Review*. **99**, 195–231.

Stuss, D.T. and Benson, D.F. (1986). *The frontal lobes*. Raven Press, New York.

Treadway, M, McCloskey, M., Gordon, B., and Cohen, N.J. (1992). Landmark life events and the organization of memory: evidence from functional retrograde amnesia. In *The handook of emotion and memory: research and theory* (ed. S. Christianson), pp. 389–410. Erlbaum, Hillsdals, NJ.

Wetzler, S.E. and Sweeney, J.A. (1986). Childhood amnesia: an empirical demonstration. In *Autobiographical memory* (ed. D.C. Rubin), pp. 202–21 Cambridge University Press.

Williams, J.M.G. (1996). Depression and the specificity of autobiographical memory. In *Remembering our past: studies in autobiographical memory* (ed. D.C. Rubin), pp. 244–70. Cambridge University Press.

Winnicott, D.W. (1953). *Playing and reality*. Routledge, London. Reprinted 1991.)

Wittgenstein, L. (1953). *Philosphoical investigations*. Blackwell, Oxford. D.

TWO

The troublesome unknowns about trauma and recovered memories

MICHAEL YAPKO

The controversy regarding the historical accuracy of memories of childhood sexual abuse which are first discovered after years or even decades of being entirely unavailable to one's conscious recall continues. As a clinician, author, and teacher who is deeply involved in the controversy, it has been a time of intense personal observation and reflection on the nature of the controversy, especially its implications for society in general and the mental health profession in particular. In this brief chapter, I will focus on what remains largely unknown despite the heated exchanges on both sides of the controversy. In so doing, I will be advocating that professionals take less extreme positions in addressing the relevant issues.

Much has changed in recent years. In 1990, when I first warned of the hazards of actively striving to uncover hidden traumas of presumed childhood sexual abuse in psychotherapy patients (see *Yapko* 1990), the controversy had not yet seemed to surface in most people's awareness. There was no such term as 'false memory syndrome' yet coined, nor was there a foundation bearing that name. The now controversial self-help book *The courage to heal* (Bass and Davis 1988) was not yet under attack. John Bradshaw's books and lectures regarding the 'wounded inner child' were at their peak of popularity. And there were no official positions, recommendations, or guidelines yet established by major professional societies.

The concerns I raised in 1990 were viewed by some at the time as 'crying wolf', i.e. warning others of a seemingly non-existent danger. However, it was clear to me then, just as it is now, that many in the clinical and research professions are unaware of developing trends until they become painfully obvious. (Consider how badly the mental health profession erred regarding the prevalence of incest as yet another example of the ability to collectively underestimate a problem.)

In early 1992, I undertook a non-scientific, yet meaningful, survey of practising clinicians from all across the United States. At that time, most clinicians still seemed to be largely unaware of the growing preoccupation with and non-critical acceptance of the notion of repressed memories of abuse presumably underlying common clinical disorders (like depression and anxiety) amongst a small but growing group of psychotherapists. Consequently, respondents' beliefs and assumptions about memory, trauma, and suggestibility could likely be revealed in their 'pristine' form, uncontaminated by the widespread and often polarized consideration the 'hot topic' of recovered memories has since received.

The survey data I gathered were published in 1994 in another book, *Suggestions of abuse* (Yapko 1994) The survey revealed that many clinicians were misinformed and underinformed about critical elements of the controversy. While I have been appropriately criticized for my less than rigorous methodology (Hammond 1995; Lynn *et al.*, 1994), few have questioned my conclusion that many psychotherapists are practising on the basis of a personal bias that may unwittingly put their patients at risk.

Interestingly, there has been a marked shift in the attitudes of the clinicians I have addressed in my recent workshops in comparison to when I first discussed these matters in the early 1990s. (This is a purely subjective observation on my part.) Now clinicians tolerate, even embrace, the information provided, better accepting the inescapable fact that any therapy that can help has an equal potential to harm. Just a few years ago, some colleagues attending my training courses in hypnosis and suggestibility would become openly angry with me for daring to suggest they could harm their patients or plant misinformation – even illusory memories – in the course of therapy. (They were often fearful that abuse survivors would be disbelieved, a legitimate concern for those clinicians too quick to discount the very real possibility that abuse did, in fact, occur.) It is encouraging to me to reflect on the observation that it has been a long time since I've had such an extreme reaction from any of my colleagues. I believe clinicians are getting clearer about the need to avoid jumping to conclusions of *any* sort without an objective basis for doing so.

Recently major professional societies (American Medical Association 1994; American Psychiatric Association 1994; American Society of Clinical Hypnosis 1995; and others) have met the challenge and provided well-considered guidelines and recommendations about the relevant issues. Debates, discussion panels, and illuminating presentations have been offered at major national and international psychotherapy conventions. Thus, it seems clear that the recovered memory controversy has fully seeped into the mental health profession's consciousness in a relatively short span of time (Butler 1995).

The controversy has also seeped into the awareness of the general public. Highly visible lawsuits involving alleged perpetrators or allegedly incompetent therapists have dominated national headlines. Highly public accusations by the famous, and not-so-famous, have been made in the media. At least half a dozen popular books have been published on the topic, with more on the way.

With all the attention the recovered memory controversy has been given, what do we know now that we didn't know before? And, as a corollary, what still remains to be known? These two questions suggest an area of consideration that is far too broad to receive full or even adequate treatment in this short chapter. Thus, in order to narrow the focus to a smaller field of consideration, I will address what I will call 'the triangle of the recovered memory controversy'.

THE CORNERS OF THE TRIANGLE

The recovered memory controversy involves a sizable amount of information, some well defined but most not, in three major areas: memory, trauma, and suggestibility. These three areas represent the corners of a triangle, a three-sided structure with each side equal in size and relative importance in maintaining the integrity of the structure (see Fig. 2.1).

To focus one's attention on only one of the sides of the triangle is to diminish the inevitable roles of the other two. Thus, to focus on memory research, i.e. the mechanisms and the relative accuracy of human memory under varying conditions (for example high or low stress, before and following hypnotic induction, high or low task motivation, etc.), as if such research could reliably determine the validity of recovered memories in a given individual, is simply unrealistic (Loftus 1993; Lynn *et al.* 1989; McConkey *et al.* 1990). Likewise, to focus only on trauma, i.e. the roles of dissociation and amnesia in coping with episodes of sexual abuse (for example the process of encapsulation and burial of traumatic material, the role of hidden memories in the formation of clinical signs and symptoms such as 'body memories', and the relative value of 'structured abreaction' in treatment) provides little insight into the mechanisms by which memory can be wholly illusory or how therapy can produce iatrogenic outcomes in a given individual (Briere and Conte 1993; Terr 1994).

The third side of the triangle is suggestibility. Just as focusing on either of the other two sides exclusively is sure to yield an incomplete understanding of the phenomenon of illusory memories which are recovered in response to an external influence (like the media or psychotherapy), the same is true when one focuses only on suggestibility. Suggestibility as an *inter*personal phenomenon involves absorbing the patient into a frame of mind – a belief, a philosophy, a perspective – that creates certain possibilities while precluding others. Suggestibility research has thus far focused on questions of susceptibility to hypnotic influence, the fact of patients frequently conforming to the demand

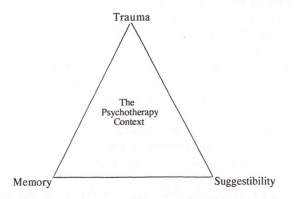

Fig. 2.1 The triangle of the recovered memory controversy.

characteristics of their therapy, and the role of social and contextual demands on subjects (Belli 1989; Christianson 1992*a*; Lindsay and Read, 1994). It is my firm belief that suggestibility has received too little consideration overall when social influence is, in my view, the primary issue in cases involving illusory memories.

There has been a double-bind ('no win') problem associated with research in each of the areas that continues to hamper progress. Specifically, the issue of 'ecological validity' has yet to be addressed adequately to the satisfaction of all (or, at least, most) involved (Yuille and Wells 1991). Laboratory experiments are often criticized as having little or no bearing on what happens in 'real life' (Briere 1992; Christianson 1992*b*; Courtois 1992). Clinical observations are frequently dismissed as anecdotal and unscientific (Loftus and Ketcham 1994; Ofshe and Watters 1994). I believe this represents the first of the 'troublesome unknowns'. How will we arrive at a coherent understanding of the controversy if controlled experimentation and clinical vignettes are deemed unacceptable evidence to opposing sides?

THE ULTIMATE RESEARCH NEVER CAN AND NEVER SHOULD HAPPEN

What might well be the only truly ecologically valid study that could satisfy extremists on both sides of the controversy is an experiment that *can never* and *should never* be done. I offer it here simply for the sake of illuminating that whatever we might learn about memory and trauma means little without determining the role of external suggestive influences in specific cases.

The forbidden experiment would simply be this: have a thousand (or more) people seek psychotherapy voluntarily and with the positive motivation typical of therapy clients to obtain relief. Have their symptoms represent those typically included on the common symptom checklists of incest or abuse survivors published in various recovery literature. All subjects must be magically but accurately certified as having absolutely no sexual abuse anywhere in their individual histories. Expose all subjects to persuasive therapists who are *genuinely* staunch believers that a history of abuse that is apparently repressed *must* be present (despite the subject's denial) in order to account for their symptoms. Expose the subjects to various memory recovery techniques (for example hypnotic age regression, guided imagery, visualization, etc.) that are regularly and enthusiastically applied in treatment to 'bring up and resolve' repressed memories. Following some reasonable length of time in treatment, say six months or a year, determine how many members of the research population are now convinced utterly and completely that they were abused as children and have repressed the memories.

For the extremists, i.e. those who are convinced no one would or could be convinced that abuse happened when it never really did, or those who believe it happens in huge proportions, this impossible experiment might be the ultimate convincer that the truth is likely to be that many subjects *can* be convinced, but only a minority of them. They likely represent a significant minority, however.

This outrageous experimental scenario, involving obvious and gross violations of every ethical issue conceivable, can serve to highlight that ultimately *our focus must be on the individual, case by case*. Knowing, for example, that dissociation may be a response to trauma doesn't say *anything* about what actually happened in a given case (Herman 1992; Spiegel 1989; Spiegel and Cardena 1991). After all, not everyone dissociates during traumatic experiences to the point of developing amnesia. Knowing that traumatic memories may be encoded differently from other memories says nothing about the variables affecting memory which might influence the recovery of specific memories of abuse in a given individual (Olio 1989; van der Kolk and van der Hart 1991). Knowing it may be possible to suggest illusory memories to some individuals does not indicate whether, for a given individual, recovered memories are true or not (Brown 1995; Claridge 1992; Coleman 1992). This represents the next 'troublesome unknown'. How will the statistical possibilities regarding memory, trauma, and suggestibility which are discovered through current and future research serve clinicians in better managing their individual cases?

WHAT DO WE KNOW?

With respect to each of the three sides of the recovered memory triangle, it now seems safe to say we know at least this much:

1. We know that child abuse and sexual trauma happen too frequently *no matter what* the frequency is (Briere 1992; Courtois 1988; Dolan 1991).
2. We know that traumatic memories are formed in some ways that are different from normal memories (Cahill *et al.* 1994; Christianson 1992*a*; van der Kolk and Saporta 1993).
3. We know that dissociation is a capacity that can be used defensively, giving rise to amnesia which may lift at a later time (Briere and Conte 1993; Hornstein 1992; Spiegel 1989).
4. We know that memory can be highly reliable, we know that memory can be highly unreliable, and we know that memory can be influenced by a variety of factors, including suggestion and misinformation (Barclay and Wellman 1986; Gudjonsson 1992; Rich 1990).
5. Regarding suggestibility, we know that people can be influenced by others even to the extreme. We know that misinformation provided by credible authorities with no apparent motive to deceive can be absorbed and responded to as though it were true (McConkey 1992; Scheflin and Shapiro 1989; Sheehan *et al.* 1991; Spiegel 1974; Weekes 1992).

Given just these few apparent but poorly defined truths regarding memory, trauma, and suggestibility, it is simply beyond question that there are many diverse possibilities in dealing with these inherently ambiguous issues. To hold *any* position that fully excludes other possibilities simply seems unreasonable at this point in time. I believe the controversy has continued because, simply put, both sides 'have a point'.

THE TROUBLESOME UNKNOWNS

The spectre of confabulation looming behind memories of abuse that arose in response to a psychotherapist's (or some other external influence, like a book or television programme) influence can cause a patient self-doubt, splits within families, suspicion of one's therapist, and fears of facing potentially painful historical facts. The uncertainty in specific clinical cases involving real people's lives has to be acknowledged and carefully managed. As I have said elsewhere (Yapko 1994), I think a fundamental injunction to practitioners and clients alike is to 'tolerate the ambiguity', and seek progress in spite of it.

Thus far, I have referred to the 'troublesome unknowns' of how the issue of 'ecological validity' can be satisfactorily resolved, and how psychotherapists will integrate new insights into individual interventions. In this section, I pose questions that I believe need to be answered, but which I recognize are perhaps unanswerable in a definitive way. I encourage readers to note their personal responses to the questions I raise, carefully considering the distinctions between objective facts and subjective inferences. Though I am current with much of the relevant literature, I obviously do not believe the questions I pose have been sufficiently answered to date.

In this section I will describe some of the specific troublesome unknowns evident in each of the three sides of the repressed memory triangle. These unknowns represent some of the most clinically challenging issues to address, requiring one to 'walk the tightrope' between historical truth and narrative truth. Each of these questions represents a potential area of meaningful inquiry. Each area is ambiguous enough to generate a range of plausible responses, while 'truth' will likely remain elusive.

Some trauma unknowns

There is a growing body of persuasive evidence that traumatic experiences are encoded differently from more routine experiences (Christianson 1992*a*; Horowitz and Reidbord 1992). The associated assumption is that traumatic memories can be preserved at a higher level of integrity than normal memories for later recall. However, some basic questions about this phenomenon remain unanswered: how many buried traumatic memories remain intact, and how many deteriorate? If buried memories of trauma decay over time, is it because of natural deterioration of some sort, or is it due to a defensive self-protection?

Why do some memories of known trauma never return in some people while other people do recover such memories? There seems to be considerably more than the mere biochemistry at work here.

Trauma experts are striving to clarify the structural differences and associated practical implications between repression, forgetting, amnesia, and dissociation. The assumption is that the child employs dissociation as a defence mechanism to cope with the overwhelming nature of abuse (Briere and Conte 1993; Terr 1994). Via the dissociation, amnesia for the abusive events permits the child to cope by leaving the conscious mind essentially unaware of the traumatic episodes. This raises several key questions yet to be satisfactorily answered: do children repress memories after each specific incident of abuse, or as a whole set of experiences at some later point in time? If children forget each traumatic episode instantly, as it happens, how exactly do they do this? How does the child lose continuity such that the event loses both its antecedents and immediate aftermath? If children store many memories of abuse and then later develop amnesia for them all, then what generates the amnesia if not the abusive episodes themselves? And, finally, why do some people repress a particular type of trauma and others do not?

Some memory unknowns

Our knowledge of memory relative to the recovered memory controversy remains incomplete. It is widely accepted that memory is not perfect, nor is it inherently unreliable. The phrase 'memory is reconstructive, not reproductive', seems to capture the essence of what is known in a general way. What remains unclear, though, is the role of memory in organizing an autobiographical narrative of childhood experience. How do infants and babies learn and remember? Preverbally, is there a valid phenomenon colloquially known as the 'body memory'? If so, how reliable are they in pointing the way to a history of abuse that pre-dates verbal ability? Are 'body memories' formed and retained throughout one's lifespan? What relationship is there between physical symptoms and body memories associated with trauma? How do we distinguish body memories from other psychosomatic symptoms unrelated to abuse?

Dissociation and amnesia are the essential elements underlying the repression, or forgetting, that may be associated with trauma. Preverbally, the 'body memory' is considered the major mechanism of stored memory. But, this raises other related questions: from what age is repression even possible? How common or uncommon is total amnesia (repression, dissociation) for trauma? And, finally, how do we reliably distinguish between repression and forgetting?

At this point in time, there is no reliable means for distinguishing a genuine memory from a confabulation or illusory memory. Without external corroborating evidence, like medical records or photographs, there is simply no way to tell whether a memory has been artificially suggested or skillfully recovered. Perhaps the most important of all the unknowns is this one: how do we learn to reliably distinguish true memories from illusory memories in the absence of external corroboration?

Some suggestibility unknowns

The presence of suggestion, both direct and indirect, is inevitable in the context of psychotherapy to one degree or another (Yapko 1990, 1995). One need not formally induce hypnosis in order for suggestibility to be evident (Erdelyi 1994; Watzlawick 1985). One need not question whether someone is suggestible, but instead assess the degree of suggestibility at a given point in time or in a given context. One need not employ formal hypnotic or suggestive techniques for the purpose of recovering presumably repressed memories in order to impart the assumption that such memories exist and the expectation that such memories can and will be found.

Suggestibility motivated by the desire to be relieved of one's symptoms is the primary reason for therapy patients routinely getting absorbed in their psychotherapists' philosophical and practical therapeutic framework. Can people be led to believe they were abused when, in fact, they never were? Case examples of virtually impossible forms of abuse that are vividly 'remembered' make it clear that the answer is yes (Baker 1992; Gardner 1992; Lindsay and Read 1994).

The suggestibility of some therapy clients who are highly motivated to accept the therapist's diagnosis and treatment plan, indefensible as it may be by objective standards, is often responsible for the iatrogenic effects of psychotherapy. What characterological and situational variables account for the willingness to redefine non-abusive family members (or others) as perpetrators? How does a history of reasonably normal interactions with family members become altered in such a way as to view all those who deny what seem to be illusory memories of abuse as part of a conspiracy or as being 'in denial'? How should clinicians treat individuals who present narratives that suggest virtually impossible forms of abuse? (For example, one woman told me in graphic detail her clear 'memories' of having been doused in gasoline and set afire at age six months as part of a satanic ritual sacrifice. Asked where the burn scars are, she claimed the cult must have had a skilled plastic surgeon present to hide her scars. She claims she firmly believes that this event happened.) Should clinicians validate patients' beliefs in order to acquire or maintain rapport? Should they challenge such beliefs? Or, perhaps, sidestep them?

The use of specific techniques in order to actively work at recovering narratives of abuse with ever-increasing detail is in itself a highly suggestive practice. Under what conditions are such methods justifiable? How necessary is it really to uncover repressed memories in order for treatment to succeed? Which memory recovery techniques are more or less likely to contaminate recovered memories just by using them? Can the potential contaminant of suggestion somehow be filtered out and yield a distilled factual narrative under *any* circumstances? If so, how?

AMBIGUITY, FRUSTRATION, ANGER, ACCEPTANCE, PROGRESS

Projective tests like the Rorschach are based on the projective hypothesis which says, in essence, that when people are faced with an ambiguous stimulus, they structure it and give it meaning based on their own projections (Sundberg *et al.* 1983). The repressed memory controversy is a terribly ambiguous stimulus, thus encouraging *lots* of projection in interested parties. People's need for clarity leads them to make meaning out of the unknown; but, most arenas in which this process occurs are not as fragile and volatile as people's memories.

With the need for clarity as well as the need to have one's views accepted at face value frustrated, the chasm between what we know and what we don't know has led to some heated, angry debates. These have not been entirely destructive, nor have they been entirely helpful.

It is apparent that opposing sides in this controversy each have some relative 'truths' to hang on to. By accepting the wisdom in Mark Twain's observation that, 'it isn't always what we don't know that hurts us, sometimes it's what we know that isn't so', perhaps we as professionals can move to a more unified and reasonable position in addressing the controversy. The greatest danger, I believe, is the extremism that leads to the hostile, 'you're either with us or against us' posture.

It has been my intention in writing this chapter to point out that there is still much to be learned about memory, trauma, and suggestibility. I hope that by identifying some of the most 'troublesome unknowns', interested parties will accept the challenge to seek more facts and accept fewer inferences. After all, the first step toward eventual knowing is asking relevant questions.

REFERENCES

American Medical Association, Council on Scientific Affairs (1994). Memories of childhood abuse. *CSA Report* 5-1-94.

American Psychiatric Association (1994). *Statement on memories of sexual abuse*. APA, Washington, DC.

American Society of Clinical Hypnosis, Committee on Forensic Hypnosis (1995). *Clinical hypnosis and memory: guidelines for clinicians and for forensic hypnosis.* ASCH Press, Des Plaines, IL.

Barclay, C. and Wellman, H. (1986). Accuracies and inaccuracies in autobiographical memory. *Journal of Memory and Language*, **25**, 93–103.

Baker, R. (1992). *Hidden memories*. Prometheus Books, Buffalo, NY.

Bass, E. and Davis, L. (1988). *The courage to heal*. Harper & Row, New York.

Belli, R. (1989). Influences of misleading postevent information: misinformation interference and acceptance. *Journal of Experimental Psychology: General*, **118**, 72–85.

Briere, J. (1992). Methodological issues in the study of sexual abuse effects. *Journal of Consulting and Clinical Psychology*, **60**, 196–203.

Briere, J. and Conte, J. (1993). Self-reported amnesia for abuse in adults molested as children. *Journal of Traumatic Stress*, **6**, 21–31.

Brown, D. (1995). Pseudomemories: the standard of science and the standard of care in trauma treatment. *American Journal of Clinical Hypnosis*, **37:3**, 1–24.

Butler, K. (1995). Caught in the crossfire. *Family Therapy Networker*, **19**, 2, 25–79.

Cahill, L., Prins, B., Weber, M., and McGaugh, J. (1994). B-adrenergic activation and memory for emotional events. *Nature*, **371**, 702–4.

Christianson, S. (ed.) (1992a). *The handbook of emotion and memory: research and theory*. Erlbaum, Hillsdale, NJ.

Christianson, S. (1992b). Emotional memories in laboratory studies versus real-life studies: do they compare? In *Theoretical perspectives on autobiographical memory* (ed. M. Conway, D. Rubin, H. Spinner, and W. Wagenaa), pp. 339–52. Kluwer, Dordrecht.

Claridge, K. (1992). Reconstructing memories of abuse: a theory-based approach. *Psychotherapy*, **29**, 243–52.

Coleman, L. (1992). Creating 'memories' of sexual abuse. *Issues in Child Abuse Investigations*, **4**, 169–76.

Courtois, C. (1988). *Healing the incest wound: adult survivors in therapy*. Norton, New York.

Courtois, C. (1992). The memory retrieval process in incest survivor therapy. *Journal of Child Sexual Abuse*, **1**, 15–32.

Dolan, Y. (1991). *Resolving sexual abuse*. Norton, New York.

Erdelyi, M. (1994). Hypnotic hypermnesia: the empty set of hypermnesia. *International Journal of Clinical and Experimental Hypnosis*, **42**, 379–90.

Gardner, R. (1992). *True and false accusations of child abuse*. Creative Therapeutics, Cresskill, NJ.

Gudjonsson, G. (1992). *The psychology of interrogations, confessions and testimony*. Wiley, Chichester.

Hammond, D. (1995). Book review: Suggestions of abuse. *American Journal of Clinical Hypnosis*, **37(3)**, 77–9.

Herman, J. (1992). *Trauma and recovery*. Basic Books, New York.

Hornstein, G. (1992). The return of the repressed. *American Psychologist*, **47**, 254–63.

Horowitz, M. and Reidbord, S. (1992). Memory, emotion, and response to trauma. In *The handbook of emotion and memory: research and theory* (ed. S. Christianson), pp. 343–58. Erlbaum, Hillsdale, NJ.

Lindsay, D and Read, J. (1994). Psychotherapy and memories of childhood sexual abuse: a cognitive perspective. *Applied Cognitive Psychology*, **8**, 281–338.

Loftus, E. (1993). The reality of repressed memories. *American Psychologist*, **48**, 5, 518–37.

Loftus, E. and Ketcham, K. (1994). *The myth of repressed memory*. St Martin's Press, New York.

Lynn, S., Myers, B., and Sivec, H. (1994). Psychotherapists beliefs, repressed memories of abuse, and hypnosis: what have we really learned? *American Journal of Clinical Hypnosis*, **36**, (3), 182–4.

Lynn, S., Weeks, J., and Milano, M. (1989). Reality vs. suggestion: pseudomemory in hypnotizable and simulating subjects. *Journal of Abnormal Psychology*, **98**, 137–44.

McConkey, K., Labelle, L., Bibb, B., and Bryant, R. (1990). Hypnosis and suggested pseudomemory. The relevance of test context. *Australian Journal of Psychology*, **42**, 197–206.

McConkey, K. (1992). The effects of hypnotic procedures on remembering: the experimental findings and their implications for forensic hypnosis. In *Contemporary hypnosis research* (ed. E. Fromm and M. Nash), pp. 405–26. Guilford, New York.

Ofshe, R. and Watters, E. (1994). *Making monsters: false memories, psychotherapy, and sexual hysteria*. Scribner, New York.

Olio, K. (1989). Memory retrieval in the treatment of adult survivors of sexual abuse. *Transactional Analysis Journal*, **19**, 93–4.

Rich, C. (1990). Accuracy of adults' reports of abuse in childhood. *American Journal of Psychiatry*, **147**, 1389.

Scheflin, A. and Shapiro, J. (1989). *Trance on trial*. Guilford, New York.

Sheehan, P., Statham, D., and Jamieson, G. (1991). Pseudomemory effects over time in the hypnotic setting. *Journal of Abnormal Psychology*, **100**, 1, 39–44.

Spiegel, D. (1989). Hypnosis in the treatment of victims of sexual abuse. *Psychiatric Clinics of North America*, 12, 295–305.

Spiegel, D. and Cardena, E. (1991). Disintegrated experience: the dissociative disorders revisited. *Journal of Abnormal Psychology*, **100**, 3, 366–78.

Spiegel, H. (1974). The grade 5 syndrome: the highly hypnotizable person. *International Journal of Clinical and Experimental Hypnosis*, **22**, 303–19.

Sundberg, N., Taplin, J., and Tyler, L. (1983). *Introduction to clinical psychology*. Prentice-Hall, Englewood Cliffs, NJ.

Terr, L. (1994). *Unchained memories: true stories of traumatic memories lost and found*. Basic Books, New York.

van der Kolk, B. and van der Hart, O. (1991). The intrusive past: the flexibility of memo and the engraving of trauma. *American Imaqo*, **48**, (4), 425–54.

van der Kolk, B. and Saporta, J. (1993). Biological response to psychic trauma. In *International handbook of traumatic stress syndromes* (ed. J. Wilson and B Raphael), pp. 25–34. Plenum, New York.

Watzlawick, P. (1985). Hypnotherapy without trance. In *Ericksonian psychotherapy, Vol. 1: Structures* (ed. J. Zeig), pp. 5–14. Brunner/Mazel, New York.

Weekes, J., Lynn, S., Green, J., and Brentar, J. (1992). Pseudomemory in hypnotized and task-motivated subjects. *Journal of Abnormal Psychology*, **101**, 356–60.

Yapko, M. (1990). *Trancework: an introduction to the practice of clinical hypnosis*, (2nd ed). Brunner/Mazel, New York.

Yapko, M. (1994). *Suggestions of abuse: true and false memories of childhood sexual trauma*. Simon & Schuster, New York.

Yapko, M. (1995). *Essentials of hypnosis*. Brunner/Mazel, New York.

Yuille, J. and Cutshall, J. (1986). A case study of eyewitness memory of crime. *Journal of Applied Psychology*, **71**, 291–301.

Yuille, J. and Tollestrup, P. (1992). A model of diverse effects on emotion on eyewitness memory. In *The handbook of emotion and memory: Research and theory* (ed. S. Christianson), pp. 201–13. Erlbaum, Hillsdale, NJ.

Yuille, J. and Wells, G. (1991). Concerns about the application of research findings: The issue of ecological validity. In *The suggestibility of children's recollections* (ed. J. Doris), pp. 118–28. APA, Washington, DC.

THREE

Events spoken and unspoken: implications of language and memory development for the recovered memory debate

ROBYN FIVUSH, MARGARET-ELLEN PIPE,
TAMAR MURACHVER, AND ELAINE REESE

> One benefit, which I have lost, of a life where many things go unsaid, is that you don't have to remember things about yourself that are too bizarre to imagine. What was never given utterance eventually becomes too nebulous to recall. (Smiley 1994, p. 305)

What happens to memories of events that are never given utterance? Do they become 'too nebulous to recall' or are they retained, perhaps to be given voice years later? This question is at the heart of the recovered/false memory debate. Obviously, the controversy surrounding the issue of whether 'recovered' memories of early sexual abuse reflect real events that occurred in the past or are 'false' memories created in the therapy situation is quite complex, extending well beyond psychological understanding of human memory. Because historically women and children have been undervalued in Western culture, and because the prevalence and consequences of childhood sexual abuse have been so long ignored, many have argued that the disbelief of (usually women's) 'recovered' memories of early sexual abuse reflects a backlash against women finally finding their voice. On the other hand, the mounting numbers of women who 'recover' memories of early abuse in the course of therapy raises the possibility that at least some of these memories have been 'implanted' through suggestion and persuasion of well-meaning, albeit manipulative, therapists.

Any resolution of the recovered/false memory controversy will have to rely, at least in part, on our knowledge of the human memory system. In this chapter, we take a developmental perspective on the controversy. Because 'recovered' memories are of events that occurred in childhood, understanding how basic memory abilities change and develop through infancy and childhood is critical to evaluating many of these memory claims. Moreover, because 'recovered' memories are most often expressed as verbal accounts of events experienced in childhood, we focus on the ways in which language interacts with children's developing abilities to recall events from their past.

Several points need to be clarified from the outset. First, although our primary focus is on children's ability to talk about past experiences, we are not claiming that all explicit memories are verbalizable. Even as adults, some memories which are accessible to conscious recall are extremely difficult to verbalize, such as memories of odours or kinesthetic experiences. And, as we will see, young children who do not yet have the language skills to express their memories can none the less show explicit memory of past experiences through re-enacting events behaviourally (see Schacter (1987) for a discussion of explicit memory, and Bauer (in press) for a discussion of behavioural measures of explicit memory in preverbal children). Verbal recall is, however, the clearest evidence of explicit memory. Moreover, recall of the past most often occurs out of the spatial and temporal context of the original experience, and it is through language that the experience can be most clearly and unambiguously communicated.

This brings up the second, and perhaps more critical, point: recalling the past is a social activity. We reminisce about our past to or with other people. Although we also reminisce to ourselves, one of the defining features of autobiographical memories is that they are accessible for sharing socially through conversational reminiscing with others (Fivush *et al.* 1996; Nelson 1993; Pillemer and White 1989). Memories for real world events are complex compositions of the people, activities, objects, and emotions experienced, as well as aspects of the ongoing discourse during the event. In recalling a real world event verbally, the individual must coordinate these myriad sources of information and form a verbal account, or narrative, about the experience.

Our notion of 'verbal recall' goes well beyond the usual conceptualization implicit in laboratory memory experiments of an individual's verbal recall of material presented by an experimenter in a controlled, non-interactive setting. From our perspective, the development of verbal recall involves two complimentary dimensions. First, we need to consider children's developing language skills for representing and recalling the past. The transition from a non-verbal infant to a verbal child is, of course, a gradual progression, and we need to consider how children's developing linguistic skills interact with memory and, in turn, their developing abilities to recount coherent narratives about their past experiences. Second, we need to consider the ways in which adults help structure experiences for children through verbal scaffolding. This idea is best illustrated by the dialectical approach to development first outlined by Vygotsky. Vygotsky (1978) proposed that all cognitive development starts in the child's interactions with others, especially more competent partners or adults. Children eventually internalize the cognitive skills practised in those interactions to perform the task independently. Development occurs as adults lure children into interactions just beyond what they can achieve on their own. Thus, for Vygotsky, development is inherently social. In addition, Vygotsky posits language as the primary means of internalization. Children learn to instruct themselves through their representations of caretakers' verbalizations.

Our guiding assumption, consistent with Vygotsky, is that events as experienced and as recalled are inherently social, and that the ways in which they are talked about with others play a critical role in how individuals come to represent those events to themselves. Language, or talk about the past, is the primary means by which we communicate memories to others and is an important method by which we represent memories to ourselves. The focus throughout this chapter, therefore, is on the ways in which language is used to organize event memories and to report these memories to others.

Two related questions are addressed. First, what is it that preverbal infants and children recall of their past experiences and can any of these memories be 'translated' into language as children become linguistically fluent? Second, how do children's memories for personally experienced events change as they enter the language-learning years, and how does the ability to express memories verbally change the ways in which memories may be organized, represented, and recalled? In considering this issue, we discuss both how language is used to help organize and remember experiences, as well as how verbal recall of events changes both as a function of age of the child and age of the memory.

MEMORY BEFORE LANGUAGE

How and when do we begin remembering past events? We know that even very young infants are able to encode and retrieve information about their world. For example, De Casper and Fifer (1980) have demonstrated that neonates are able to discriminate their own mother's voice from a stranger's voice within the first days of life, indicating that they must have encoded and retained this auditory information while still *in utero* (see also De Casper and Spence 1986). A substantial body of research by Rovee-Collier and her colleagues has shown that in the first six months of life infants are capable of long-term remembering (for reviews, see Rovee-Collier and Hayne 1987; Rovee-Collier and Shyi 1992). Using a mobile conjugate reinforcement paradigm in which the infant learns to kick to produce movement in an interesting mobile, they have shown that even two- and three-month-old infants remember the contingency over periods of days and even weeks if the infant's memory is reactivated.

These early memories differ from those of older children in a number of ways, however. One difference is that young infants forget more quickly than do older infants and children. Even within the first three months of life there is a marked change in the time frame of forgetting. Two-month-old infants remember the mobile and respond to it after a delay of one day since training, but not after three days; three-month-old infants respond following delays as long as eight days and forgetting is not complete until nearly two weeks after initial training with the mobile (Rovee-Collier and Hayne 1987). These early memories can be reactivated, for example, if the infant is exposed to a 'reminder', seeing the mobile without the opportunity to kick, prior to the memory test. Exposure to the reminder appears to reactivate a latent or dormant memory (Rovee-Collier and Hayne 1987), extending the infant's memory over the same duration as following the original training. There may, however, be 'time windows' during which reminders are effective (Rovee-Collier 1995). For example, Greco *et al.* (1986) found that for two-month-old infants a reminder presented three weeks after training was effective in reactivating the memory but a reminder presented four weeks after training was not, whereas for three-month-olds a reminder at four weeks was still effective but one at five weeks was not. Memory reactivation therefore provides a mechanism for extending memories over meaningful time periods, perhaps helping bridge the gap between early experience and later behavior (Rovee-Collier and Hayne 1987), but not all early memories will remain available for reactivation.

The second point about early infant memories is that they are very specific and closely bound to the context in which they were acquired. Changes to the mobile or to aspects of the context in which the memory was acquired at the time of the memory test may result in failure to retrieve the memory and disruption in performance. For example, Rovee-Collier *et al.* (1985) found that when three-month-old infants were trained to kick a mobile in a crib with a highly distinctive crib bumper and were tested seven days later with a different, distinctive, bumper, there was little evidence that infants remembered the contingency, whereas infants tested with the same crib bumper as during training showed good memory over the same time period. At least over the first six months of life, infants become more sensitive to the context in which the memories were acquired (Rovee-Collier and Shyi 1992).

Moreover, these early memories are very readily modified and up-dated by subsequent experience. For example, Greco *et al.* (1990) found that three-month-old infants who had learned to kick to a series of mobiles in a distinctive context and were then exposed to a new, distinctive, mobile immediately following training but without the opportunity to kick, also responded to the new mobile when tested 24 hours later. That is, passive exposure to the new mobile in the training context was sufficient for the new mobile to be integrated with the memories of the training mobiles. The distinctive context was important for the integration of the memory in the study by Greco *et al.* (1986), but it is not the only basis for modifying early memories; modification or integration of the original memory may be based on other similarities, for example the movement of the mobile (Rovee-Collier and Shyi 1992). Moreover, with three-month-old infants, information may be integrated in this way up to four days after the original training.

The implication of these findings is that the people, objects, and events that the preverbal infants are likely to remember are those to which they are repeatedly exposed either through re-encountering the specific events or reinstatement of the contexts which would serve as reminders. Because specific memories may be readily up-dated and modified by subsequent experience, as Rovee-Collier and Shyi (1992) point out, details characterizing specific episodes are likely to become unavailable for later recall. In other words, early memories that are likely to endure may be generalized memories, consistent with the account of early memory development proposed by Nelson (1988). Even those memories which remain potentially available may be inaccessible unless very specific retrieval cues are available. Such specificity may, of course, contribute to later difficulties in accessing very early memories.

Even with these limitations on early remembering, there is evidence suggesting that memories of events experienced during the second half of the first year of life may be retained in some form over several years. In a provocative series of studies, Myers and her colleagues have explored whether events experienced between six and ten months of age are remembered as children grow older. Myers *et al.* (1987) assessed whether children aged almost three could remember a series of auditory localization experiments they participated in as six- to nine-month-old infants, and Perris *et al.* (1990) and Myers *et al.* (1994) examined whether children would recall an unusual activity (for example pulling a lever in a puppet's foot to make an interesting noise) learned in an unusual location (a tent playhouse) during infancy as they progressed through the preschool years. In all three experiments, children who experienced these events as infants behaved differently at the subsequent retention tests compared with groups of non-experienced controls. Experienced children spent more time interacting with the previously seen objects (reaching for toys in the dark, patting the puppets) than did non-experienced controls. Experienced children also showed savings in re-learning the contingency between a specific action and the interesting effect compared with non-experienced controls. There was, however, little evidence of explicit recall of the earlier experiences.

Similarly, a burgeoning body of research has demonstrated that from twelve months of age on, infants demonstrate delayed imitation of presented action sequences (see Bauer in press for a review). In this paradigm, children are shown an action, or a sequence of actions, associated with a specific object or objects. At a specified retention interval, children are again presented with the objects; if they spontaneously perform the previously modelled actions, it must be based on their memory of the modelled actions because they did not produce the actions before seeing the model in the original presentation, and because children of the same age with no experience do not produce the actions. Using this paradigm, it has been amply demonstrated that children experiencing an event when they are as young as twelve months of age are able to retain aspects of their experience for as long as one year (Bauer *et al.* 1994; McDonough and Mandler 1994; Meltzoff 1995; see Fivush 1994 for an overview). These results indicate that events experienced early in life can be remembered over very long periods of time.

A critical question, however, is whether any of these memories can be expressed verbally. A few experimental studies which have focused on trying to elicit verbal recall of events experienced preverbally have failed to demonstrate any clear indication of this kind of translation even when children were assessed at ages three to five years, when they are clearly capable of recalling events verbally (Boyer *et al.* 1994; Myers *et al.* 1994). But there are a few anecdotes in the literature that suggest such a translation is possible (Myers *et al.* 1994; Nelson and Ross 1980; Todd and Perlmutter 1980). All of these anecdotes focus on an individual child who is able to provide an isolated verbal label when placed back in the context in which the event was originally experienced. For example, in Myers *et al.* (1987), upon seeing the screen on which pictures had been displayed during the original experience, one almost three-year-old child said 'blue whale'. This was, indeed, one of the pictures that had been displayed when he had participated in this experience at the age of nine months.

Descriptions from the clinical literature of children with known histories of trauma during infancy and early childhood confirm that children's verbal recall of events occurring very early in life is quite sparse, if evident at all. Gaensbauer (1995) reports that during play therapy, in which the children were provided with all the appropriate props and encouraged and guided by the therapist who knew what had occurred, most children could re-enact their trauma. Children under the age of about eighteen months when the trauma occurred, however, could not verbally recall much, if anything, about the event, even if interviewed many years later when they were clearly capable of verbal recall. Terr (1988) also reports that children traumatized between 18 and about 36 months of age showed 'spotty', fragmentary verbal recall; only those children traumatized after the age of 36 months were able to provide a coherent verbal account of what had occurred. Similarly, Howe *et al.* (1994) assessed children's memories of medical emergency room visits. Children ranging in age from eighteen months to five years were interviewed at home both a few days after their treatment visit and again six months later. In general, children who were older at the time of the accident were able to report more information verbally both immediately and six months later. Particularly interesting was the very low level of verbal recall from children who were eighteen months old at the time of the accident, at both delays. Thus both clinical observations and more experimentally controlled studies of early event memory converge on the conclusion that events occurring before the age of about eighteen months are extremely difficult to verbalize, even as children develop more sophisticated language skills.

Research by Bauer and Werwerka (1995, in press) adds an interesting wrinkle to this conclusion. In their study, thirteen- to twenty-month-old infants imitated a series of action sequences immediately after presentation, and were able to re-enact these sequences after delays of three to twelve months. In addition, children who had better productive language skills at time of the initial experience, as assessed by maternal report, spontaneously produced more memory-related verbalizations as they were re-enacting the sequences than children with less productive vocabularies. Bauer and Werwerka (in press) assessed the memories of the children who had been twenty months old at the initial experience again twelve months later when they were 32 months of age. Intriguingly, children who had better productive language at twenty months of age and who verbalized more about the event during the intervening memory assessment now had better verbal recall of the event than children who verbalized less about the event during the intervening assessment. Thus verbal ability at time of experience is related to long-term ability to recall events verbally.

Overall, then, although there is some indication that events experienced during the second half of the first year of life may be reflected in behaviour for many years, there is no indication that these memories become accessible for verbal recall as children develop language skills. Indeed, even under highly supportive retrieval conditions, when children are back in the same spatial–temporal context as the original event, and/or are provided with appropriate props and verbal prompting, children do not seem to be able to provide more than a few fragmentary verbalizations about events experienced during the first year and a half of life. To date, there is no evidence in the literature of children being able to provide a decontextualized extended verbal account of an event experienced before the age of eighteen months, even when assessed after they have become linguistically able to recount the past. Thus it seems highly unlikely that events occurring during this early developmental period could be accessible for verbal recall during adulthood. But once children enter the language-learning years, the ability to recall past experiences verbally changes dramatically.

THE TRANSITION TO VERBAL RECALL

The development of language is an astonishing, yet gradual process (see Garton 1992 for an overview). Most children say their first word sometime between 12 and 18 months of age, and begin putting words together sometime around their second birthday. By about three years of age, children are speaking in clearly comprehensible sentences, although, of course, language skills continue to develop throughout childhood and into adulthood.

Whereas the preverbal infant may be reliant on re-encountering events, places, and people in order to reactivate and access memories, the acquisition of language offers a much more efficient means of retrieving and maintaining memories. With the acquisition of language, and the concurrent development of a rich semantic system, the child can be reminded of events through language. These developments allow for effective, self-maintained reminding, and increase the likelihood that conceptually similar memories will be activated. Language also facilitates the linking together of events separate in time and place, and allows one to refer to events in the absence of any physical cues.

A number of researchers have now conducted studies of children's naturally occurring talk about the past from near the beginning of language learning (Eisenberg 1985; Hudson 1990; Sachs 1983). The general concurrence of their findings is that talk about the past progresses from highly cued and elicited recall to children's spontaneous initiations about past events. Before eighteen months, children make few, if any, references to past events. From eighteen months to two years, children refer to past events, but most often in reference to an absent object, to a recently completed action or event, or in the context of highly routinized conversational games (for example 'Where's X?'). These conversations are almost always initiated by adults. From two to two and a half years, children participate willingly in memory conversations with adults but, again, these conversations are most often in the form of a routine in which an adult asks a question and supplies the answer, and the child imitates the answer, or in which an adult asks a yes-no question to which the child responds appropriately. By around two and a half to three years, children engage in short but frequent conversations about earlier past events, often at their own initiation. Notably, this general developmental pattern appears to hold across several different cultures. Eisenberg (1985) found similar patterns with a Hispanic sample to Hudson's (1990) and Sach's (1983) findings with white middle-class children. Miller and Sperry (1988) also concluded that the working-class South Baltimore children in their sample had achieved spontaneous talk about the past at around two and a half years. Finally, Heath (1983) found that children from white and African-American working-class communities in North Carolina talked about their own past experiences before age three.

Thus, by the time children are between two and a half and three years of age, they are able to recall verbally a good bit of accurate information about their past, and they can easily report about events that occurred more than six months ago (Fivush *et al.* 1987). At this point, however, their verbal reports are still somewhat fragmentary. Most of their recall is in the form of bits and pieces of information recalled in response to specific questions from adults. When recounting a past event, one must go beyond providing details about what occurred; one must place the event in spatial and temporal context, introduce the people involved, provide background details that connect and explain the various components of the event, and provide evaluative information that gives the event its meaning (for example Chafe 1990; Labov 1982; Peterson and McCabe 1982). Simply put, one must tell a good story. It is not until children are about three to three and a half years old that they are able to provide a reasonably coherent narrative about a past experience. At this point in development, most children will spontaneously provide orienting information to help place the event in spatial–temporal context, and they will also include a wide variety of evaluative devices to portray the event's personal meaning (Fivush *et al.* 1995; Miller and Sperry 1988; Umiker-Seboek 1979). Narrative skills continue to develop, with children including more background explanation, more explicit temporal and causal information (using words such as *first*, *next*, *because*, *when*, and so forth), and more descriptive information as they grow older (Fivush *et al.* 1995; Hudson and Shapiro 1991; Peterson and McCabe 1982). Additionally, whereas younger children rely heavily on adults' questions to help structure their recall, as children progress through the preschool years, they need fewer and fewer prompts and less verbal guidance from adults in order to give a coherent account of a past event (Hamond and Fivush 1990; Todd and Perlmutter 1980; see Pillemer and White 1989 for a review).

Over the preschool years, then, children's abilities to give an independent, coherent account of a past experience develop dramatically, suggesting that children are learning to use language to help them structure their understanding of events. Following Vygotsky (1978), we maintain that, although language and thought are not isomorphic, language becomes the dominant mode in which thought can be expressed both externally to others and internally to oneself. The implication is that the narrative form the child adopts can shape and change the memory representation, just as more complex event representations can be talked about with more advanced narrative forms. In this way, narrative forms organize the experience of the event and its subsequent representation in memory (see Fivush and Haden (in press) for further discussion of this point).

Given this theoretical framework, several questions arise as to how events come to be represented in memory. First, how does talking about a specific event, either before, during, or after its occurrence, influence children's developing representation and memory of that experience? Second, how does talking about past events in general help children learn the forms and function of talking about the past? Each of these issues is addressed, before we turn to a third question, the fate of these early memories as children grow older.

LANGUAGE AND MEMORIES OF SPECIFIC EVENTS

Even verbally competent children may rely on external narration to understand and remember events. Talk about an event may influence the way in which it is encoded and its accessibility for later retrieval. In a series of studies, Pipe *et al.* (in preparation) have examined the effects of narrative structure on children's event recall. In these studies children aged five to six years took part in an hierarchically organized event, 'Visiting the Pirate'. When the actions, objects, and goals were described and explained as part of the joint interaction between researcher and child (for example.'Now we are going to make the pirate map. First we have to make the special paint, then . . .' etc.), verbal recall was more complete and more accurate than when children participated in the same event but with only 'empty language' accompanying the interaction (for example 'Now we are going to do this.'). It may not be simply the labelling of objects or actions that is important for later recall. Marche and Howe (1995), for example, narrated every second action of a story presented via slides, and found no effect on children's memory of whether or not details were labelled. Rather, recall may be influenced by the way in which adult conversation provides structure and helps the child comprehend the event and relations among its actions.

Another way in which narration might facilitate recall is by making memories more accessible on the basis of verbal prompts and cues provided during the recall interview. If the event descriptions match the questions or prompts provided at recall, this may facilitate the process of memory retrieval. It appears, however, that the effects of talking about events may have more far-reaching effects, influencing the memory representation itself, not only its retrieval. In the Pipe *et al.* (in preparation) study, for example, the effects of narration on children's event recall were observed not only when children were verbally prompted to recall actions relating to specific sub-goals, but also in free recall prior to prompting. The pattern of errors further suggested that narration during the event provided children with something more than the verbal codes for specific event actions. Children who experienced the event without specific descriptions of objects, actions, and the goals of the event not only recalled less information but also included more extraneous information in their accounts. The difference is not simply that children who did not have the event narrated for them could not describe the event as accurately as those who did; the increase in errors was primarily due to the intrusion of actions and objects that were not part of the particular event rather than distorted descriptions of the event itself. Moreover, even in re-enactment, children who experienced the event without narration made more intrusions. These results indicate that narration provided a more easily understood framework in which children could interpret the event. Children without this framework, without meaningful narration, intruded erroneous details in much the same way as Bartlett's (1932) adults behaved when recalling stories from another culture. With meaningful narration, children are able to organize the event representation by forming coherent relations among actions and by understanding why actions occur when they do.

Children's encoding of events might be influenced by narration in other, related ways. Adult narration may facilitate recall by encouraging children to organize groups of actions into coherent units, which young children may not do spontaneously (Rather *et al.* 1990). Moreover, adult narration during the unfolding of an event may focus the child's attention towards central actions and away from peripheral ones. Children might be learning not only what to encode, but also what to ignore. Tessler and Nelson (1994), for example, found that only those items that were labelled by the child or the parent during the occurrence of the event were mentioned when children were interviewed about the event a week later.

Narration might sometimes serve to highlight a particular episode in memory, or conversely, to highlight similarities across different experiences. In many naturally occurring interactions, the aspects of an event that are highlighted are likely to be those unique to the particular episode or occurrence. In this way, narration can help define a specific instance so that the experience can be remembered with less interference from other, similar experiences. On other occasions, however, the purpose of narration may be to highlight the similarities between experiences, to make links with previous or familiar experiences. Thus, narration may also encourage the child to relate the present event to past experiences, helping the child to construct a meaningful, self-relevant representation.

Events given utterance as they unfold, by the child or an adult interacting with the child, facilitate the child's retelling of the event. A similar benefit might also occur even if narration was not present during the event but instead took place either before or after the event. Baker-Ward *et al.* (1994) found that the amount and quality of preparation children received before their first dental examination had a modest facilitating effect on their later recall of the event. Results from Pipe *et al.* (in preparation) also indicate that the effect of narration before an event is experienced is very similar to that of providing narration during the event; children who were read a story before the event recalled more information and made fewer errors in their accounts than children who only experienced the event without narration. Particularly for unfamiliar, novel events, narration prior to experience appears to provide children with a framework in which to interpret the event. It must be noted, however, that in both of these studies, prior narration was accompanied by either a video or an illustrated picture book of the event. It is not clear at present whether narration alone would have the same facilitating effect.

Just as narration prior to an event can provide a framework for interpreting the event, subsequent narration can equip the child with a framework for retrieving and reminiscing about the event. Goodman *et al.* (1994) assessed children's memories for a voiding cystourethrogram (VCUG), an extremely unpleasant medical procedure involving catherization, fluoroscopic filming, and voiding of the bladder while still on the examination table. Parental willingness to discuss the VCUG with children after the event was related to children's accurate reporting of the event. Consistent with this finding, results from Pipe *et al.* (in preparation) show that when children receive narration a few days after a non-narrated event, their performance is identical to that of children receiving the narration during the event, and is superior to that of children receiving no narration. Providing narrative information after the experience also highlights what information should be remembered and recalled. For example, Anderson and Pichert (1978) have demonstrated that a change in perspective after the event can influence what is reported. In their study, adults read a story about two boys playing in a house. Participants were asked to take the perspective of a home buyer or a burglar before they read the passage, and were then asked to recall the passage. Later, they were asked to take another perspective and recall the passage again. With this change in perspective, some new information was recalled and some of the earlier recalled information was forgotten.

Providing children with the appropriate framework can be beneficial, but frameworks can also have biasing, distorting effects on memory. In the context of abusive experiences, the framework provided by adult narration may not be an accurate reflection of the actual experience. What happens to children's recall when they receive distorted narration? Indeed, the question most frequently addressed with respect to the effects of post-event narration on children's event reports is whether young children are more suggestible than older children and adults; that is, are they more likely to include the misinformation in their subsequent accounts (see Ceci and Bruck 1993 for a review).

It is useful to distinguish here between two phenomena which frequently are both referred to as suggestibility, namely, compliance with misleading information at the time it is presented, for example in the form of a question, and misinformation acceptance, that is, incorporation of the misinformation into the child's own account. There are clear age differences, at least up until age eight years, in children's willingness to comply with misleading questions at the time they are asked (for example Goodman and Reed 1986; King and Yuille 1987; Ornstein *et al.* 1992). In many instances compliance with misleading questions clearly reflects the operation of social factors in the interview situation rather than those relating to memory for the event and may depend on such factors as the content of the question, the way in which the question is phrased, whether the interview is supportive or intimidating, the strength of the memory for the event, and the delay between the event and the interview (Batterman-Faunce and Goodman 1993; Dent 1990; Gee and Pipe, 1995; Goodman and Clarke-Stewart, 1991; Greenstock Pipe 1996; Rudy and Goodman 1991). Although important in the context of children's testimony, issues relating to compliance are outside the scope of the current chapter. We are concerned here with the more general question of the effects of post-event information, including misinformation, on children's memory of the event.

Only a few studies have directly addressed the question of how talking about an event afterwards affects the underlying memory representation of that event (for example *et al.* 1995; Ceci *et al.* 1987; Leichtman and Ceci 1995; Poole and Lindsay 1995). Although young children can clearly be misled about the details contained in a story on the basis of a single exposure to misinformation (Ceci *et al.* 1987), we know of no evidence that their accounts of their own experiences are so easily manipulated. It is also clear, however, that under some conditions, biased information about an event may distort children's understanding and interpretation of events and lead to errors in their accounts, especially for confusing, unfamiliar experiences.

For example, Clarke-Stewart *et al.* (1989) showed that a biased interrogation may have a marked influence on children's accounts, in particular on children's interpretation of what happened (see also Goodman and Clarke-Stewart 1991). In Clarke-Stewart *et al.*'s study, children interacted with a confederate posing as a janitor. The janitor followed one of two scripts, either cleaning and arranging some toys, including a doll, or playing with them roughly and suggestively. When children were interviewed shortly after, their accounts were generally accurate regardless of whether the interview was neutral, comprising open-ended, non-suggestive questions, or biased to be consistent with the child's experience. When the interrogation was inconsistent with the child's experience, suggesting that the janitor who had cleaned the doll had actually been playing and was bad, there was a marked decrease in accuracy in response to the interpretive questions (for example, was the janitor cleaning the toys or playing with them? Was he doing his job or was he being bad?). The effect of a second biased interview immediately after the first was even stronger, with the majority of children accepting the interrogator's interpretations of the janitor's behaviour. Moreover, children maintained these interpretations even when questioned by their parents at the end of the interview session. In general, however, children who were interrogated with a biased interview answered the factual questions just as accurately as those children interviewed without such a bias.

Leichtman and Ceci (1995) have similarly shown that providing a biased context for interpreting an event can have marked effects on children's subsequent accounts. Three- and five-year-old children were provided with a stereotype of Sam Stone, a nice but bumbling stranger. Later, they had a chance to briefly meet Sam Stone when he visited their pre-school. In addition, some of the children received repeated suggestions about two stereotype-consistent behaviours that had not occurred during his visit. During a later interview, over one-third of the responses made by the younger children who had received only the prior stereotype information agreed that Sam Stone had done at least one specific bad action. When children received both the prior stereotype and subsequent, repeated suggestions about the two bad actions, close to half of the responses of the younger children, and nearly one-third of the responses of the older children incorporated these stereotype consistent actions into their free recall. When young children are exposed to biased narration repeatedly or following very long delays, it appears that their accounts may be especially vulnerable (Bruck *et al.* 1995; Poole and Lindsay 1995).

However, in the absence of suggestive or misleading information, young children seem remarkably immune to post-event information provided by adults. Fivush and her colleagues (Fivush *et al.* 1991; Fivush 1994) examined the extent to which preschool children would incorporate information originally provided by adults during discussions of past events into their own subsequent recall of those events.

Across ages two and a half six years and a large variety of events, there was little evidence that children reported information originally reported by adults; only about 9 to 12 per cent of the information children recounted was information provided by either the mother or an experimenter on a previous recall. Thus, whereas it is clear that strong, repeated misinformation can have a deleterious effect on children's event memories, it is equally clear that young children's memories are not so fragile as to be completely open to even vague suggestions.

LANGUAGE AND MEMORIES OF EVENTS IN GENERAL

Thus far, we have seen that the content of what children recall may sometimes be influenced by information provided by adults under some conditions. In addition, a growing body of research demonstrates that children learn how to organize their recall of past experiences through participating in reminiscing with adults. Moreover, adults show individual differences in the way they talk about the past across many different kinds of events. These general 'styles' of conversing about the past, regardless of the specific event discussed, have implications for children's verbal recall and for their developing memory systems.

Specifically, individual parents differ in the extent and type of support they provide for their children during memory conversations (Engel 1986; Fivush and Fromholf 1988; Hudson 1990; McCabe and Peterson 1991; Reese and Fivush 1993). Some parents provide a great deal of contextual support for their children's recall by asking questions and giving more and more information when children cannot recall an event. When children do provide a part of the memory, these high-elaborative parents confirm children's responses and then elaborate further (for example, child recalls eating ice-cream at a birthday party and mother responds. 'Ice-cream. It was an ice-cream cake. And what was on the ice-cream cake?'). In contrast, low-elaborative parents tend to repeat the same question over and over to the child in an attempt to get the 'correct' memory response (for example, mother asks child who was at the event; child does not answer; and mother asks again 'Do you remember who was there?' without further elaboration). These parents provide less information, and thus less contextual support, for their children overall. Their conversations also tend to be shorter.

Parents' styles of talking about the past generalize across the specific events talked about and are consistent over several years (Reese *et al.* 1993) and across siblings (Haden 1996). Importantly, early in development, children are not consistent in their style of reminiscing. By the time children are five or six years of age, however, through a process of mutual accommodation between parent and child, children have internalized a relatively stable style of talking about the past with their parents (Reese *et al.* 1993).

There are at least three implications of style of reminiscing for the study of autobiographical memory and the recovered memory debate. First, parents' styles of talking about the past may be influential in how well children maintain event representations over lengthy delays. Events that are discussed in greater depth and perhaps with greater frequency after their occurrence may be less vulnerable to decay and to the intrusion of additional information than events that are not discussed in detail. Thus, an elaborative parental style may result in children's stronger representations for a variety of events.

Suggestive evidence supports this idea. Williams (1995) reports that of a sample of adult females with known histories of childhood sexual abuse, about one-third recalled their abuse when interviewed as adults, and a subset (12 of 75) claimed that there was a period of time during which they did not recall their abuse but now do. Women who always remembered their abuse also recalled more supportive interactions surrounding their abuse experience from their mothers than those women claiming to have forgotten their abuse for a period of time. Similarly, in the Goodman *et al.* (1994) study discussed earlier in which children were asked to recall their VCUG experiences, the researchers report that children's memories were positively related to maternal 'warmth'. Although it is not clear exactly what maternal support and warmth is indexing in these studies, it seems quite likely that one aspect of maternal support would be talking about the event with the child. Mothers who talk in more supportive ways with their children about traumatic experiences may help their children form more organized and more enduring memories of those events.

Second, internalizing a style of remembering may eventually influence the way in which children encode events. A parent's style of reminiscing may largely serve to instruct children in the aspects of events that are interesting and important to remember; this may eventually be translated into the aspects of events that are important to notice as events are taking place. Third, and finally, a child's style of reminiscing is most clearly reflected in their skill at verbally recalling events. An elaborative style is simply a more effective way of communicating to others than a low-elaborative style. Children with an elaborative style of reminiscing provide lengthy, fluent, and detailed accounts of the past. It is conceivable that the richness of their accounts may render them more believable than the sparse, unevaluated narratives of children with a low-elaborative style.

The research on individual differences in adult–child talk about the past thus demonstrates that by the end of the preschool period children are adopting a more general style of talking about past events. This style may influence the strength of their memory representations, what is attended to during encoding, and the efficacy of their verbal accounts. It is important to note, however, that styles of talking about the past appear to vary across cultures. White middle-class parents are likely to be more elaborative on the whole than adults in some other cultures, as Eisenberg (1985) noted with her Hispanic sample and Mullen and Yi (1995) with a Korean population. Cultural differences in reminiscing styles probably have a great deal to do with the value placed on memory and the reason for which memories are discussed in the culture: whether primarily for purposes of entertainment, reminiscing, or moral lessons (for example Miller *et al.* 1992; Mullen and Yi 1995).

Thus far, we have argued that the ways in which events are talked about as they are occurring, in preparation, and in retrospect all play a role in how those events will be understood, represented, and ultimately recalled by young children. Moreover, the ways in which adults talk about events with their young children in general will have enduring effects on the ways in which children come to represent and recount their past experiences overall, with some children developing a more elaborative autobiographical style than others. Of obvious concern is the ultimate fate of these memories. To date, research has not examined whether the way in which events are talked about with young children has implications for the long-term retention of those memories. But over the past ten years there has been a growing body of research on the more general question of it and how children recall specific experiences across long delays.

LONG-TERM RECALL OF CHILDHOOD EXPERIENCES

Certainly, as adults, we remember personal experiences across decades, and these memories are often highly accurate, whether it is memories of mundane events such as our high-school classmates (Bahric *et al.* 1975) or more emotional and traumatic events such as concentration camp experiences (Wagenaar and Groenig 1990) or memories of highly significant personal and historical events (Conway 1995). Very few studies have examined long-term recall in children, but the few that have confirm that children are able to recall experiences over long delays. In the first study of its kind, Sheingold and Tenney (1982) examined memories for the birth of a sibling occurring when the participant was aged four. Four-year-olds were able to recall accurate details about the birth occurring just a few months ago, and older children and adults continued to recall accurate information even as time since the event increased. Although providing evidence that some salient events may be very well recalled across childhood, this study was limited in at least two ways. First, birth of a sibling is an event that many families talk about frequently, and individuals may be recalling the family story, rather than their own experience. Second, the study was cross-sectional in design. To truly assess long-term retention and forgetting of personal memories, it is necessary to conduct longitudinal research.

Although children may be able to remember their experiences over very long time periods, they may recall significantly less information about them as time goes on (for example Flin *et al.* 1992; Hudson and Fivush 1991; Ornstein *et al.* 1992; Pipe 1992; Salmon and Pipe 1996). Salmon and Pipe (1996), for example, re-interviewed children who had taken part in a quasi-medical event one year earlier, at the age of three or five years. Both age groups recalled significantly fewer items of accurate information about the event following the one-year delay than they had when interviewed one week after the event. The younger children also made more errors at the long delay although the accounts of the older children remained highly accurate. Pipe (1992) also reported follow-up interviews with children who had taken part in a novel event, 'visiting the magician', one or two years previously. Children interviewed following the two-year delay provided much briefer free recall reports than they had when interviewed ten days or ten weeks after the event. This was the case even when the original event context was reinstated fully at the time of the interview. The effects of very long delays may, however, depend on the nature of the interview. In a one-year follow-up of six and nine year-old children who had participated in the magician event as part of another study, children were directly prompted to recall aspects of the event, and recalled as much information after the one-year delay as they had soon after the event (Pipe 1992). In fact, the younger children reported more information overall following the longer delay.

Poole and White (1993) examined whether children's responses to repeated questioning within an interview session showed the same patterns as they had two years earlier. As was the case when interviewed shortly after the event, children were less consistent in response to repeated yes–no questions than were adults. In addition, at the longer delay there was some evidence that children were less accurate in their accounts, in particular, in response to open-ended questions than they had been two years earlier.

Few studies have examined the effects of much longer delays on children's event recall. Goodman *et al.* (1989) found that very few children recalled a 'mundane social interaction' in which they had participated when aged between three and six years, when interviewed four years later (see also Goodman and Clarke-Stewart, (1991) for a description). Indeed, when initially asked for free recall, only one of the 15 subjects recalled any information relating to the original event. Following extensive questioning, which presumably provided more specific retrieval cues, several more children recalled the event, although in general they recalled relatively little information. Despite their difficulty in retrieving the memory, children were none the less not easily mislead about things that did not happen, in particular by questions which might lead to the implication that abuse had occurred during the original event.

Hudson and Fivush (1991) similarly found that children had difficulty accessing a memory from six years earlier until provided with more specific retrieval cues. They assessed children's memories for a kindergarten class trip to a museum of archaeology immediately, six weeks, one year, and six years after the event. Even after a six-year delay, children were able to report accurate details of their experiences and there were few errors or intrusions. However, whereas there was little evidence of forgetting up to one year after the event, children did not recall as much after six-years as they had on previous interviews, and often needed very specific cues, such as photographs of the event, in order to recall any information at all. Thus, although it is clear that children can often recall their experiences over long periods of time, it is also clear that forgetting does occur, and events may become more difficult to access as time since the experience increases.

Long-term recall of past experiences is likely to depend on a number of variables in addition to the length of time that has passed, such as the nature and distinctiveness of the event (Hudson *et al.* 1992), intervening experiences, additional experiences or interviews (Fivush and Schwarzmueller 1995; Poole and White 1995), and the memory interview itself, in particular, the retrieval cues provided. We also need to consider the age of the child at the time of experience. In particular, there is reason to speculate that memories from the preschool years may follow a different course from memories from later childhood. We have already seen how memories of events experienced before the age of about eighteen months may be inaccessible for verbal recall, but what of events occurring between the ages of two and four years? Most adults have difficulty recalling events from their childhood that occurred before this age, a phenomenon that has been labelled childhood amnesia (for reviews see Pillemer and White 1989; Wetzler and Sweeney 1986). The fact that adults have particular difficulty recalling events from this early period of life might suggest that children also have difficulty retaining memories from this period. Yet the few studies that have examined long-term retention of preschool memories have found results quite similar to the results with older children. Fivush and her colleagues (Fivush and Hamond 1990; Fivush and Shukat 1995; Hamond and Fivush 1990; see Fivush 1993 for a review) have demonstrated that four- to six-year-old children are able to give accurate, extended accounts of events experienced one to two-years in the past. For example, both four- and six-year-old children gave long detailed accounts of a family trip to Disneyworld that occurred either six or eighteen months earlier (Hamond and Fivush 1990). Moreover, four-year-old children who went to Disneyworld eighteen months earlier reported as much information as six-year-old children who had been to Disneyworld six months earlier, although younger children needed more cues and prompts in order to recall as much as the older children recalled spontaneously.

Most impressive, in a five-year longitudinal study, Schwarzmueller and Fivush (in preparation) found that children aged eight are able to recall events that they had reported in a previous interview when they were between three and four years of age. It must be noted, however, that the events recalled over this long delay were special, distinctive events, such as being a flower girl at an aunt's wedding, or the death of a pet. It may very well be that distinctiveness is essential for recalling a specific event over long delays, as these events can be more easily cued and accessed than more routine or mundane events (see Hudson *et al.* (1992) for a full discussion of this issue).

In a related finding, Pillemer *et al.* (1994) examined memory for a unique preschool experience, both immediately and seven years later. Children were evacuated from their preschool when a fire alarm went off, which was subsequently determined to be due simply to burning popcorn. All of the three-and-a-half- and four-and-a-half-year old children could report this experience when interviewed immediately afterward. Seven years later, the children who had been four and a half at the time of experience could still recall the event, but the children who had been three and a half years had much more difficulty. Pillemer *et al.* attribute this age difference to the fact that at the time of experience the four-and-a-half-year-olds understood the causal structure of the event which allowed them to retain the memory, whereas the three-and-a-half-year-olds did not appreciate the causal structure at the time of experience, and so had a more disorganized memory to begin with.

It is perhaps not surprising that, overall, the research indicates that there is substantial forgetting for some events over long periods of time. On the other hand, some events seem to be remarkably well remembered even over periods of many years. Especially when events are distinctive, personally meaningful, and well organized, preschool children are able to verbally recall them over long periods of time, and can retain these memories across the transition into childhood. Because traumatic events are often quite distinctive, they may be especially memorable. Traumatic events are also, by definition, stressful, and this may also affect their memorability. It is clear, however, that the relation between stress and memory is not a simple one (see Christianson 1992 for a review). Although it is reasonable to assume that stress will frequently influence children's memories of their experiences, the relation is unlikely to be simply that trauma either enhances memory or leads to poorer recall. Indeed, both positive (for example Goodman *et al.* 1991; Ornstein *et al.* 1992) and negative (for example Oates and Shrimpton 1991; Peters 1991) effects on memory have been reported for children interviewed about stressful events.

A number of clinical case studies have also documented children's memories of traumatic experiences ranging from a dog bite (Terr 1988) to being kidnapped (Terr 1979, 1983) or witnessing a homicide (Pynoos and Eth 1984; Pynoos and Nader 1989). In general, these case studies indicate that the majority of children aged older than three years at the time of the trauma are likely to remember the experience, in some cases over quite long time periods. Terr (1979, 1983), for example, concluded that the majority of children who had been kidnapped from a school bus when aged between five and fourteen years could still give '. . . a fully detailed account of the experience' when interviewed four years later (Terr 1983, p.1545). Similarly, in a study focusing on children who experienced trauma before age five years, the majority of children aged between three and five years at the time of the trauma could give a verbal account when interviewed following delays of six months to twelve years. As noted earlier, however, children who were younger than age three at the time of the traumatic experience were not generally able to verbally recall the experience, even once they had clearly developed language.

More experimentally controlled studies have focused on painful and stressful medical procedures. For example, Goodman *et al.* (1994) and Ornstein (1995) investigated children's memories for a VCUG. Goodman *et al.* report that three- to four-year-old children did not recall this event as well as five- to six-year-old children, although almost all children could provide some accurate information. Ornstein reports that children between the ages of three and seven years demonstrated impressive memory for this event both immediately and six weeks later. Not only was there virtually no forgetting among these children over this relatively short delay, but most of the information was given in response to the first, open-ended question, in contrast to the more general finding that young children need many questions and prompts in order to help them retrieve information.

Similarly, Baker-Ward and Burgwyn-Bailer (in preparation) have found that three- to seven-year-old children who experienced facial laceration requiring suturing recalled details of their experiences quite well immediately, six weeks and one year later. In fact, there was almost no forgetting over the one-year period, although the amount recalled in response to open-ended questions declined over time and that recalled in response to yes/no questions increased. Intriguingly, those children who asked more questions of the physician during the procedure showed better memory for the event, when this was assessed at the six-week delay (Baker-Ward *et al.* 1995). This finding fits with our general framework that the ways in which an event is talked about and explained to the child during its occurrence will affect subsequent memory.

Clearly, even young children can recall traumatic experiences relatively well over time, a least when they were older than two and a half years at the time of experience. However, as is the case for non-traumatic experiences, few traumatic experiences occurring before the age of two and a half years are likely to be available for verbal recall. For example, as discussed earlier, Howe *et al.* (1994) interviewed children ranging in age from eighteen months to five years about an emergency room visit both immediately and after a six month delay. Children in the youngest group recalled little verbally either immediately or at the six month delay. But from thirty months of age on, although older children recalled more verbally than did younger children, all children recalled as much after the six month delay as at the immediate interview. The only decline in memory was for peripheral information in free recall, but once open-ended prompts were introduced, even peripheral information was as well recalled after six months as at immediate recall.

Although all of these experiences can be assumed to be stressful, individual differences in stress level may play a role in how well an experience is recalled. Findings to date are equivocal. Howe *et al.* (1994) found no relation between stress, as judged by the child's mother, and children's recall. Ornstein (1995) reports a negative relationship between behavioural ratings of stress and children's memory, but no relation between memory and cortisol measures of stress. Goodman *et al.* (1994) report that children showing symptoms related to post-traumatic stress disorder (PTSD), such as nightmares and specific fears, tended to be more inaccurate in their recall of the VCUG procedure. Finally, Parker *et al.* (in press) found a curvilinear relation between stress and memory. They interviewed three- and four-year-old children about their experiences during Hurricane Andrew, a devastating storm that hit the Florida coast, between three and six months after the event. Children recalled a remarkable amount of accurate information about their experiences, and there was no relation between amount of recall and retention interval. However, those children who experienced high stress during the storm, as judged by objective damage to their house (for example, the roof caved in, trees came into the house) recalled less than children experiencing moderate stress (for example, broken windows, trees down in their yard).

In summary, although the relation between stress and memory is still not clear, it is obvious is that even very young children can recall very stressful experiences extremely well even after delays of several months or a year. Moreover, it seems that children report more about stressful experiences than about more mundane experiences. For example, Ornstein (1995) reports that children's recall of a VCUG was more complete than their memories for a well-doctor visit. Similarly, children recalled substantially more information about Hurricane Andrew (about 100 propositions) compared with comparably aged children recalling an extended family trip to Disneyworld (about 40 propositions) (Hamond and Fivush 1991). Because no study has directly compared memories for traumatic and mundane experiences, we must be cautious in drawing conclusions about the effects of trauma on either the initial memory, or the longevity of the memory.

It must be noted that in studies examining the effects of trauma on children's memory, the stressful or traumatic experiences are likely to have been 'socially validated' and discussed with the children at the time of occurrence, prior to or following the event. The contribution of these sources of information additional to the children's generally detailed recall is only beginning to be studied. It is, of course, possible that some memories for traumatic experiences may be maintained in the absence of any such discussions. Children may well rehearse events to themselves, even when they are not discussed or disclosed to anyone else. But absence of discussion may contribute to forgetting even of traumatic experiences. We know that narratives provide a structure for organizing memories, and possibly provide the basis for maintaining integrated memories over long time periods. When there is no narrative framework, or a framework at odds with the child's experience, this may well change children's understanding and organization of the experience, and ultimately their ability to provide a detailed and coherent account. None the less, it is clear that memories for stressful and traumatic events are at least as good if not better than memories for more mundane events. Of course, we do not know the ultimate fate of these traumatic memories. Even though children seem to recall these events extremely well for months or even years, this does not mean that these events will be retained or easily accessible in the adult years.

CONCLUSIONS AND IMPLICATIONS

In this chapter, we considered the developing relations between language and memories for personally experienced events. In keeping with the purpose of this book, we are especially interested in how this research informs the recovered/false memory debate. Some of the implications have been foreshadowed, but in this section we draw the comparisons more explicitly, and speculate on the fate of early memories, spoken and unspoken. Again, we must stress that our focus is on verbal recall. Whereas many experiences may have long-lasting effects on personality and behaviour, they may not necessarily be accessible for conscious recollection or recounting. However, it is also our contention that language gives memories a particular coherence, through narrative structure, that may not be possible outside of language.

It seems quite clear that memories for events that occur before the age of about eighteen months are particularly difficult to verbalize. Even as children become competent narrators of their own experience, they are unable to provide more than a few fragmentary labels about these early experiences, and even these fragments seem to be retrieved only in highly supportive contexts which provide rich and detailed cues about the event. Thus it is highly unlikely that experiences from this early developmental period are accessible for verbal recall as children grow into adulthood.

Between eighteen months and three years of age, children begin to reference past experiences and can participate in conversations about the past, but again, only under highly supportive conditions. Adults provide most of the content and structure of past narratives, with young children providing bits and pieces of information in response to direct requests. Although experiences from this period of life can be recalled verbally, children's reports are 'spotty' and fragmentary. Intriguingly, children seem to retain at least some of these memories over extended periods of time, but their verbal reports remain quite fragmented and limited, and this is true for both mundane and traumatic events. Given this pattern, it seems possible that memories for events from this age period are accessible in adulthood, but these memories are likely to be unorganized, and quite sparse. Moreover, young children are highly dependent on adults to provide specific cues and prompts in order to retrieve memories, and thus as adults, these memories would probably only be accessible with very specific cues. Most important, because the memories are so fragmentary, and because poorly organized and comprehensible event memories are more susceptible to misleading information and suggestion, memories from this period of life would be especially prone to reconstruction and suggestion if recalled in adulthood.

During the preschool years, children's memory skills develop dramatically. They become able to provide organized narratives about their past experiences and begin to rely less on adults cues and prompts. Still, until about five or six years of age, children remain somewhat dependent on adults to help them form organized memories of experienced events. Obviously, event memories are based on the experience itself, and the actions performed, the objects interacted with, and the emotions felt will all be part of the evolving representation. Children can and do recall accurate details about events that are not narrated. But the ways in which events are talked about by adults before, during and after they occur, play a fundamental role in how events are remembered in at least two ways. First, language can serve to highlight specific aspects of an ongoing event, drawing the child's attention to those aspects, while downplaying others. Aspects attended to are more likely to be encoded whereas aspects not attended to are less likely to be encoded. In this case, certain aspects of events may never be retrievable because they were never encoded. Second, language helps provide the interpretive structure for an event. Although much of the event may be encoded and retained, only those aspects of the event that fit with the narrative may be recalled. This is essentially the classic schema model of memory first outlined by Bartlett (1932). However, from a developmental perspective, we would argue that young children, who are more reliant on adults to help them provide this organizing narrative, may be more susceptible to the adult's narrative interpretation of the event than are older children and adults.

This position has interesting implications for memories of abuse. It is highly unlikely that adults provide accurate narrative accounts of abusive experiences they are perpetrating on children. Rather, adults are likely to either not talk about the event at all or to provide a distorting narrative account (for example, 'we're playing a special game'). Moreover, most children who are abused are threatened or cajoled into not talking about the experience with anyone. Children experiencing abuse may, therefore, have great difficulty forming a coherent account of the experience. Again, we must stress that we are not arguing that children do not recall experiences that are not talked about. Many children do recall abuse and many adults who were abused as children retain these memories intact from childhood. Rather, we would argue that the ways in which these experiences are organized and remembered may depend, in part, on how they are or are not talked about. Experiences never talked about may be less coherently organized overall than experiences which are talked about. Again, this would mean that these experiences may be particularly difficult to access as children grow older, as less organized memories are generally more difficult to retrieve. Experiences during which adults provide a distorting narrative may lead to memories focusing on what the narrative highlights, thus rendering the abusive aspects more difficult to recall because they do not fit with the organizing structure. It is possible that children remember the abusive aspects of the experience but that they will be unable to provide a coherent verbal account of these aspects of the event. The ultimate fate of such memories remains uncertain. In the short term, we know that events unspoken are not as well recalled and are more prone to error than events spoken, but it seems possible that as children develop more appropriate narrative frameworks for their abuse experiences, they may be able to remember aspects of the events not previously integrated with their narrative accounts. It may also be the case that these memories will be more subject to distortion and suggestion because they are more fragmented. This is clearly a critical question for future research.

As children continue to develop more sophisticated narrative skills, they become less reliant on adults to help them organize and understand their experiences. In a sense, children become able to narrate their own experiences to themselves. But there are interesting individual differences in this process. Children of elaborative parents become better narrators of their own experience than children of less elaborative parents. Children who develop more elaborated ways of talking about their experiences, both to others and to themselves, may be more likely to retain experiences over long periods of time and to be able to provide detailed accounts of their experiences even after long delays. Children of less elaborative parents may have more poorly organized memories that become more difficult to access as they grow older, and may be more dependent on external cues to retrieve these memories. Although quite speculative at this point, individual differences in autobiographical memory skills may play an important role in understanding the fate of early memories.

Finally, we must emphasize that all of the research indicates that childhood events from about the age of three on are remarkably well recalled across the childhood years. Certainly there are differences in how individual children recall individual events, but most studies have found a great deal of accurate information is recalled even after long delays for both mundane and traumatic events. Whatever our ultimate conclusions about the recovered memory debate, the issue must be placed in the context of an impressive ability to recall our past.

REFERENCES

Anderson, R.C. and Pichert J.W. (1978). Recall of previously unrecallable information following a shift in perspective. *Journal of Verbal Learning and Verbal Behavior.* **17**, 1–12.

Bahrick, H., Bahrick, P.O., and Wittlinger, R.P. (1975). Fifty years of memory for names and faces: a cross-sectional approach. *Journal of Experimental Psychology: General*, **104**, 54–75.

Baker-Ward, L. and Burgwyn-Bailer, E. *One-year follow-up of children interviewed regarding treatment of facial lacerations*. (In preparation.)

Baker-Ward, L., Burgwyn, E.O., and Parrish, L.A. (1994). Does knowledge affect young children's memory for a very first dental visit? In *Young children's accounts of medical and dental examinations: Remembering and reporting personal experiences*, symposium presented at the biennial meetings of the Conference on Human Development, Pittsburgh.

Baker-Ward, L., Burgwyn, E., Ornstein, P.A. and Gordon, B.N. (1995). Children's reports of a minor medical emergency. In *Children's memory for emotional and traumatic experiences*, symposium presented at the biennial meetings of the Society for Research in Child Development, Indianapolis.

Bartlett, F.C. (1932). *Remembering: a study in experimental and social psychology*. Cambridge University Press, New York.

Batterman-Faunce, J.M. and Goodman, G.S. (1993). Effects of context on the accuracy and suggestibility of child witnesses. In *Child victims, child witnesses: Understanding and improving testimony* (ed. G.S. Goodman and B.L. Bottoms), pp. 301–30. Guilford Press, New York.

Bauer, P.J. Recalling past events: from infancy to early childhood. *Annals of Child Development*. (In press.)

Bauer, P. and Wewerka, S. (1995). One- to two-year olds' recall of events: the more expressed the more impressed. *Journal of Experimental Child Psychology*, **59**, 475–96.

Bauer, P. and Wewerka, S. Saying is revealing: verbal expression of event memory in the transition from infancy to early childhood. In *Developmental spans in event comprehension and representation: Bridging fictional and actual events* (ed. P van den Broek, P.J. Bauer, and T. Bourg). Erlbaum, Hillsdale, NJ. (In press.)

Bauer, P.J., Hertsgaard, L.A. and Dow, G.A. (1994). After 8 months have passed: long-term recall of events by 1- to 2-year-old children. *Memory*, **2**, 353–82.

Boyer, M.E., Barron, K.L. and Farrar, M.J. (1994). Three-year-olds remember a novel event from 20 months: evidence for long-term memory in children? *Memory*, **2**, 417–46.

Bruck, M., Ceci, S.J., Francoeur, E., and Barr, R. (1995). 'I hardly cried when I got my shot!' Influencing children's reports about a visit to their pediatrician. *Child Development*, **66**, 193–208.

Chafe, W. (1990). Some things that narratives tell us about the mind. In *Narrative thought and narrative language* (ed. B.K. Britton and A.D. Pelligrini), pp.79–98. Erlbaum, Hillsdale, NJ.

Ceci, S.J. and Bruck, M. (1993). Suggestibility of the child witness: a historical review and synthesis. *Psychological Bulletin*, **113**, 403–39.

Ceci, S.J., Toglia, M.P., and Ross, D.F. (1987). *Children's eyewitness memory*. Springer, New York.

Christianson, S.A. (1992). Emotional stress and eyewitness memory: a critical review. *Psychological Bulletin*, **112**, 284–309.

Clarke-Stewart, A., Thompson, W., and Lepore, S. (1989). *Manipulating children's interpretations through interrogation*. Paper presented at the biennial meeting of the Society for Research in Child Development, Kansas City.

Conway, M. (1995). *Flashbulb memories*. Erlbaum, Hillsdale, NJ.

De Casper, A.J. and Fifer, W.P. (1980). Of human bonding: newborns prefer their mother's voices. *Science*, **208**, 1174–6.

De Casper, A.J. and Spence, M.J. (1986). Prenatal maternal speech influences newborn's perception of speech sounds. *Infant Behavior and Development*, **9**, 133–50.

Dent, H.R. (1990). Interviewing. In *The suggestibility of children's recollections* (ed. J.L. Doris), pp. 138–44. American Psycholocal Association, Washington. DC.

Eisenberg, A.R. (1985). Learning to describe past experience in conversation. *Discourse Processes*, **8**, 177–204.

Engel, S. (1986). *Learning to reminisce: A developmental study of how young children talk about the pass*. Unpublished doctoral dissertation, City University of New York.

Fivush, R. (1993). Developmental perspectives on autobiographical recall. In *Child victims, child witnesses: Understanding and improving testimony*, (ed. G.S. Goodman and B.L. Bottoms), pp. 1–24. Guilford Press, New York.

Fivush, R. (1994) (ed.). *Long-term retention of infant memories: a special issue of memory*. Erlbaum, Hillsdale, NJ.

Fivush, R. Young children's event recall: are memories constructed through discourse? *Consciousness and Cognition*, **3**, 356–73. (In press.)

Fivush, R. and Fromhoff, F. (1988). Style and structure in mother–child conversations about the past. *Discourse Processes*, **8**, 177–204.

Fivush, R. and Haden, C. Narrating and representing experience: preschooler's developing autobiographical recounts. In *Developmental spans in event comprehension and representation: bridging fictional and actual events* (ed. P. van den Broek, P.J. Bauer, and T. Bourg). Erlbaum, Hillsdale, NJ., (In press.)

Fivush, R. and Hamond, N. (1990). Autobiographical memory across the preschool years: towards reconceptualizing childhood amnesia. In *Knowing and remembering in young children*, (ed. R. Fivush and J.A. Hudson), pp. 223–48. Cambridge University Press, New York.

Fivush, R. and Schwarzmueller, A. (1995). Say it once again: effects of repeated questions on children's event recall. *Journal of Traumatic Stress*, **8**, 555–80.

Fivush, R. and Shukat, J. (1995). Content, consistency and coherency of early autobiographical recall. In *Memory and testimony in the child witness children's and adults' eyewitness testimony* (ed. M.S. Zaragozza, J.R. Graham, G.C.N. Hall, R. Hirschman, and Y.S. Ben-Porath). Sage, Thousand Oaks, CA.

Fivush, R., Gray, J.T., and Fromhoff, F.A. (1987). Two year olds talk about the past. *Cognitive Development*, **2**, 393–410.

Fivush, R., Hamond, N.R., Harsch, N., Singer, N., and Wolf, A. (1991). Content and consistency of young children's autobiographical recall. *Discourse Processes*, **14**, 373–88.

Fivush, R., Haden, C., and Adam, S. (1995). Preschooler's developing narrative structure: implications for childhood amnesia. *Journal of Experimental Child Psychology*, **60**, 32–56.

Fivush, R., Haden, C., and Reese, E. (1996). Remembering, recounting and reminiscing: the development of autobiographical memory in social context. In *Reconstructing our past: an overview of autobiographical memory* (ed. D. Rubin), pp. 341–59. Cambridge University Press, New York.

Flin, R., Boon, J., Knox, A., and Bull, R. (1992). The effect of a five-month delay on children's and adults' eyewitness testimony. *British Journal of Psychology*, **83**, 323–36.

Gaensbauer, T. (1995). Trauma in the preverbal period: symptoms, memories and developmental impact. *The Psychoanalytic Study of the Child*, **17**, 86–103.

Garton, A.F. (1992). *Social interaction and the development of language and cognition*. Erlbaum, Hillsdale, NJ.

Gee, S. and Pipe, M.E. (1995). Helping children to remember: the influence of object cues on children's accounts of a real event. *Developmental Psychology*, **31**, 746–58.

Goodman, G.S. and Clarke-Stewart, A. (1991). Suggestibility in children's testimony: Implications for child sexual abuse investigations. In *The suggestibility of children's recollections* (ed. J.L. Doris), pp. 92–105. American Psychological Association, Washington, DC.

Goodman, G.S. and Reed, R.S. (1986). Age differences in eyewitness testimony. *Law and Human Behavior*, **10**, 317–32.

Goodman, G.S., Wilson, M.E., Hazan, C., and Reed, R.S. (1989). Children's testimony nearly four years after an event. Unpublished manuscript.

Goodman, G.S., Hirschman, J.E., Hepps, D., and Rudy, L. (1991). Children's memory for stressful events. *Merrill-Palmer Quarterly*, **37**, 109–58.

Goodman, G.S., Quas, J.A., Batterman-Faunce, J.M., Riddlesberger, M.M., and Kuhn, J. (1994). Predictors of accurate and inaccurate memories of traumatic events experienced in childhood. *Consciousness and Cognition*, **3**, 269–94.

Greco, C., Hayne, H., and Rovee-Collier, C. (1990). The roles of function, reminding, and variability in categorization by 3-month-old infants. *Journal of Experimental Psychology: Learning, Memory, and Cognition*, **16**, 617–33.

Greco, C., Rovee-Collier, C., Hayne, H., Griesler, P. and Earley, L. (1986). Ontogeny of early event memory: I. Forgetting and retrieval by 2- and 3-month-olds. *Infant Behavior and Development*, **9**, 441–60.

Greenstock, J. and Pipe, M.-E. (1996). Interviewing children about past events: the influence of peer support and misleading questions. *Child Abuse and Neglect*, **20**, 69–80.

Haden, C. (1996). *Different stories?: Relating patterns of maternal stylistic consistency and sibling similarity in talk about the past*. Submitted manuscript.

Hamond, N.R. and Fivush, R. (1990). Memories of Mickey Mouse: young children recount their trip to Disneyworld. *Cognitive Development*, **6**, 433–48.

Heath, S.B. (1983). *Ways with words: language, life, and work in communities and classrooms*. Cambridge University Press.

Howe, M.L., Courage, M.L., and Peterson, C. (1994). How can I remember when 'I' wasn't there? Long-term retention of traumatic memories and emergence of the cognitive self. *Consciousness and Cognition*, **3**, 327–55.

Hudson, J.A. (1990). The emergence of autobiographic memory in mother-child conversations. In *Knowing and remembering in young children* (ed. R. Fivush and J.A. Hudson), pp. 166–96, Cambridge University Press, New York.

Hudson, J.A. and Fivush, R. (1991). As time goes by: sixth graders remember a kindergarten event. *Applied Cognitive Psychology*, **5**, 346–60.

Hudson, J.A. and Shapiro, L. (1991). Effects of task and topic on children's narratives. In *New directions in developing narrative structure* (ed. A. McCabe and C. Peterson), pp. 89–136. Erlbaum, Hillsdale, NJ.

Hudson, J.A., Fivush, R. and Kuebli, J. (1992). Scripts and episodes: the development of event memory. Applied Cognitive Psychology, **6**, 483–505.

King, M.A. and Yuile, J.C. (1987). Suggestibility and the child witness, In *Children's eyewitness memory* (ed. S.J. Ceci, M.P. Toglia, and D.F. Ross), pp. 24–35. Springer, New York.

Labov, W. (1982). Speech actions and reaction in personal narrative. In *Analyzing discourse: text and talk* (ed. D. Tannen). Georgetown University Press, Washington, DC.

Leichtman, M.D. and Ceci, S.J. (1995). The effects of stereotypes and suggestions on preschoolers reports. *Developmental Psychology*, **31**, 58–578.

Marche, T.A. and Howe, M.L. (1995). Preschoolers report misinformation despite accurate memory. *Developmental Psychology*, **31**, 554–67.

McCabe, A. and Peterson, C. (1991). Getting the story: a longitudinal study of parental styles in eliciting narratives and developing narrative skill. In *Developing narrative structure* (ed. A. McCabe and C. Peterson), pp. 217–53. Erlbaum, Hillsdale, NJ.

McDonough, L. and Mandler, J.M. (1994). Very long-term recall in infants: infantile amnesia reconsidered. *Memory*, **2**, 339–52.

Meltzoff, A.N. (1995). What infant memory tells us about infantile amnesia: long-term recall and deferred imitation. *Journal of Experimental Child Psychology*, **59**, 497–515.

Miller, P.J. and Sperry, L.L. (1988). Early talk about the past: the origins of conversational stories of personal experience. *Journal of Child Language*, **15**, 293–315.

Miller, P.J., Mintz, J., Hoogstra, L., Fung, H., and Potts, R. (1992). The narrated self: young children's construction of self in relation to others in conversational stories of personal experience. *Merrill–Palmer Quarterly*, **38**, 45–67.

Mullen, M.K. and Yi, S. (1995). The cultural context of talk about the past: implications for the development of autobiographical memory. *Cognitive Development*, **10**, 417–20.

Myers, N.A., Clifton, R.G., and Clarkson, M.G. (1994) When they were very young: almost threes remember two years ago. *Infant Behavior and Development*, **10**, 128–32.

Myers, N.A., Perris, E.E., and Speaker, C.J. (1994). Fifty months of memory: a longitudinal study in early childhood. *Memory*, **2**, 383–416.

Nelson, K. (1988). The ontogeny of memory for real events. *Remembering reconsidered: traditional and ecological approaches to the study of memory* (ed. U. Neisser and E. Winograd), pp. 244–77. Cambridge University Press, New York.

Nelson, K. (1993). The psychological and social origins of autobiographical memory. *Psychological Science*, **1**, 1–8.

Nelson, K. and Ross, G. (1980). The generalities and specific of long-term memory in infants and young children. In *New directions for child development: children's memory* (ed. M. Perlmutter), pp. 87–101. Jossey–Bass, San Francisco.

Oates, K. and Shrimpton, S. (1991). Children's memory for stressful and non-stressful events. *Medicine, Science and the Law*, **31**, 4–10.

Ornstein, P.A. (1995). Children's long-term retention of salient personal experiences. *Journal of Traumatic Stress*, **8**, 581–606.

Ornstein, P.A., Gordon, B., and Laurus, D. (1992). Children's memory for a personally experienced event: implications for testimony. *Applied Cognitive Psychology*, **6**, 49–60.

Parker, J., Bahrick, L., Lundy, B., Fivush, R. and Levitt, M. Effects of stress of children's memory for a natural disaster. *Proceedings of the first annual conference of the Society for Applied Research on Memory and Cognition*. (In press.)

Perris, E.E., Myers, N.A., and Clifton, R.K. (1990). Long-term memory for a single infancy experience. *Child Development*, **61**, 1796–807.

Peters, D. (1991). The influence of stress and arousal on the child witness. In *The suggestibility of children's recollections* (ed. J.L. Doris), pp 60–76. Washington: American Psychological Association, Washington, DC.

Peterson, C. and McCabe, A. (1982). *Developmental psycholinguistics: three ways of looking at a narrative*, Plenum, New York.

Pillemer, D.B. and White, S.H. (1989). Childhood events recalled by children and adults. In *Advances in child development and behavior, Vol. 22* (ed. H.W. Reese). Academic, New York.

Pillemer, D.B., Picariello, M.L., and Pruett, J.C. (1994). Very long-term memories of a salient preschool event. *Applied Cognitive Psychology*, **8**, 95–106.

Pipe, M.-E. (1992). Recalling events one and two years later: Cues, props and reminiscence. Paper presented at the NATO Advanced Studies Institute Conference on the Child Witness in Context: Cognitive, Social and Legal Perspectives, Lucca, Italy.

Pipe, M.-E. and Wilson, J.C. (1994). Cues and secrets: influences on children's event reports. *Developmental Psychology*, **30**, 515–25.

Pipe, M-E., Dean, J., Canning, J., and Murachver, T. Telling it like it is, was and will be: the impact of talking about events on memory. (In preparation.)

Poole, D.A. and Lindsay, D.S. (1995). Interviewing preschoolers: effects of nonsuggestive techniques, parental coaching and leading questions on reports of experienced events. *Journal of Experimental Child Psychology*, **60**, 129–54.

Poole, D.A. and White, L.T. (1991). The effects of question repetition on the eyewitness testimony of children and adults. *Developmental Psychology*, **27**, 975–86.

Poole, D.A. and White, L.T. (1993). Two years later: effects of question repetition and retention interval on the eyewitness testimony of children and adults. *Developmental Psychology* **29**, 844–53.

Pynoos, R.S. and Eth, S. (1984). The child as witness to homicide. *Journal of Social Issues*, **40**, 87–108.

Pynoos, R.S. and Nader, K. (1989). Children's memory and proximity to violence. *Journal of the American Academy of Child and Adolescent Psychiatry*, **28**, 236–41.

Ratner, H.H., Smith, B.S., and Padgett, R.J. (1990). Children's organization of events and event memories. In *Knowing and remembering in young children* (ed. R. Fivush and J. Hudson), pp. 65–93. Cambridge University Press, New York.

Reese, E. and Fivush, R. (1993). Parental styles of talk about the past. *Developmental Psychology*, **29**, 596–606.

Reese, E., Haden, C.A. and Fivush, R. (1993). Mother–child conversations about the past: Relationships of style and memory over time. *Cognitive Development*, **8**, 403–30.

Rovee-Collier, C. (1995). Time windows in cognitive development. *Developmental Psychology*, **31**, 147–69.

Rovee-Collier, C.K and Hayne, H. (1987). Reactivation of infant memory: implications for cognitive development. In *Advances in child development and behavior*, Vol. 20 (ed. H.W. Reese), pp. 185–238. Academic, New York.

Rovee-Collier, C.K. and Shyi, G.C.W. (1992). A functional and cognitive analysis of infant long term retention. In *The development of long-term retention* (ed. C.J. Brainerd, M.L. Howe, and V.F. Reynal), pp. 3–55. Springer, New York.

Rovee-Collier, C., Griesler, P.C., and Earley, L.A. (1985). Contextual determinants of retrieval in three-month-old infants. *Learning and Motivation*, **16**, 139–57.

Rudy, L. and Goodman, G.S. (1991). Effects of participation on children's reports: implications for children's testimony. *Developmental Psychology*, **27**, 527–38.

Sachs, J. (1983). Talking about the there and then: the emergence of displaced reference in parent-child discourse. In *Children's language*, Vol. 4 (ed. K. Nelson), pp. 1–28. Erlbaum, Hillsdale, NJ.

Salmon, K. and Pipe, M.-E. (1996). One year later, how effective are cues and props in facilitating children's event reports? Unpublished

Schacter, D.L. (1987). Implicit memory: history and current status. *Journal of Experimental Psychology: Learning, Memory and Cognition*, **13**, 501–18.

Schwarzmueller, A. and Fivush, R. Children recall childhood: autobiographical memories from age 3 through 8. (In preparation.)

Sheingold, K. and Tenney, Y.J. (1982). Memory for a salient childhood event. In *Memory observed* (ed. V. Neisser), pp. 201–12. Freeman, San Francisco.

Smiley, J. (1994). *A thousand acres*. Harper Collins, New York.

Terr, L.C. (1979). Children of Chowchilla: a study of psychic trauma. *The Psychoanalytic Study of the Child*, **34**, 547–623.

Terr, L.C. (1983). Chowchilla revisited: the effects of psychic trauma four years after a school-bus kidnapping. *American Journal of Psychiatry*, **140**, 1543–50.

Terr, L.C. (1988). What happens to early memories of trauma? a study of twenty children under age five at the time of documented traumatic events. *Journal of the American Academy of Child and Adolescent Psychiatry*, **27**, 96–104.

Tessler, M. and Nelson, K. (1994). Making memories: the influence of joint encoding on later recall by young children. *Consciousness and Cognition*, **3**, 307–26.

Todd, C. and Perlmutter, M. (1980). Reality recalled by preschool children. In *New directions for child development*, No.10: Children's memory (ed. M. Perlmutter), pp.69–86. Jossey-Bass, San Francisco.

Umiker-Seboek, D.J. (1979). Preschool children's intraconversational narratives. *Journal of Child Language*, **6**, 91–109.

Vygotsky, L.S. (1978). *Mind in society: the development of higher psychological processes*, (ed. M. Cole, V. John-Steiner, S. Scribner, and E. Souberman). Harvard University Press, Cambridge, MA.

Wagenaar, W.A. and Groeneweg, J. (1990). The memory of concentration camp survivors. *Applied Cognitive Psychology*, **4**, 77–87.

Wetzler, S.E. and Sweeney, J.A. (1986). Childhood amnesia: an empirical demonstration. In *Autobiographical memory* (ed. D. Rubin), pp. 202–21. Cambridge University Press, New York.

Williams, L.M. (1995). Recovered memories of abuse in women with documented child sexual victimization histories. *Journal of Traumatic Stress*, **8**, 649–74.

FOUR

The recovered memories debate:
a cognitive neuroscience perspective

DANIEL L. SCHACTER, KENNETH A. NORMAN,
and WILMA KOUTSTAAL

The recovered memories debate is the most passionately contested battle
that has ever been waged about the nature of human memory. Students
of memory are no strangers to controversy: arguments about single versus
multiple memory systems (Schacter and Tulving 1994), storage failure versus
retrieval failure theories of forgetting (Loftus and Loftus 1980), and laboratory
versus naturalistic methodologies (Banaji and Crowder 1989) have persisted for
years. But all of these debates have been restricted to academic participants and
are largely unrelated to the concerns of people in everyday life. Controversies
over recovered memories, in contrast, have touched the lives of thousands of
families; the emotional stakes for all involved are incalculably high. Parents
who have been falsely accused of sexual abuse on the basis of recovered memories
are faced with a personal – and sometimes legal – nightmare. People who come
to accept memories of abuse that never occurred may needlessly endure the
trauma that results from believing that one has been betrayed by parents
or other trusted caregivers. Others who recover genuine memories of sexual
abuse are likely to encounter doubts about the validity of their recollections,
thereby further intensifying the pain of an already difficult experience. And
professionals on both sides of the debate may find their competence, motives,
and even integrity called into question. These are some of the reasons why
the recovered memories debate has been consistently characterized by strong
emotions and often by outright acrimony (see Crews *et al.* 1995; Harvey and
Herman 1994; Kihlstrom 1995; Lindsay and Read 1994; Loftus and Ketcham
1994; Ofshe and Watters 1994; Olio 1994; Pendergrast 1995; Schacter 1995*b*;
Whitfield 1995).

Debates typically conclude with winners and losers, so it is natural to
assume that one side in the recovered memories debate will turn out to
be right and the other will turn out to be wrong. Indeed, participants on
both sides of the argument have characterized the debate in this manner.
Ofshe and Watters (1994, p. 5) noted that 'The options for those taking
sides in this debate are quite unambiguous . . . this professional debate
is not likely to be settled amicably or on some mutually agreed upon
middle ground.' They proceeded to mount a blistering attack on therapists
who actively seek repressed memories of sexual abuse. Speaking from the

other side of the issue, Whitfield (1995) claimed that virtually all members of the False Memory Syndrome Foundation, an organization composed largely of families who claim to have been falsely accused of abusing their children, are in fact perpetrators who cannot face the reality of what they have done. In the face of such radically different visions of what has happened, it is difficult to avoid the conclusion that one or the other of these two warring camps will be vindicated and the other humiliated. But as argued elsewhere (Schacter, 1995a, b, 1996), this all-or-none depiction of the debate is an overly simplistic view of an issue that is comprised of several different questions, each of which needs to be separately considered and evaluated.

From the perspective of memory researchers, there are three broad areas in which questions need to be posed about the state of evidence relevant to the recovered memories debate. The first set of questions concerns the issue of 'forgetting'. What do we know about the forgetting and recovery of traumatic experiences? Can people forget traumatic experiences and, if so, what kinds of traumas are most susceptible to forgetting? If traumatic experiences can be forgotten, can they subsequently be remembered accurately? What memory processes are implicated in the forgetting and recovery of trauma? The second set of questions concerns the issue of 'distortion'. What is the evidence for implantation of illusory memories of sexual abuse? What do data concerning memory distortion imply about the conditions under which people are most likely to construct pseudomemories of abuse? The third set of questions concerns the relation between recovered memories of actual abuse and illusory memories of abuse: how can 'true' and 'false' memories be distinguished? Are accurate recovered memories preceded by signs and symptoms of abuse – non-conscious or implicit memories – that are not observed in connection with illusory recollections? What is the evidence that people can exhibit implicit memories for traumas that they do not remember?

In this chapter we examine evidence that pertains to each set of questions. For each set, we summarize briefly the state of knowledge regarding memories of childhood sexual abuse. We also broaden the frame of analysis to consider relevant evidence from other areas of research, including clinical observations of traumatic memory as well as current cognitive psychology and cognitive neuroscience. Our goals are twofold. The first is to provide our own assessment of the state of the evidence in the recovered memories debate. Here we emphasize that answers to the various questions we have posed need not all point toward the same side of the debate. For instance, it is perfectly possible to conclude, as we do, that illusory memories of abuse exist yet at the same time concede that some traumatic experiences can be forgotten and later recovered. The second goal is to seek guidance and direction for future research from current work on remembering and forgetting.

FORGETTING AND RECOVERY OF TRAUMA

Is it possible to forget a traumatic experience such as being sexually abused? This question is fundamental to the recovered memories debate, because if the answer is negative, then it follows that all recovered memories of abuse are illusory. The most directly relevant evidence is provided by studies that have examined the memories of sexual abuse survivors. In several studies, therapy patients who claim to remember being sexually abused were asked whether there was ever a time in the past that they could not remember the abuse. In every one of these studies, a significant proportion of respondents – ranging from approximately 20 per cent to 60 – answered the question affirmatively (Briere and Conte 1993; Herman and Schatzow 1987; Loftus *et al.* 1994*a*). Elliott and Briere (1995) report similar findings from a sampling of the general population that included only a small percentage of people who were involved in any form of psychological treatment (see also Feldman-Summers and Pope 1994). Taken together, these results may appear to provide definitive evidence for forgetting of abuse. However, critics have pointed out several serious methodological flaws in the studies (Kihlstrom 1995; Loftus 1993; Ofshe and Watters 1994; Pendergrast 1995; Pope and Hudson 1995). One significant problem is that none of these studies provided corroborative evidence that the remembered abuse actually occurred. Without such evidence, we must be cautious about interpreting the estimates of forgetting. It may also be difficult for participants in such studies to retrospectively assess what they could and could not remember at various points in the past. When people are asked to indicate whether there was ever a time when they 'could not' remember a particular event, a variety of possible interpretations are available, ranging from 'preferred not to think about it' to 'tried my best to recall it but (despite such efforts) was unable to do so'. Clearly, the status of 'forgotten' memories would be very different in these two scenarios. It is difficult to ascertain which of these or of other possible interpretations is most applicable to participants in the aforementioned studies.

Two recent studies provide more convincing evidence that people can forget episodes of abuse. Grassian (personal communication) analysed questionnaire responses from 42 people who claimed to have been abused by a Massachusetts priest. Although there was no direct evidence that these individuals had been abused, the priest admitted to abusing one man during a tape-recorded phone confession, thus providing independent evidence consistent with the conclusion that abuse had in fact occurred. When asked how often they had thought about the abuse after it occurred, eight of the 42 respondents (19 per cent) said that they never had any thoughts about the abuse until it became publicized in the media during the early 1990s. Although suggestive, this study still suffers from the problem that people are asked to retrospectively assess the extent of their prior thoughts about an abusive incident; the accuracy of such retrospective estimates is unknown.

In a significant methodological advance over previous studies, Williams

(1994) interviewed 128 women who – some 17 years earlier – had been brought to a hospital emergency room because of an abusive episode. Thus, there could be little doubt that abuse had in fact occurred. Thirty-eight percent failed to remember the index admission. Most of these women recalled other incidents of abuse from their childhoods. However, 12 per cent of them remembered no abuse at all (for detailed discussion of this study, see Loftus *et al.* 1994*b* and Pope and Hudson 1995).

The foregoing observations show clearly that some incidents of abuse can be forgotten. However, the evidence from the studies of Grassian and Williams is concerned with experiences that occurred more than a decade prior to the time that subjects were questioned. Such forgetting might be the result of the same decay or interference processes that make it difficult to recall many episodic memories from the distant past. In contrast, for some instances of recovered memories, the apparent forgetting cannot be easily attributed to ordinary decay or interference processes. For example, cases have been described in which patients recover memories of having endured years of horrific abuse, including repeated rapes and even ritualistic torture (see Loftus and Ketcham 1994; Ofshe and Watters 1994; Pendergrast 1995). If such memories are accurate, then special mechanisms must be invoked in order to account for the observed forgetting. Most of the discussion and debate has centred on whether a mechanism of repression exists that could operate to suppress extreme traumas, experienced repeatedly and over an extended period of time.

Research on repression has been fraught with difficulty and controversy almost from the time that Freud first introduced the concept (for a variety of viewpoints see Singer 1990). One fundamental issue concerns the way in which repression is defined. As Erdelyi (1985) points out, Freud initially viewed repression as a kind of conscious turning away from an unpleasant experience. Given that thinking and talking about a past event constitutes a powerful means for enhancing subsequent recall of that event, it follows that events that are not thought about or talked about will not derive the usual mnemonic benefits of rehearsal. Indeed, many experiments have shown that instructing subjects not to rehearse an event lessens the probability of subsequent recall or recognition (for example Bjork 1989; Johnson 1994; Koutstaal and Schacter in press *b*). However, there is no evidence that simple lack of rehearsal, motivated by a conscious attempt to avoid an unpleasant memory, can result in total amnesia for repeated traumatic experiences that would normally be well remembered. A more powerful mechanism is needed.

Erdelyi (1985) describes how Freud came to conceptualize a more potent form of repression than simple conscious avoidance of unpleasant materials. In his later writings, Freud came to view repression as an unconscious, defensive process that protects the ego from threatening material. A central – and as yet unanswered – question concerns the strength of the evidence for the existence of such a mechanism. Sceptics point to the lack of experimental evidence for defensive repression from controlled laboratory studies (Holmes 1990; Loftus and Ketcham 1994). However, the relevance of such studies to the construct of defensive repression is unclear because of the inherent limitations of laboratory research. If defensive repression occurs only in response to highly threatening or even traumatizing situations, then laboratory research may have little that is relevant to say about the matter.

Clinical studies of psychogenic amnesias provide evidence that is pertinent to questions concerning the reality of defensive repression, and also to the related question of whether and in what sense psychological trauma is associated with amnesia. Several different forms of psychogenic amnesia can be distinguished. In cases of fugue and functional retrograde amnesia, psychological trauma results in a massive but temporary amnesia for large sectors of a patient's personal past. Although cases of this kind have been reported in the clinical literature for over a century, only a few patients have been carefully studied with formal memory tests. For example, Schacter *et al.* (1982) studied one patient who lost access to nearly all episodic and autobiographical memories for several days following a traumatic event. With the exception of memories relating to a single preserved 'island' of episodic memory from about a year prior to the trauma, the patient was unable to recall any events from his past. Yet this same patient had no difficulty recalling semantic knowledge from all previous time periods (for reviews of other cases see Kihlstrom and Schacter 1995; Schacter and Kihlstrom 1989).

Several points need to be made about the relation between such far-reaching functional retrograde amnesias and the concept of repression on the one hand and forgetting of childhood sexual abuse on the other. First, repression is only one of several possible explanations of functional retrograde amnesias. Since repression is usually assumed to operate on particular experiences, and functional retrograde amnesias involve most or all of a patient's past, it has been suggested that dissociative processes, rather than repression, are responsible for the disorder (for example Spiegel 1995). Second, a significant proportion of functional retrograde amnesia patients have a prior history of brain damage (for review and discussion see Schacter 1996 and Schacter and Kihlstrom 1989). Thus, psychological or dynamic explanations alone may not account for these disorders. Third, extensive functional retrograde amnesias are often short-lasting and profoundly disrupt a patient's entire life. By contrast, in some reported cases of recovered memories of childhood trauma, particularly those involving alleged satanic ritual abuse, patients are seemingly amnesic for numerous horrific episodes that occurred across a span of years while at the same time leading relatively normal lives – until they recover traumatic memories in therapy (Loftus and Ketcham 1994; Ofshe and Watters 1994; Pendergrast 1995). Thus, although extensive functional retrograde amnesias are important because they indicate that traumatic events are sometimes associated with profound and extensive forgetting, they do not provide a direct model for the kinds of amnesias that have been considered in the recovered memories controversy. Nor do they clearly provide support for the theoretical notion of defensive repression, as opposed to dissociation or some similar process.

In contrast to these far-reaching psychogenic amnesias, people sometimes forget single traumatic episodes, a condition sometimes referred to as limited amnesia (Schacter 1986; Schacter and Kihlstrom 1989). As noted earlier, Williams' work shows that people can forget single childhood traumas that occurred decades earlier, but it does not demonstrate that a special repression mechanism is needed to account for this finding. In other kinds of limited amnesias, people forget traumatic events from the recent past. Because recent emotional traumas are usually well remembered, evidence indicating an absence of memory for a recent trauma implies that mechanisms above and beyond ordinary decay and interference must be operating (for reviews see Christianson 1992; Schacter 1996, Chapter 7). What are these mechanisms? Let us consider some possibilities in the context of relevant evidence.

Limited amnesias are frequently observed in perpetrators of violent crimes. In various studies of accused and convicted murderers, roughly 25 to 65 per cent claim amnesia for their crimes (for review see Schacter 1986). As Schacter (1986) pointed out, however, interpretation of these amnesias is difficult because: (1) a significant proportion of them are feigned and (2) those that are not consciously simulated are often attributable to alcohol intoxication. An important and still unanswered question is whether amnesia for a violent crime on the part of a perpetrator is ever attributable solely to defensive repression, as opposed to faking, alcohol intoxication, or other factors such as brain injury or loss of consciousness. One prominent case of emotionally induced amnesia for a violent murder – Sirhan Sirhan's assassination of Robert F. Kennedy – now appears likely to be attributable to conscious simulation on Sirhan's part (Moldea 1995). Sirhan has consistently claimed amnesia for the event. When he was hypnotized and re-entered the frenzied emotional state in which he committed the crime, Sirhan reportedly recalled and re-enacted the murder, which seemed to suggest that his amnesia for the crime was produced by state-dependent retrieval (Bower 1981). However, he has since let slip details of the incident that suggest he has remembered the event all along (see Moldea 1995).

Tayloe (1995) has recently reported one of the few cases of dense amnesia for a violent crime that cannot be easily attributed to alcohol intoxication or faking. Marvin Bains, a 50-year-old machinist, appeared on a neighbour's doorstep with the lower right side of his jaw destroyed by a gun blast. Police found Bains' wife in her kitchen, dead from a shotgun blast. Bains claimed no knowledge of the incident and could not say how his jaw had been damaged, but he was eventually charged with murder. According to Bains' recollection when hypnotized, he had intended to shoot himself and had killed his wife by accident. After the termination of hypnosis, Bains professed no memory for what he had said and continued to claim amnesia for the murder. However, his account under hypnosis provided specific information about the fate of a missing bullet that, up until that point, no one could explain. The defence attorney and a prosecution expert returned to the scene of the murder and found a buckled beam above the kitchen ceiling, exactly where Bains' testimony indicated that the missing bullet had passed. The charge of murder was then reduced to manslaughter. Bains served three years in prison and shot himself shortly after his release.

Simulation of amnesia is unlikely in this case, because Bains' own memory contained the crucial information about the missing bullet that could have corroborated a defence that he had murdered his wife accidentally in an ill-fated attempt to kill himself. (Bains later was able to remember the incident outside of the hypnotic state.) Further, no evidence of alcohol intoxication was reported. Nonetheless, Bains' jaw was seriously damaged by the shotgun blast and it is possible that the gunshot could have caused him to lose consciousness or in some way contributed to his amnesia. Defensive repression, though a possible contributor to Bains' amnesia, is not the only potential cause of it.

Amnesias have also been reported for victims of violent crimes. For example, Christianson and Nilsson (1989) described a case of amnesia for a terrible rape. However, this case resembles the psychogenic amnesias described earlier, insofar as the victim forgot large portions of her personal past in addition to being unable to recollect the trauma. Likewise, war-related amnesias frequently involve fugue states and extensive forgetting of the soldier's past (Sargent and Slater 1941; Thom and Fenton 1920).

Other studies of individuals suffering from various forms of trauma suggest that some sort of memory loss is often associated with trauma. For instance, Herman (1995) notes the seemingly paradoxical fact that trauma can lead both to excellent memory and extensive forgetting. As evidence for a link between trauma and amnesia, she cites Carlson and Rosser-Hogan's (1994) study of Cambodian war refugees. Carlson and Rosser-Hogan report that 90 per cent of these refugees endorsed as applicable to themselves a checklist item, 'amnesia for past traumatic experiences'. Does this mean that 90 per cent of these refugees experienced dense amnesia for a trauma, in the same sense that Marvin Bains did? If so, how could the respondents have *known* that they were amnesic for past traumatic experiences unless they now remembered them? How did the refugees interpret the term 'amnesia', which was translated for them into their native Cambodian language? And how would other non-traumatized Cambodians of a similar age and background respond to this question? Without an appropriate control group and a better understanding of how the respondents understood the checklist item, it is hard to say what kind of amnesia the respondents were describing and whether this study provides evidence of a link between trauma and amnesia. Clearly, it does not provide any direct evidence for the operation of defensive repression.

In a recent article that notes the prevalence of traumatic amnesia, van der Kolk and Fisler (1995) cite (among many others) a study by Wilkinson (1983) concerning people who witnessed the collapse of the skywalks in the Kansas City Hyatt Regency. Wilkinson found that nearly all of these people were plagued by intrusive recollections of the trauma; none of them reported amnesia for the episode in which the skywalks collapsed. About half of them said they attempted to avoid being reminded of the disaster, and about one-third reported post-traumatic 'memory difficulties', referring to problems remembering ongoing events. Presumably these are the reasons why van der Kolk and Fisler refer to this study as evidence pertinent to traumatic amnesia. However, we must not confuse these effects of trauma on general memory performance or capacity with amnesia for the traumatic episode itself. The participants' attempts to avoid being reminded of the incident reflect the use of conscious suppression strategies. However, these strategies were apparently not successful, since virtually everyone reported intrusive recollections of the traumatic event. And while the post-traumatic 'memory difficulties' reported by many respondents likely reflect a lingering disruptive effect of the traumatic episode, this is still a long way from repressing the trauma. Wilkinson's report and similar studies of memory for naturally occurring traumas provide little or no evidence for the operation of an automatic, defensive form of repression that creates total amnesia for a traumatic experience (for further review and discussion see Schacter 1996 and Spiegel 1995).

Perhaps because there is little evidence that repression can produce severe amnesia for events that would ordinarily be well remembered, some have suggested that amnesia only tends to occur for repeated traumatic experiences. This idea is most closely identified with Terr (1994), who suggests that 'Type I' traumas (single shocking events) are well remembered, but 'Type II' traumas are poorly remembered. As a consequence of repeated abuse, suggests Terr, a child might become increasingly practiced at blocking out stressful episodes, with the result that all memory of the abuse may be lost. There is no evidence from clinical research to support this idea and several reasons to doubt it (for critiques and discussion see Loftus and Ketcham 1994, Pendergrast 1995 and Schacter 1996). Grassian (personal communication) found that people who reported having been abused repeatedly were less likely – not more likely – to temporarily forget about the abuse. This finding is perhaps not surprising, because numerous studies of non-traumatic memory have shown that repetition of an event tends to increase, not decrease, memory for that event. A repeatedly abused person may have difficulty remembering the particulars of any one episode of abuse, because many similar episodes tend to merge and blend with one another into a general event schema (Linton 1975; Neisser 1982). Indeed, some survivors of sexual abuse report sketchy memories of the abuse, which could reflect the merging of various episodes (Harvey and Herman 1994). But these normal forgetting processes would not produce total amnesia for the existence of abuse.

What kinds of processes might produce extensive amnesia for repeated abuse? There is some reason to believe that people suffering from dissociative disorders may exhibit extensive forgetting of childhood experiences, including traumatic ones. Much has been written lately regarding multiple personality disorder, now known as dissociative identity disorder. Sceptics on one side claim that multiple 'personalities' are, in fact, iatrogenic creations of suggestive therapies (see Merskey 1992; Ofshe and Watters 1994; Pendergrast 1995), whereas those on the other side argue that extensive childhood sexual abuse plays a causal role in creating a genuine and debilitating illness (for example Putnam 1989). Morton (in press) has distinguished between a developmental form of multiple personality disorder, which may be related to sexual abuse and involves long-standing dissociative processes, and an acquired form, which can involve iatrogenesis. As discussed elsewhere, and consistent with Morton's view, iatrogenesis is probably involved in many, but not all, cases of dissociated identities (Schacter 1996). More to the point, Schacter *et al.* (1989) reported a patient, IC, who exhibited dissociated identities prior to any therapy and had a history of sexual abuse that was corroborated by family members. Extensive testing of IC's autobiographical memory revealed that she was unable to recall a single incident from her childhood prior to age 10. Matched control subjects, by contrast, had little difficulty remembering numerous childhood incidents. If these problems in recalling childhood experiences shown by IC are typical of other patients with dissociative disorders (Bliss 1986), then it is conceivable that extensive forgetting of repeated abusive episodes might be observed in many members of this population. However, a true dissociative disorder causes a profound disruption in patients' everyday lives. As Putnam and his colleagues observe (Putnam 1993), children with dissociative disorders exhibit severe behaviour problems at school and at home, and are almost invariably brought to the attention of mental health professionals. Thus, there are reasons to expect that patients who claim to have forgotten years of repeated abuse due to dissociative pathology also would have a documented childhood history of severe psychological problems. In the absence of evidence indicating childhood psychopathology, it seems reasonable to remain sceptical of claims of amnesia for extended and severe sexual abuse.

In summary, the most convincing evidence for forgetting of sexual abuse involves individual incidents from the distant past. Such forgetting may be attributable to normal processes of decay and interference, together with the use of conscious avoidance or suppression. More extensive forgetting of repeated abusive episodes may occur, but such amnesia is likely to be linked with the presence of some dissociative pathology. There is scant evidence for the operation of a defensive, unconscious form of repression that results in dense amnesia for specific experiences. Evidence from psychogenic amnesias indicates that trauma can be associated with far-reaching amnesias, but these amnesias are poorly understood and differ in various ways from the kind of forgetting that is at issue in cases of sexual abuse.

It must also be emphasized that just because some traumatic experiences can be forgotten, it does not logically follow that they can be recovered. Forgotten traumas, like many other experiences that seemingly vanish from memory, might be permanently unavailable to conscious recollection. In cases of extensive functional retrograde amnesia, memories are usually recovered after just a few days or weeks, although some may persist for longer time periods (Kritchevsky *et al.* in press). This distinguishes such cases from instances of recovered memories of sexual abuse, where recollections return decades later. None the less, several cases of recovered memories of sexual abuse have been reported in which external corroboration was available to confirm the accuracy of the memory (for example Grassian, personal communication; Nash 1994; Schooler 1994; Williams 1995). These cases tend to involve specific abusive episodes – as opposed to years of repeated abuse – although some reports of the latter have been noted (Harvey and Herman 1994). The fact that some forgotten traumas can later be recovered should not be entirely surprising. Numerous laboratory studies of non-traumatic memory have revealed that providing appropriate retrieval cues can lead to recall of aspects of seemingly forgotten experiences (for a recent review see Koutstaal and Schacter in press *a*). There is no reason to assume that the same does not apply to inaccessible traumatic memories.

The foregoing observations should make it clear that recovered memories of sexual abuse can be accurate. How often are they accurate? This is a crucial question, but there is little evidence that directly bears on it. The literature on memory for traumas that are known to have occurred, such as earthquakes, sniper attacks, or kidnappings, indicates that memory is usually persistent and accurate, although some distortion can occur (see Pynoos and Nader, 1989; Terr, 1988; for review, see Schacter 1996). Laboratory research on emotion and memory also indicates that memory for emotionally arousing events is generally accurate, with distortion occurring at the level of specific details (for a review of these findings see Heuer and Reisberg 1992). However, none of these literatures specifically addresses the accuracy of memories that are temporarily forgotten and only later recovered. Some have raised the possibility that such memories might be especially accurate, because they are shielded from the potentially distorting effects of post-event rehearsal that can influence easily accessible memories (van der Kolk 1994). However, we are unaware of any data showing that forgotten-and-recovered memories of traumatic events are especially accurate. Likewise, we are unaware of any data showing that such memories are any more susceptible to distortion than are continuously available memories. Furthermore, we are still left with the separate question of whether people can 'remember' a traumatic experience when none occurred, which we take up later in the chapter.

Forgetting and recovery of trauma: what can cognitive neuroscience add?

In the preceding section we pointed out that some incidents of sexual abuse, particularly those that occurred in the distant past, might be forgotten and recovered for the same reasons that non-traumatic experiences are sometimes forgotten and recovered: decay or interference processes may render an experience inaccessible, and provision of appropriate retrieval cues might lead to recall of aspects of the inaccessible memory. In cases such as these, there may be no need to seek special mechanisms in order to understand how forgetting and recovery occur. But when large portions of the past are forgotten, as in instances of dissociative disorders or functional retrograde amnesia, appealing to 'ordinary' forgetting-and-recovery processes is not sufficient. Although it remains unclear as to whether such 'extraordinary' forgetting does occur in cases of sexual abuse, it is useful to consider whether present knowledge of the brain and memory can illuminate matters. We next briefly review recent evidence concerning the possible effects of extreme stress on hippocampal function on the one hand, and frontal lobe functioning (especially as evidenced in memory encoding and retrieval) on the other.

Hippocampus and glucocorticoids

Stein *et al.* (1995) recently reported a study of abused women that revealed volume reductions in the hippocampal region, which is known to be critically important for explicit or declarative memory (Cohen and Eichenbaum 1993; Moscovitch 1994; Schacter *et al.* 1995*b*, 1996*a*; Squire 1992; Squire *et al.* 1992). Stein *et al.* performed structural magnetic resonance imaging (MRI) in 22 women with a history of prolonged and severe sexual abuse. They found a significant reduction (5 per cent) of left hippocampal volume in abused women compared with non-abused women; the magnitude of hippocampal volume reduction was associated with increasing evidence of psychiatric symptoms. Similarly, two recent studies employing MRI with Vietnam veterans revealed reduced hippocampal volume in veterans with post-traumatic stress disorder (PTSD) compared with veterans without PTSD (Gurvitz *et al.* in press) and with healthy comparison subjects (Bremner *et al.* 1995). Bremner *et al.* found an 8 per cent reduction in right hippocampal volume in traumatized veterans, whereas Gurvitz *et al.* found bilateral hippocampal reductions. Also, Bremner *et al.* (1995) documented significant deficits in explicit memory for recently presented materials in veterans with PTSD, with some evidence of a correlation between memory deficit and hippocampal volume reduction.

One interpretation of these findings is that people with unusually small hippocampi are predisposed to developing psychiatric symptoms or PTSD in response to traumatic stress. Alternatively, decreased hippocampal volume might be related to the toxic effects of the class of hormones known as glucocorticoids, which are released in response to prolonged stress and can damage the hippocampus (Sapolsky *et al.* 1990; Sapolsky 1992). Indeed, De Bellis *et al.* (1994*a*) found that sexually abused girls and adolescents suffer from dysregulation of the hypothalamic-pituitary-adrenal axis, the brain system responsible for releasing cortisol (the principal glucocorticoid of primates). Also, it has been shown that experimental and therapeutic exposure to glucocorticoids can produce memory deficits on standard explicit memory tests (Keenan *et al.* 1995; Newcomer *et al.* 1994; Wolkowitz *et al.* 1990).

This collection of findings raises the possibility that prolonged stress, resulting in excess exposure to glucocorticoids, could damage the hippocampus and thereby create memory problems in survivors of sexual abuse and other traumatized people. However, none of the women in Stein *et al.*'s study were amnesic for their abuse, and as a group they showed normal performance on laboratory tests of explicit memory for recently studied information – tests that are usually sensitive to hippocampal damage. Thus, the observed hippocampal volume reductions in Stein *et al.*'s study were not related to memory performance. Other studies of women with reported histories of sexual abuse have revealed some deficits in recalling autobiographical incidents (Kuyken and Brewin, 1995; Parks and Balon 1995). These deficits involve the failure to retrieve specific episodic childhood memories in response to single-word cues or the tendency to retrieve 'overgeneral' memories that do not refer to a single episode. This is a very different pattern of results from that observed in patients with damage to the hippocampus and nearby medial temporal lobe structures. Hippocampal damage in humans can produce some impairment for events that occurred prior to the onset of hippocampal damage but, unlike abuse survivors, these patients tend to remember events and facts from the distant past better than events that occurred relatively more recently (for reviews, see Cohen and Eichenbaum 1993; Parkin and Leng 1993; Squire 1992). This leads us to conclude that documented difficulties remembering childhood episodes in abuse survivors are probably not specifically linked to hippocampal function. They may instead reflect a combination of deficient encoding and retrieval strategies (Williams 1992). The precise relation – if any – of hippocampal volume reductions in survivors of sexual abuse to the forgetting and recovery of traumatic experiences thus remains unclear.

Moreover, the exact role of the hippocampus in memory is still being debated, partly as a result of studies with non-human primates that suggest that damage to the hippocampus proper does not produce severe memory loss, whereas damage to the adjacent perirhinal and entorhinal cortices does (see Murray *et al.* 1993; Zola-Morgan *et al.* 1989). In addition, neuroimaging studies of memory, using such blood flow measurement techniques as positron emission tomography, have produced a mixed pattern of results, with some studies documenting hippocampal activation during encoding or retrieval, and others failing to observe any hippocampal activation (for discussion see Buckner and Tulving, 1995; Schacter *et al.* 1995*b*, 1996; Ungerleider 1995). Schacter *et al.* (1996*a*) have recently provided evidence that hippocampal activation during retrieval is related to the experience of recollecting a past event: on a stem-cued recall task, hippocampal activation was greater in a 'high-recall' condition (characterized by deep, semantic encoding of target words at study) than in a 'low-recall' condition (where subjects performed a shallow, t-junction encoding task at study). But it remains uncertain exactly how such findings relate, if at all, to evidence of reduced hippocampal volumes in traumatized people.

Stress and disrupted encoding

It has been suggested that traumatic experiences may be encoded differently from non-traumatic ones (Krystal *et al.* 1995a, b; Spiegel 1995; van der Kolk 1994). The most common outcome of emotionally traumatic experiences is intrusive and repetitive recollection of the traumatic event (for recent reviews, see Schacter 1996; Spiegel 1995). Laboratory studies of both rats and people suggest that enhanced memory for traumatic events is mediated by stress-related hormones such as epinephrine (Cahill *et al.* 1994). However, other substances released by the brain in stressful situations, such as opioid peptides, have inhibitory effects on retention (for a review see Cahill and McGaugh 1996; McGaugh 1995). Many of these neurochemical influences on memory act via what has been termed the 'final common pathway' by increasing or decreasing the release of the adrenergic neuromodulator norepinephrine (NE) in the amygdala, an important component of the limbic system. For example, epinephrine increases the release of NE, and opiates inhibit NE release (McGaugh *et al.* 1993). It is conceivable that neurochemicals whose effects on memory are inhibitory might be related in some way to forgetting of sexual abuse or other traumatic events.

In order for the memory-inhibiting effects of stress-related hormones to be relevant to the recovery of traumatic memories, such substances must somehow create an available but inaccessible memory trace (rather than only a very weak, and thus unavailable, trace). This would be the case if opioid peptides or other neurochemicals that are released in response to extreme stress led to highly state-dependent memories – traces that are 'locked into' (Colpaert 1990) the neurochemical and neurophysiological state that was present at encoding, and are only retrievable when the organism is again in a similar biological state. Kandel and Kandel (1994) speculated that the release of opioid peptides during a stressful experience such as sexual abuse might lead to temporary inability to remember the trauma but then, later, another arousing experience could result in release of neurochemicals that activate the formerly inaccessible memory. Evidence pertaining to these state dependent explanations of opiate effects on memory is equivocal. Izquierdo and his colleagues have found evidence consistent with state-dependency using large doses of β-endorphin, an endogenous opiate (see Izquierdo 1984 for representative studies). However, interpretation of these studies is complicated by their use of an inhibitory avoidance task, where long response latencies are taken as evidence for memory; locomotor retardation caused by administration of β-endorphin at test might be mistaken for state-dependent memory (McGaugh, personal communication). Using a different opiate peptide (morphine), Castellano and McGaugh (1989) failed to find evidence for state dependency. Finally, other neurochemicals have been linked with state dependency. For example, Colpaert (1990) obtained evidence consistent with the claim that benzodiazepines (which inhibit memory performance when administered post-training) induce state-dependent memory. This study used a lever-pressing task and therefore is not subject to the methodological criticisms discussed above (for recent work implicating the amygdaloid complex in benzodiazepine-induced amnesia and evidence pointing to the existence of endogenous benzodiazepines see Cahill and McGaugh (1996).

Another approach to explaining how memories for trauma might come to be 'available but inaccessible' focuses on the link between trauma and dissociation. Many clinicians and researchers have argued that traumatic experiences can produce a dissociative state in some individuals (cf. our earlier discussion); in this state, mechanisms that normally lead to integrated perceptual experience and memory traces are disrupted, resulting in fragmentary engrams that are difficult to retrieve (see Krystal *et al.* 1995*a*, *b*; Terr 1994; van der Kolk 1994). Experimental analogues of dissociative states have been produced in human subjects using the NMDA receptor antagonist ketamine, which disrupts glutamatergic transmission and produces impairments in thinking and problem solving that resemble deficits observed after frontal lobe lesions (Krystal *et al.* 1994*a*, *b*). The frontal lobes play an important integrative role in memory, both by promoting elaborative encodings in which new experiences become integrated with preexisting knowledge (Demb *et al.* 1995; Kapur *et al.* 1994; Shimamura 1995), and by allowing effortful, strategic search of memory (Kapur *et al.* 1995; Moscovitch 1994, 1995; Schacter *et al.* 1996*a*). Administration of ketamine may disrupt frontal contributions to elaborative encoding and strategic retrieval. To the extent that the frontal lobes enable an individual to expand on, refine, or otherwise appropriately modify retrieval cues when the cues fail to directly trigger the sought-after trace, eliminating the frontal contribution to memory should make retrieval state dependent – more dependent than usual on an exact initial match between the sensory and physiological states that prevail at encoding and retrieval. The fact that ketamine leads to characteristic distortions in perception, most probably by interfering with NMDA-receptor-dependent thalamo-cortical sensory relays (Krystal *et al.* 1995*a*), could also increase state dependency by decreasing the match between perceptions occurring in ketamine and non-ketamine states. Consistent with these suggestions, Jackson *et al.* (1992) found evidence for state-dependent memory for a learned lever-pressing response following administration of ketamine and other NMDA antagonists. The logical next step would be to directly test whether ketamine also makes memory state-dependent in humans, using standard explicit memory tasks.

It is not known whether the effects of ketamine mimic the effects of stress during a traumatic experience. However, DeBellis *et al.* (1994*b*) found evidence for excessive levels of catecholamines in the urine of sexually abused girls, and evidence exists demonstrating that catecholamines (in particular, dopamine and norepinephrine) regulate the activity of glutamatergic neurons in frontal cortex (Goldman-Rakic 1987; Williams and Goldman-Rakic 1995). Thus, excessive amounts of catecholamines released during a stressful event might be expected to result in abnormal patterns of glutamatergic transmission (Krystal *et al.*

1995*a*). Apart from the issue of whether stress disrupts frontal lobe functioning, however, we emphasize that we know of no evidence that disrupted frontal lobe functioning could produce total amnesia for repeated traumatic experiences, as has been reported in some alleged cases of recovered memories. And, as with observations concerning glucocorticoids and the hippocampus, these findings from neuroscience have not yet been tied directly to forgetting of sexual abuse, so they must be viewed as intriguing but speculative possibilities that merit exploration in future research (see Schacter 1996).

ILLUSORY MEMORIES OF ABUSE: FACT OR FICTION?

Just as it is difficult to estimate precisely how many recovered memories of abuse are accurate, it is also difficult to estimate precisely how many are illusory. Widely varying estimates have been offered by those on opposite sides of the debate. Pendergrast (1995), for example, suggests a virtual epidemic of recovered memories involving hundreds of thousands of cases, whereas Whitfield (1995) contends that only a few scattered cases exist. There is little good evidence on which to base an estimate of the incidence of false memories of abuse. However, several kinds of observations converge on the conclusion that illusory memories of sexual abuse can and do occur.

Illusory memories of trauma: converging evidence

The existence of recovered memories involving satanic ritual abuse provides strong evidence that some memories of abuse can be illusory. Survey data indicate that a significant number of mental health professionals have reported treating clients who recover memories of satanic ritual abuse (Goodman *et al.* 1994; Wakefield and Underwager 1994). But no corroborated cases have ever been reported and extensive efforts by law enforcement agencies to find hard evidence of satanic abuse have consistently failed to uncover anything (Nathan and Snedeker 1995; Ofshe and Watters 1994; Wright 1994).

The most reasonable interpretation of these facts is that most (and quite possibly all) recovered memories of satanic abuse are illusory. If false memories of satanic abuse can be created, then it seems likely that illusory memories of non-satanic abuse can be created, too. The fact that people can remember with great conviction seemingly impossible events such as alien abductions (Baker 1992; Mack 1994) and abuse in past lives (Spanos *et al.* 1991) is consistent with this possibility, and indicates that people can develop illusory recollections of significant traumas.

Although ethical considerations preclude investigation of whether false memories of significant traumas can be implanted experimentally, recent evidence for implantation of mildly distressing events has been reported.

Loftus and Pickrell (1995) reported that 20 to 25 per cent of participants 'remembered' a particular – but fabricated – incident of getting lost in a shopping mall as a child after being queried repeatedly about such an event by a family member; family members agreed that the event had never occurred. Hyman *et al.* (1995) conducted a similar study, in which college students were asked to recall seemingly distinctive childhood events (for example an overnight hospitalization for an ear infection) that, according to their parents, never happened. Approximately 25 per cent developed some sort of illusory recollection after being asked several times about the event. Although clearly still a far distance from falsely remembering sexual abuse, these studies are certainly consistent with the idea that some people can develop illusory memories of significant personal events.

Relevant evidence is also provided by people who have disavowed or 'retracted' their recovered memories. Nelson and Simpson (1994) report a survey of 20 women who retracted their recovered memories of sexual abuse. Ninety-five per cent of them recovered their memories during therapy, and all of them reported that their therapists influenced the development of their memories. Ninety per cent reported that some sort of trance induction was used in therapy to recover memories. Hypnosis was the most common technique, reported by 85 per cent of the women. Trance writing, regression, and suggestions of abuse were also widely reported. The majority of the women (70 per cent) also indicated that group therapy influenced their recovered memories.

The fact that someone retracts a recovered memory need not mean that the memory is illusory. Difficulties handling the psychological pain of a recovered memory, social pressures, and related factors could possibly be involved in some retractions. None the less, given the similarities among the retractors in Nelson and Simpson's study, and the improbable nature of the memories that are retracted in some instances (for example satanic ritual abuse), we believe that retractions should generally be taken at face value.

Nelson and Simpson's (1994) observations are also noteworthy because the techniques mentioned by the retractors could all be considered risky ones that might be expected to produce illusory recollections (Lindsay and Read 1996). Indeed, the fact that such risky techniques appear prominently in the writings of some therapists who advocate seeking out supposedly 'repressed' memories of abuse (see Bass and Davis 1988; Frederickson 1992) constitutes further evidence for the likely existence of illusory memories (Lindsay and Read 1994, 1996; Loftus 1993; Ofshe and Watters 1994; Pendergrast 1995). In a recent survey of 145 doctoral level psychotherapists in the United States, Poole *et al.* (1995) found that nearly one-third of those who responded sometimes use hypnosis in order to help clients remember child sexual abuse, and about the same percentage reported using guided imagery related to abuse situations.

There is now a large literature linking hypnosis and illusory memories. When highly hypnotizable subjects are given suggestions to 'remember' events that never occurred, many of them do (for reviews, see Kihlstrom in press; Lynn and

Nash 1994; Spiegel 1995). Although the exact contributions of hypnotizability and hypnosis *per se* can be debated (Brown 1995), there is no evidence that hypnosis increases the accuracy of memory, and considerable evidence that it either leads people to develop excessively liberal response criteria that result in false recollections or alters the experience of retrieval in a way that produces confident recollections (for discussion see Dywan 1995). Likewise, asking people to imagine abuse that may or may not have occurred could be considered a risky technique in view of extant data showing that: (1) imagination and memory can be confused (Johnson *et al.* 1979), (2) imagining events can increase one's subjective confidence that they actually occurred (Garry *et al.* 1996) and can also increase the likelihood of producing a false recollection (Hyman and Pentland 1996), and (3) visual imagery depends on some of the same brain mechanisms that are involved in visual perception (Kosslyn *et al.* 1993, 1995), which might contribute to a heightened sense of reality for some imagined events.

All of these lines of evidence converge on the conclusion that illusory memories of sexual abuse can and do occur. None the less, we must also point out that there is no direct evidence that specific techniques used in therapy are the sole or primary cause of these false recollections, although it seems reasonable to assume that they do contribute to the development of inaccurate memories. Other factors, such as individual differences in proneness to suggestive influences, might also play a role. For example, Hyman and Billings (1995) found that people who provided false memories of childhood events (for example a visit to a hospital) scored higher than people who did not provide false memories on two measures: the Creative Imagination Scale (Wilson and Barber 1978), which measures vividness of imagination in various sensory modalities and is related to hypnotic susceptibility, and the Dissociative Experiences Scale (Bernstein and Putnam 1986), which measures reported tendencies toward lapses in attention and memory. Lynn and Nash (1994) point out that individuals who exhibit medium or high hypnotic susceptibility are especially prone to producing illusory memories in response to suggestions. And Gudjonnsson (1991) has found that people who exhibit high levels of 'interrogative suggestibility' – the tendency to provide positive responses to an interviewer's leading questions – are especially likely to offer false confessions in response to social pressure. Interrogative suggestibility appears to be unrelated to hypnotic susceptibility (Register and Kihlstrom 1988). We do not yet know whether patients who have developed false memories of childhood sexual abuse would exhibit high scores on any of these dimensions, but the possibility seems plausible and merits investigation.

Illusory memories: perspectives from cognitive neuroscience

There is general agreement that memory does not preserve an exact or 'photographic' representation of all aspects of past experiences. Students of the mind and brain both view memory as a fundamentally constructive process. A number of cognitive psychologists have argued that memories of past experiences are constructed from a combination of stored fragments of an event, pre-existing knowledge, beliefs, and expectations that the rememberer brings to an experience, and properties of the environment in which the experience is retrieved (cf. Bartlett 1932; Conway and Rubin 1993; Jacoby *et al.* 1989*a*; Johnson *et al.* 1993; Neisser 1967; Schacter 1989, 1996; Tulving 1983). Similarly, neuroscientists contend that memories are constructed on the basis of stored fragments of experiences that are distributed throughout a variety of cortical regions; there is no single place in the brain that contains 'the memory' of a particular experience. The distributed components of a memory are linked or bound together by medial temporal and other systems that work cooperatively with cortical storage areas during encoding and retrieval (cf. Damasio 1989; McClelland *et al.* 1995; Squire 1987, 1992). The fact that memories are constructed need not mean that they are inaccurate; memory is quite accurate in many situations. But from the perspectives of both cognitive psychology and neuroscience, illusory recollections are a natural potential by-product of the fundamentally constructive nature of memory (Schacter 1996).

Recent research has begun to illuminate the cognitive and neurobiological factors that contribute to illusory memories. One important phenomenon is known as source memory or source monitoring – remembering when, where, and how a memory was acquired (Johnson *et al.* 1993). Confusions between real and imagined events can be construed as source monitoring failures (Hyman and Pentland 1996; Johnson *et al.* 1979). Visual imagery may be an especially powerful contributor to source confusions because access to visual information about an event provides an important basis for the subjective conviction that an event occurred in one's own past (Brewer 1988; Dewhurst and Conway 1994). Although memories of actual, perceived events generally contain more visual/perceptual details than do memories of merely imagined events (Johnson and Raye 1981), the act of creating visual images may lend an imagined event the recollective 'feeling' of an actual one, making it very difficult for people to correctly identify the source of this compelling subjective experience of remembering.

Loss of source information renders one vulnerable to a variety of other memory distortions and illusions. Recent research has revealed that source memory problems are involved in memory distortions that occur when people are exposed to misleading post-event suggestions, as observed initially in studies by Loftus and colleagues (for example Loftus *et al.* 1978). When people witness a particular event, such as a car stopped at a stop sign, and are later given misleading information about it – the car stopped at a give way sign – they often later 'remember' seeing a give way sign. Although Loftus and colleagues originally contended that the misleading post-event information had its effect by 'overwriting' memory for the original event, McCloskey and Zaragoza (1985) showed clearly that information about the original event remains available in memory when appropriate tests are given. A variety of more recent studies have revealed that effects of misleading information arise in large part because of source memory failure: people do not recollect whether the critical information was part of the original event or was only suggested to them later (for example Belli *et al.* 1994; Lindsay 1990; Zaragoza and Lane 1994). Although source memory failure is not the sole basis for the misinformation effect (Loftus *et al.* 1995), it is clearly a major contributor.

Failures of source memory are also implicated in the 'false fame' illusion, where subjects mistakenly claim that a recently encountered non-famous name (Jacoby *et al.* 1989*b*) or face (Bartlett *et al.* 1991) is famous. The illusion occurs when people forget that the name or face was presented during a study episode, thus misattributing familiarity or fluent processing of the item to the person's (non-existent) fame. Likewise, Gilbert and colleagues (Gilbert 1991; Gilbert *et al.* 1993) have reported experiments in which people are shown arbitrary statements about made-up words (for example 'A bilicar is a spear'), and are told that some of the statements are true whereas others are false. Gilbert has found that when people forget the source information associated with each statement (whether it is true or false), they show a bias to remember the statements as 'true'. Similarly, Begg *et al.* (1992) have found that subjects tend to believe statements made by discredited sources when they forget relevant information about the source.

Source memory has also been implicated in the studies mentioned earlier showing that some young adults can be induced to create false memories of childhood experiences in response to repeated questioning (Hyman *et al.* 1995; Loftus and Pickrell 1995). Hyman *et al.* (1995) suggest that with repeated questioning, subjects may recall various aspects or portions of actual childhood events and misattribute them to the fabricated target event. Consistent with this idea, Hyman *et al.* found that individuals who thought about the false event in the context of general knowledge about their childhood selves during the first interview were more likely to construct false memories in subsequent interviews. Thinking about the false event in relation to other knowledge about oneself may serve to create a difficult source monitoring problem for later interviews: the false event seems related to, or integrated with, general self-knowledge, and subjects may be unable to determine whether the emerging sense that the memory 'belongs' to their pasts derives from having thought about it during the prior interview, or from the actual occurrence of the event during their childhoods.

Source memory appears to depend critically on the functioning of frontal lobe systems that are involved in strategic retrieval and monitoring of past experiences. Patients with frontal lobe damage are especially prone to forgetting the source of newly acquired information (Janowsky *et al.* 1989; Schacter *et al.* 1984; Shimamura and Squire 1987), and exhibit a variety of memory illusions and distortions (DeLuca and Cicerone 1991; Johnson 1991; Moscovitch 1995; Schacter and Curran 1995; Schacter *et al.* 1996*b*). Elderly adults often exhibit poor source memory, and the degree of impairment has been related to signs and symptoms of age-related frontal lobe impairment (Craik *et al.* 1990; Glisky *et al.* 1995; Schacter *et al.* 1991, 1994). Schacter *et al.* (1995a) have reviewed a number of studies showing poor source memory in young children, who also exhibit patterns of performance that are similar to patients with frontal lobe damage on a variety of tasks. Recent studies by Ceci and collaborators have shown clearly that source memory failures play a key role in the development of false memories in preschool children (for review of these studies see Ceci 1995).

It is not yet known whether source memory failures play a role in illusory memories of abuse. However, some false memories may be created when elements of actual experiences are recalled and their source is forgotten, with the result that something that was said, suggested, or imagined is mistaken as an actual event from one's past. Because a person is indeed recollecting parts of an actual experience, the person may be more likely to develop a strong conviction that the entire recollected experience actually occurred.

In a related vein, memory distortions also occur when people rely inappropriately on their memories for the general gist of an episode, as opposed to specific information about the details of an event. This point has been made convincingly by Reyna and Brainerd (1995), who have proposed a 'fuzzy trace' theory that distinguishes between a 'gist trace' that captures general properties of past experiences and a 'verbatim' trace that represents detailed, specific information.

This idea, combined with ideas about source memory, appears to provide a good account of one recently described memory distortion. Roediger and McDermott (1995; see also Read 1996) used a procedure originally introduced by Deese (1959) in which people who study a list of words, each associated to a non-presented theme word, subsequently very often falsely recognize the non-presented theme word. Thus, for example, subjects who study 'drowsy', 'bed', 'tired', 'pillow', 'rest', 'pyjamas', and other related words later claim with high confidence to remember having been exposed to the theme word 'sleep', even though it was not presented. Subjects in these experiments were asked to indicate whether they actually 'remember' specific details of their encounters with a test word on the study list, or just 'know' that the word was presented earlier because it seems familiar (see Gardiner and Java 1993; Tulving 1985). Roediger and McDermott (1995) found that subjects often claimed to 'remember' the non-presented critical lure, making as many 'remember' responses to critical lures as to words that were actually studied. Payne *et al.* (1996) have found that subjects will often attribute these memories to a specific source. In their experiments, subjects heard studied words spoken by several speakers, and were later asked to indicate whether they remembered which speaker said each word that they indicated was on the study list; subjects were given the option of not designating a speaker.

None the less, subjects frequently 'remembered' the source of non-presented critical lures.

One way to think about this pattern of results is that false recognition of critical lure words is based on retention of the semantic gist of the studied items, together with deficient source monitoring. Schacter *et al.* (1996*c*) have recently provided some support for this view in a study that examined false recognition of critical lures in patients with organic amnesic syndromes. Such patients typically exhibit poor explicit memory for recent experiences, despite normal intelligence, perception, and language (for a review see Parkin and Leng 1993). In the Schacter *et al.* study, both amnesic patients and matched controls heard a series of lists of words, with each of the words in a given list highly associated to a non-presented critical lure; later, they made recognition decisions about studied words, critical lures, and unrelated lures (i.e. non-presented words that had no obvious associations to any previously presented words). As expected, amnesic patients less often correctly recognized the studied words and more often incorrectly recognized completely unrelated lures than did controls, thus reflecting their impaired memory for which words had appeared on the list. Importantly, however, amnesic patients also made fewer false alarms to critical lures than did control subjects (see Fig. 4.1). Based on this finding, Schacter *et al.* suggested that false alarms to critical lures depend on access to a semantic gist representation that is impaired in amnesic patients. In normal subjects, false recognition of critical lures occurs when the gist representation is retained and subjects interpret gist activation as evidence that the item itself was presented.

More recent work in our laboratory has used the same paradigm to examine false recognition of critical lures in elderly adults. We found that older adults showed less accurate recognition of studied words than did younger adults, although their impairment was not nearly as large as that observed in amnesic patients (Norman and Schacter in press *a*). In contrast to amnesic patients, however, the elderly made just as many false alarms to critical lures as younger people did (Fig. 4.2). Older adults apparently had problems recollecting specific information from the study list, but retained as much gist information as young subjects did. Consistent with these observations, Tun *et al.* (1995) found that older adults intruded critical lures in free recall just as often as young people, even though they remembered fewer list items.

We have recently studied a patient with frontal damage who exhibits a striking form of false recognition involving an even more extreme contrast between preserved retention of general or gist information and impaired retention of specific information. Patient BG suffered a stroke in 1993 that caused extensive damage in his right frontal lobe (Curran *et al.* in press; Schacter *et al.* 1996*b*). Schacter *et al.* tested BG on a variety of recognition memory paradigms and found that he consistently exhibited much higher rates of false recognition than do age-matched controls. Most strikingly, when asked to indicate whether he 'remembers' or 'knows' that an item appeared on an earlier list, BG frequently claimed to 'remember' having encountered new (never presented) words, sounds, pictures, or pseudowords – much more often than do elderly controls. BG exhibits pathological false recognition even after studying materials that are not associatively related to, or physically similar to, items he has encountered previously. However, BG virtually stopped false alarming when he studied items from specific categories and was then tested with new items from non-studied categories.

Schacter *et al.* suggested that BG is likely to exhibit pathological false recognition when the general features of studied and non-studied items are similar (for example, in an experiment where all of the items at study and at test are non-categorized words). BG's ability to remember specific information from the study episode is poor, perhaps because he has difficulty engaging in effortful retrieval strategies that depend on frontal regions (for example Moscovitch 1995; Schacter *et al.* 1996*a*). Accordingly, he relies heavily on his relatively preserved memory for the gist of what he has encountered. In subsequent testing, we have asked BG exactly what he recollects when he says that he 'remembers' encountering studied words (Curran *et al.* in press). BG provides fairly specific explanations of his 'remember' responses to non-studied words that probably reflect source memory problems – he generates thoughts or

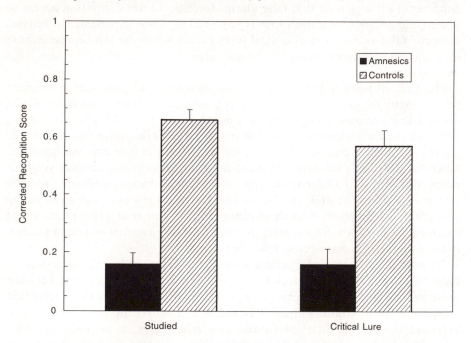

Fig. 4.1, Recognition data from the Schacter *et al.* (1996*c*) study, comparing amnesics and controls. Corrected recognition scores were obtained by taking the proportion of 'Old' responses and subtracting the baseline false alarm rate for that group and item type. The error bars indicate the standard error.

reactions to a word that he mistakenly believes he experienced during a prior study episode. BG's false recognition problem may result from his generating an 'unfocused' retrieval description at test (i.e. an insufficiently specific mental representation of the characteristics of the study episode), which matches the recollective experiences triggered by non-studied distractor items just as well as it matches memories elicited by the studied items themselves (Norman and Schacter in press *b*).

We do not yet know whether any of these findings and ideas concerning false recognition and gist versus specific information bear directly on illusory memories of childhood trauma. To the extent that some false memories accurately reflect the gist of past experience, however, it is possible that illusory memories of sexual abuse are accurate representations of some aspect of a patient's past – abuse suffered at the hands of a perpetrator other than the one that the patient remembers, or emotional distress that never culminated in actual physical or sexual abuse. While these determinations may be difficult to make in any one case, they serve to remind us that the relations between memory and reality are often complex and that it is sometimes difficult to categorize memories as either 'true' or 'false' (cf. Hacking 1995; Schacter 1996).

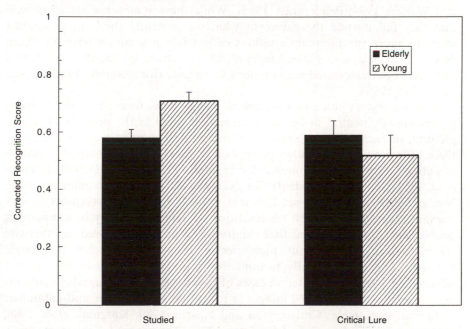

Fig. 4.2 Data from Norman and Schacter (in press *a*, Expt. 1), comparing false recognition of non-studied 'critical lure' words in elderly and young subjects. The general procedure was identical to that of Roediger and McDermott (1995, Expt. 2). Corrected recognition scores were obtained by taking the proportion of 'Old' responses and subtracting the baseline false alarm rate for that group and item type. The error bars indicate the standard error.

IMPLICIT MEMORY AND THE SYMPTOMS OF FORGOTTEN ABUSE

The distinction between explicit memory (conscious recollection of past experiences) and implicit memory (non-conscious effects of past experience on subsequent behaviour) (for example Schacter 1987) has been explored intensively in cognitive psychology and neuroscience during the past decade (for reviews see Richardson-Klavehn and Bjork 1988; Roediger and McDermott 1993; Schacter *et al.* 1993). Although we have focused on explicit memory thus far, implicit memory is highly relevant to the recovered memories debate. A number of therapists have suggested that even when people cannot explicitly remember prior abuse, they may none the less exhibit implicit memory for the abusive episodes in symptoms and behaviours (for example, Bass and Davis 1988; Frederickson 1992; Terr 1994; van der Kolk 1994). A number of critics have pointed out that some of the symptoms cited as signs of unremembered abuse, such as problems with intimacy, eating disorders, and the like, are not specifically associated with sexual abuse (Pope and Hudson 1992) and could have any number of causes (Kihlstrom, Chapter 5 this volume; Ofshe and Watters 1994; Pendergrast 1995). While these symptoms are so general that they fall outside the rubric of what we generally think of as implicit memory, more specific manifestations of possible past abuse have also been described, such as unexplained fears of, or attractions to, specific objects that may have been associated with an abusive episode (for example, Frederickson 1992; Terr 1994).

Most laboratory research on implicit memory has focused on the learning of emotionally neutral or benign information, such as the priming of words, pictures, or faces, and perceptual and motor skill acquisition. None the less, there have been several studies of implicit memory for emotional information in patients with organic amnesia (for example, Damasio *et al.* 1989; Johnson *et al.* 1985) and college students (for example, Bargh and Pietromonaco 1982; Niedenthal 1992; for review see Tobias *et al.* 1992). Evidence that is more directly relevant comes from clinical observations of implicit memory in traumatized people. Terr (1988) reported that children who had been abused or otherwise traumatized often 'acted out' memories of the abuse even when they could not (or would not) explicitly recount the traumatic event or events. Similar effects have been documented in cases of psychogenic amnesia, where patients may generate trauma-related images or ideas that seem strange and unfamiliar to them (for example, Christianson and Nilsson 1989; Kaszniak *et al.* 1988; for review see Kihlstrom and Schacter 1995; Schacter and Kihlstrom 1989). Indeed, some of the earliest evidence of implicit memory for traumatic events comes from turn-of-the-century descriptions of psychogenic amnesias by such well known clinicians as Freud, Janet, and Prince (see Schacter 1987; Schacter and Kihlstrom 1989).

Converging evidence from studies of animals and humans suggests that the amygdala may play a key role in such implicit emotional memories. Studies with rats, for instance, indicate that the amygdala is clearly involved in the acquisition of conditioned fear (LeDoux 1995). Importantly, amygdala-based learning in rats has been dissociated experimentally from hippocampus-based learning (McDonald and White 1993). Consistent with these findings, Bechara *et al.* (1995) have recently shown that a patient with amygdala damage failed to exhibit a form of fear conditioning, but had no difficulty remembering the circumstances of the conditioning episode itself; conversely, a patient with hippocampal damage showed normal conditioning but failed to remember the conditioning episode. A patient with damage to both the amygdala and the hippocampus neither remembered the conditioning episode nor exhibited any conditioning.

All of these findings indicate that it is possible that people who have forgotten about an episode of abuse explicitly could still exhibit some form of implicit memory for it, perhaps because of emotional representations that in some way involve or depend on the amygdala. Likewise, the idea that traumatic experiences can result in poorly integrated memories also relates to evidence implicating the amygdala in implicit forms of memory. If traumatic stress can disrupt integrative processes during encoding, it is conceivable that some effects of trauma might be expressed implicitly in affective states, independently of any recollection of the context surrounding the traumatic episode (Jacobs and Nadel 1985).

At the same time, however, we must also stress some important cautionary notes. Perhaps most important, in all of the aforementioned clinical and experimental examples, there was no doubt about the existence of the event that provided the basis for implicit memory. In laboratory studies, researchers can present specified target materials, and later compare subjects' reactions to these materials with their reactions to new, non-presented information. Implicit memory is inferred when people respond faster, more accurately, or in some way differently to studied or previously presented materials compared with non-studied materials. Similarly, in clinical cases of psychogenic amnesia, implicit memory was exhibited for traumas that were known to have occurred. The situation is fundamentally different, however, when someone does not recollect being abused and a therapist (or anyone else) interprets a specific behaviour, fear, or attraction as evidence for the existence of abuse. While the inference might be correct in some instances, it is probably incorrect in others. When no abuse has in fact occurred, unjustified interpretation of fears, attractions, or other behaviours as signs of implicit memory for forgotten abuse could provide a basis for constructing an illusory recollection. Because inferring the existence of implicit memories requires carefully controlled comparisons that are typically not available in clinical settings, attempting to work backwards from symptoms to hypothetical or merely possible events is a highly risky and unjustified practice (see also Kihlstrom, Chapter 5 this volume; Pendergrast 1995).

We also note that the existence of implicit memory for abuse need not imply that a person will ever be able to remember a forgotten trauma explicitly. If a traumatic experience was poorly encoded because of stress or other inhibitory or disruptive influences, and all that remains is implicit memory of some form, there is no basis for assuming that explicit recollection of the trauma will follow. Thus, the issue of whether victims of sexual abuse might show implicit memory for traumatic events – and if so, what it might mean for recovery – remains open and requires systematic study.

CONCLUDING COMMENTS

Our review and assessment of the evidence suggests that some experiences of childhood abuse, especially those involving only one or a few incidents may, indeed, be forgotten for a time but then later remembered. However, the possibility that numerous highly traumatic incidents occurring over a period of years might likewise be completely forgotten and then later recovered is considerably less likely – and very unlikely in the absence of any previous signs of dissociative pathology. Further, there is clear evidence pointing to the possibility of engendering illusory memories through the use of techniques that may make source monitoring difficult or that may alter an individual's subjective confidence that an event actually occurred. An enormous body of results from cognitive psychology and cognitive neuroscience demonstrates that memories are vulnerable to distortion, and that confidence and vividness do not always go hand in hand with accuracy. Similarly, we have acknowledged the possibility that memory for previous traumatic experiences might be expressed implicitly, in the absence of conscious recollection of those events, and have noted clinical and experimental findings consistent with that possibility. Yet we have also pointed to the extreme hazards of attempting to use behaviours or symptoms to draw inferences about earlier traumatic events in the absence of any independent knowledge that they had, in fact, occurred.

In evaluating the plausibility of any particular case of recovered memory, all aspects of the situation merit consideration. These aspects include not only the nature of the memory itself, but also the circumstances surrounding the return of the memory (for example, whether specific cues may have facilitated retrieval, or whether risky therapeutic practices were employed), the initial plausibility of the content of the memory as determined from other sources (for example, if the memory involves satanic abuse, then independent evidence suggests that the memory is very likely illusory), and characteristics of the individual (for example, other evidence of a tendency to have dissociative experiences or the presence of a high level of interrogative suggestibility may be risk factors for illusory memories). Furthermore, in evaluating any one case, it would be a mistake to necessarily assume that the memory is either 'all true' or 'all false'. Memories that are 'mostly true' can contain inaccurate details, just as memories that are 'mostly false' can be comprised of fragments of memories of actual episodes that are unwittingly, but incorrectly, conjoined together. Some recovered memories may be essentially accurate, some may be largely inaccurate but none the less partially based on experiences of the individual other than actual abuse (for example, imagined abuse, or situations involving emotional abuse), and still others wholly inaccurate. The tremendous human costs involved in the recovered memories debate demand that all aspects of the situation be considered and evaluated against knowledge derived from both clinical and experimental sources.

ACKNOWLEDGEMENTS

Preparation of this chapter was supported by National Institute on Aging grant AG08441–06, National Institute of Neurological Disorders and Stroke grant PO1 NS27950, and a National Defense Science and Engineering Graduate Fellowship.

REFERENCES

Baker, R. (1992). *Hidden memories*. Prometheus Books, Buffalo, NY.

Banaji, M.R. and Crowder, R.O. (1989). The bankruptcy of everyday memory. *American Psychologist*, **44**, 1185–93.

Bargh, J.A. and Pietromonaco, P. (1982). Automatic information processing and social perception: the influence of trait information presented outside of conscious awareness on impression formation. *Journal of Personality and Social Psychology*, **43**, 437–49.

Bartlett, F.C. (1932). *Remembering*. Cambridge University Press, New York.

Bartlett, J.C., Strater, L., and Fulton, A. (1991). False recency and false fame of faces in young adulthood and old age. *Memory & Cognition*, **19**, 177–88.

Bass, E. and Davis, L. (1988). *The courage to heal: a guide for women survivors of child sexual abuse*. HarperPerennial, New York.

Bechara, A., Tranel, D., Damasio, H., Adolphs, R., Rockland, C., and Damasio, A.R. (1995). Double dissociation of conditioning and declarative knowledge relative to the amygdala and hippocampus in humans. *Science*, **269**, 1115–18.

Begg, I.M., Anas, A., and Farinacci, S. (1992). Dissociation of processes in belief: source recollection, statement familiarity, and the illusion of truth. *Journal of Experimental Psychology: General*, **121**, 446–58.

Belli, R.F., Lindsay, D.S., Gales, M.S., and McCarthy, T.T. (1994). Memory impairment and source misattribution in postevent misinformation experiments with short retention intervals. *Memory & Cognition*, **22**, 40–54.

Bernstein, E.M. and Putnam, F.W. (1986). Development, reliability, and validity of a dissociation scale. *Journal of Nervous and Mental Disease*, **174**, 727–35.

Bjork, R.A. (1989). Retrieval inhibition as an adaptive mechanism in human memory. *Varieties of memory and consciousness*, pp. 309–30. Erlbaum, Hillsdale, NJ.

Bliss, E.L. (1986). *Multiple personality, allied disorders, and hypnosis.* Oxford University Press, New York.

Bower, G.H. (1981). Mood and memory. *American Psychologist*, **36**, 129–48.

Bremner, J.D., Randall, P., Scott, T.M., Bronen, R.A., Seibyl, J.P., Southwick, S.M., *et al.* (1995). MRI-based measurement of hippocampal volume in patients with combat-related posttraumatic stress disorder. *American Journal of Psychiatry*, **152**, 973–81.

Brewer, W.F. (1988). Memory for randomly sampled autobiographical events. In *Remembering reconsidered: ecological and traditional approaches to the study of memory* (ed. U. Neisser and E. Winograd), pp. 21–90. Cambridge University Press, New York.

Briere, J. and Conte, J. (1993). Self-reported amnesia for abuse in adults molested as children. *Journal of Traumatic Stress*, **6**, 21–31.

Brown, D. (1995). Pseudomemories: the standard of science and the standard of care in trauma treatment. *American Journal of Clinical Hypnosis*, **37**, 1–24.

Buckner, R.L. and Tulving, E. (1995). Neuroimaging studies of memory: theory, and recent PET results. In *Handbook of neuropsychology*, Vol. 10 (ed. F. Boller and J. Grafman). pp. 439–66. Elsevier, Amsterdam.

Cahill, L. and McGaugh, J.L. (1996). Modulation of memory storage. *Current Opinion in Neurobiology* **6**, 237–42.

Cahill, L., Prins, B., Weber, M., and McGaugh, J.L. (1994). β-Adrenergic activation and memory for emotional events. *Nature*, **371**, 702–4.

Carlson, E.B. and Rosser-Hogan, R. (1994). Cross-cultural response to trauma: a study of traumatic experiences and posttraumatic symptoms in Cambodian refugees. *Journal of Traumatic Stress*, **7**, 43–58.

Castellano, C. and McGaugh, J.L. (1989). Effect of morphine on one-trial inhibitory avoidance in mice: lack of state-dependency. *Psychobiology*, **17**, 89–92.

Ceci, S.J. (1995). False beliefs: some developmental and clinical considerations. In *Memory Distortion* (ed. D.L. Schacter, J.T. Coyle, G.D. Fischbach, M.-M. Mesulam, and L.E. Sullivan), pp. 91–128. Harvard University Press, Cambridge, MA.

Christianson, S.-Å. (1992). Remembering emotional events: potential mechanisms. In *The handbook of emotion and memory: research and theory* (ed. S.-Å. Christianson) pp. 307–40. Erlbaum, Hillsdale, NJ.

Christianson, S.-Å. and Nilsson, L.G. (1989). Hysterical amnesia: a case of adversively motivated isolation of memory. In *Aversion, avoidance, and anxiety: perspectives on aversively motivated behavior* (ed. T. Archer and L.-G. Nilsson), pp. 289–310. Erlbaum, Hillsdale, NJ.

Cohen, N.J. and Eichenbaum, H. (1993). *Memory, amnesia, and the hippocampal system.* MIT Press, Cambridge, MA.

Colpaert, F.C. (1990). Amnesic trace locked into the benzodiazepine state of memory. *Psychopharmacology*, **102**, 28–36.

Conway, M.A. and Rubin, D.C. (1993). The structure of autobiographical memory. In *Theories of memory* (ed. A.F. Collins, S.E. Gathercole, M.A. Conway, and P.E. Morris), pp. 103–37. Erlbaum, Hillsdale, NJ.

Craik, F.I.M., Morris, L.W., Morris, R.G., and Loewen, E.R. (1990). Relations between source amnesia and frontal lobe functioning in older adults. *Psychology and Aging*, **5**, 148–51.

Crews, F. *et al.* (1995). *The memory wars: Freud's legacy in dispute.* New York Review Bk, New York.

Curran, T., Schacter, D.L., Norman, K.A., and Galluccio, L. (in press). False recognition after a right frontal lobe infarction: Memory for general and specific information. *Neuropsychologia.*

Damasio, A.R. (1989). Time-locked multiregional retroactivation: a systems-level proposal for the neural substrates of recall and recognition. *Cognition*, **33**, 25–62.

Damasio, A.R., Tranel, D., and Damasio, H. (1989). Amnesia caused by herpes simplex encephalitis, infarctions in basal forebrain, Alzheimer's disease and anoxia/ischemia. In *Handbook of neuropsychology,* Vol. 3 (ed. F. Boller and J. Grafman), pp. 149–66. Elsevier, Amsterdam.

De Bellis, M.D., Chrousos, G.P., Dorn, L.D., Burke, L., Helmers, K., Kling, M.A., Trickett, P.K., and Putnam, F.W. (1994*a*). Hypothalamic–pituitary–adrenal axis dysregulation in sexually abused girls. *Journal of Clinical Endocinology and Metabolism*, **78**, 249–55.

De Bellis, M.D., Lefter, L., Trickett, P.K., and Putnam, F.W. (1994*b*). Urinary catecholamine excretion in sexually abused girls. *Journal of the American Academy of Child and Adolescent Psychiatry*, **33**, 320–7.

Deese, J. (1959). On the prediction of occurrence of particular verbal intrusions in immediate recall. *Journal of Experimental Psychology*, **58**, 17–22.

DeLuca, J. and Cicerone, K.D. (1991). Confabulation following aneurysm of the anterior communicating artery. *Cortex*, **27**, 417–23.

Demb, J.B., Desmond, J.E., Wagner, A.D., Vaidya, C.J., Glouer, G.H., and Gabrieli, J.D.E. (1995). Semantic encoding and retrieval in the left inferior prefrontal cortex: a functional MRI study of task difficulty and process specificity. *Journal of Neuroscience*, **15**, 5870–8.

Dewhurst, S.A. and Conway, M.A. (1994). Pictures, images, and recollective experience. *Journal of Experimental Psychology: Learning, Memory, and Cognition*, **20**, 1088–98.

Dywan, J. (1995). The illusion of familiarity: an alternative to the report-criterion account of hypnotic recall. *International Journal of Clinical and Experimental Hypnosis*, **53**, 194–211.

Elliot, D.M. and Briere, J. (1995). Posttraumatic stress associated with delayed recall of sexual abuse: a general population study. *Journal of Traumatic Stress*, **8**, 629–47.

Erdelyi, M.H. (1985). *Psychoanalysis: Freud's cognitive psychology*. Freeman, New York.

Feldman–Summers, S. and Pope, K.S. (1994). The experience of 'forgetting' childhood abuse: a national survey of psychologists. *Journal of Consulting and Clinical Psychology*, **62**, 636–9.

Frederickson, R. (1992). *Repressed memories*. Simon & Schuster, New York.

Gardiner, J.M. and Java, R.I. (1993). Recognising and remembering. In *Theories of memory* (ed. A.F. Collins, S.E. Gathercole, M.A. Conway, and P.E. Morris), pp. 163–88. Erlbaum, Hove, East Sussex.

Garry, M., Manning, C., Loftus, E.F., and Sherman, S.J. (1996). Imagination inflation: imagining a childhood event inflates confidence that it occurred. *Psychonomic Bulletin and Review*, **3**, 208–14.

Gilbert, D.T. (1991). How mental systems believe. *American Psychologist*, **46**, 107–19.

Gilbert, D.T., Tafarodi, R.W., and Malone, P.S. (1993). You can't not believe everything you read. *Journal of Personality and Social Psychology*, **65**, 221–33.

Glisky, E.L., Polster, M.R., and Routhieaux, B.C. (1995). Double dissociation between item and source memory. *Neuropsychology*, **9**, 229–35.

Goldman–Rakic, P.S. (1987). Circuitry of primate prefrontal cortex and regulation of behavior by representational memory. In *Handbook of physiology: Vol. V, Higher functions of the brain* (ed. F. Plum), pp. 373–417. American Physiology Society, Bethesda, MD.

Goodman, G.S., Qin, J., Bottoms, B.L., and Shaver, P.R. (1994). *Characteristics and sources of allegations of ritualistic child abuse*, final report to the National Center on Child Abuse and Neglect.

Gudjonsson, G.H. (1991). The application of interrogative suggestibility to police interviewing. In *Human suggestibility: advances in theory, research, and application* (ed. J.F. Schumaker), pp. 279–88. Routledge, New York.

Gurvitz, T. V., Shenton, M. E., Hokama, H., Ohta, H., Lasko, N. B., Gilbertson, M. W., *et al.* Magnetic resonance imaging study of hippocampal volume chronic, combat-related posttraumatic stress disorder. *Biological Psychiatry*. (In press).

Hacking, I. (1995). *Rewriting the soul: multiple personality and the sciences of memory*. Princeton University Press.

Harvey, M.R., and Herman, J.L. (1994). Amnesia, partial amnesia, and delayed recall among adult survivors of childhood trauma. *Consciousness and Cognition*, **3**, 295–306.

Herman, J.L. (1995). Crime and memory. *Bulletin of the American Academy of Psychiatry Law*, **23**, 5–17.

Herman, J.L. and Schatzow, E. (1987). Recovery and verification of memories of childhood sexual trauma. *Psychoanalytic Psychology*, **4**, 1–14.

Heuer, F. and Reisberg, D. (1992). Emotion, arousal, and memory for detail. In *The handbook of emotion and memory: research and theory* (ed. S.-Å. Christianson), pp. 151–80. Erlbaum, Hillsdale, NJ.

Holmes, D.S. (1990). The evidence for repression: an examination of sixty years of research. In *Repression and dissociation* (ed. J.L. Singer) pp. 85–102. University of Chicago Press.

Hyman, I.E., Jr. and Billings, F.J. (1995). *Individual differences and the creation of false childhood memories*. (Submitted.)

Hyman, I.E., and Pentland, J. (1996). The role of mental imagery in the creation of false childhood memories. *Journal of Memory and Language*, **35**, 101–17.

Hyman, I.E., Husband, T.H., and Billings, F.J. (1995). False memories of childhood experiences. *Applied Cognitive Psychology*, **9**, 181–7.

Izquierdo, I. (1984). Endogenous state dependency: memory depends on the relation between neurohumoral and hormonal states present after training and at the time of testing. In *Neurobiology of learning and memory*, (ed. G. Lynch, J.L. McGaugh, and N.M. Weinberger), pp. 333–50. Guilford Press, New York.

Jackson, A., Koek, W., and Colpaert, F.C. (1992). NMDA antagonists make learning and recall state-dependent. *Behavioral Pharmacology*, **3**, 415–21.

Jacobs, W.J., and Nadel, L. (1985). Stress-induced recovery of fears and phobias. *Psychological Review*, **92**, 512–31.

Jacoby, L.L., Kelley, C.M., and Dywan, J. (1989*a*). Memory attributions. In *Varieties of memory and consciousness: essays in honour of Endel Tulving* (ed. H.L. Roediger III and F.I.M. Craik), pp. 391–422, Erlbaum, Hillsdale, NJ.

Jacoby, L.L., Woloshyn, V., and Kelley, C.M. (1989*b*). Becoming famous without being recognized: unconscious influences of memory produced by dividing attention. *Journal of Experimental Psychology: General*, **118**, 115–25.

Janowsky, J.S., Shimamura, A.P. and Squire, L.R. (1989). Source memory impairment in patients with frontal lobe lesions. *Neuropsychologia*, **27**, 1043–56.

Johnson, H.M. (1994). Processes of successful intentional forgetting. *Psychological Bulletin*, **116**, 274–92.

Johnson, M.K. (1991). Reality monitoring: evidence from confabulation in organic brain disease patients. In *Awareness of deficit after brain injury: clinical and theoretical issues* (ed. G.P. Prigatano and D.L. Schacter), pp. 176–97. Oxford University Press, New York.

Johnson, M.K. and Raye, C.L. (1981). Reality monitoring. *Psychological Review*, **88**, 67–85.

Johnson, M.K., Raye, C.L., Wang, A.Y., and Taylor, T.H. (1979). Fact and fantasy: the roles of accuracy and variability in confusing imaginations with perceptual experiences. *Journal of Experimental Psychology: Human Learning and Memory*, **5**, 229–40.

Johnson, M.K., Kim, J.K., and Risse, G. (1985). Do alcoholic Korsakoff's syndrome patients acquire affective reactions? *Journal of Experimental Psychology: Learning, Memory, and Cognition*, **11**, 27–36.

Johnson, M.K., Hashtroudi, S., and Lindsay, D.S. (1993). Source monitoring. *Psychological Bulletin*, **114**, 3–28.

Kandel, E. and Kandel, M. (1994). Flights of memory. *Discover*, **15**, (May) 19, 10, 32–38.

Kapur, S., Craik, F.I.M., Jones, C., Brown, G.H., Houle, S., and Tulving, E. (1995). Functional roles of prefrontal cortex in retrieval of memories: a PET study. *NeuroReport*, **6**, 1880–4.

Kapur, S., Craik, F.I.M., Tulving, E., Wilson, A.A., Houle, S., and Brown, G.M. (1994). Neuroanatomical correlates of encoding in episodic memory: Levels of processing effect. *Proceedings of the National Academy of Science*, **91**, 2008–11.

Kaszniak, A.W., Nussbaum, P.D., Berren, M.R., and Santiago, J. (1988). Amnesia as a consequence of male rape: a case report. *Journal of Abnormal Psychology*, **97**, 100–4.

Keenan, P.A., Jacobson, M.W., Soleymani, R.M., and Newcomer, J.W. (1995). Commonly used therapeutic doses of glucocorticoids impair explicit memory. *Annals of the New York Academy of Sciences*, **176**, 400–2.

Kihlstrom, J.F. (1995). The trauma-memory argument. *Consciousness and Cognition*, **4**, 63–7.

Kihlstrom, J.F. Hypnosis, memory, and amnesia. In *Biological and psychological perspectives on memory and memory disorders* (ed. L.R. Squire and D.L. Schacter). American Psychiatric Press, Washington, DC. (In press.)

Kihlstrom, J.F. and Schacter, D.L. (1995). Functional disorders of autobiographical memory. In *Handbook of memory disorders* (ed. A. Baddeley, B. Wilson, and F. Watts), pp. 337–64. Wiley, Chichester.

Kosslyn, S.M., Alpert, N.M., Thompson, W.L., Chabris, C.F., Rauch, S.L., and Anderson, A.K. (1993). Visual mental imagery activates topographically organized visual cortex: PET investigations. *Journal of Cognitive Neuroscience* **5**, 263–87.

Kosslyn, S.M., Thompson, W.L., Kim, I.J., & Alpert, N.M. (1995). Topographical representations of mental images in primary visual cortex. *Nature*, **378**, 496–8.

Koutstaal, W. and Schacter, D.L. Inaccuracy and inaccessibility in memory retrieval: contributions from cognitive psychology and cognitive neuropsychology. In *Trauma and memory: clinical and legal controversies* (ed. P.S. Appelbaum, L. Uyehara, and M. Elin), Oxford University Press, New York. (In press *a*.)

Koutstaal, W. and Schacter, D.L. Intentional forgetting and voluntary thought suppression: two potential methods for coping with childhood trauma. In *Review of Psychiatry*, Vol. 16 (ed. L.J. Dickstein, M.B. Riba, and J.M. Oldham). American Psychiatric Press, Washington, DC. (In press *b*.)

Kritchevsky, M., Zouzounis, J.A., and Squire, L.R. Transient global amnesia and functional amnesia: contrasting examples of episodic memory loss. In *Biological and psychological perspectives on memory and memory disorders* (ed. L.R. Squire and D.L. Schacter). American Psychiatric Press, Washington, DC. (In press.)

Krystal, J.H., Karper, L.P., Bennett, A., Abi-Dargham, A., D'Souza, D.C., Gil, R., and Charney, D.S. (1994*a*). Modulation of frontal cortical function by glutamate and dopamine antagonists in healthy subjects and schizophrenic patients: a neuropsychological perspective. *Neuropsychopharmacology*, **10**, S-43–198.

Krystal, J.H., Karper, L.P., Seibyl, J.P., Freeman, G.K., Delaney, R., Bremner, J.D., *et al.* (1994*b*). Subanesthetic effects of the NMDA antagonist, ketamine, in humans: psychotomimetic, perceptual, cognitive, and neuroendocrine effects. *Archives of General Psychiatry*, **51**, 1994–214.

Krystal, J.H., Bennett, A.L., Bremner, J.D., Southwick, S.M., and Charney, D.S. (1995*a*). Toward a cognitive neuroscience of dissociation and altered memory functions in post-traumatic stress disorder. *Neurobiological and clinical consequences of stress: from normal adaptation to PTSD* (ed. M.J. Friedman, D.S. Charney, and A.Y. Deutch), pp. 239–69. Lippincott-Raven, Philadelphia.

Krystal, J.H., Southwick, S.M., and Charney, D.S. (1995*b*). Post traumatic stress disorder: psychobiological mechanisms of traumatic rememberance. *Memory distortion: how minds, brains, and societies reconstruct the past* (ed. D.L. Schacter, J. T. Coyle, G.D. Fischbach, M.-M. Mesulam, and L.E. Sullivan), pp. 150–72. Harvard University Press, Cambridge, MA.

Kuyken, W. and Brewin, C.R. (1995). Autobiographical memory functioning in depression and reports of early abuse. *Journal of Abnormal Psychology*, **104**, 585–91.

LeDoux, J.E. (1995). Emotion: clues from the brain. *Annual Review of Psychology*, **46**, 209–35.

Lindsay, D.S. (1990). Misleading suggestions can impair eyewitnesses' ability to remember event details. *Journal of Experimental Psychology: Learning, Memory, and Cognition*, **16**, 1077–83.

Lindsay, D.S. and Read, J.D. (1994). Psychotherapy and memories of childhood sexual abuse: a cognitive perspective. *Applied Cognitive Psychology*, **8**, 281–338.

Lindsay, D.S. and Read, J.D. (1996). 'Memory work' and recovered memories of childhood sexual abuse: scientific evidence and public, professional, and personal issues. *Psychology, Public Policy, and the Law*, **1**, 1–61.

Linton, M. (1975). Memory for real word events. *Explorations in cognition* (ed. D.A. Norman & D.E. Rumelhart), pp. 376–404. Freeman, San Francisco.

Loftus, E.F. (1993). The reality of repressed memories. *American Psychologist*, **48**, 518–37.

Loftus, E.F. and Coan, D. (1995). The construction of childhood memories. In *The child witness in context: cognitive, social and legal perspectives* (ed. D. Peters). Kluwer, New York.

Loftus, E.F. and Ketcham, K. (1994). *The myth of repressed memory: false memories and allegations of sexual abuse*. St Martin's Press, New York.

Loftus, E.F. and Loftus, G.R. (1980). On the permanence of stored information in the human brain. *American Psychologist*, **35**, 409–20.

Loftus, E.F. and Pickrell, J.E. (1995). The formation of false memories. *Psychiatric Annals*, **25**, 720–5.

Loftus, E.F., Miller, D.G., and Burns, H.J. (1978). Semantic integration of verbal information into a visual memory. *Journal of Experimental Psychology: Human Learning and Memory*, **4**, 19–31.

Loftus, E.F., Polonsky, S., and Fullilove, M.T. (1994*a*). Memories of childhood sexual abuse: remembering and repressing. *Psychology of Women*, **18**, 67–84.

Loftus, E.F., Garry, M., and Feldman, J. (1994*b*). Forgetting sexual trauma: what does it mean when 38% forget? *Journal of Consulting and Clinical Psychology*, **62**, 1177–81.

Loftus, E.F., Feldman, J., and Dashiell, R. (1995). The reality of illusory memories. In *Memory distortion: how minds, brains and societies reconstruct the past* (ed. D.L. Schacter, J.T. Coyle, G.D. Fischbach, M.-M. Mesulam, and L.F. Sullivan), pp. 47–68. Harvard University Press, Cambridge, MA.

Lynn, S.J. and Nash, M.R. (1994). Truth in memory: ramifications for psychotherapy and hypnotherapy. *American Journal of Hypnosis*, **36**, 194–208.

Mack, J.E. (1994). *Abduction: human encounters with aliens.* Scribner's, New York.

McClelland, J.L., McNaughton, B.L., and O'Reilly, R.C. (1995). Why there are complementary learning systems in the hippocampus and neocortex: insights from the successes and failures of connectionist models of learning and memory. *Psychological Review*, **102**, 419–57.

McCloskey, M. and Zaragoza, M. (1985). Misleading postevent information and memory for events: arguments and evidence against memory impairment hypotheses. *Journal of Experimental Psychology: General*, **114**, 1–16.

McDonald, R.J. and White, N.M. (1993). A triple dissociation of memory systems: hippocampus, amygdala, and dorsal striatum. *Behavioral Neuroscience*, **107**, 3–22.

McGaugh, J.L. (1995). Emotional activation, neuromodulatory systems and memory. In *Memory distortion: how minds, brains, and societies reconstruct the past* (ed. D.L. Schacter, J.T. Coyle, G.D. Fischbach, M.-M. Mesulam, and L.E. Sullivan), pp. 255–73. Harvard University Press, Cambridge, MA.

McGaugh, J.L., Introini-Collison, I.B., Cahill, L.F., Castellano, C., Dalmaz, C., Parent, M.B., and Williams, D.L. (1993). Neuromodulatory systems and memory storage: role of the amygdala. *Behavioral Brain Research*, **58**, 81–90.

Merskey, H. (1992). The manufacture of personalities: the production of multiple personality disorder. *British Journal of Psychiatry*, **160**, 327–40.

Moldea, D.E. (1995). *The killing of Robert F. Kennedy: an investigation of motive, means, and opportunity.* Norton, New York.

Morton, J. Cognitive perspectives on recovered memories. In *Recovered memories of abuse: true or false?* (ed. J. Sandler). Karnac Books, London. (In press.)

Moscovitch, M. (1994). Memory and working-with-memory: evaluation of a component process model and comparisons with other models. In *Memory systems 1994* (ed. D.L. Schacter and E. Tulving), pp. 269–310. MIT Press, Cambridge, MA.

Moscovitch, M. (1995). Confabulation. In *Memory distortion: how minds, brains, and societies reconstruct the past* (ed. D.L. Schacter, J.T. Coyle, G.D. Fischbach, M.-M. Mesulam, and L.E. Sullivan), pp. 226–54. Harvard University Press, Cambridge, MA.

Murray, E.A., Gaffan, D., and Mishkin, M. (1993). Neural substrates of visual stimulus-stimulus association in Rhesus monkeys. *Journal of Neuroscience*, **13**, 4549–61.

Nash, M.R. (1994). Memory distortion and sexual trauma: the problem of false negatives and false positives. *International Journal of Clinical and Experimental Hypnosis*, **42**, 346–62.

Nathan, D. and Snedeker, M. (1995). *Satan's silence: ritual abuse and the making of a modern American witch hunt.* Basic Books, New York.

Neisser, U. (1967). *Cognitive psychology.* Appleton-Century-Crofts, New York.

Neisser, U. (1982). John Dean's memory: a case study. In U. Neisser (Ed.), *Memory observed: remembering in natural contexts* (ed. U. Neisser), pp. 139–59. Freeman, San Francisco.

Nelson, E.L. and Simpson, P. (1994). First glimpse: an initial examination of subjects who have rejected their recovered visualizations as false memories. *Issues in Child Abuse Accusations,* **6,** 123–33.

Newcomer, J.W., Craft, S., Hershey, T., Askins, K., and Bardgett, M.E. (1994). Glucocorticoid-induced impairment in declarative memory performance in adult humans. *Journal of Neuroscience,* **14,** 2047–53.

Niedenthal, P.M. (1992). Affect and social perception: on the psychological validity of rose-colored glasses. In *Perception without awareness: cognitive, clinical, and social perspectives* (ed. R.F. Bornstein and T.S. Pittman), pp. 211–35. Guilford, New York.

Norman, K.A. and Schacter, D.L. False recognition in younger and older adults: exploring the characteristics of illusory memories. *Memory & Cognition.* (In press *a.*)

Norman, K.A. and Schacter, D.L. Implicit memory, explicit memory, and false recollection: a cognitive neuroscience perspective. In *Implicit memory and metacognition,* (ed. L.M. Reder). Erlbaum, Hillsdale, NJ. (In press *b.*)

Ofshe, R. and Watters, E. (1994). *Making monsters: false memories, psychotherapy, and sexual hysteria.* Scribner's, New York.

Olio, K.A. (1994). Truth in memory. *American Psychologist,* **49,** 442–3.

Parkin, A.J. and Leng, N.R.C. (1993). *Neuropsychology of the amnesic syndrome.* Erlbaum, Hillsdale, NJ.

Parks, E.D. and Balon, R. (1995). Autobiographical memory for childhood events: patterns of recall in psychiatric patients with a history of alleged trauma. *Psychiatry,* **58,** 199–208.

Payne, D.G., Elie, C.J., Blackwell, J.M., and Neuschatz, J.S. (1996). Memory illusions: recalling, recognizing, and recollecting events that never occurred. *Journal of Memory and Language,* **35,** 261–85.

Pendergrast, M. (1995). *Victims of memory: incest accusations and shattered lives.* Upper Access, Hinesburg, VT.

Poole, D.A., Lindsay, S.D., Memon, A., and Bull, R. (1995). Psychotherapy and the recovery of memories of childhood sexual abuse: US and British practitioners' opinions, practices, and experiences. *Journal of Consulting and Clincial Psychology,* **63,** 426–87.

Pope, H.G., Jr. and Hudson, J.I. (1992). Is childhood sexual abuse a risk factor for Bulimia Nervosa? *American Journal of Psychiatry,* **149,** 455–63.

Pope, H.G., Jr. and Hudson, J.I. (1995). Can memories of childhood sexual abuse be repressed? *Psychological Medicine,* **25,** 121–6.

Putnam, F.W. (1989). *Diagnosis and treatment of multiple personality disorder.* Guilford, London.

Putnam, F.W. (1993). Dissociative disorders in children: behavioral profiles and problems. *Child Abuse & Neglect,* **17,** 39–45.

Pynoos, R.S. and Nader, K. (1989). Children's memory and proximity to violence. *Journal of the American Academy of Child and Adolescent Psychiatry,* **28,** 236–41.

Read, J.D. (1996). From a passing thought to a false memory in 2 minutes: confusing real and illusory events. *Psychonomic Bulletin and Review.,* **3,** 105–111.

Register, P.A. and Kihlstrom, J.F. (1988). Hypnosis and interrogative suggestibility. *Personality and Individual Differences*, **9**, 549–58.

Reyna, V.F. and Brainerd, C.J. (1995). Fuzzy-trace theory: an interim synthesis. *Learning and Individual Differences*, **7**, 1–75.

Richardson-Klavehn, A. and Bjork, R.A. (1988). Measures of memory. *Annual Review of Psychology*, **36**, 475–543.

Roediger, H.L., III and McDermott, K.B. (1993). Implicit memory in normal human subjects. In *Handbook of neuropsychology*, Vol. 8 (ed. H. Spinnler and F. Boller), pp. 63–131. Elsevier, Amsterdam.

Roediger, H.L., III and McDermott, K.B. (1995). Creating false memories: remembering words not presented in lists. *Journal of Experimental Psychology: Learning, Memory, and Cognition*, **21**, 803–14.

Ross, B.M. (1991). *Remembering the personal past*. Oxford University Press, New York.

Sapolsky, R.M. (1992). *Stress, the aging brain, and the mechanisms of neuron death*. MIT Press, Cambridge, MA.

Sapolsky, R.M., Uno, H., Rebert, C.S., and Finch, C.E. (1990). Hippocampal damage associated with prolonged glucocorticoid exposure in primates. *Journal of Neuroscience*, **10**, 2897–902.

Sargent, W. and Slater, E. (1941). Amnesic syndromes in war. *Proceedings of the Royal Society of Medicine*, **34**, 757–64.

Schacter, D.L. (1986). Amnesia and crime: how much do we really know? *American Psychologist*, **41**, 286–95.

Schacter, D.L. (1987). Implicit memory: history and current status. *Journal of Experimental Psychology: Learning, Memory, and Cognition*, **13**, 501–18.

Schacter, D.L. (1989). Memory. In *Foundations of cognitive science* (ed. M.I. Posner), pp. 683–725. MIT Press, Cambridge, MA.

Schacter, D.L. (1995a). Memory distortion: history and current status. In *Memory distortion: how minds, brains and societies reconstruct the past* (ed. D.L. Schacter, J.T. Coyle, G.D. Fischbach, M.-M. Mesulam, and L.E. Sullivan), pp. 1–43. Harvard University Press, Cambridge, MA.

Schacter, D.L. (1995b). Memory wars. *Scientific American*, **272**, 135–9.

Schacter, D.L. (1996). *Searching for memory: the brain, the mind, and the past*. Basic Books, New York.

Schacter, D.L. and Kihlstrom, J.F. (1989). Functional amnesia. In *Handbook of neuropsychology*, Vol. 3 (ed. F. Boller and J. Grafman), pp. 209–31. Elsevier, Amsterdam.

Schacter, D.L. and Tulving, E. (1994). What are the memory systems of 1994? In *Memory systems 1994* (ed. D.L. Schacter and E. Tulving), pp. 1–38. MIT Press, Cambridge, MA.

Schacter, D.L., Wang, P.L., Tulving, E., and Freedman, M. (1982). Functional retrograde amnesia: a quantitative case study. *Neuropsychologia*, **20**, 523–32.

Schacter, D.L., Harbluk, J.L., and McLachlan, D.R. (1984). Retrieval without recollection: an experimental analysis of source amnesia. *Journal of Verbal Learning and Verbal Behavior*, **23**, 593–611.

Schacter, D.L., Kihlstrom, J.F., Kihlstrom, L.C., and Berren, M.B. (1989). Autobiographical memory in a case of multiple personality disorder. *Journal of Abnormal Psychology*, **98**, 508–14.

Schacter, D.L., Kaszniak, A.K., Kihlstrom, J.F., and Valdiserri, M. (1991). The relation between source memory and aging. *Psychology and Aging*, **6**, 559–68.

Schacter, D.L., Chiu, C.Y.P., and Ochsner, K.N. (1993). Implicit memory: a selective review. *Annual Review of Neuroscience*, **16**, 159–182.

Schacter, D.L., Osowiecki, D.M., Kaszniak, A.F., Kihlstrom, J.F., and Valdiserri, M. (1994). Source memory: extending the boundaries of age-related deficits. *Psychology and Aging*, **9**, 81–9.

Schacter, D.L., Kagan, J., and Leichtman, M.D. (1995*a*). True and false memories in children and adults: a cognitive neuroscience perspective. *Psychology, Public Policy, and Law*, **1**, 411–28.

Schacter, D.L., Reiman, E., Uecker, A., Polster, M.R., Yun, L.S., and Cooper, L.A. (1995*b*). Brain regions associated with retrieval of structurally coherent visual information. *Nature*, **376**, 587–90.

Schacter, D.L., Alpert, N.M., Savage, C.R., Rauch, S.L., and Albert, M.S. (1996*a*). Conscious recollection and the human hippocampal formation: evidence from positron emission tomography. *Proceedings of the National Academy of Sciences*, **93**, 321–5.

Schacter, D.L., Curran, T., Galluccio, L., Milberg, W., and Bates, J. (1996*b*) False recognition and the right frontal lobe: a case study. *Neuropsychologia*, **34**, 793–808.

Schacter, D.L., Verfaellie, M., and Pradere, D. (1996*c*) The neuropsychology of memory illusions: false recall and recognition in amnesic patients. *Journal of Memory and Language*, **35**, 319–34.

Schacter, D.L. and Curran, T. (1995). The cognitive neuroscience of false memories. *Psychiatric Annals*, **25**, 726–30.

Schooler, J.W. (1994). Seeking the core: the issues and evidence surrounding recovered accounts of sexual trauma. *Consciousness and Cognition*, **3**, 452–69.

Shimamura, A.P. (1995). Memory and frontal lobe function. In *The cognitive neurosciences* (ed. M. Gazzaniga), pp. 803–13. MIT Press, Cambridge, MA.

Shimamura, A.P. and Squire, L.R. (1987). A neuropsychological study of fact memory and source amnesia. *Journal of Experimental Psychology: Learning, Memory, and Cognition*, **13**, 464–73.

Singer, J.L. (ed.). (1990). *Repression and dissociation: implications for personality theory, psychopathology, and health*. University of Chicago Press.

Spanos, N.P., Menary, E., Gabora, N., DuBreuil, S., and Dewhirst, B. (1991). Secondary identity enactments during hypnotic past-life regression: a sociocognitive perspective. *Journal of Personality and Social Psychology*, **61**, 308–20.

Spiegel, D. (1995). Hypnosis and suggestion. In *Memory distortion: how minds, brains, and societies reconstruct the past* (ed. D.L. Schacter, J.T. Coyle, G.D. Fischbach, M.-M. Mesulam, and L.E. Sullivan), pp. 129–149, Harvard University Press, Cambridge, MA.

Squire, L.R. (1987). *Memory and brain*. Oxford University Press, New York.

Squire, L.R. (1992). Memory and the hippocampus: a synthesis from findings with rats, monkeys, and humans. *Psychological Review*, **99**, 195–231.

Squire, L.R., Ojemann, J.G., Miezin, F.M., Petersen, S.E., Videen, T.O., and Raichle, M.E. (1992). Activation of the hippocampus in normal humans: a functional anatomical study of memory. *Proceedings of the National Academy of Sciences*, **89**, 1837–41.

Stein, M.B., Koverala, C., Hanna, C., Torchia, M.G., and McClarty, B. (1995). Neurobiological correlates of childhood sexual abuse: II. MRI-based measurement of hippocampal volume in adult women. (Submitted.)

Tayloe, D.R. (1995). The validity of repressed memories and the accuracy of their recall through hypnosis: a case study from the courtroom. *American Journal of Hypnosis*, **3**, 25–31.

Terr, L. (1988). What happens to early memories of trauma? *Journal of the American Academy of Child Adolescent Psychiatry*, **27**, 96–104.

Terr, L. (1994). *Unchained memories*. Basic Books, New York.

Thom, D.A. and Fenton, W. (1920). Amnesia in war cases. *American Journal of Psychiatry*, **76**, 437–48.

Tobias, B.A., Kihlstrom, J.F., and Schacter, D.L. (1992). Emotion and implicit memory. In *The handbook of emotion and memory: research and theory* (ed. S.-Å. Christianson), pp. 67–92. Erlbaum, Hillsdale, NJ.

Tulving, E. (1983). *Elements of episodic memory*. Clarendon, Oxford.

Tulving, E. (1985). Memory and consciousness. *Canadian Psychologist*, **26**, 1–12.

Tun, P.A., Wingfield, A., and Rosen, M. (1995). *Age effects on false memory for words*, paper presented at the 36th Annual Meeting of the Psychonomic Society, Los Angeles, CA.

Ungerleider, L. G. (1995). Functional brain imaging studies of cortical mechanisms for memory. *Science*, **270**, 769–75.

van der Kolk, B.A. (1994). The body keeps the score: memory and the evolving psychobiology of PTSD. *Harvard Review of Psychiatry*, **1**, 253–65.

van der Kolk, B.A. and Fisler, R.E. (1995). Dissociation and the fragmentary nature of traumatic memories: overview and exploratory study. *Journal of Traumatic Stress*, **8**, 505–25.

Wakefield, H. and Underwager, R. (1994). *Return of the furies: an investigation into recovered memory therapy*. Open Court, Chicago.

Whitfield, C.L. (1995). *Memory and abuse: remembering and healing the effects of trauma*. Health Communication, Deerfield Beach, FL.

Wilkinson, C.B. (1983). Aftermath of a disaster: the collapse of the Hyatt Regency Hotel skywalks. *American Journal of Psychiatry*, **140**, 1134–9.

Williams, G.V. and Goldman-Rakic, P.S. (1995). Modulation of memory fields by dopamine D_1 receptors in prefrontal cortex. *Nature*, **376**, 572–5.

Williams, J.M.G. (1992). Autobiographical memory and emotional disorders. In *The handbook of emotion and memory: research and theory* (ed. S.-Å. Christianson), pp. 451–77. Erlbaum, Hillsdale, NJ.

Williams, L.M. (1994). Recall of childhood trauma: a prospective study of women's memories of child sexual abuse. *Journal of Consulting and Clinical Psychology*, **62**, 1167–76.

Williams, L.M. (1995). Recovered memories of abuse in women with documented child sexual victimization histories. *Journal of Traumatic Stress*, **8**, 649–73.

Wilson, S.C. and Barber, T.X. (1978). The Creative Imagination Scale as a measure of hypnotic responsiveness: applications to experimental and clinical hypnosis. *American Journal of Clinical Hypnosis*, **20**, 235–49.

Wolkowitz, O.M., Reus, V.I., Weingartner, H., Thompson, K., Breier, A., Doran, A., Rubinow, D., and Pickar, D. (1990). Cognitive effects of corticosteroids. *American Journal of Psychiatry*, **147**, 1297–303.

Wright, L. (1994). *Remembering Satan: a case of recovered memory and the shattering of an American family*. Knopf, New York.

Zaragoza, M.S. and Lane, S.M. (1994). Source misattributions and the suggestibility of eyewitness memory. *Journal of Experimental Psychology: Learning, Memory, and Cognition*, **20**, 934–45.

Zola-Morgan, S., Squire, L.R., Amaral, D.G., and Suzuki, W.A. (1989). Lesions of perirhinal and parahippocampal cortex that spare the amygdala and hippocampal formation produce severe memory impairment. *Journal of Neuroscience*, **9**, 4355–70.

FIVE

Suffering from reminiscences: exhumed memory, implicit memory, and the return of the repressed

JOHN F. KIHLSTROM

In one of his earliest psychoanalytic essays, 'Further remarks on the neuro-psychoses of defence', Freud introduced the concept of 'the return of the repressed' (Freud 1896, p. 170) as a mechanism underlying neurotic symptoms. Discussing the nature and mechanisms of obsessional neurosis, he wrote (Freud, 1896, pp. 169–70):

[The illness] is characterized by the *return of the repressed memories* – that is, therefore, by the failure of the defence ... The re-activated memories, however, and the self-reproaches formed from them never re-emerge into consciousness unchanged: what become conscious as obsessional ideas and affects, and take the place of the pathogenic memories so far as conscious life is concerned, are structures in the nature of a *compromise* between the repressed ideas and the repressing ones ...

The notion of *the return of the repressed* did not apply just to obsessional neurosis, however; it was also implicated in hysteria and paranoia (Freud 1892–9; 1896), hysterical attacks (Freud 1909*b*, p. 111), psychical (secondary) impotence (Freud 1909*c*, p. 183), obsessions (Freud 1911*b*, p. 323) and other forms of mental illness. In Draft K on 'The neuroses of defense', enclosed with his 1896 New Year letter to Fliess, Freud wrote that 'The main differences between the various neuroses are shown in the way in which the repressed ideas return . . .' (Freud 1892–9, p. 223; see also Freud 1924, p. 183).

As psychoanalytic theory evolved, Freud made use of 'the return of the repressed' time and time again. The concept lies behind Breuer and Freud's pre-psychoanalytic assertion that 'hysterics suffer mainly from reminiscences' (Breuer and Freud 1893–5, p. 7). Freud saw in a young child's sleep ceremonials a representation of a repressed episode of sexual abuse by a servant-girl (Freud 1896, n.1, pp. 172–3). He attributed a child's interest in mathematics, and his puzzling inability to solve certain problems, to his repressed sexuality (Freud 1907, p. 36). He saw a parallel between the return of the repressed and forensic lie detection (Freud 1909*a*, p. 111). The concept comes up in the analysis of the Schreber case (Freud 1911*a*, p. 68), and in Freud's criticisms of Jung – who dared to substitute the return of complexes for the return of the repressed (Freud 1914, p. 30).

In his major statement on repression, Freud (1915, p. 154, italics original) wrote:

The mechanisms of a repression becomes accessible to us only by our deducing that mechanism from the *outcome* of the repression. Confining our observations to the effect of repression on the ideational portion of the representative, we discover that as a rule it creates a *substitutive formation* . . . Further, we know that repression leaves *symptoms* behind it. May we then suppose that the forming of substitutes and the forming of symptoms coincide, and, if this is so on the whole, is the mechanism of forming symptoms the same as that of repression? The general probability would seem to be that the two are widely different, and that it is not the repression itself which produces substitutive formations and symptoms, but that these latter are indications of a *return of the repressed* and owe their existence to quite other processes.

And he repeated the formulation in *Moses and monotheism*, the last of Freud's works to appear in his lifetime (Freud 1939, p. 127):

All the phenomena of the formation of symptoms may justly be described as the 'return of the repressed'.

THE RETURN OF THE REPRESSED, REDUX

More recently, Freud's essential ideas have been revived by proponents of the view that unconscious memories of childhood incest, sexual abuse, and other trauma underlie many forms of adult maladjustment and psychopathology (see, for example, Bass and Davis 1988, 1994; Blume 1990; Frederickson 1992; Herman 1992; Terr 1994; for a detailed analysis of the parallels between Freud's theories and later clinical practices, see Bowers 1995; Crews 1995; Kihlstrom 1994). The modern version of the trauma-memory argument (Kihlstrom 1995) runs approximately as follows:

- A child (or adult, for that matter), victimized by trauma, invokes repression or dissociation as a psychological defence mechanism;
- this repression or dissociation renders the child amnesic for the trauma itself;
- nevertheless, unconscious representations of the trauma are encoded and stored in memory;
- these unconscious memories affect conscious experience, thought, and action in the form of mental and behavioural symptoms such as intrusive images, somatic feelings, and dreams;
- such symptoms are signs that a traumatic event occurred, a representation of which is available in memory;
- restoration of conscious access to the traumatic memory is an important ingredient in psychotherapy for trauma victims;
- where attempts to exhume the traumatic memory do not succeed, it is important for the patient to acknowledge that the trauma occurred.

Thus, just as Freud asserted a century ago, many current practitioners argue that unconscious memories express themselves as symptoms. Bass and Davis (1988) clearly have the trauma-memory argument and the return of the repressed in mind when they write in their best-selling self-help book, *The courage to heal*, of flashbacks, sense memories, and body memories as if they were representations of past episodes of abuse. Blume (1990), another popular self-help author, echoes this view:

'Hysterical symptoms'. . . represent unremembered trauma or unacknowledged feelings. Because there is a physical distraction, the survivor is at once protected and blocked . . . Her body remembers, but her mind does not. (p. 93)

Flashbacks are memories of past traumas. They may take the form of pictures, sounds, smells, body sensations, feelings or the lack of them (numbness). Many times there is no actual visual or auditory memory. (p. 102)

Frederickson (1992) offers an elaborate classification of five kinds of memory, four of which seem to reflect the return of the repressed (italics added):

Recall memory is a consciously retained memory of events accompanied by the sense of having experienced those events. It involves a series of related images organized around time and space into a logical sequence. (p. 88)

Imagistic memory is a memory that breaks through to the conscious mind in the form of imagery. This imagery is actually an incomplete picture of events that happened. The images are like a slide show. They pop up and are gone in an instant, often leaving the person wondering, 'Now, where did *that* come from?' . . . When the images from repressed memories do come spilling out, they are persistent and uniquely compelling . . . Images that surface from the unconscious can be from any part of the abuse scene . . . Some aspects of the imagery may be exaggerated, even though each image represents an accurate slice of the abuse . . . The most confusing thing about the images is that they seem unrelated to what is happening at the present moment. They are, in fact, triggered by something in the environment that reminds their unconscious of the buried memory. The associated memory breaks through the unconscious as an image. (pp. 89–91).

Feeling memory is the memory of an emotional response to a particular situation. If the situation we are being triggered to remember is a repressed memory, we will have the feelings pertaining to the event without any conscious recall of the event itself. Feeling memory is often experienced as a flood of inexplicable emotion, particularly around abuse issues . . . A felt sense that something abusive has happened is a common form of a feeling memory. Some survivors will say, 'Yes, I think I was sexually abused, but it's just a gut feeling.' These clients are experiencing a feeling memory about being abused, even though at that moment they can recall nothing about their abuse. (p. 92)

Our bodies react to everything that happens to us, and *body memory* is the physical manifestation of a past incident. The more significant the incident is, the greater the impact on the body. Our physical bodies always remember sexual abuse, just as our feelings and our minds do . . . Like imagistic and feeling memory, body memory often emerges in conjunction with other forms of unconscious memory processes . . . The body memories, alone or with other forms of memory, tell the story of the sexual abuse. (pp. 93–4)

Acting-out memory is a form of unconscious memory in which the forgotten incident is spontaneously acted out through some physical action. It involves either a verbal or bodily act in response to something that reminds one of the original episode . . . Perhaps the most common kind of acting-out memory is when survivors suddenly say something about their abuse that they had no intention of saying . . . Physically acting out part of an abuse memory is another manifestation of this kind of memory . . . Acting-out memory can occur even when you are asleep. A dream may contain a fragment of an abuse memory, triggering an acting-out memory . . . Similar reactions can also occur under the influence of drugs and alcohol.

Comparing conscious recollection with the return of the repressed, Frederickson (1992) further writes:

If an abuse memory does not materialize spontaneously, it rarely surfaces as a recall memory. The memory instead returns through the unconscious memory processes. Survivors will have a series of realizations about their abuse that they find clear and believable, but rarely do they have a sense of having lived what is being felt or pictured. They call it a memory because the pieces fit into their sense of reality, not because they actually now remember experiencing the abuse. What most people call spontaneous recall usually involves memories that have been denied, not repressed. (pp. 95–6)

In a recent television interview, Leore Terr, a prominent authority on childhood trauma (Terr 1991, 1994) argued that a particular patient's inability to eat whole bananas or pickles, white sauces, or mayonnaise was evidence that she had been sexually abused as a child, and justified therapeutic attempts to exhume memories of the abuse (interview on the Maury Povich Show, 25 May 1994). This vulgar Freudianism – even Freud admitted that sometimes a cigar is a cigar – epitomizes the present-day doctrine of the return of the repressed.

It is important to note that the return of the repressed is not just the stuff of popular-press books and tabloid television. Respected academic psychologists and psychiatrists have argued that cognitive and neuropsychological research on memory supports the idea that trauma can be repressed, and return as symptoms. For example, Terr (1991, 1994) has drawn a distinction between two types of trauma: type I refers to unanticipated, single events, while type II refers to exposure to multiple events and chronic conditions. According to Terr, victims of type I trauma typically have full, detailed memory of their experiences, while the memories of type II victims are impaired:

Children who experience type II traumas often forget. They may forget whole segments of childhood – from birth to age 9, for instance. (Terr 1991, p. 16)

If they are repeatedly traumatized, children can be expected to 'forget' much of what happened . . . Holes in memory are created by defensive operations, such as the very common defense of repression. When repression lifts, the memories may come back relatively intact. (Terr 1994, p. 30).

In her original paper on this subject, Terr (1991, p. 15) attributed the memory failures in type II trauma victims to psychological defences and coping operations such as denial, repression, and dissociation. In her later book, however, Terr (1994, pp.44ff.) draws on the distinction, now familiar in cognitive neuropsychology, between explicit and implicit memory (Schacter 1987, 1995). Explicit memory is conscious recollection, as evidenced by the individual's ability to recall or recognize some event from his or her past. Implicit memory, by contrast, refers to any effect of a past event on the person's ongoing experience, thought, or action, independent of conscious recollection. Accordingly, Terr argues that people can reveal in their behaviour memories for traumatic experiences that are not accessible to conscious recollection and verbal report:[1]

The mystery that flows from this division of memory – when it comes to traumatized people – is how something taken into memory explicitly eventually behaves so similarly to the memories that are entirely implicit. These lost, no-longer-verbal memories drive action just as effectively as would a conditioning experiment (Terr 1994, p. 45).

Another trauma researcher who has made use of the explicit – implicit memory distinction is van der Kolk (1994; van der Kolk and van der Hart 1991), who has proposed that traumatic experiences are stored in somatic memory, in the form of visual images and physical sensations, even when they are not available in declarative memory as consciously accessible verbal reports. Reflecting on the contributions of Freud and Janet to understanding memory for trauma, van der Kolk and van der Hart (1991) clearly opted for the position which Breuer and Freud (that is, Freud before the hypothesis of infantile seduction was replaced by the hypothesis of infantile sexuality) shared with Janet: that current symptoms are unconscious expressions of memories of the past.

For the past 75 years, psychoanalysis, the study of repressed wishes and instincts, and descriptive psychiatry, virtually ignored the fact that actual memories may form the nucleus of psychopathology and continue to exert their influence on current experience by means of the process of dissociation ... Lack of proper integration of intensely emotionally arousing experiences into the memory system results in dissociation and the formation of traumatic memories ... Though subconscious, they continue to influence current perceptions, affect states, and behavior; they are usually accessible under hypnosis. (van der Kolk and van der Hart 1991, pp. 426, 431–2.)

Van der Kolk and van der Hart (1991) went on to propose that traumatic memories, because they are not accessible to consciousness, exist in a kind

---

1 Terr (1994) actually uses the explicit–implicit and declarative–non-declarative distinctions (Squire *et al.* 1993) interchangeably. Terr (1994, pp. 48–50), also distinguishes between six major forms of memory – immediate, short-term, knowledge and skills, priming, associative, and episodic – although her definitions and examples of each type do not always match the standard terminology within cognitive psychology.

of frozen state, unaltered by subsequent experience or even the passage of time. In particular, these authors have proposed that the feelings of terror associated with traumatic events persist, even though the victim is unable to express them verbally; and that the retrieval of such somatosensory, iconic, or motoric memories is state dependent, so that they are especially likely to be evoked when the person is once again exposed to stress or trauma. Therapeutic recovery, in their view, requires that the person remember, or at least accept the fact of, the traumatic event(s) that precipitated the person's illness in the first place.

More recently, van der Kolk (1994) has drawn on neuroscientific research and theory to support his position that unconscious memories of trauma are expressed as somatic symptoms:

Research into the nature of traumatic memories indicates that trauma interferes with declarative memory (i.e., conscious recall of experience) but does not inhibit implicit, or nondeclarative, memory, the memory system that controls conditioned emotional responses, skills and habits, and sensorimotor sensations related to experience. (p.258, references omitted)

Van der Kolk (1994) further proposes that stress-induced increases in corticosteroids interfere with hippocampal function, and thus the storage of a declarative (or explicit) memory, but have no effect on the storage of non-declarative (implicit) emotional associations, which is mediated by the amygdala. Thus, the traumatized person responds emotionally to objects and events reminiscent of the original trauma, without consciously remembering the trauma itself.

Similarly, Kandel and Kandel (1994) proposed that children who cannot escape repeated abuse dissociate from the experience while it is happening, or repress the experience afterward. They further invoked the difference between explicit and implicit memory in order to explain how the emotional feelings associated with abuse could persist, while conscious recollection of abuse was lost. In the absence of independent corroboration, Kandel and Kandel suggested that 'particularly compelling behavioral clues . . . might sometimes help support a case' (p. 38). Thus, behavioural symptoms, construed as implicit memories, are held out as the means by which uncorroborated memories of historical events can be confirmed.

INFERRING HISTORY FROM SYMPTOMS

Part and parcel of the doctrine of the return of the repressed, for Freud as well as for the current promoters of recovered memory therapy, is the idea that a whole host of mental and behavioural symptoms are reflections – implicit memories, if you will – of childhood abuse. Those who present symptoms of 'Post-Incest Syndrome' (Blume 1990, p. xxi) or 'Repressed Memory Syndrome'

(Frederickson 1992, p. 40) are indeed, as Breuer and Freud would have said, 'suffering from reminiscences'. Thus, Bass and Davis (1988, pp. 34–54) offered a list of 74 symptoms representing the long-term effects of child sexual abuse. By suggesting that their readers evaluate themselves in terms of this list, Bass and Davis imply that people who display these symptoms are likely to have been victims of child sexual abuse. In the third edition of their book, Bass and Davis (1994, p. 15) state that this material 'was never designed to be a checklist of symptoms by which readers could determine whether or not they'd been sexually abused' (see also their cautionary note on p. 38).

Because other authors have followed the lead of Bass and Davis (1988, 1994) without being quite so circumspect, it seems likely that this is precisely what has happened. Thus, Blume (1990, pp. xviii–xxi) printed a 34-item 'Incest Survivors' After Effects Checklist', along with the statement that it 'can serve as a diagnostic device for suggesting childhood sexual victimization when none is remembered. It also serves as a roadmap for a therapist treating someone whose amnesia or denial is total. Whether or not actual memories are recovered, the checklist then presents a structure for identifying and addressing the consequences of incest' (1990, p. xvi). Similarly, Frederickson (1992, pp. 47–51) has published a list of 63 'symptoms that many survivors with buried memories have experienced' (p. 47). The lists include such attributes as feeling different from other people, having trouble expressing one's feelings, difficulty in accepting one's own body, relationships that don't work out, using sex to meet needs that aren't sexual, difficulty in setting boundaries with one's children, and dissatisfaction with family relationships.

Despite the attention given to such checklists in the media and popular press (not to mention therapists' offices),[2] there are several reasons why it is not possible to infer, from patients' patterns of symptoms and complaints, that they were, or even are likely to have been, victims of incest, sexual abuse, or other trauma as children. In order to appreciate what is wrong with such inferences, it is important to examine them in detail. In the absence of independent, objective corroboration of the patient's history, retrospective diagnosis of incest, sexual abuse, or other childhood trauma from images, dreams, bodily feelings, and other symptoms seems to be based on the following sort of argument:

Child abuse causes symptom X.
This person has symptom X.
Therefore, this person was abused as a child.

For example, a clinician presented with a bulimic patient might infer that he or she was subject to abuse as a child. If the patient does not remember the abuse, then the further inference would be that he or she had repressed (or dissociated) these memories, rendering them inaccessible to conscious

2 The items of Blume's (1990) checklist were included in a professional guide to abuse-survivor therapy published by the American Psychological Association (Walker 1994), without any reference to evidence validating the association between these 'common symptoms' (p. 113) and abuse.

recollection. According to this logic, the bulimic symptoms represent what Freud called the return of the repressed, or what we would now call an implicit memory of the abuse. On the basis of this evidence, then, the patient might come to believe that he or she had in fact been abused, interpret other symptoms as evidence of the abuse as well, and eventually be led to reconstruct conscious recollections of the abuse itself.

For the purposes of analysing the syllogism above, let us assume that the premise is true: that some symptom, such as bulimia, occurs as a consequence of child abuse. Are we then permitted to infer child abuse as a likely historical fact when presented with a symptom such as bulimia? No. Logically, conditional reasoning of the sort characterized above involves a logical hypothesis, connecting an antecedent, p, with a consequent, q, as in the following statement:

$$\text{If } p, \text{ then } q.$$

Such a hypothesis permits two types of conditional argument, known as *modus ponens* and *modus tollens*:

Modus ponens: IF p is true THEN q is true; p is true;
               THEREFORE, q is also true.
Modus tollens: IF p is true THEN q is true; q is not true;
               THEREFORE, p cannot be true.

For purposes of exposition only, let us assume now that the premise that child abuse causes bulimia is true. Then, if we know that the person has been abused (p), modus ponens permits us to infer (or predict) that he or she is also bulimic (q), or at least is at risk for this disorder. And if we know that the person is not bulimic (*not q*), modus tollens permits us to infer (or postdict) that he or she was not abused (*not p*).

However, if a person is bulimic, we are not permitted to infer that he or she was abused. To make this inference would be to commit a common logical error known as *affirming the consequent*. The error is to infer that the antecedent is true from the fact that the consequent is true – in the case of our example, that the person has been abused (p) from the fact that he or she is bulimic (q). The consequent might be true for other reasons. The only exception to the prohibition on affirming the consequent is when the 'if' is biconditional – that is, when the symptom in question is pathognomonic of abuse. This is unlikely to be the case for the sorts of behavioural and psychosocial symptoms included on the lists proposed by Bass and Davis (1988), Blume (1990), and Frederickson (1992) – not least because the symptoms in question seem to exemplify what Meehl (1956) called the 'Barnum effect', in which personality predicates are so general that they are applicable to some extent to almost anyone.

Moreover, there are at present no reasons to think that premises of this sort are actually true in the first place. For example, the specific connection between abuse and eating disorder is highly dubious (Pope *et al.* 1994).

Somewhat surprisingly, given all the attention to the problem of abuse and its consequences, there appears to be very little good evidence that any psychological symptom, or indeed any particular cluster of symptoms, is associated with trauma *per se* (Beitchman *et al.* 1991, 1992). It may be true that many abused children grow up to be bulimic adults, but that is not enough to establish a connection between past and present. We also need to know how many abused children *do not* become eating disordered, how many eating disordered patients were *not* abused. The true association between child abuse and eating disorder can only be determined once we have filled in all the cells in the 2×2 table implied by the premise that abuse causes eating disorder (Dawes 1993).

And, of course, the table itself must be properly constructed: subjects must be classified on the basis of the antecedent variable (i.e. whether they were abused), and the table must take into account the population base rates for the antecedent. Failure to do this – for example, simply examining histories of abuse in eating-disordered patients versus controls – can severely distort the relations in question, compared to what we might learn by following representative samples of abused and non-abused children into adulthood. Suppose we discovered, for example, that 60 per cent of abused children, but only 20 per cent of non-abused children, suffer an eating disorder as adults. On the surface, this might look like evidence of an association between abuse and eating disorder, but then suppose that the incidence of abuse in the population is 10 per cent. Based on these assumptions, Table 5.1 shows how a representative sample of 1000 individuals would be cast into the cells of a 2×2 table relating abuse and eating disorder. Note that while most of the abused children would be found to have an eating disorder as adults, most of the eating-disordered adults *would not* have been abused as children. Even with a strong prospective relation between childhood abuse and adult eating disorder, retrospective inference of childhood abuse from adult eating disorder would be incorrect in 75 per cent (160 of 240) cases. This analysis underscores the dangers associated with the practice, endorsed by Kandel and Kandel (1994), of construing symptoms as evidence supporting uncorroborated memories.

Table 5.1 Hypothetical relation between childhood abuse and adult eating disorder

Child abuse	Eating disorder		Total
	Present	Absent	
Present	60	40	100
Absent	180	720	900
Total	240	760	1000

The table assumes that the incidence of child abuse is 10 per cent, and that 60 per cent of abused children, compared with 20 per cent of non-abused children, suffer eating disorder as adults.

It should also be noted that even if the correlation between abuse (or other trauma) and eating disorder (or other behavioural or psychosocial symptoms) were established on the basis of a proper prospective, the interpretation of this association would be unclear because we know so little about the processes mediating the relations. In order to demonstrate a causal link (or just a statistical association) with abuse and trauma *per se*, not to mention repressed or dissociated traumatic memories, we must be in a position to evaluate the separate and combined effects of a number of factors which are inevitably confounded with abuse and trauma – for example:

1. A history of child sexual abuse *per se*. This, of course, raises the difficult question of how abuse is to be defined. All abuse is wrong, of course, and all abuse is illegal, but to say this does not mean that qualitative and quantitative differences among cases should be ignored. It is not at all clear that a single instance of fondling should be treated as equivalent to acts of intercourse or sodomy engaged over an extended period.

2. The family environment. If the perpetrators of child sexual abuse frequently abuse alcohol or other drugs, or abuse commonly occurs in families that are 'dysfunctional' in other ways, then it is possible that an individual adult's symptoms are attributable to these factors, rather than to sexual abuse *per se*. Do the adult children of alcoholic child abusers have different outcomes from the adult children of alcoholics who did not sexually abuse their children?

3. Whether the abuse is remembered or forgotten. This is, of course, the central issue in arguments about 'the return of the repressed'. For Breuer and Freud (1893–5), and for modern proponents of the trauma-memory argument as well, it is *forgotten* abuse which is transformed into symptoms, and remembering the abuse is the first step to recovery. Abuse for which the person is amnesic should be more pathogenic than abuse which is remembered.

4. The mechanism by which the forgetting occurs. For Breuer and Freud (1893–5), trauma is forgotten because it is repressed; for Janet (1907), trauma is forgotten because it is dissociated. Some proponents of recovered memory therapy treat these terms as loosely synonymous, while others appear to favour dissociation over repression; but the two mechanisms are not identical – that is why Freud and Janet fought with each other so much! – and it is not clear that their effects will be identical. Of course, there are other mechanisms by which incidents of abuse may be lost to memory, and it is not at all clear that ordinary forgetting and normal infantile and childhood amnesia should have the same pathogenic effects as repression and dissociation.

5. Whether abuse is remembered, inferred, or simply believed in. It is not at all clear what is remembered in recovered memory therapy. It is one thing to remember an incident of abuse, or a string of incidents, which had been previously forgotten (especially when these events can be confirmed by independent evidence). It is quite another thing to interpret (i.e. redefine) certain

incidents, which were always remembered perfectly well, as examples of abuse. And it is something else entirely to come to believe that abuse occurred, in the absence of any memory for any specific incidents of abuse at all. Moreover, it should be understood that recovering a memory of an abuse incident is not itself evidence that repression or dissociation has occurred. Cued recall or recognition procedures commonly yield memories that are inaccessible under conditions of free recall; and even when the type of memory test is unchanged, memory naturally fluctuates from one retrieval attempt to another (Tulving 1964); and there are conditions under which memory can improve with repeated testing (for reviews see Erdelyi 1984; Kihlstrom and Barnhardt 1993; Payne 1987). But nobody would say that these phenomena of memory, observed in college students remembering lists of pictures and words, reflect the lifting of repression or dissociation.

6. Whether remembered abuse is disclosed or kept secret. Recovered memory therapy implies that previously inaccessible memories are brought into conscious awareness, not merely that someone has agreed to disclose something that he or she has always remembered. Disclosure of trauma may have positive effects (Pennebaker 1990), but this is not the same as the recovery of a repressed or dissociated traumatic memory.

7. Whether the individual is identified by others as a victim of child sexual abuse, and

8. Whether the individual identifies *him-* or *herself* as a victim. These issues are two sides of the same coin. Although it seems intuitively plausible, even likely, that incest and other forms of trauma, abuse, and neglect would have adverse consequences for adjustment, it is also important to consider the possibility that at least some of these consequences are products of the social perception of the victim, rather than of victimization *per se*. That is, once a victim of abuse has been identified, other people (including family members, teachers, social service workers, and the like), believing that early trauma inevitably has certain effects on personality, may treat that individual in such a way as to elicit symptoms of maladjustment where none would appear otherwise; or alternatively, such a process might be instigated by the victim's identification of *him-* or *herself* as a victim. We know too much about the self-fulfilling prophecy (Darley and Fazio 1980; Jones 1986; Merton 1948; Miller and Turnbull 1986) to reject out of hand the possibility that identifying someone as a victim of abuse might create symptoms even in the absence of any actual history of abuse.

INFERRING HISTORY FROM IMPLICIT MEMORIES

What Freud called *the return of the repressed* we now call *implicit memory*. Even though cognitive psychologists usually think of implicit memory in terms of priming effects, the symptoms attributed to childhood incest or sexual abuse do meet the formal criterion of implicit memories: changes in experience, thought, and action (in this case, complaints and symptoms) that are attributable to past events (in this case, episodes of incest or abuse). Of course, the notion of implicit memory enjoys considerably more support than the return of the repressed ever did (for concise summaries see Schacter (1987, 1995) and Schacter *et al.* (1993); for comprehensive surveys of the literature see Graf and Masson (1993) and Lewandowsky *et al.* (1989).

The classic illustrations of the dissociation between explicit and implicit memory are seen in brain-damaged patients with the amnesic syndrome (Schacter 1987, 1995). Other examples are surgical patients who have received general anaesthesia (Kihlstrom 1993) or conscious sedation (Polster 1994), and psychiatric patients who have been administered electroconvulsive therapy (Dorfman *et al.* 1995). The fact that implicit memory can be spared while explicit memory is profoundly impaired lends plausibility to the argument that images, feelings, bodily sensations, and behaviours can represent the unconscious influence of past traumatic experiences which have been repressed, dissociated, or otherwise forgotten. Put another way: it is not possible to argue against concepts like body memories, or feeling memories, simply on the ground that there is no evidence for unconscious memory. There is plenty of such evidence.

The case for implicit memory in the trauma-memory argument is strengthened by the fact that explicit and implicit memory can be dissociated even in the absence of any evidence of brain insult, injury, and disease. Consider, for example, the phenomenon of post-hypnotic amnesia (reviewed by Kihlstrom and Barnhardt 1993). After just a few words of suggestion on the part of the hypnotist, some subjects (those who are most highly hypnotizable) find themselves unable to remember the events and experiences that transpired while they were hypnotized. When the hypnotist administers a pre-arranged reversibility cue to cancel the amnesia suggestion, these memories come flooding back into awareness, and the once-amnesic subject is now able to remember what happened perfectly well. The fact that access to memories can be impaired and restored simply by means of suggestion shows that memories can be rendered unconscious, and later recovered to conscious awareness, by means of purely psychological processes.

Moreover, during the time that the amnesia suggestion is in effect, the events of hypnosis can influence the subject's ongoing experience, thought, and action, even though he or she cannot consciously remember these same experiences (for reviews see Kihlstrom 1995; Kihlstrom and Barnhardt 1993). For example, hypnotic subjects show priming effects on word-association and category-generation tasks, even though they cannot remember studying the targets while they were hypnotized (Kihlstrom 1980). Similarly, a problem-solving set established during hypnosis continues to influence the subjects' post-hypnotic problem-solving behaviour, even though they do not remember the trials by which that set was established (Huesman *et al.* 1987). In fact, post-hypnotic amnesia is the only example of an amnesia in which explicit memory can be abolished, at the same time sparing implicit memory, and then later restored. In the organic amnesias, the failure of explicit memory is permanent and irreversible.

Similarly, the clinical literature contains several cases of functional amnesia which appear to reveal dissociations between explicit and implicit memory – although it is not always clear that the patients eventually recovered memory for the instigating trauma (for complete reviews see Kihlstrom and Schacter, 1995; Kihlstrom *et al.* 1993; Schacter and Kihlstrom 1989) For example, M.R., a victim of homosexual rape, became distressed and suicidal after viewing a Thematic Apperception Test card which could be interpreted as one person attacking another from behind (Kaszniak *et al.* 1988). C.M., another rape victim, became upset when she visited the brick path on which she had been assaulted, and reported the intrusion of words such as 'bricks' and 'bricks and the path' into her stream of consciousness – even though she had no conscious recollection of being assaulted; furthermore, her memory returned when she later went jogging on a path whose physical features resembled the one on which she had been attacked (Christiansen and Nilsson 1989). Experimental studies of two cases of multiple personality disorder (also known as dissociative identity disorder) show that implicit memory can transfer across personalities, even when explicit memory does not (Ludwig *et al.* 1972; Nissen *et al.* 1988).

Although much more extensive experimental study will be necessary before we fully understand the vicissitudes of memory in these cases, the available research lends some support to some assertions, which are central to the trauma-memory argument and recovered memory therapy. In the first place, it is clear that dissociations between explicit and implicit memory can occur in functional as well as organic amnesias. Moreover, at least in post-hypnotic amnesia and genuine cases of multiple personality disorder, memories expressed only implicitly can be restored to explicit recollection. At the same time, the available research does not support other claims – such as that traumatic stress typically induces dissociative or repressive processes resulting in amnesia, or that children subjected to repeated trauma engage in defensive dissociation, or that exhumation of traumatic memories is important to therapeutic outcome.

Moreover, and this is a critical point, the research on explicit and implicit memory lends no support whatsoever to the notion that historical events can be *inferred* on the basis of mental and behavioural phenomena such as images and dreams, emotional feelings, bodily sensations, and intrusive behaviours. Such complaints and symptoms may be important elements of the patient's clinical presentation, and they may well have to be dealt with therapeutically, but in the absence of independent corroboration it is not legitimate to treat them as if they were implicit memories of the past. Nor, of course, is it legitimate to refer to these complaints and symptoms as evidence that the patient was in fact abused, in the absence of independent, objective evidence concerning the abuse itself.

In linking the clinical literature on the 'return of the repressed' to the research literature on implicit memory, it is important to remember that we know about explicit and implicit memory only because we already know the past, and it is this knowledge which allows us to make sense of what is happening in the present. Because we already know which items a laboratory subject has studied on a particular occasion, we are able to distinguish a genuine priming effect from a random fluctuation in test performance. Without such knowledge, we must remain agnostic. Where, as in many if not most clinical situations, the past is unknown or uncertain, the inference that a patient's images, feelings, or behaviours represent implicit memories of trauma is simply untenable. Given objective evidence of trauma for which the person is amnesic, the hypothesis that certain images, emotional feelings, somatic sensations, intrusive behaviours, and the like represent implicit memories of trauma is interesting and may well be true. In the absence of such corroboration, however, the same hypothesis is simply speculation. In the clinic as in the cognitive laboratory, the only way to test the hypothesis is to seek independent, objective corroboration.

Perhaps the most distressing aspect of the trauma-memory argument and recovered memory therapy is the apparent ease with which many of its proponents and practitioners reach the conclusion that incest and abuse occurred in the lives of their patients, in the absence of any objective corroboration of the inferred trauma. Once the practitioner has communicated this inference to the patient, or the patient arrives at it him- or herself on the basis of portrayals in the media and the popular press, the belief that one was abused can instigate additional images and feelings, which are also taken as implicit memories, providing further support for the belief that the patient was in fact abused, and instigating a process of reinterpreting the remembered past, and reconstructing new recollections around suppositions which, while perhaps making for a satisfactory narrative explanation, may not have been valid in the first place. The result can be that both patient and practitioner get enmeshed in a vicious cycle from which there can be no escape without shattering the most deeply held beliefs of both parties (this is, in part, the problem of false memory syndrome; see Kihlstrom (1994). Freud made this mistake 100 years ago (Bowers and Farvolden 1996; Crews 1995; Macmillan 1991), and there is every reason to think that it is being repeated today. The only way to prevent this mistake from recurring is to insist on independent corroboration of hypothetical implicit memories, and ostensible recovered explicit memories, of abuse.

IN CONCLUSION, A CAUTIONARY TALE

Jane Doe, a patient admitted to the hospital with psychogenic fugue, was unable to identify herself or give any helpful information about her identity. During routine interviews, Lyon (1985) performed some informal tests of her ability to recognize and use common objects. When Lyon asked Jane Doe to show him how to use a telephone, he noticed that she dialled the same number repeatedly. When he called the number himself, the person who answered quickly proved to be the patient's mother. Thus, Jane Doe's telephone-dialling behaviour was, in fact, an implicit expression of knowledge which she could not consciously recollect. Lyon's idea, that Jane Doe might be dialling a particular person whom she knew, was a brilliant clinical intuition, and resolved the case. But the intuition could only be confirmed by the truth on the ground – the objective fact of whether the person on the other end of the line knew Jane Doe. In the absence of such objective corroboration, Lyon was in no position to tell Jane that she was obviously trying to dial someone she knew – nor could he inform the person who answered that she did in fact know Jane Doe, but was in denial about it. The crucible of memory, whether explicit or implicit, is the truth of history.

ACKNOWLEDGEMENTS AND AUTHOR NOTES

The point of view represented here is based on research supported by Grant MH-35856 from the National Institute of Mental Health. I thank Robert Crowder, Marilyn Dabady, Elizabeth Phelps, and Katherine Shobe for their comments. I also thank Daniel McCracken for drawing my attention to the Maury Povich interview.

Address correspondence to John F. Kihlstrom, Department of Psychology, Yale University, PO Box 208205, New Haven, CT 06520–8205, USA. Internet: kihlstrm@minerva.cis.yale.edu.

REFERENCES

Bass, E. and Davis, L. (1988). *The courage to heal: a guide for women survivors of child sexual abuse*. Harper & Row, New York.

Bass, E. and Davis, L. (1994). *The courage to heal: a guide for women survivors of child sexual abuse*, 3rd edn. Harper & Row, New York.

Beitchman, J.H., Zucker, K.J., Hood, J.E., daCosta, G.A., and Akman, D. (1991). A review of the short-term effects of child sexual abuse. *Child Abuse & Neglect*, **15**, 537–56.

Beitchman, J.H., Zucker, K.J., Hood, J.E., daCosta, G.A., Akman, D., and Cassavia, E. (1992). A review of the long-term effects of child sexual abuse. *Child Abuse & Neglect*, **16**, 101–18.

Blume, E.S. (1990). *Secret survivors: Uncovering incest and its aftereffects on women*. Wiley, New York.

Bowers, K.S. and Farvolden, P. (1996). Revisiting a century-old Freudian slip – from suggestion disavowed to the Truth repressed. *Psychological Bulletin*, **19**, 355–80.

Breuer, J. and Freud, S. (1893–5). *Studies on hysteria*. In *The standard edition of the complete psychological works of Sigmund Freud*, Vol. 2, (ed. J. Strachey). Hogarth Press, London.

Christianson, S.-A. and Nilsson, L.-G. (1989). Hysterical amnesia: a case of aversively motivated isolation of memory. In *Aversion, avoidance, and anxiety*, (ed. T. Archer & L.-G. Nillson), pp. 289–310. Erlbaum, Hillsdale, NJ.

Crews, F. (1995). *The memory wars: Freud's legacy in dispute*. New York Review Imprints, New York.

Darley, J.M. and Fazio, R.H. (1980). Expectancy confirmation processes arising in the social interaction sequence. *American Psychologist*, **35**, 867–81.

Dawes, R.M. (1993). Prediction of the future versus an understanding of the past: a basic asymmetry. *American Journal of Psychology*, **106**, 1–24.

Dorfman, J., Kihlstrom, J.F., Cork, R.C., and Misiaszek, J. (1995). Priming and recognition in ECT-induced amnesia. *Psychonomic Bulletin & Review*, **2**, 244–8.

Erdelyi, M.H. (1984). The recovery of unconscious (inaccessible) memories: laboratory studies of hypermnesia. In *The psychology of learning and motivation*, Vol. 18, (ed. G.H. Bower), pp. 95–127). Academic, New York.

Frederickson, R. (1992). *Repressed memories: a journey to recovery from sexual abuse*. Simon & Schuster, New York.

Freud, S. (1892–1899). Draft K. The neuroses of defense (A Christmas fairy tale). In *The standard edition of the complete psychological works of Sigmund Freud*, Vol. 1, (ed. J. Strachey), pp. 220–8. Hogarth Press, London.

Freud, S. (1896). Further remarks on the neuro-psychoses of defence. In *The standard edition of the complete psychological works of Sigmund Freud*, Vol. 3, (ed. J. Strachey), pp. 159–85. Hogarth Press, London.

Freud, S. (1907). Delusions and dreams in Jensen's *Gradiva*. In *The standard edition of the complete psychological works of Sigmund Freud*, Vol. 9, (ed. J. Strachey), pp. 7–95. Hogarth Press, London.

Freud, S. (1909a). Psycho-analysis and the establishment of the facts in legal proceedings. In *The standard edition of the complete psychological works of Sigmund Freud*, Vol. 9, (ed. J. Strachey), pp. 103–14. Hogarth Press, London.

Freud, S. (1909b). Some general remarks on hysterical attacks. In *The standard edition of the complete psychological works of Sigmund Freud*, Vol. 9, (ed. J. Strachey), pp. 229–34. Hogarth Press, London.

Freud, S. (1909c). On the universal tendency to debasement in the sphere of love (Contributions to the psychology of love II). In *The standard edition of the complete psychological works of Sigmund Freud*, Vol. 11, (ed. J. Strachey), pp. 179–90. Hogarth Press, London.

Freud, S. (1911a). Psycho-analytic notes on an autobiographical account of a case of paranoia (dementia paranoides). In *The standard edition of the complete psychological works of Sigmund Freud*, Vol. 12, (ed. J. Strachey), pp. 9–82. Hogarth Press, London.

Freud, S. (1911b). The disposition to obsessional neurosis: A contribution to the problem of choice in neurosis. In *The standard edition of the complete psychological works of Sigmund Freud*, Vol. 12, (ed. J. Strachey), pp. 317–26. Hogarth Press, London.

Freud, S. (1914). On the history of the psycho-analytic movement. In *The standard edition of the complete psychological works of Sigmund Freud*, Vol. 14, (ed. J. Strachey), pp. 7–66. Hogarth Press, London.

Freud, S. (1915). Repression. In *The standard edition of the complete psychological works of Sigmund Freud*, Vol. 14, (ed. J. Strachey), pp. 146–58. Hogarth Press, London.

Freud, S. (1924). The loss of reality in neurosis and psychosis. In *The standard edition of the complete psychological works of Sigmund Freud*, Vol. 19, (ed. J. Strachey), pp. 183–7. Hogarth Press, London.

Freud, S. (1939). *Moses and monotheism*. In *The standard edition of the complete psychological works of Sigmund Freud*, Vol. 23, (ed. J. Strachey), pp. 7–137. Hogarth Press, London.

Graf, P. and Masson, M.E.J. (1993). *Implicit memory: new directions in cognition, development, and neuropsychology*. Erlbaum, Hillsdale, NJ.

Herman, J.L. (1992). *Trauma and recovery*. Basic Books, New York.

Huesman, L.R. Gruder, C.L., and Dorst, G. (1987). A process model of posthypnotic amnesia. *Cognitive Psychology*, **19**, 33–62.

Janet, P. (1907). *The major symptoms of hysteria*. Macmillan, New York.

Jones, E.E. (1986). Interpreting interpersonal behavior: the effects of expectancies. *Science*, **234**, 41–6.

Kandel, M. and Kandel, E. (1994). Flights of memory. *Discover*, (May), 32–8.

Kaszniak, A.W., Nussbaum, P.D., Berren, M.R., and Santiago, J. (1988). Amnesia as a consequence of male rape: a case report. *Journal of Abnormal Psychology*, **97**, 100–4.

Kihlstrom, J.F. (1980). Posthypnotic amnesia for recently learned material: Interactions with 'episodic' and 'semantic' memory. *Cognitive Psychology*, **12**, 227–51.

Kihlstrom, J.F. (1993). Implicit memory function during anesthesia. In *Memory and Awareness in Anesthesia* (ed. P.S. Sebel, B. Bonke, and E. Winograd), pp. 10–30. Prentice-Hall, New York.

Kihlstrom, J.F. (1994). Exhumed memory. In *Truth in memory*, (ed. S.J. Lynn and N.P. Spanos). Guilford, New York.

Kihlstrom, J.F. (1995). The trauma-memory argument and recovered memory therapy. In *The recovered memory/false memory debate*, (ed. K. Pezdek and W.P. Banks), pp. 297–311. Academic, San Diego, CA.

Kihlstrom, J.F. and Barnhardt, T.M. (1993). The self-regulation of memory, for better and for worse, with and without hypnosis. In *Handbook of mental control*, (ed. D.M. Wegner and J.W. Pennebaker), pp. 88–125. Prentice-Hall, Englewood Cliffs, NJ.

Kihlstrom, J.F. and Schacter, D.L. (1995). Functional disorders of autobiographical memory. In *Handbook of memory disorders*, (ed. A. Baddeley, F. Watts, and B. Wilson), pp. 337–64. Wiley, London.

Kihlstrom, J.F., Tataryn, D.J., and Hoyt, I.P. (1993). Dissociative disorders. In *Comprehensive handbook of psychopathology*, 2nd edn, (ed. P.J. Sutker & H.E. Adams), pp. 203–34. Plenum, New York.

Lewandowsky, S., Dunn, J. and Kirsner, K. (1989). *Implicit memory: theoretical issues*. Erlbaum, Hillsdale, NJ.

Ludwig, A.M., Brandsma, J.M., Wilbur, C.B., Bendfeldt, F., and Jameson, D.H. (1972). The objective study of multiple personality: or, are four heads better than one? *Archives of General Psychiatry*, **26**, 298–310.

Lyon, L.S. (1985). Facilitating telephone number recall in a case of psychogenic amnesia. *Journal of Behavior Therapy & Experimental Psychiatry*, **16**, 147–9.

Macmillan, M.B. (1991). *Freud evaluated: the completed arc*, Advances in Psychology no 75. North-Holland, Amsterdam.

Meehl, P. (1956). Wanted – a good cookbook. *American Psychologist*, **11**, 263–72.

Merton, R.K. (1948). The self-fulling prophecy. *Antioch Review*, **8**, 193–210.

Miller, D.T. and Turnbull W. (1986). Expectancies and interpersonal processes. *Annual Review of Psychology*, **37**, 233–56.

Nissen, M.J., Ross, J.L., Willingham, D.B., Mackenzie, T.B., Schacter, D.L. (1988). Memory and awareness in a patient with multiple personality disorder. *Brain & Cognition*, **8**, 117–34.

Payne, D.G. (1987). Hypermnesia and reminiscence in recall: a historical and empirical review. *Psychological Bulletin*, **101**, 5–27.

Pennebaker, J.W. (1990). *Opening up: the healing power of confiding in others*. Morrow, New York.

Polster, M.R. (1994). Drug-induced amnesia: implications for cognitive neuropsychological investigations of memory. *Psychological Bulletin*, **114**, 477–93.

Pope, H.G., Mangweth, B., Negrao, A.B., Hudson, J.I., and Cordas, T.A. (1994). Childhood abuse and bulimia nervosa: a comparison of American, Austrian, and Brazilian women. *American Journal of Psychiatry*, **151**, 732–7.

Schacter, D.L. (1987). Implicit memory: history and current status. *Journal of Experimental Psychology: Learning, Memory, and Cognition*, **13**, 501–18.

Schacter, D.L. (1995). Implicit memory: a new frontier for cognitive neuroscience. In *The cognitive neurosciences*, (ed. M.S. Gazzaniga), pp. 815–24. MIT Press, Cambridge, MA.

Schacter, D.L., Chiu, C.-Y.P., and Ochsner, K.N. (1993). Implicit memory: a selective review. *Annual Review of Neuroscience*, **16**, 159–82.

Schacter, D.L. and Kihlstrom, J.F. (1989). Functional amnesia. In *Handbook of neuropsychology*, Vol. 3, (ed. F. Boller and J. Graffman), pp. 209–31.

Squire, L.R., Knowlton, B.J., and Musen G. (1993). The structure and organization of memory. *Annual Review of Psychology*, **44**, 453–95.

Terr, L. (1991). Childhood traumas: an outline and overview. *American Journal of Psychiatry*, **148**, 10–20.

Terr, L. (1994). *Unchained memories: true stories of traumatic memories, lost and found*. Basic Books, New York.

Tulving, E. (1964). Intratrial and intertrial retention: notes toward a theory of free recall verbal learning. *Psychological Review*, **71**, 219–37.

van der Kolk, B.A. (1994). The body keeps the score: memory and the evolving psychobiology of posttraumatic stress. *Harvard Review of Psychiatry*, **1**, 253–65.

van der Kolk, B.A. and van der Hart. (1991). The intrusive past: the flexibility of memory and the engraving of trauma. *American Imago*, **48**, 425–54.

Walker, L.E.A. (1994). *Abused women and survivor therapy: a practical guide for the psychotherapist*. American Psychological Association, Washington, DC.

SIX

Recovery of true and false memories: paradoxical effects of repeated testing

HENRY L. ROEDIGER, III,
KATHLEEN B. MCDERMOTT, AND LYN M. GOFF

The issue of recovered memories is central to this volume. The current meaning of the term *recovered memory* resides within the context of therapeutic practice. In a typical case, an adult, while in therapy, recovers a distant memory of a childhood event; at issue is whether the memory represents an event that actually occurred in the individual's past or instead is a construction that seems plausible to the individual but never actually happened. (Of course, the recovered memory could be partly true and partly false, too, especially if a complex event has been recovered.) Experimental psychologists have applied knowledge derived from laboratory and field research to the issue of recovered memories in therapy (for example Ceci and Bruck 1995; Lindsay and Read 1994; Loftus 1993). We continue this tradition in the present chapter; in addition, we examine some evidence that has not yet been introduced to explore memory recovery.

The reports of memories recovered under therapy often reveal a piecemeal process. Rarely does an individual recover all memories suddenly. Rather, the process is typically spread out over time, with numerous attempts to retrieve certain events. Often people recover additional details over repeated attempts, and their confidence in the accuracy of the memories similarly increases over time. We explore these aspects of recovered memories in this chapter, and we introduce laboratory research that is relevant to the issue of recovered memories over repeated retrieval attempts.

THE PLAN OF THE CHAPTER

The purpose of this chapter is to explore what psychologists have learned about repeated testing of memory in laboratory paradigms and to consider applications of this knowledge to thorny issues arising from cases of recovered memories in therapy. The study of recovered memories (in the laboratory) dates almost from the turn of the century, and yet the huge body of evidence from several lines of experimental investigation has played almost no part in attempts to understand recovered memories in the current controversies. In almost all cases of recovered memories in therapy, it is impossible to discern which memories are true and which are false; the events that might verify or disprove the validity of the disputed memories have long been lost in the dim mists of time. Although events presented in the laboratory may suffer the drawback of differing from 'real life' events on a number of dimensions, they have the definite advantage of being under experimental control. This advantage is absolutely critical because without relatively precise knowledge of the events that actually occurred, claims about the accuracy or inaccuracy of later memories are nothing but that – claims. If the researcher does not know what originally happened, then it is impossible to tell if a recovered memory is true or false. Overlooking (or ignoring) this simple fact accounts in part for the great confusion and debate surrounding the study of recovered memories arising outside the laboratory (Roediger 1996; Schacter 1995).

In this chapter, we cover four related topics. First we consider evidence from experimental investigations that shows that memories can be recovered over time in laboratory situations. In particular, we consider the phenomena of reminiscence, hypermnesia, and spontaneous recovery. In the case of each phenomenon (explained below), we see evidence that retrieval of a collection of events is spread out in time. Of course, recovery of memories is never complete in repeated testing experiments, but such experiments do show that recovery of previously inaccessible memories often occurs. In fact, some amount of 'memory recovery' occurs in virtually all experiments examining the topic, although the gains are usually rather modest. We consider the relevance of this experimental work for the current 'recovered memory controversy' and find that few strong generalizations can be made about recovery from years in the past.

Second, we consider the effects of retrieving information from memory on later retrieval. Retrieval attempts (or tests) are not neutral events, leaving retention of the retrieved event unaffected. Rather, retrieval of an event alters the course of its future retention. For events that actually occurred and are retrieved, the process of recall makes the event more likely to be recalled at a later point in time. However, for events that are erroneously retrieved (that is, for false memories) the act of retrieval also consolidates the memory and confers easier (and more confident) access later. Therefore, repeated retrieval (or repeated testing) will be shown to have paradoxical effects, enhancing accurate retention while sometimes leading to increased recall of wrong information (that is, to the development of false memories).

In a third section of the chapter, we consider the effect of response criterion on remembering. In particular, what effects do instructions to guess (or to free associate) have on remembering? To preview our findings, research shows that instructions to guess usually cause people to produce little additional accurate information but can cause considerable confusion. Rememberers who guess may suffer problems in monitoring which of their responses refer to events that actually occurred and which were simply guesses they generated.

In the fourth and final section of the chapter, we ask why people may come to accept and to believe memories recovered from early in their lives. If one slowly recovers a memory of an horrific event of which one was previously unaware, why believe it? The answer to this question is doubtless complex, but we suggest that one piece to the puzzle is that most people (including psychologists who study memory) have adopted misleading ways of thinking about the issue by accepting erroneous metaphors of how memory works (Roediger 1980).

The thrust of the chapter is that although repeated retrieval of events can lead to recovery of accurate memories, the processes involved also constitute powerful forces for the development of false memories. We deal with this paradox – the benefits and drawbacks of repeated retrieval – throughout the chapter. We omit one important set of topics as outside the bounds of this chapter, although it is relevant to the recovered memory debate: effects of external retrieval cues. In the present chapter we consider only cases in which people attempt to retrieve memories on two or more occasions under the same conditions, typically free recall. There is a separate (and generally relevant) literature on the effects of external retrieval cues in probing latent memories; often retrieval cues have the power to invoke memories for events that could not be recalled under other circumstances. Roediger and Guynn (1996) provide a partial review of the literature on the effect of retrieval cues, but its application to the claims surrounding the recovered memory debate must await a different occasion.

RECOVERED MEMORIES IN LABORATORY SETTINGS

Ballard (1913) reported one of the first major experimental studies of recovered memories. He gave schoolchildren passages of poetry to learn and tested their memories both soon after learning and then again at various periods up to a week later. His major finding was that children frequently reported lines of poetry on later tests that had not been recalled on the earlier test. He called the phenomenon reminiscence and defined it as 'the remembering again of the forgotten without relearning' (Ballard 1913, p. v). Reminiscence is then defined in the way that today is (loosely) used for recovered memories: an event that cannot be recalled for a period of time (even with effort) is recovered on a later retrieval attempt.

When people are given repeated memory tests, they not only recover items on later tests that had not been recalled earlier, but they also forget items between tests. That is, events recalled on a first test may be forgotten on the second test. In some of Ballard's (1913) original experiments, the reminiscence or recovery between tests outweighed the intertest forgetting, and he sometimes used the net difference in recall levels between tests as an index of reminiscence. That is, overall recall on a second test was actually greater than that on the first test and this amount of gain between tests was used as an index of item recovery.

This practice led to some confusion in the definition of reminiscence, with some later researchers failing to replicate the overall gain in recall between tests and therefore concluding that they had failed to obtain reminiscence.

Buxton (1943) reviewed the literature and concluded that reminiscence was not a reliable phenomenon. However, if Ballard's original definition of reminiscence (as quoted above) is maintained, this conclusion is not warranted. Interestingly, the source of the confusion lies in Ballard's different practices of reporting the effect. That is, Ballard sometimes reported the number of items recalled on a second test that could not be recalled on a first test (this measure accurately indexes reminiscence as defined above), but at other times he reported the gain in total items recalled between tests (which underestimates true reminiscence because forgetting between tests is included). If recall is greater on a second test than on a first test, reminiscence must have occurred. However, even if overall recall is the same on two successive tests (or even if it is worse on the second test), reminiscence might still have occurred but been offset or masked by forgetting between tests. Indeed, when reminiscence is considered as recall of events on a second (or later) test that could not be recalled on an earlier test, it is found in virtually all experiments. In this limited sense, the existence of recovered memories is indisputable: we can often recover information on a later occasion that we could not recall on a first occasion.

These considerations may be a bit abstract, so let us consider data from another classic experiment of this genre to flesh out the details. Brown (1923) asked the question (which formed the title of his paper), 'To what extent is memory measured by a single recall?' In his first experiment, he asked US college students to recall as many as possible of the (then) 48 states during a five-minute test. About half an hour later, without any warning, he gave the same test again, requiring subjects to recall the 48 states for five minutes. The second experiment was similar, except in this case he presented students a list of 48 words (four times) and then asked them to recall as many words as possible during two five-minute tests that were again separated by half an hour. Brown's interest was in how performance would change between tests.

Brown's results are given in Table 6.1. The first two rows show the total number of items correctly recalled on the first (T_1) and second (T_2) tests, respectively, with the difference $(T_2 - T_1)$ in the third row. The fact that performance on the second test was better than that on the first is the pattern that sparked the interest of Ballard and others. After all, in the case of the word list (or episodic memory) the second test occurred at a longer delay from the original experiences, so forgetting between tests might be expected. However, the data actually show improvement both in retrieval of the list (episodic memory) and in the states (semantic memory). (Although Brown (1923) and Ballard (1913) reported no inferential statistics, data like those in Table 6.1 have been reported many times more recently, and their reliability is not in doubt.) The net improvement between tests is now called hypermnesia

(Erdelyi and Becker 1974), and this phenomenon will be discussed further below.

Table 6.1 Results from Brown's (1923) experiments

	States	Word list	
Test 1 (T_1)	36.31	25.48	
Test 2 (T_2)	39.66	26.77	
Difference (T_2–T_1)	3.35	1.29	Hypermnesia
Intertest forgetting	1.94	3.04	
Intertest recovery	5.29	4.33	Reminiscence

Brown (1923) also broke down his data into the components of intertest recovery (or reminiscence) and intertest forgetting. Forgetting occurred between tests for both states and words, but the forgetting was offset and overcome by item recovery. Obviously, whenever there is overall improvement between tests, the intertest recovery must outweigh the intertest forgetting, as occurred (at least numerically) in Brown's (1923) experiment for both types of material. As noted above, intertest recovery is observed in virtually all experiments in which people are given more than one free recall test. However, net improvement between tests is only observed some of the time, and depends on the magnitude of intertest forgetting. One point to be drawn from Brown's experiment and many more like it is that what is called 'a memory test' and what performance is achieved on such a test is not immutable; give another test (even of the same kind) and the estimate of what can be remembered will differ, sometimes in important ways. We shall see this lesson illustrated repeatedly in the remainder of the chapter.

The study of reminiscence and hypermnesia languished for a time but returned to the fore in the late 1960s and early 1970s when free recall returned as a favoured method of study, and researchers became interested in retrieval processes *per se*. Tulving (1967) reported impressive levels of both intertest recovery and intertest forgetting in free recall experiments (establishing reminiscence again as an object of study). He argued that his results showed people have a 'limited capacity retrieval system' because although the overall recall levels were fairly stable in his experiments, the particular items recalled were quite different between tests. Recall of some events seemed to preclude recall of others, as was later documented (for example Roediger 1978).

With somewhat different procedures, Erdelyi and Becker (1974) reported that total recall of pictures (but not words) increased over three successive tests, each lasting seven minutes (thereby establishing hypermnesia). Reminiscence occurred for both pictures and words, although it was greater for pictures. In a later experiment, Erdelyi *et al.* (1976) had different groups of subjects study

(a) pictures, (b) words – the names of the pictures – or (c) words as in the previous condition, but with instructions for subjects to form mental images of the words' referents. Subjects were given three successive tests. These tests were forced recall tests; subjects were given sheets with 60 boxes and told to write one item in each box (i.e. to fill all 60), guessing when necessary. (The rationale for forced recall is to hold the response criterion constant; subjects provide a fixed number of responses on each recall of the material so changes across tests cannot be due to simple guessing effects.) The results are shown in Fig. 6.1, which indicates total correct recall over the three tests. Hypermnesia occurred for pictures and for the words recoded as images, but not for words presented without imagery instructions. (More recently, others have found significant hypermnesia for words, although it is usually a small effect.) For present purposes, the important point is that hypermnesia – improvement in overall recall over repeated free or forced recall tests – is now a well-established (if not well-understood) phenomenon.

Both the topics of reminiscence and hypermnesia have enjoyed continued study to this date. An exhaustive review of this literature is outside the bounds of this chapter, but reviews from different perspectives can be found in Erdelyi (1984), Payne (1987), and Roediger and Challis (1989). Here we describe several prominent studies that illustrate points that may illuminate some of the current discussion about recovered memories.

Studies of reminiscence and hypermnesia show that retrieval of a complex collection of events (such as a set of pictures or words) does not occur all at once but is extended over time. Roediger and Thorpe (1978) presented two groups of subjects with 60 pictures that could be easily named. One group was given three seven-minute free recall tests on the pictures, with the recall indicated by subjects writing down the names of the pictures. After the first seven-minute test, sheets were collected, subjects were given a new blank page,

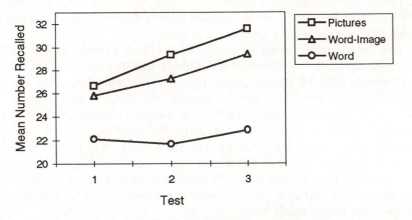

Fig. 6.1 Mean number of items recalled as a function of presentation mode and test number. Data are taken from Erdelyi *et al.* (1976).

and the process was repeated, with the subjects starting again. The third test was given the same way, except subjects were told that it was their last test. A second group of subjects who had studied the pictures got a single long test lasting 21 minutes. The interest was in comparing recall of the two groups over the entire 21-minute test period. Would the subjects who received the three seven-minute tests (using the procedure Erdelyi and Becker had introduced) recall more than the subjects given the single long test of equivalent duration? The experiment included two other groups of subjects who were tested in the same two ways (three seven-minute tests or one 21-minute test) after seeing a list of 60 words (the names of the pictures). Therefore, a total of four groups were tested, using two different types of materials (pictures or words) and two different methods of testing (three seven-minute tests or one 21-minute test).

Figure 6.2 shows the cumulative recall results for the four conditions. Cumulative recall is simply the plot of the number of items correctly recalled over time, a cumulative record of remembering. Subjects who were given three tests were scored as recalling an item when it was first produced and repetitions in recall (on the later tests) were ignored in this measure. Three facts are apparent from Fig. 6.2. First, pictures are better recalled than words, at least after the second or third minute of recall. Second, in terms of cumulative recall of the entire set, subjects receiving three seven-minute tests performed about the same as those receiving the single 21-minute test. The slight differences apparent in the figure were small, and not statistically reliable; later research comparing several shorter tests with a longer test of equivalent total duration has also upheld this lack of difference between these test conditions (for example Payne 1986). The third point, and the most interesting one for present purposes, is how recall of the set of items is extended over time. Even a relatively long recall period – such as seven-minutes for 60 items – is insufficient for permitting subjects to reveal their knowledge. Considerably more information was recalled during the last 14 minutes, although the relation among the conditions remained stable. Recovery of memories is spread out in time.

This incremental nature of retrieval over long periods can be seen even more dramatically in other results. Erdelyi and Kleinbard (1978) presented six subjects with 60 stimuli, either pictures of simple figures or words that named the pictures. Three subjects received the pictures and three the words. After seeing the stimuli once at a 5 s rate, subjects were given three successive free recall tests, as described earlier. After the third test subjects were given a set of envelopes, and three times a day, for a week, they tested themselves by forced recall for the set of pictures or words they had originally seen. (Keep in mind that the pictures or words were seen only once, at the beginning of the experiment.) After a week, subjects came back to the lab and took a final set of three forced recall tests.

Erdelyi and Kleinbard's basic results are shown in the two panels of Fig. 6.3. On the top is cumulative recall across all the tests, so the improvements represent reminiscence or recovered memories – recall of items on later tests that could not be recalled on earlier tests. It is clear that pictures were generally better recalled than words and that great amounts of recovery occurred beyond the first test – about 21 items for the subjects recalling pictures and 14 for those recalling words. The number of items correctly recalled on each test is shown in the bottom panel. This measure reflects both recovery and forgetting between tests and shows greater hypermnesia for pictures and little or none in recall of words over the week. These results complement those above by showing that recall can increase incrementally over longer periods of time than in usual laboratory settings.

This extended nature of retrieval is also manifested in semantic memory tasks, those that tap relatively permanent knowledge (Tulving 1972). Bousfield and Sedgewick (1944) reported continuously increasing recall over 18 minutes when students were asked to recall the names of college students they knew, and when they recalled US cities, pleasant objects, and other similar categories. Roediger *et al.* (1982) reported increasing recall over 30 minutes when subjects were asked to produce all the types of sports, birds, and US presidents they could recall. The results are shown in Fig. 6.4, where it can be seen that the gains over time correlate positively with the overall category size. Gains after the first few minutes in recall of a finite category such as presidents, where students could recall only about half of all members, were relatively slight

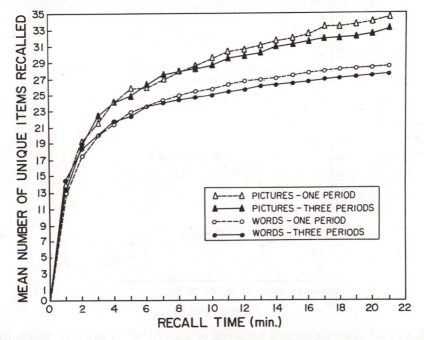

Fig. 6.2 Cumulative recall in Roediger and Thorpe's (1978) experiment as a function of study and test condition.

(but statistically significant). Cumulative recall curves such as those in Figs. 6.1–6.4 are fitted reasonably well by exponential functions, and researchers have proposed various models of underlying processes (for example Indow and Togano 1970; Wixted and Rohrer 1994). For present purposes, we use these cumulative records only to illustrate how recall of even a relatively circumscribed set of events (a picture or word list, or a semantic category) extends over time. Items can be accurately recovered even after relatively long times since retrieval was initiated.

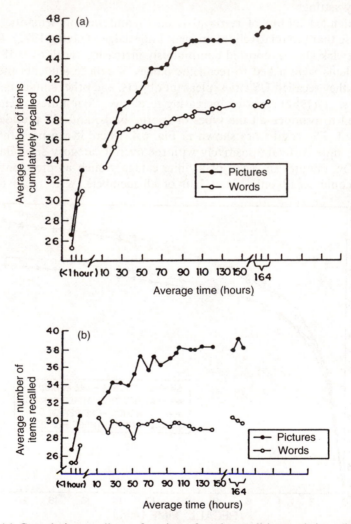

Fig. 6.3 (a) Cumulative recall as a function of study condition and time. (b) The mean number of items recalled on individual tests as a function of study condition and time. Figures taken from Erdelyi and Kleinbard (1978).

The laboratory evidence reviewed in this section suggests support for a limited notion of 'recovered memories', but the limits are great indeed. The studies reviewed here have the following properties, all which distinguish the laboratory cases from those of allegedly recovered memories in therapeutic situations. One critical variable is the retention interval. The retention interval in these laboratory experiments is relatively short (usually measured in minutes or, at most, days), whereas in recovered memory cases in therapy the retention interval is usually very long (measured in years or decades). Could memories for specific events be accurately recovered over repeated tests if the first attempt was not made until decades later? We know of only one relevant study, conducted by Williams and Hollan (1981). They asked four subjects to retrieve the names of people who had been in their senior class in high school some years previously. The people were tested repeatedly over several sessions and were told to think out loud while they were recalling. (Williams and Hollan obtained the subjects' high school yearbooks, so that they could determine the subjects' accuracy in

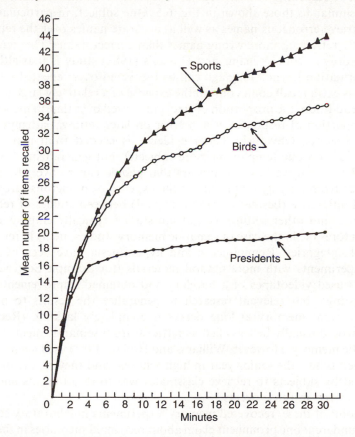

Fig. 6.4 Cumulative recall curves as a function of item type and time. From Roediger *et al.* (1982).

retrieving.) Two subjects (numbers 1 and 3 in their report) were tested for one hour a day on weekdays on two successive weeks. Therefore, each subject recalled for ten hours over ten separate sessions. Their results are shown in the two panels in Fig. 6.5, with both correct recall and errors plotted cumulatively over sessions. As we have seen in previous figures displaying recall of recently learned lists, correct recall of classmates increased steadily over sessions. However, unlike in the recall of lists, the number of names recalled in error also increased systematically over sessions. The errors in this case were usually names of people that the subject knew, but who had not been in the subject's senior class in high school. These errors presumably represent proactive and retroactive interference exerted by learning of people before and after those in the senior year in high school. Stated differently, the recall of these names represents source monitoring errors (Johnson *et al.* 1993).

Two other subjects in Williams and Hollan's (1981) study were tested repeatedly, but according to a less regular schedule. None the less, their results were quite similar to those shown in Fig. 6.5. One subject, in particular, was prone to retrieve erroneous names as well as accurate names over the repeated tests, actually retrieving more wrong names than correct names! One tentative point to be drawn from Williams and Hollan's (1981) study is that although correct information learned long ago can be recovered over repeated retrieval attempts, this extra recall comes only at the expense of a relatively large number of errors. In addition, the proportion of errors increased over time in their study, a larger proportion of responses was in error on later retrieval attempts than on earlier attempts. Obviously, better evidence is needed from many more studies such as this one (employing more subjects), but generalizing from the limited evidence that we have, it appears that people can recover the names of classmates from long ago, but only at the expense of numerous errors.

A second difference (besides retention interval) between studies of retrieval in lab settings and other settings is that lab studies typically employ sets of words or pictures or, in the case of semantic memory studies, items in relatively well-learned categories. Reminiscence and hypermnesia have been observed in a few experiments with more natural materials (for example Scrivner and Safer (1988) used videotapes of a burglary and obtained improvements with repeated testing), but relevant research to generalize the results to natural materials of event memory at long delays is completely lacking. (Recall of classmates would usually be classified as retrieval from semantic memory than from episodic memory. However, Williams and Hollan (1981) used a temporally circumscribed time – the senior year in high school – and they report that one strategy used by subjects to retrieve classmates was to recall events and then who was involved in those events.)

A third point of these 'recovered memory' experiments in laboratory settings is that they undercut one prominent claim about recovered memories in therapy, namely that recovered memories represent the 'return of the repressed', or that recovered memories are a hallmark of threatening material that has been

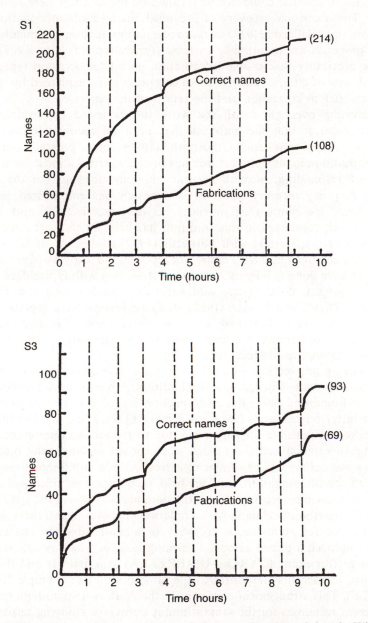

Fig. 6.5 Cumulative number of names recalled as a function of time in Williams and Hollan's (1981) study.

banished to an unconscious state. In the experiments described above, and in many more, material that was inaccessible on one test was recovered on a later test, but no one has proposed that the pictures, words, names of sports, and names of classmates that could not be recalled on the first test were somehow repressed. The occasional recovery of previously inaccessible information has been known, since Ballard's (1913) work, to be a natural feature of remembering. Retrieval processes are notoriously variable (for example Tulving 1967), and recovering previously inaccessible information on a later occasion represents the normal state of affairs, rather than an exception to be explained by special mechanisms such as repression and the return of the repressed.

An interesting oversight in all the work just reviewed on reminiscence and hypermnesia is that the emphasis has been on recovery of accurate information. As Koriat and Goldsmith (1996) have pointed out, the laboratory tradition in memory research has been concerned almost exclusively with correct responding, or with accuracy in remembering. On the other hand, the everyday memory tradition of research has emphasized general correspondence (or non-correspondence) between recollections and actual events. Research conducted in this tradition has been much more concerned with memory errors, starting with Bartlett's (1932) studies. Most laboratory experiments using free recall have either not reported the recovery of erroneous memories or have done so only as an aside, to show that with typical free recall instructions, subjects do not guess wildly (for example Roediger and Thorpe 1978). The Williams and Hollan (1981) study reviewed above represents an exception to this claim, but there are few others. Indeed, in hypermnesia research with forced recall, it is impossible to measure false recall, because subjects are required to produce guesses.

Before leaving this section, we need to mention one other type of memory recovery that is studied in laboratory conditions: spontaneous recovery. In the study of human memory, this phenomenon played a large role in classic two-factor interference theory (see Crowder (1976) for a review). Briefly, one factor believed responsible for forgetting due to retroactive interference was 'unlearning' of original material as one was exposed to interfering material. Unlearning was believed to be similar to extinction of a conditioned response in Pavlovian conditioning; if the analogy held, then responses unlearned might also show spontaneous recovery after extinction, just as Pavlov (1927, pp.48–9) had shown. Therefore, beginning with Underwood (1948), researchers sought to find evidence for spontaneous recovery in human subjects. The typical paradigm employed a paired associate learning task, in which people learned pairs of items (for example XRG – UMBRELLA) in a first list and then, in a second list, learned new responses to the same stimuli (for example XRG – MANATEE). This arrangement conforms to the A–B, A–D paradigm (people learn different responses for the same stimulus terms) for studying retroactive interference. After learning the second list, subjects are given the stimulus term (XRG, or the A term) and asked to recall (depending on the instructions) only the first list response, either the first or second list response (whichever first comes to mind), or both the first and second list responses. Retroactive interference occurs with all three instructions; that is, recall of B responses when cued by A is worse after A–D learning than in a control condition in which there is no new learning. In addition, such interference is greatest just after learning the A–D list. However, at issue here is spontaneous recovery: are B responses recovered over time so that they will be recalled better after a long interval than after a short interval?

The data on this question are mixed, with some researchers obtaining the effect and others not. However, Brown (1976) reviewed the literature and concluded that spontaneous recovery was a real phenomenon, if somewhat fragile. More recently, Wheeler (1995) reached the same conclusion and buttressed it with evidence from several new experiments. His subjects, better remembered B responses at retention intervals from 16 to 36 minutes after A–D learning than only one minute afterwards. Therefore, the phenomenon of spontaneous recovery seems established, although it is admittedly not an overpowering effect. In addition, the laboratory paradigms used thus far differ dramatically from cases of recovered memories in therapy; to our knowledge, no one has shown analogous phenomena (i.e. recovery of memories that have suffered interference) after very long delays. None the less, a possible avenue for promising new research might be to conduct spontaneous recovery experiments with long delays between A–D learning and subsequent testing. Our prediction is that no recovery will be discovered (relative to performance at short delays) because the effect will be swamped by forgetting caused by events during the long delay. If so, then the phenomenon would still be of interest to researchers, but would provide little support for any notion of recovered memories at long delays.

In summary, evidence from laboratory experiments shows the recovery of memories over time and over repeated tests under the same (nominally identical) testing conditions. People frequently recall information on a later test that they could not recall on an earlier test (reminiscence, or intertest recovery). Sometimes this recovery outweighs intertest forgetting, resulting in better recall on a later test than on an earlier test (hypermnesia). In addition, some experiments have shown spontaneous recovery over short intervals for material that has been subjected to retroactive interference. So the recovery of (previously unrecallable) memories in the lab is well established. However, whether such recoveries are germane to the issue of recovered memories in therapy remains to be demonstrated. In order to extend the conclusions, the research must be extended along a number of dimensions. Probably the most important (but certainly not the only) feature that differs between recovered memory experiments and memories recovered in therapy is the retention interval. To our knowledge, only one study has examined recovery of memory for known events over extended retrieval attempts years after the information had been acquired (Williams and Hollan 1981). Although they did report significant recovery over repeated retrieval attempts, they also documented large numbers of erroneous memories (presumably arising from interference of names learned in other contexts). These erroneous memories represented as many as half of all the recollections in the later retrieval attempts. Further experiments like this one need to be conducted to explore the possibility of recovering memories at long delays and assessing their accuracy. We also need to know if subjects can tell the difference between accurate and erroneous memories. We might suspect that the answer will often be no; otherwise subjects would not make the errors at all. However, it may well be that people could be more confident of accurate than inaccurate memories. These interesting possibilities await future research.

EFFECTS OF RETRIEVAL ON LATER RETRIEVAL

The process of retrieving information is not a neutral act, but also modifies the memory of the information that is retrieved (Bjork 1975). The effect of testing can be either positive or negative. The positive effect is often called the testing effect and has been documented repeatedly, dating from experiments conducted over many years (for example Gates 1917; Raffel 1934; Spitzer 1939). In their simplest form, experiments revealing a testing effect provide two groups of subjects material to be memorized; then one group receives an immediate test and the other group does not. When both groups are tested later, the one receiving the immediate test performs better than the group that was not tested earlier. As just one example of such an experiment, we consider data reported by Wheeler and Roediger (1992). In some conditions, subjects heard a story and, simultaneously, saw pictures projected on a screen. The pictures represented objects mentioned in the story, and subjects were told that they would be tested on the pictured objects by being asked to recall their names. After study, different groups of subjects took either three successive forced

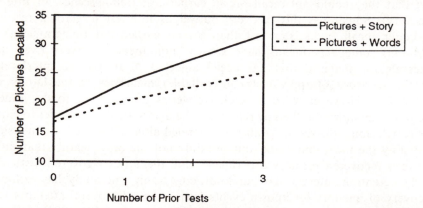

Fig. 6.6 Mean number of items recalled in Wheeler and Roediger's (1992) study as a function of number of prior tests and study condition.

recall tests, one forced recall test, or no test. A week later subjects returned to the same room and were given a final forced recall test. The number of items correctly recalled on the delayed test is shown in Fig. 6.6 as a function of the number of initial tests. It is clear that the number of prior tests exerted a powerful effect on later recall. The same outcome has been reported in many other experiments. However, when tests involve cued recall, the effect of one test on another is determined by the types of cues used and the relation between cues used on the tests (McDaniel *et al.* 1989).

The testing effect just described is relatively robust: a first test generally has a positive effect when the same information is tested later. However, the effects of testing are not always positive. Testing some information can interfere with retrieval of other information, a phenomenon known as output interference (Tulving and Arbuckle 1963). For example, when categorized lists are presented and then their testing order occurs sequentially (in a randomized or counterbalanced arrangement), recall of items from a category declines with the output position of the category (Roediger and Schmidt 1980; Smith 1971). Similarly, if subjects are given cues for some categories but asked to recall all the categories later, recall of the other categories is worse than for control subjects who are given no cues (Roediger 1980). Finally, retrieval practice on some items of information makes recall of that information quite likely, but interferes with recall of other information learned at about the same time (Anderson *et al.* 1994).

The research reviewed briefly in this section shows that the effects of testing can be positive or negative, depending on the conditions. Being tested on information typically improves recall of that information but may harm recall of other information. In the next section we consider evidence that the act of testing can also lead to false memories.

CREATION OF FALSE MEMORIES IN REPEATED RECALL

The evidence reviewed above indicates that retrieving information generally increases the likelihood of accurately retrieving the same material again. Recall on a first test makes that material more recallable later (the testing effect) and the later tests may even reveal recall of additional information (the phenomena of reminiscence and hypermnesia). Because of these powerful phenomena, it is not surprising that some researchers have concluded that the effect of testing is largely beneficial and have noted the stability of reports in repeated recall. For example, in the study of children's memories for events, Fivush *et al.* (1995) examined children's recollections of personally experienced events over repeated testings and noted the stability and coherence of the children's accounts. Dent and Stephenson (1979) tested children's memories for events witnessed via videotapes. Children interviewed five times over a two month interval recalled more accurate information than children interviewed once or twice.

Poole and White (1996) reviewed the evidence with respect to children's repeated recall and concluded that children's recollections can be stable and that a test can facilitate later recollection. The facilitating effect of testing is especially likely when the test occurs shortly after the child experienced the event. However, at longer delays repeated testing sometimes leads to inaccuracy and error (for example Flin *et al.* 1992; Poole and White 1993). In this section we consider a different tradition of the repeated testing literature, one that shows how false memories can arise over repeated testing. (At the end of the chapter we attempt to reconcile the disparate effects of repeated testing.)

If testing has enhancing effects on veridical memories – and it generally does – then we might expect that the same effect would occur on false memories. That is, if a person makes an error in recalling an event, this act of recall may serve to increase the future recall of the false memory. Exactly this pattern occurred in an experiment reported by Roediger and McDermott (1995, Experiment 2). They presented subjects with 16 lists of 15 words. Each list was comprised of words associatively related to a critical non-presented word. For example, one list consisted of words such as *bed, rest, awake, tired, dream, wake,* and *snooze,* all of which are associatively related to *sleep.* A previous experiment using this paradigm (Deese 1959) had shown that subjects falsely recalled the missing word with a high probability shortly after study of the list, so the paradigm is useful for inducing the experience of false memories in a laboratory setting. Subjects in Roediger and McDermott's experiment either took a recall test immediately after list presentation, or they worked math problems after list presentation. (Eight lists occurred in the recall condition and eight in the math condition.) When an immediate free recall test occurred, subjects recalled the missing items at a high rate (after 0.55 of the lists).

After subjects had studied all 16 lists, they were given a recognition test in which studied items were mixed in with lures (either the critical missing items from the 16 studied lists or comparable items from eight other lists that had not been studied). During the recognition test subjects judged each item as old (studied) or new (non-studied) and then, for each item deemed old, they judged whether they remembered the occurrence of the item on the list or simply knew that it had been on the list but did not remember the moment of its occurrence. The remember/know paradigm was introduced by Tulving (1985) as a way to measure the rememberer's conscious experience during recollection. In the present context, having subjects say that they actually remember an event's occurrence provides a useful index of false remembering (if the remembered event did not occur). That is, recognition judgments can be made merely on the basis of an event seeming familiar (Mandler 1980; Jacoby *et al.* 1989), so observing subjects making *remember* judgments provides a firmer basis for claims of false remembering.

Roediger and McDermott's (1995) recognition results are shown in Fig. 6.7 as a function of whether the relevant list had been studied and whether or not a recall test occurred prior to the recognition test. The results for list items are on the left and those for critical (non-studied) lures are on the right. The entire column represents overall recognition (the proportion of items to which subjects said *old*) and the filled part represents the part of overall recognition that constituted *remember* responses. The first point to notice is that the false alarm rates for the lures were equal to the hit rates, both for lists that were studied and not previously tested (the middle bars in both panels) and for lists that were studied and tested (the right bars). False recognition equalled veridical recognition: subjects could not distinguish veridical from illusory memories. More importantly for present purposes is the effect of testing. For both veridical and illusory memories, a prior recall test increased both overall recognition responses and *remember* responses. Prior testing led to increased false remembering.

Attempts to replicate the testing effects found by Roediger and McDermott (1995) by using the same paradigm, with a few modifications, have generally confirmed its existence (for both veridical and false recall). McDermott (1996*a*) analysed data from 11 experiments, all of which conformed closely to the procedures used by Roediger and McDermott. Several independent variables, in addition to initial test condition, were manipulated in these experiments. Most of the results show that recall has a positive effect on later recognition, although some studies fail to show the effect at statistically reliable levels (for example Schacter *et al.* 1996). McDermott (1996*a*) found that in 17 of 22 relevant comparisons between the Study + Recall and Study + Math conditions, there was a numerical advantage for the Study + Recall condition, with one tie (significant by a sign test, $p<0.05$). Therefore, it seems safe to conclude that taking an initial test enhances the probability with which people will classify the studied and critical items as having been presented.

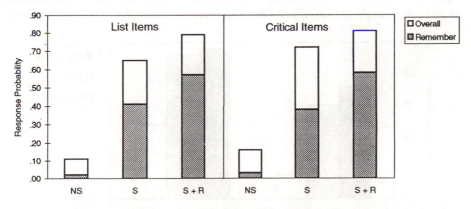

Fig. 6.7 Overall recognition and remember responses as a function of prior testing history and item type (list or critical) in Roediger and McDermott's (1995) Experiment 2. NS corresponds to the non-studied condition, S to the condition in which the list was studied but no initial recall test occurred, and S + R to the study plus recall condition.

In a variation of this paradigm, McDermott (1996*b*, Experiment 1) obtained a testing effect on a free recall test given two days after study of the lists. Subjects heard 24 lists; after each of eight lists, they took immediate free recall tests, after each of eight other lists, they worked math problems for 30 seconds and then took a free recall test, and after eight lists, there were no initial tests at all. Subjects returned two days later and took a final free recall test, on which they were asked to recall as many words as possible from the 24 lists presented in the first phase. Subjects were told to recall as many words as possible, regardless of whether the words had been recalled on the first day. In addition, subjects were explicitly warned against guessing.

Data from McDermott's (1996*b*) experiment are depicted in Fig 6.8. The testing effects manifested in these data were very robust: The probability of recalling a studied item was about four times greater for lists that had been tested previously (either immediately or after a 30 s filled delay) than for lists not previously tested; the probability of false recall increased two-fold as a result of prior testing. Evidence for the critical role that test delay can play in producing false memories lies in the finding that after this two-day delay, the probability of erroneously recalling a critical item exceeded the probability of correct recall (of the studied items). Therefore, as mentioned earlier, retention interval seems to be a critical factor in determining the likelihood of false recall.

In a later experiment, McDermott (1996*c*), replicated this finding and added a new twist. If taking a test enhances later veridical and false memory, then it seems logical to extrapolate and predict that the more tests previously taken the larger the effect. McDermott's (1996*c*) experiment tested this hypothesis by having subjects take either zero, one, or three tests prior to a final free recall test. Subjects heard 18 lists, taken from Roediger and McDermott's (1995) materials. After six of the lists, they took three successive (2 min) recall tests; after six lists, they took a single (2 min) recall test, and after six lists there was no initial test.

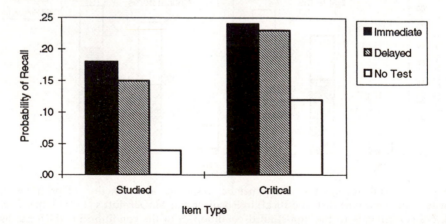

Fig. 6.8 The probability of recall on a final free recall test as a function of initial test condition and item type in McDermott's (1996*b*) Experiment 1.

Immediately following this phase, subjects took a final free recall test over all
the lists; the results are shown in Fig 6.9. If subjects had initially taken three
tests on a list, the probability of veridical recall and false recall was enhanced
relative to the condition in which only one test had occurred initially. Again,
the effect of taking one test (relative to the zero test condition) was evident in
these data. Thus, McDermott's (1996c) data lend credence to the claim that
the more times subjects attempt to retrieve an event, the more likely they will
be to recollect what occurred; however, this increase comes at the expense of
an increase in false recall.

Roediger *et al.* (1996) examined the role of repeated testing in the misinformation paradigm developed by E. Loftus and her colleagues (for example
Loftus *et al.* 1978). We consider selected conditions of their Experiment 1
here. Subjects saw a slide sequence depicting a crime in an office where
a workman stole money from a woman's purse. Afterwards, they received
a narrative description (supposedly written by an observer) that contained
mostly correct information, but which inserted several pieces of misleading
information. Subjects then received a short-answer cued recall test in which
they were cued, item by item, as to the source from which they were to recall
information. For some questions, subjects were told to recall only information
recollected from the slide sequence (i.e. not information recollected from the
narrative). For other items, they were told to recall information either from
the slides or from the narrative. (Other items were not initially tested.) Not
surprisingly, subjects were more likely to produce misleading information
from the narrative on this first test if they had been told that they could
recall from either source (0.62) than if they had been told to recall from only
the slides (0.33).

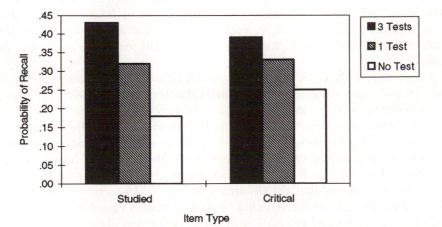

Fig. 6.9 The probability of recall of studied items and critical non-presented items on
a final free recall test as a function of number of prior tests in McDermott's (1996c)
Experiment 1.

The primary interest in the experiment was recall on a second test that occurred two days later. Subjects received a similar cued recall test, but now they were instructed to recall only information from the slides In addition, for each item recalled, subjects were asked to make remember/know judgments, to indicate whether they remembered the actual occurrence of the information in the slides or simply knew it had been there, but did not actually remember its occurrence. The results of this second, delayed, test are shown in Fig. 6.10 for the misinformation items. The total column represents overall recall and the filled part constitutes *remember* responses. The control condition represents items for which no misinformation was given (and which had not been previously tested). False recall in the control condition indicates that the items we used were somewhat likely to be guessed by subjects, but *remember* responses were low. False recall was reliably higher for the items that had received misinformation and that had not been previously tested, but obviously the difference did not appear in *remember* responses. The control/no test comparison constitutes the standard misinformation effect, and false recall was reliably greater in the misinformation condition (0.19) than in the control condition (0.09). However, the other two columns show that the magnitude of the misinformation effect was much greater if subjects had received a prior test on the items. Subjects who had previously tried to confine their recall to information in the slides showed false recall on 0.38 of the items (0.23 remember responses), whereas those who had recalled from either source falsely recalled details for 0.48 of the items (0.31 remember responses).

The act of false recall on a first test greatly increased false recall on a later test and also increased the likelihood of subjects saying that they remembered the actual occurrence of the (non-presented) information. Therefore, the results of this experiment converge on the same conclusion derived from the other experiments with word lists: the act of testing enhances false recall just as it does veridical recall. In addition, recalling false information makes subjects more likely to judge later that they remember its occurrence during the actual event.

As mentioned above, it has been concluded that repeated testing helps to stabilize children's accurate event memories (Poole and White 1995). However, other evidence indicates that repeated testing also stabilizes inaccurate information in children's memories (for example Ceci and Bruck 1993). In addition the mere fact of repeatedly testing children about events that never occurred sometimes seems to lead children to believe that the events did occur. Ceci *et al.* (1994*a*) had children repeatedly think about non-events, events that were generally unusual and that the children's parents said had never occurred to the children. The false events were interwoven in the interviews with true events, and children were asked to recall as much as they could about each event on seven to ten separate occasions with seven to ten days occurring between each interview. The children were told that the events they were judging may or may not have happened and they were asked to recall as much as possible about each. In this experiment, the children falsely recalled 25–44 per cent of the non-events, but there was no trend for false recall to increase over the interview sessions. However, in a similar experiment conducted later, Ceci *et al.* (1994*b*) had the interviewers tell the children before each test that all the fictitious events had actually occurred. Under these conditions, there was a reliable increase in children's remembering of the events over the twelve-week period of testing; 80 per cent more of the non-events were remembered during the eleventh session than in the first. In addition, when children were told at the end of the experiment that some of the events had not actually happened, it was difficult in many cases to shake the children's faith in their memories. Repeatedly recollecting the events seems to 'freeze' them in memory, to use Kay's (1955) expression, making the memories quite real to the children. However, as these studies indicate, it may be necessary for the children to believe that the events actually occurred to see the increased levels of false remembering over the repeated tests.

Several interesting experiments have similarly shown that simply asking adult subjects to describe childhood events multiple times increases the likelihood that they will describe an event that never happened, even when no misinformation is provided (Hyman *et al.* 1995; Loftus 1993). However, as with the evidence from children, the data are not entirely consistent. For example, Hyman *et al.* (1995, Experiment 2) asked college student subjects to describe childhood events, some of which were true and one of which was false (according to the subjects' parents). At the time of the first interview, none of the subjects remembered the false event. During the second interview, 18 per cent of the subjects described the false event as having occurred. By the time of the third interview, 25 per cent of the subjects indicated that they remembered the event that never happened. In a similar paradigm, Loftus and Coan (described in

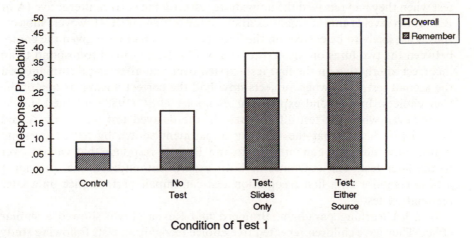

Fig. 6.10 Probability of overall recall and remember responses on a final recall test as a function of initial test condition in Roediger *et al.* (1996) study.

Chapter 7 of Loftus and Ketcham (1994)) found that the memory of a false event can develop and become more detailed over multiple interviews. However, in a similar experiment, Loftus and Pickrell (1996) did not find such an increase. Clearly, further work is required with this paradigm to see if repeatedly testing for recollections of events that did not happen can lead to false memories, without provision of misinformation. As with the Ceci *et al.* experiments conducted with children, it seems likely that the psychological set induced in subjects will turn out to play a critical role; if people believe that the events really occurred and they perceive their task as one of trying to recover these events, then the increase in recall (of non-events) over repeated testing is more likely. One possible mechanism that could account for such increases is that subjects imagine how the events may have happened on the first few retrieval attempts and later their repeated imaginings turn into memories, exemplifying the process of source misattribution (Johnson *et al.* 1993).

The paradigms described above examined the effect of a recall test (free or cued recall) on later recall and recognition. We can also ask if a recognition test affects later recall and recognition. Schooler *et al.* (1988) tested subjects repeatedly in an eyewitness memory situation on recognition tests. Subjects saw a slide sequence depicting a crime scene. For purposes of exposition, let us consider a critical detail A that was assessed on one or more recognition tests. On an initial recognition test, some subjects were tested by being given a choice between the correct detail and a lure (A or B?), whereas others were tested with two lures and forced to pick between them (B or C?). A third group simply engaged in an unrelated filler task. On a final recognition test, all subjects were given another multiple choice test with four alternatives (A, B, C, or D?).

Schooler *et al.* (1988) found that subjects were most accurate on the delayed test when they had received the immediate test with the correct alternative (A or B?), which reveals another manifestation of the testing effect. However, subjects were least likely to be correct on the later test if they had been given the choice between the two lures on the first test (B or C?). Being forced to respond to an incorrect alternative on the first test carried over and affected performance on the second test, even when subjects now had the correct answer as one of the four choices. In a second experiment, Schooler *et al.* (1988) obtained similar results even when the test alternatives on the delayed test were only A and D, which indicates that the memory impairment shown by forced guessing is not only the prior commitment to the B or C response that carries over to the later test. The outcomes of both experiments indicate that providing a false response on a first recognition test can impair performance on a later recognition test.

In a list learning paradigm, Brainerd and Reyna (1996) showed a similar effect. They gave children repeated free choice recognition tests following study of a list of words. Compared with appropriate control groups, children who correctly recognized words on earlier tests showed greater recognition on later tests. However, children who falsely recognized words on the first test – who made false alarms – also recognized those words later. Once again, testing has facilitating effects on accurate recognition but can lead to false recognition as the lures are repeatedly exposed.

To summarize this section, results from many experiments show quite consistently that (1) the act of recall enhances accurate recall and (2) recalling an event in error similarly increases erroneous recall later. Accurate and false recognition on a first test similarly lead to increased recognition of both types on later tests. Some evidence suggests that simply testing repeatedly for recollections of non-events can lead to false memories, but further data are needed to support this conclusion. In the next section, we examine evidence on a related issue, the effect of guessing on recall.

EFFECTS OF GUESSING ON RECALL

Bartlett (1932) pointed out that recollections in natural circumstance rarely place the premium on accurate, verbatim recall that occurs under laboratory conditions. Indeed, in light of later evidence (Gauld and Stevenson 1967), it seems likely that Bartlett's (1932) instructions to his subjects did not emphasize accurate remembering. When people try to re-create complex events, they may often guess and fill in details. We can ask what effect such guessing might have on later remembering.

We have considered some evidence relevant to the subject in the previous section. Roediger *et al.* (1996) showed that erroneous recall of misinformation from a narrative on a first test carried over and was remembered with confidence on a later test. Similar results occurred in Schooler *et al.*'s (1988) experiments when their subjects were forced to guess between two incorrect answers on a forced choice recognition test; performance was impaired on a later recognition test as compared with appropriate control conditions. Although these results are relevant, they do not precisely address the question raised here: if subjects guess about possible answers on a first recall test, will they later come to remember the information they guessed (and were wrong about) as actually having occurred during the original event?

The issue of guessing, or of going beyond the information that can be confidently retrieved, has figured most prominently in the literature asking if hypnosis can aid memory retrieval. Some psychologists and police organizations believe hypnosis has the power to help people retrieve information that could not be recovered in a normal waking state. However, this issue has been researched for 20 to 30 years and practically no evidence exists that retrieval attempts under hypnosis unlock memories that could not be otherwise recalled (Lynn and Nash 1994; Smith 1983).

During hypnosis people are often encouraged to generate everything they can think of, to free associate about the event they are trying to retrieve.

Although such guessing does not seem to lead to increased accurate recall, there is mounting evidence that it can lead people to various memory illusions. Much of the evidence people generate while hypnotized is false and, when subjects are back in their normal waking state and asked to retrieve information about the original event, they can become confused about what actually happened during the original event because of the misinformation they generated. Basically, the people are asked to distinguish between what events actually happened and ones they imagined while under hypnosis, a source monitoring problem. Johnson and Suengas (1988) have shown that internally generated or imagined events are potent sources of interference in such source monitoring situations. The available evidence shows that subjects who score high on hypnotic suggestibility scales often confuse events they retrieved under hypnosis with those that actually occurred (Lynn and Nash 1994; Sheehan 1988; Whitehouse *et al.* 1991). In addition, because people under hypnosis are often encouraged to believe that what they retrieve really happened, they may be more likely to accept the information as actually having occurred. In a sense, subjects provide themselves with their own misinformation and the act of generation may make the misinformation even more potent than when it is externally presented (Roediger 1996). As Schacter (1995, p.17) has noted in this context, 'The evidence suggests that hypnosis creates a retrieval environment in which people are more willing than usual to call a mental experience a "memory" and, in which they express a great deal of confidence in both true and false memories'

Although most work on the effects of guessing on memory have occurred in hypnosis paradigms, the dangers of guessing may go well beyond the context of hypnosis. Any time people guess during remembering, whether consciously embellishing the event or simply making honest errors while going beyond the information they can accurately retrieve, the generated information may later come to be accepted as a veridical memory. Hastie *et al.* (1978) had people guess during an eyewitness testimony experiment and discovered that guesses were later judged to be part of the original event. Other experiments reported by McDermott (1996c), Jacoby *et al.* (1989, p.413), and Roediger *et al.* (1993, pp. 114–22) also lead to the conclusion that when subjects are forced to guess on a first test, they will often accept guesses from the first test as true memories on a second test given at a later point in time. Therefore, it seems quite likely that the act of guessing while retrieving information about an event can lead to false memories even when subjects are not hypnotized. However, further evidence is needed to document this point more conclusively.

RECOVERED MEMORIES

This chapter has primarily addressed how false memories develop through repeated retrieval. We finish by asking why people believe memories that are objectively false. In the lab, people will often claim to actually remember the moment of occurrence of an event that did not happen (Roediger and McDermott 1995), or they will judge with great confidence that it did (even betting money on its occurrence – Weingardt *et al.* (1994)). Outside the lab, people in therapy will sometimes come to believe that they were sexually abused years ago, even if they have never had memories of abuse prior to therapy. In all these cases, we may ask 'Why?'

The answer to this question is doubtless complex and probably involves the social psychology of belief and attitude change at least as much (and probably more than) the cognitive psychology of remembering. However, we make one suggestion here that may serve as a piece to solving this puzzle. Briefly, people (both psychologists and laypeople alike) have developed metaphors for memory that are ill-suited for discussing false memories. Roediger (1979) noted that just as people have implicit theories of personality and intelligence, so do they for memory. These implicit theories of memory are embedded in the language people commonly use to describe memorial phenomena. Briefly, the general theory of memory in Western culture involves the assumptions of spatial storage and search. Memory is conceived as a large space, discrete memories are like objects deposited in this space, and the process of accessing those memories involves searching for them (just as one would search through a physical space). This metaphor seems natural when we use expressions such as memories being in the front or back of our minds, of events sinking into memory or penetrating it, and of memories being easy or hard to find, or memories that are lost.

Cognitive psychologists have generally employed the same spatial storage and search metaphor when constructing either formal or informal models (Roediger 1980). Thus, from the time of Plato, memories have been conceived as being engraved on a wax tablet or as birds being placed in an aviary. More recently, psychologists have conceived of memory as a library (with books as memories), as rooms in a house (with objects in the rooms as memories), as a conveyer belt (with suitcases representing the memories) and many more (see Roediger 1980). Each of these metaphors preserves the spatial storage and search assumptions that are embedded in our implicit memory theory as expressed in our everyday language.

These metaphors for memory obviously serve some useful function, otherwise they would not have persevered all these years. However, they seem fundamentally ill-suited and unnatural to characterize memory errors. If we think of our memories as (to pick but one typical example) books in a library, the metaphor is useful for representing distinctions about encoding (original purchase of the book), storage (placing it in the library), decay (its falling apart and becoming unreadable with age), and the critical role of retrieval processes (the book being hard to find due to being misshelved). So far so good. But how would one find a book that was never brought into the library in the first place? How could a false memory arise – remembering an event (retrieving a book) that was not 'there'?

The spatial storage and search metaphors break down here and we need to seek alternative ways of understanding. For example, Loftus and Ketcham (1994) have used the metaphor of memory being like water in a bowl. Just after an event, we can remember its details clearly, just as we can see in clear water. But interfering events occurring over time are like pouring milk into the bowl. The water becomes milky and what was once remembered with clarity can become cloudy and confused. Who can tell, after a long interval, which is the water and which the milk? Similarly, who of us can tell, if we are trying to recall a childhood event after many years and much interference, if the remembrance really reflects the event or rather reflects the interfering activities over time? Now, the milk-in-water metaphor, while capturing the aspect of how false remembering may arise, could well be completely inappropriate for other purposes. However, our point here is that most of the dominant metaphors of memory, whether implicitly supposed by laypeople, or explicitly proposed by psychologists, are generally ill-suited to explain false remembering. The spatial storage and search metaphors generally all leave the impression that what is recalled from some time in the past must have been stored during that time. However, much current research (both from laboratory studies and more natural field experiments) documents the fact that people can develop full-blown memories of events that never happened and, even for events that did happen, people can remember them quite differently from their actual occurrence.

We believe that the spatial storage and search metaphors that dominate thinking about memory may contribute to people's acceptance of false memories as true: we suppose that events we remember must have been stored and had previously been hard to find. The idea that memory is like a videotape recording (never seriously believed by psychologists but occasionally endorsed by others) is even more misleading. Such misleading metaphors may partly cause acceptance of recovered memories as veridical, but as we stated previously, this factor is surely only one of many.

CONCLUSION

This chapter has focused on repeated retrieval as a prime factor in both the consolidation of accurate memories and as a source of false memories. Although more research is warranted, the results reviewed here clearly indicate that repeated retrieval can lead to false memories and can make erroneous recall on a first occasion seem even more real on later occasions, when the event is recalled again. False responding on a recognition test will also alter later recognition. It is interesting that repeated testing seems to resemble other factors – imaginal processing and repetition, to mention two – that both improve memory for actual events and yet, under the right circumstances, can lead to the development of false memories. The resolution of this paradox may not be complex: one hypothesis is that factors that enhance accurate remembering can, through the same mechanisms, lead to false memories. So repeatedly retrieving, or repeatedly imagining, or being repeatedly exposed to false information, can all lead to remembering of events that never happened.

REFERENCES

Anderson, M.C., Bjork, R.A., and Bjork, E.L. (1994). Remembering can cause forgetting: exploring the retrieval dynamics of long-term memory. *Journal of Experimental Psychology: Learning, Memory, and Cognition*, **20**, 1063–87.

Ballard, P.B. (1913). Oblivescence and reminiscence. *British Journal of Psychology Monograph Supplements*, **1**, 1–82.

Bartlett, F.C. (1932). *Remembering: a study in experimental and social psychology.* Cambridge University Press.

Bjork, R.A. (1975). Retrieval as a memory modifier: an interpretation of negative recency and related phenomena. In *Information processing and cognition*, (ed. R.L. Solso), pp. 123–144. Wiley, New York.

Bousfield, W.A. and Sedgewick, C.H.W. (1944). An analysis of sequences in restricted associative responses. *Journal of General Psychology*, **30**, 149–65.

Brainerd, C.J. and Reyna, V.F. Mere memory testing creates false memories in children. *Developmental Psychology*, **32**, 467–78.

Brown, A.S. (1976). Spontaneous recovery in human learning. *Psychological Bulletin*, **83**, 321–38.

Brown, W. (1923). To what extent is memory measured by a single recall trial? *Journal of Experimental Psychology*, **6**, 377–82.

Buxton, C.E. (1943). The status of research in reminiscence. *Psychological Bulletin*, **40**, 313–40.

Ceci, S.J. and Bruck, M. (1993). Suggestibility of the child witness: a historical review and synthesis. *Psychological Bulletin*, **113**, 403–39.

Ceci, S.J. and Bruck, M. (1995). *Jeopardy in the courtroom: a scientific analysis of children's testimony.* American Psychological Association Press, Washington, DC.

Ceci, S.J., Huffman, M.L.C., Smith, E. and Loftus, E.F. (1994a). Repeatedly thinking about non-events. *Consciousness and Cognition*, **3**, 388–407.

Ceci, S.J., Loftus, E.F., Leichtman, M.D., and Bruck, M. (1994b). The possible role of source misattributions in the creation of false beliefs among preschoolers. *International Journal of Clinical and Experimental Hypnosis*, **42**, 304–20.

Crowder, R.G. (1976). *Principles of learning and memory.* Erlbaum, Hillsdale, NJ.

Deese, J. (1959). On the prediction of occurrence of particular verbal intrusions in immediate recall. *Journal of Experimental Psychology*, **58**, 17–22.

Dent, H.R. and Stephenson, G.M. (1979). An experimental study of the effectiveness of different techniques of questioning child witnesses. *British Journal of Social and Clinical Psychology*, **18**, 41–51.

Erdelyi, M.H. (1984). The recovery of unconscious (inaccessible) memories: Laboratory studies of hypermnesia. In *The psychology of learning and motivation: advances in research and theory*, Vol. 18, (ed. G.H. Bower), pp. 95–127. Academic, New York.

Erdelyi, M.H. and Becker, J. (1974). Hypermnesia for pictures: incremental memory for pictures but not for words in multiple recall trials. *Cognitive Psychology*, **6**, 159–71.

Erdelyi, M.H. and Kleinbard, J. (1978). Has Ebbinghaus decayed with time? The growth of recall (hypermnesia) over days. *Journal of Experimental Psychology: Human Learning and Memory*, **4**, 275–89.

Erdelyi, M.H., Finkelstein, S., Herrell, N., Miller, B., and Thomas, J. (1976). Coding modality vs. input modality in hypermnesia: is a rose a rose a rose? *Cognition*, **4**, 311–19.

Fivush, R., Haden, C., and Adam, S. (1995). Structure and coherence of preschooler's personal narratives over time: implications for childhood amnesia. *Journal of Experimental Child Psychology*, **60**, 32–56.

Flin, R., Boon, J., Knox, A., and Bull, R. (1992). The effect of a five-month delay on children's and adults' eyewitness memory. *British Journal of Psychology*, **83**, 323–36.

Foster, R.A., Schooler, J.W., and Loftus, E.F., (1988). Some deleterious consequences of the act of recollection. *Memory and Cognition*, **16**, 243–51.

Garry, M., Manning, C.G., Loftus, E., and Sherman, S.J. (1996). Imagination inflation: imagining a childhood event inflates confidence that it occurred. *Psychonomic Bulletin and Review* **3**, 208–14.

Gates, A.I. (1917). Recitation as a factor in memorizing. *Archives of Psychology*, **40**, 104.

Gauld, A. and Stephenson G.M. (1967). Some experiments related to Bartlett's theory of remembering. *British Journal of Psychology*, **58**, 39–49.

Hastie, R., Landsman R., and Loftus, E.F. (1978). Eyewitness testimony: the dangers of guessing. *Jurimetrics Journal*, **19**, 1–8.

Hyman, I.E., Husband, T.H., and Billings, F.J. (1995). False memories of childhood experiences. *Applied Cognitive Psychology*, **9**, 181–97.

Indow, T. and Togano, K. (1970). On retrieving sequence from long term memory. *Psychological Review*, **77**, 317–31.

Jacoby, L.L., Kelley, C.M., and Dywan, J. (1989). Memory attributions. In *Varieties of memory and consciousness: Essays in honour of Endel Tulving*, (ed. H.L. Roediger and F.I.M. Craik), pp. 391–422. Erlbaum, Hillsdale, NJ.

Johnson, M.K., Hashtroudi, S., and Lindsay, D.S. (1993). Source monitoring. *Psychological Bulletin*, **114**, 3–28.

Kay, H. (1955). Learning and retaining verbal material. *British Journal of Psychology*, **46**, 81–100.

Koriat, A. and Goldsmith, M. (1996). Memory metaphors and the everyday-laboratory controversy: the correspondence versus storehouse conceptions of memory. *Behavioral and Brain Sciences*, **19**, 167–88.

Lindsay, D.S. and Read, J.D. (1994). Psychotherapy and memories of childhood sexual abuse: A cognitive perspective. *Applied Cognitive Psychology*, **8**, 281–338.

Loftus, E.F. (1993). The reality of repressed memories. *American Psychologist*, **48**, 518–37.

Loftus, E.F. and Ketcham, K. (1994). *The myth of repressed memory*. St Martin's Press, New York.

Loftus, E.F. and Pickrell, J.E. (1996). The formation of false memories. *Psychiatric Annals*, **25**, 720–5.

Loftus, E.F., Miller, D.G., and Burns, H.J. (1978). Semantic integration of verbal information into a visual memory. *Journal of Experimental Psychology: Learning, Memory, and Cognition*, **4**, 19–31.

Lynn, S.J. and Nash, M.R. (1994). Truth in memory: ramifications for psychotherapy and hypnotherapy. *American Journal of Hypnosis*, **36**, 194–208.

McDaniel, M.A., Kowitz, M.D., and Dunay, P.K. (1989). Altering memory through recall: The effects of cue-guided retrieval processing. *Memory & Cognition*, **17**, 423–34.

McDermott, K.B. (1996*a*). Remembering words not presented in lists: the role of testing in producing a memory illusion. Doctoral dissertation, Rice University, Houston.

McDermott, K.B. (1996*b*). The persistence of false memories in list recall. *Journal of Memory and Language*, **35**, 212–30.

McDermott, K.B. (1996*c*). Guessing and testing magnify memory illusions. (Manuscript in preparation.)

Mandler, G. (1980). Recognizing: the judgment of previous occurrence. *Psychological Review*, **87**, 252–71.

Norman, K.A. and Schacter, D.L. False recognition in younger and older adults: Exploring the characteristics of illusory memories. *Memory & Cognition*. (In press.)

Pavlov, I.P. (1927). *Conditioned reflexes* (transl. G.V. Anrep). Oxford University Press, London.

Payne, D.G. (1986). Hypermnesia for pictures and words: testing the recall level hypothesis. *Journal of Experimental Psychology: Learning, Memory, and Cognition*, **12**, 6–29.

Payne, D.G. (1987). Hypermnesia and reminiscence in recall: A historical and empirical review. *Psychological Bulletin*, **101**, 5–27.

Payne, D.G., Elie, C.J., Blackwell, J.M., and Neuschatz, J.S. (1996). Memory illusions: recalling, recognizing, and recollecting events that never occurred. *Journal of Memory and Language*, **35**, 261–85.

Poole, D.A. and White, L.T. (1993). Two years later: effects of question repetition and retention interval on the eyewitness testimony of children and adults. *Developmental Psychology*, **29**, 844–53.

Poole, D.A. and White, L.T. (1995). Tell me again: stability and change in the repeated testimonies of children and adults. In *Memory, suggestibility, and eyewitness testimony in children and adults,* (ed. M. Zaragoza, J.R. Graham, G.N.N. Hall, R. Hirschman, and Y.S. Ben-Porath), pp. 24–43. Sage, Thousand Oaks, CA.

Raffel, G. (1934). The effect of recall on forgetting. *Journal of Experimental Psychology*, **17**, 828–38.

Roediger, H.L. (1978). Recall as a self-limiting process. *Memory & Cognition*, **6**, 54–63.

Roediger, H.L. (1979). Implicit and explicit memory models. *Bulletin of the Psychonomic Society*, **13**, 339–42.

Roediger, H.L. (1980). Memory metaphors in cognitive psychology. *Memory & Cognition*, **8**, 231–46.

Roediger, H.L. (1996). Memory illusions. *Journal of Memory and Language*, **35**, 76–100.

Roediger, H.L. and Challis, B.H. (1989). Hypermnesia: improvements in recall with repeated testing. In *Current issues in cognitive processes: the Tulane Flowerree Symposium on cognition*, pp. 175–99. Erlbaum, Hillsdale, NJ.

Roediger, H.L. and Guynn, M.J. Retrieval processes. In *Handbook of perception and cognition*, Vol. 10, (ed. E.L. Bjork and R.A. Bjork), pp. 197–236. Academic Press, San Diego, CA.

Roediger, H.L. and McDermott, K.B. (1995). Creating false memories: remembering words not presented in lists. *Journal of Experimental Psychology: Learning, Memory, and Cognition*, **21**, 803–14.

Roediger, H.L. and Schmidt, S.R. (1980). Output interference in the recall of categorized and paired associate lists. *Journal of Experimental Psychology: Human Learning and Memory*, **6**, 91–105.

Roediger, H.L. and Thorpe, L.A. (1978). The role of recall time in producing hypermnesia. *Memory & Cognition*, **6**, 296–305.

Roediger, H.L., Payne, D.G., Gillespie, G.L., and Lean, D.S. (1982). Hypermnesia as determined by level of recall. *Journal of Verbal Learning and Verbal Behavior*, **21**, 635–65.

Roediger, H.L., Wheeler, M.A., and Rajaram, S. (1993). Remembering, knowing and reconstructing the past. In *The psychology of learning and motivation advances in theory and research*, Vol. 30, (ed. D.L. Medin), pp. 97–134. Academic, New York.

Roediger, H.L., Jacoby, J.D. and McDermott, K.B. (1996). Misinformation effects in recall: creating false memories through repeated retrieval. *Journal of Memory and Language*, **35**, 300–18.

Schacter, D.L. (1995). Memory distortion: history and current status. In *Memory distortion*, (ed. D.L. Schacter, J.T. Coyle, G.D. Fischbach, M.M. Mesulam, and L.E. Sullivan), pp. 1–43. Harvard University Press, Cambridge, MA.

Schacter, D.L., Verfaellie, M., and Pradere, D. (1996). The neuropsychology of memory illusions: false recall and recognition in amnesic patients. *Journal of Memory and Language*, **35**, 319–34.

Scrivner, E. and Safer, M.A. (1988). Eyewitnesses show hypermnesia for details about a violent event. *Journal of Applied Psychology*, **73**, 371–7.

Sheehan, P.W. (1988). Memory distortion in hypnosis. *International Journal of Experimental and Clinical Hypnosis*, **36**, 296–311.

Smith, A.D. (1971). Output interference and organized recall from long-term memory. *Journal of Verbal Learning and Verbal Behavior*, **11**, 24–32.

Smith, M.C. (1983). Hypnotic memory enhancement of witnesses: does it work? *Psychological Bulletin*, **94**, 387–407.

Spitzer, H.F. (1939). Studies in retention. *Journal of Educational Psychology*, **30**, 641–56.

Suengas, A.G. and Johnson, M.K. (1988). Qualitative effects of rehearsal on memories for perceived and imagined complex events. *Journal of Experimental Psychology: General*, **117**, 377–89.

Tulving, E. (1967). The effects of presentation and recall in free recall learning. *Journal of Verbal Learning and Verbal Behavior*, **6**, 175–84.

Tulving, E. (1972). Episodic and semantic memory. In *Organization of memory*, (ed. E. Tulving and W. Donaldson), pp. 381–403. Academic, New York.

Tulving, E. (1985). Memory and consciousness. *Canadian Psychologist*, **26**, 1–12.

Tulving, E. and Arbuckle, T.Y. (1963). Sources of intratrial interference in paired-associate learning. *Journal of Verbal Learning and Verbal Behavior*, **1**, 321–34.

Underwood, B.J. (1948). 'Spontaneous recovery' of verbal associations. *Journal of Experimental Psychology*, **38**, 429–39.

Weingardt, K.R, Toland, H.K., and Loftus, E.F. (1994). Reports of suggested memories: do people truly believe them? In *adult eyewitness testimony: current trends and developments* (ed. D.F. Ross, J.D. Read, and M.P. Toglia), pp. 3–26. Cambridge University Press, New York.

Wheeler, M.A. (1995). Improvement in recall without repeated testing: spontaneous recovery revisited. *Journal of Experimental Psychology: Learning, Memory, and Cognition*, **21**, 173–84.

Wheeler, M.A. and Roediger, H.L. (1992). Disparate effects of repeated testing: reconciling Ballard's (1913) and Bartlett's (1932) results. *Psychological Science*, **3**, 240–5.

Whitehouse, W.G., Orne, E.C., Orne, M.T., and Dinges, D.F. (1991). Distinguishing the source of memories reported during waking and hypnotic recall attempts. *Applied Cognitive Psychology*, **5**, 51–9.

Williams, M.D. and Hollan, J.D. (1981). The process of retrieval from very long-term memory. *Cognitive Science*, **5**, 87–119.

Wixted, J.T. and Rohrer, D. (1994). Analyzing the dynamics of free recall: an integrative review of the empirical literature. *Psychonomic Bulletin & Review*, **1**, 89–106.

SEVEN

*P*ast and present: recovered memories and false memories

MARTIN A. CONWAY

> There is in general no guarantee of the correctness of our
> memory; and yet we yield to the compulsion to attach
> belief to its data far more often than is objectively justified.
> (Freud 1900)

Memories can be wrong – sometimes very wrong. Memories can also be
'forgotten' for long periods of time and later remembered with surprise.
These are *facts* of memory, they are not hypotheses, speculative beliefs,
or 'folk' psychology. They merely reflect two characteristics of everyday
remembering: all rememberers will have experienced surprise at retrieving
memories they previously thought forgotten and, similarly, all rememberers
will on some occasions have had demonstrated to them that a memory they
believed to be accurate was incorrect in some or all its details. Another 'fact' of
memory, first commented on by Ribot (1882), is that memories are incomplete –
as Ribot put it they are 'time compressed'. Thus, memories are not literal records
of experiences rather they are *interpretations* of experiences and they preserve
what is relevant to the individual at the time of particular experiences and, later,
when they are remembered (Conway 1990a,b, 1992, 1996). Fluctuating access,
errors, and incompleteness, portray a sorry picture of human episodic memory
or, as I shall refer to it here, *autobiographical memory* (Tulving 1972, 1983,
1985; see also Conway 1990a,b, 1991, 1992, 1996; Conway and Rubin 1993).
But autobiographical memory (AM) also has other (redeeming) properties,
two of which are that the representations of the past which the system creates
are often *basically*[1] accurate and the remememberer has some, limited, ability
to assess memory accuracy. Volatility of access, errors, incompleteness, and
even wholly false memories in the context of basic accuracy are the hallmarks
of AM. Autobiographical memories, then, represent personal interpretations
of experience, or personal meanings, which are more or less faithful to the
events from which they were derived. But personal meanings change with the
changing self and AMs, when retrieved, are further interpreted in terms of the
current goals and plans of the self. Taking this view, accessibility and accuracy

---

1 By 'basic accuracy' I mean only that some event or some class of event that was actually
experienced is remembered. The specific details of an event or of events may vary, considerably,
in their veridicality.

are properties determined as much by the present as the past.

In this chapter I first describe a cognitive model of the AM system and consider the process of autobiographical remembering. This model, which proposes that memories are transitory mental constructions compiled from different types of autobiographical knowledge, is then applied to the notion of memory recovery. Memory recovery has become a highly contentious issue in the area of recovered memories of childhood traumas and especially in recovered memories of childhood sexual abuse (CSA) (Lindsay and Reed 1994, 1995; Loftus 1993; Loftus and Ketcham 1994; Ofshe and Watters 1994; Pendergrast 1995; Schooler 1994; Terr 1994; Weiskrantz 1995). Memory recovery, however, as a 'fact' of AM is ubiquitous (see Rodiger *et al.*, Chapter 6 this volume) and the issue is whether this takes a different form in the recovery of CSA memories compared with more 'everyday' memories. Proponents of the view that AMs of CSA are radically different from other AMs argue that the two classes of memory are not comparable and, consequently, that explanations of less traumatic memories cannot be applied to memories of CSA (for example Terr 1994). I suggest that this is not the case and show that cognitive models of AM and the somewhat less developed models of AM in the psychoanalytic literature, particularly the models of Freud (Breuer and Freud 1893; Freud 1900) and Kris (1956), are in fact highly compatible. Moreover, the processes of memory recovery suggested by the cognitive model can be easily and profitably extended to memories for trauma (see Conway 1995a). The phenomenon of false memory is considered next, and various ways in which false memories can arise are outlined: it is a property of the cognitive model that AMs are, in certain respects, always 'false'. Finally, conscious states associated with the construction of true and false memories are discussed and it is proposed that states of conscious awareness characteristic of the two types of memory construction might provide important clues to memory accuracy.

CONSTRUCTING A MEMORY

One model of AM proposes that AMs are transitory mental representations dynamically generated by a complex retrieval process (Anderson and Conway 1993; Conway 1992, 1993, 1995a,b, 1996; Conway and Bekerian 1987; Conway and Rubin 1993). According to this model, retrieval processes channel activation through an *autobiographical knowledge base* that contains AM knowledge structures in which knowledge at different levels of abstraction is used to index knowledge at other levels of abstraction (more specific or less specific) or knowledge in other knowledge structures. A memory is constructed once a stable pattern of activation is established in the knowledge base. The constructed memory includes the activated knowledge *and* the retrieval model used to create that memory in that episode of construction. Thus, there are two important components to the model: the AM knowledge base and central control process which mediate retrieval.

As regards the autobiographical knowledge base, Conway and Rubin (1993) in their review of AM described three broad classes of autobiographical knowledge persistently identified in recent research (for example Anderson and Conway 1993; Barsalou 1988; Brown *et al.* 1986; Conway 1992; Conway and Bekerian 1987; Linton 1986; Schooler and Herrmann 1992; Treadway *et al.* 1992). *Lifetime periods* are the most general, most abstract, or most inclusive type of knowledge, and denote time periods typically measured in units of years; *general events* represent more specific types of event knowledge typically measured in units of months, weeks, and days; and finally, *event-specific knowledge* refers to memory for highly specific knowledge unique to a single event and typically measured in units of seconds, minutes, or, possibly, hours. These types of knowledge are organized into knowledge structures within the AM knowledge base and indices between different levels of a knowledge structure mediate the construction of patterns of activated knowledge which constitute AMs. Figure 7.1 (from Conway 1996) illustrates this scheme for two thematically organized sets of lifetime periods, a work theme and a relationship theme.

Lifetime periods, such as *when I was at school*, *when I was at university*, *working for company X*, *when the children were little*, *when I lived with Y*, and so forth, contain general knowledge about significant others, common locations, actions, activities, plans, and goals, characteristic of a period. Lifetime periods also name distinct periods of time with identifiable beginnings and endings although these, of course, may be fuzzy rather than discrete. The content of a lifetime period represents *thematic* knowledge about common features of that period (Conway 1996), as well as *temporal* knowledge about the duration of a period (Anderson and Conway 1993). For any given period of time there may be a number of lifetime periods. For instance, *when I lived with Y* may overlap in time with *when I worked at X* but this temporal overlap does not necessarily give rise to an overlap between knowledge structures in AM. The thematic knowledge of the two time periods may be sufficiently different to lead to knowledge structures that index different parts of the autobiographical knowledge base (Barsalou 1988; Conway and Bekerian 1987; Linton 1986). Thus, the significant others, common locations, actions, activities, plans, and goals, characteristic of *when I lived with Y* may not be characteristic of *when I worked at X*, which features a different set of others, locations, actions, activities, plans, and goals. In this case cues which are effective in accessing knowledge indexed by one lifetime period may not be effective in accessing knowledge indexed by another lifetime period *even thought the two periods refer to the same time*. Alternatively, lifetime periods may be thematically linked together (as shown in Fig. 7.1) to form higher-order themes (Conway 1992; Linton 1986). When this occurs then the same cues can be used to access multiple lifetime periods, although once accessed knowledge specific to a single period will then constrain access to associated knowledge.

General events, shown in the ellipses in Fig. 7.1, are more specific and at the same time more varied than lifetime periods. Thus, general events encompass repeated events, for example *evening hikes to meadows*, and single events, for example *sharing a bottle of wine with a friend in a cafe in Paris*, (cf. Barsalou 1988). Repeated general events might be thought of as types of highly detailed personal scripts (Schank and Abelson 1977; Schank 1982). Single general events, on the other hand, are summaries of series of minor events or action sequences (Barsalou 1988), which are often organized chronologically, from first to last occurring actions, and frequently feature a thematic distinctive detail (Anderson and Conway, 1993; Conway 1996). Thus, in the 'bottle of wine' example a thematic distinctive detail might be *my friend reveals to me the 'real' reason for his trip to France*. According to Anderson and

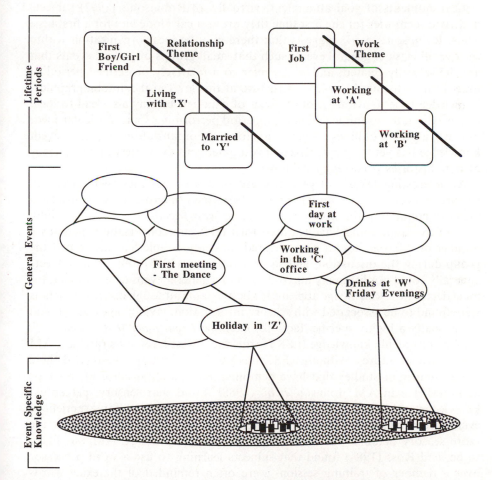

Fig. 7.1 Structure of the autobiographical knowledge base.

Conway (1993) such distinctive details can be used to access single general events directly from lifetime periods because they correspond to knowledge held at that level, for example about significant others characteristic of the indexing lifetime period. In addition to repeated and single general events Robinson (1992) pointed out that general events may also represent sets of associated events and so encompass a series of memories linked together by a theme. For example, Robinson (1992) studied what he called 'mini-histories' for activities such as *learning to drive a car* and *first romantic relationship*. Initial findings suggested that these were organized around single general events featuring goal-attainment knowledge (both positive and negative) that appeared to convey significant information for the self, for example about how easily a skill was acquired, and about success and failure in intimate interpersonal relations. Interestingly, both types of mini-history featured highly vivid recollections of critical moments of goal attainment: virtually all Robinson's (1992) subjects had vivid memories for the first time they drove a car alone and for a first kiss. Thus, Robinson's work suggests that there may be local organization within the overall class of general events such that small groups of general events that are thematically related, and which refer to a relatively proscribed period of time, form a distinct knowledge structure at this level in the autobiographical knowledge base. Obviously, other types of experiences may also lead to local organization, for example a holiday, a period performing some particular piece of work, a period of illness, and so on. However, organization of general event knowledge has yet to be extensively investigated and the variety and frequency of mini-histories is currently unknown.

An interesting feature of general event details is that they themselves can be further decomposed into what might be termed 'micro-details'. Consider a memory containing the micro-detail *talking with friends*, (cf. Conway 1996). This micro-event could have featured turn taking in conversation, perhaps a number of different topics were covered, possibly people left and joined the group during the discussion, and so on. Anderson (1993) found that subjects generally could not list many micro-details of a general event detail. In fact, for most details little knowledge appeared to be available although distinctive details were found to be associated with sensory information, vivid images, affect, and occasionally a highly specific 'fact', for example *I remember that X said '. . .'*. This event-specific knowledge (ESK) forms the lowest level in hierarchical AM knowledge structures. Although ESK has not been directly investigated there are a number of studies that have demonstrated the importance of this type of knowledge in AM. Johnson *et al.* (1988) found that sensory, perceptual knowledge was the key feature that distinguished memory for experienced events from memory for imagined events. Brewer (1988) observed that the more sensory detail available at recall the more accurate an AM was likely to be, and Ross (1984) found that subjects learning to use a word processor over a number of training sessions were often reminded of the exact words they had edited in a previous session. These findings all suggest that ESK is central to AMs, and may play a critical role in convincing a rememberer that they have in fact 'remembered' an event (see Conway *et al.* 1996).

One intriguing possibility is that ESK, although indexed by structures in the autobiographical knowledge base, is not itself part of that knowledge base. This is illustrated in Fig. 7.1 where ESK is depicted as an undifferentiated pool of event-specific details accessed by cues held at the general event level. According to this scheme the part of the autobiographical knowledge base that comprises lifetime periods and general events is part of a much larger general-purpose knowledge base (Conway 1990*a,b*, 1992; Anderson and Conway 1993), whereas ESK may be part of a separate memory system. Certainly, it is notable that patients suffering from organic retrograde amnesia often appear to have some preserved access to lifetime periods and, to some extent, general event knowledge, but usually have difficulty in retrieving ESK from the periods covered by their amnesia (for reviews see Conway, 1993, 1995*b*). Moreover, this proposal is at least partly compatible with recent studies of implicit memory that clearly demonstrate that highly specific sensory knowledge can be retained and can influence subsequent behaviour (for review see Roediger and McDermott 1993; Schacter 1987; also Kinlstrom, Chapter 5 this volume; Schacter *et al.*, Chapter 4 this volume). Indeed, Tulving and Schacter (1990) proposed that implicit memory may be mediated by a pre-semantic perceptual memory system. Such a system, when indexed by cues from AM knowledge structures, might give rise to the recall of sensory details, vivid images, and so forth, that appear to characterize ESK.

The autobiographical knowledge base and the knowledge structures it contains provide the basis for the construction of specific AMs. The knowledge base, however, has to be accessed and, once accessed, activation channelled by the indices of the knowledge structures has to be monitored and evaluated (Anderson and Conway 1993; Burgess and Shallice 1995; Conway 1992, 1996; Norman and Bobrow 1979; Williams and Hollan 1981). Early models of AM retrieval processes (for example Williams and Hollan 1981) conceptualized this process taking place in a series of discrete stages which were iteratively cycled through until the sought-for memory had been located. A cue would provide initial *access* to autobiographical knowledge, followed by a *search* phase, which in turn was thought to be followed by a stage in which the outputs of the search were *evaluated* against some set of preset criteria. If accessed knowledge was consistent with the criteria then the whole process was terminated and a memory was retrieved. If, instead, the criteria were not met then the whole process was cycled through again. In this and subsequent cycles each access stage was initiated with a new cue that was an elaboration of the preceding cue, with each elaboration being determined by the outcome of the prior evaluation or verification stage. Thus, memories were located and retrieved by successive approximations of staged cyclic retrieval process.

The access–search–verify model does capture, in broad outline, the comparatively effortful process of AM retrieval and Fig. 7.2 (from Conway 1996) shows two protocols taken from subjects thinking aloud while retrieving memories to the cue words *chair* and *restaurant*. These protocols and others collected in different studies (Burgess and Shallice 1995; Reiser *et al.* 1986; Williams and Hollan 1981) illustrate the way in which autobiographical knowledge is accessed and elaborated as a memory is generated. Importantly, the two examples in Fig. 7.2 feature lifetime periods, general events, and ESK. This is a common feature of AMs (cf. Conway and Bekerian 1987; Conway 1992) which rarely seem to consist of only lifetime period knowledge, only general event knowledge, or only ESK. Rather AMs are compilations of knowledge at different levels of abstraction. However, in order to conceptualize how such compilations are created an account of the control processes that modulate memory construction is required. Norman and Shallice (1980), Shallice (1988), and, more recently, Burgess and Shallice (1995) (see also Baddeley 1986) have proposed a number of ways in which central control process might modulate the process of memory construction, (Burgess and Shallice (1995) and Conway and Tacchi (1996) present the most recent views on this). Rather than review these in detail here we will simply note that the main feature of these proposals is that some set of central processes monitor patterns of activations arising and dissipating in long-term memory and schedule how and when these are to be used in various processing sequences. There are a number of ways this can be achieved. For instance, control processes might increase or decrease (inhibit) activation in long-term knowledge structures either in some direct way or more indirectly by determining which cues will be used to probe the system (cf. Anderson and Bjork 1996). Selection of one cue over another could have the effect of increasing, maintaining, or decreasing, already established patterns of activation, and in this way central processes control areas of activated knowledge. Of course, once the knowledge base is accessed the indices between different layers of knowledge and between different knowledge structures constrain and channel the spread of activation and so, independently, determine the emergence of stable patterns of activated knowledge.

It now seems clear that for central control processes to have this effect in memory construction they must themselves be guided and constrained by some type of model. At the highest level the cognitive system must have models of the environment and of the cognitive system itself (Johnson-Laird 1983), including knowledge of capacities and intentions. One important point for the present discussion is that the central system also have access to, or incorporate, the current self concept and the active themes, goals, and plans, of that self. Conway (1996) proposes that goals and plans are generated to solve existential problems facing the individual. Goals and plans are cognitive representations which act to reduce self-discrepancies (Higgins 1987) and in their attainment or failure create new self-discrepancies and, hence, new plans and goals. Goal attainment is determined by the effects of plans as these are enacted in actual behaviour. Both successful and unsuccessful outcomes lead to

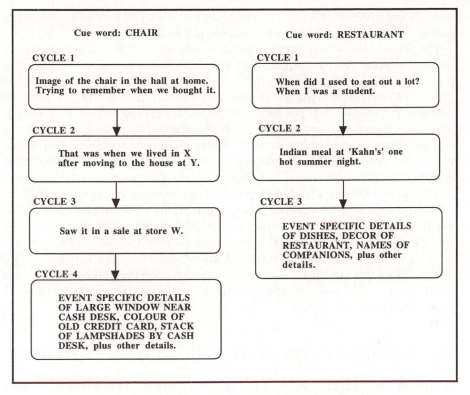

Fig. 7.2 Two protocols to cued memory retrieval.

the encoding of associated experiences in the autobiographical knowledge base and in this sense autobiographical knowledge is a record of past selves in that it preserves[2] knowledge of experiences which featured the self-discrepancies of previous selves (cf. Strauman 1990). Plan implementation and realization is also associated with emotional experience which may serve a specific function in plan repair and plan generation (Oatley and Johnson-Laird 1987; Oatley 1992) and give rise to the detailed representations in long-term memory of times when personal plans required urgent change or abandonment (Conway 1995*a*). By this view central control process, which modulate memory construction (at both encoding and retrieval), are intrinsically part of a pattern of self-discrepancies expressed as interlinked goals and plans for discrepancy reduction and which constitute the current self. With these resources the central system is able to generate mental models which place effective and self-relevant constraints on

2 Note that the representation of goals and plans need not be conscious although, possibly, at some point some part or all of a goal or plan may have been conscious. Also note that autobiographical knowledge held in long-term memory will not necessary contain any explicit knowledge of the discrepancies associated with the encoding of that knowledge. Instead the the knowledge and the way it is retained, i.e. other knowledge to which it is linked, support inferences concerning the goals and plans that guided encoding.

memory construction, i.e. what can be accepted as part of a memory, and what cannot, and when the retrieval process should be terminated.

The process of memory construction consists, then, of a dynamic and cyclic retrieval process that is modulated by a mental model generated by a central process which places constraints on, and provides control over, the retrieval process. Retrieval is dynamic because the model changes in response to accessed knowledge and, possibly, to other task demands which arise during the course of memory construction. The eventual memory which is constructed is a conjunction of a stable pattern of activation in the autobiographical knowledge base, encompassing autobiographical knowledge at different levels of specificity, with the centrally held retrieval model used to modulate construction (see Ericsson and Kintsch (1995) for a related proposal). The conjoined patterns of activation in long-term memory and central processing areas are transitory and effortful to maintain: but while they endure they constitute that memory in that processing episode. Such transitory mental representations may themselves be encoded, in some way, into the autobiographical knowledge base, and Conway (1996) considers how this same process of memory construction might function to create autobiographical knowledge of previous memory constructions and knowledge of external experiences.

THE CUE SENSITIVITY OF AUTOBIOGRAPHICAL MEMORY

A critically important feature of the model outlined in the previous section is that the construction process is almost wholly determined by the cues or memory descriptions elaborated during the course of establishing a memory. If appropriate cues are not initially present in the retrieval environment or cannot be elaborated into effective memory descriptions during the cycles of retrieval then the sought-for information either cannot be accessed or, if accessed, cannot be constructed into a memory, i.e. a stable pattern of activation cannot be established. An example of this later type of *construction failure* has been investigated in clinically depressed patients by J.M.G. Williams and his colleagues (Williams and Broadbent 1986; 1992; Williams and Scott 1988; see for a review). Typically such patients experience difficulties in constructing fully detailed memories and often terminate the construction process at the level of general events. For example, a patient may recall taking walks in the park after Sunday lunch but be unable to construct a memory of any specific walk. Similar problems have been noted in certain patients with neurological damage to the frontal lobes who may present with 'clouded' AMs (Baddeley and Wilson 1986). In both cases it seems possible that the failure to construct fully detailed AMs of specific events is related to malfunction of central control process: in both patient groups there may be insufficient cognitive resources to support either the generation of elaborated descriptions with which to search the AM knowledge base or the subsequent construction of a specific memory.

Another component of the model is that memories, because of their cue dependency and transitory nature, are highly unstable. The critical component in establishing a memory is the incremental development of an effective memory description. But, development of a description is itself dependent on many factors which are dynamic and, therefore, change over time rendering the generation of similar descriptions progressively more unlikely as time between retrievals increases. So, for example, if the subject who retrieved the memory to the cue word *chair* shown in Fig. 7.2 were asked to retrieve that memory again then they would necessarily have to start the memory search with a different memory description: one, which at a minimum, included the knowledge that they had 'retrieved' the memory before. Of course, the initial and subsequent memory descriptions would also differ in that the constraints of the task model would also be different due to changes to the self, the subject's developing understanding of the retrieval task, and other perhaps purely endogenous and local factors such as motivation or time of day and so on (see Mullin *et al.* 1993).

All cues which correspond to prestored autobiographical knowledge have the potential to activate the knowledge with which they are associated (Tulving and Thomson 1973). It is assumed that this activating effect is non-conscious and automatic. Indeed, the model specifies that patterns of activation continuously arise and dissipate in the autobiographical knowledge base in response to internally generated and externally presented cues (Conway 1992, 1996; Conway and Rubin 1993). Not all cues will, however, lead to the emergence of *stable* patterns of activation. When a cue corresponds to knowledge held at the level of lifetime periods then activation will quickly dissipate over the many general events indexed by the period. The net effect being no distinct and stable pattern of activation. In contrast, when a cue corresponds to general event information then an associated lifetime period will receive some activation and event-specific knowledge may also be activated, depending on the nature of the general event and upon other general event knowledge to which the cue is associated. Similarly, associated general events may receive activation as this spreads and dissipates over the indices of the AM knowledge base. Thus, in the case of cues which correspond to general event information more distinct and, possibly, more stable patterns of activation may be established.

The most potent cues for inducing stable patterns that can lead directly to memories without further cycles of the retrieval process are those which directly correspond to ESK. The occurrence of cues with a direct correspondence to pre-stored ESK will, however, be infrequent. This is because they must be processed in a way that produces a representation which has a one-to-one mapping with pre-stored ESK (cf. Kolers and Roediger 1984; see Crowder (1993) for a recent statement on the procedural view of memory retrieval). Event-specific knowledge is conceived as being close to a literal record of prior processing (Conway 1992). It is a fragmentary record which preserves a sample of the configuration of processes that were present at some point in the encoding environment and consequently contains sensory-perceptual information and information of cognitive/affective operations. For a subsequently presented cue to activate a record it must itself be both represented and processed in a way that is highly similar to the way in which the ESK it indexes was originally represented and processed.[3] Thus, simply generating an image of an item, for example a house in which one lived, will not lead to the rapid formation of a memory. In addition to this the model specifies that the actual process of mapping a cue (or memory description) directly onto pre-stored ESK takes place non-consciously. That is to say that when a cue is processed in a way that corresponds uniquely to the way in which an item of pre-stored ESK was processed, then activation of the pre-stored knowledge proceeds automatically, outside conscious awareness (cf. Moscovitch 1992). In the case of direct activation of ESK, activation spreads from highly specific to less specific AM knowledge, traversing the indices of the specific general event with which the ESK is associated to a lifetime period which indexes the now activated general event. This spread of activation from specific to general knowledge activates a unique route from an item of ESK to a general event, and from the general event to a lifetime period. In this way a stable pattern of activation in the knowledge base is rapidly and automatically established. In contrast, for activation spreading in the reverse direction, from lifetime period to general event, there are many indices and therefore many routes. Similarly, general events have multiple indices to ESK (see Fig. 7.1) which afford many different ways of access. By this view, only activation spreading from ESK can rapidly establish a single and distinct pathway through autobiographical memory knowledge structures and, effectively, by-pass the cyclic retrieval process. Thus, cues which activate specific items of ESK have a potent effect in generating stable patterns of activation in the knowledge base.

It is, of course, one of the prime functions of central control processes to either inhibit or facilitate access to such endogenous patterns of activation in the knowledge base. However, a cue which is processed in a particular and unique way will necessarily be integrated with current processing sequences modulated by the operation of central control processes. This is because control processes coordinate processing sequences and, therefore, information that enters into a (cognitive) task will become, perhaps briefly, a part of the control sequence. Consequently, when a centrally processed cue directly

3 This conception of ESK is similar to other proposals concerning the representation of specific knowledge. In particular, Brewin (1989) proposed that emotional experiences are represented by two distinct types of memories: verbally accessible memories and situationally accessible memories. Verbally accessible memories consist of consciously mediated knowledge present at the time of experience and closely related to current plans and goals of the self. Situationally accessible memories, in contrast, retain highly specific records of non-conscious processing occurring during the experience of emotion. Brewin *et al.* (1995) use these distinctions in their recent account of post-traumatic stress disorder, one aspect of which focuses on the association of 'flashbacks' with situationally accessible memories. In the present model, verbally accessible knowledge would be derivable from the lifetime period–general event structure whereas situationally accessible knowledge would be represented as ESK (see Conway (1995a) for an application of the model to flashbulb and traumatic memories).

accesses ESK the probability that a memory will be rapidly constructed, enter into central processing sequences and, perhaps, consciousness, is higher than when ESK is not directly accessed. This partly automatic process of memory construction contrasts with the more effortful construction evident in intentional acts of remembering. In intentional memory construction the retrieval process, which is driven by central control processes, proceeds in a more incremental fashion, sampling and evaluating knowledge activated in lifetime periods and general events, as a stable pattern of activation is gradually established in the knowledge base (see Conway and Bekerian 1987). A further possibility here is that intentional retrieval may commence by detecting a pattern of activation currently present in the knowledge base. If this pattern makes available knowledge relevant to the retrieval model then a memory can be rapidly constructed. In later sections we will see that these forms of rapid memory construction have been noted by a number of investigators. In summary, the elaboration of cues during memory construction, the changing interpretation of cues across different episodes of retrieval, and cue-compatibility with the organization of autobiographical knowledge, all act to determine memory specificity, stability, and automaticity of construction.

PSYCHOANALYTIC MODELS OF AUTOBIOGRAPHICAL MEMORY

The constructivist model of AM was principally developed to account for findings from laboratory experiments, questionnaire studies, and, more recently, impairments of AM arising from brain damage (Conway 1990, 1992, 1993, 1995b, 1996; Conway and Bekerian 1987; Conway and Rubin 1993). In contrast, models of autobiographical memory proposed by psychoanalysts were developed as part of a larger project to understand and treat psychogenic disorders. Consequently, models in this latter area tend to be less well developed and subordinate to theoretical constructs that generate effective intervention and treatment procedures. Despite this there are close parallels between cognitive and psychoanalytical models of AM, which suggest a convergence rather divergence of theory. Freud (in Breuer and Freud 1895) proposed specific ways in which memories might be organized in long-term memory, and in the *Interpretation of dreams* (Freud 1900) put forward an account of memory retrieval in which control processes played a critical role (see Erdelyi 1985; Erdelyi and Goldberg 1979). Freud considered memories to be organized thematically and within each theme to be stored in a linear sequence, 'like a file of documents' (Freud 1895, p.288). For pathogenic memories of trauma (including CSA) Freud proposed that thematically related memories were concentrically arranged around trauma memories rather than represented in a linear sequence. Freud conceived of this form of organization as an outer layer formed by memories that had always been accessible to consciousness and inner layers which were progressively less accessible. These layers of memories surrounded the core traumatic memories which were wholly inaccessible but which, nevertheless, remained available (Tulving and Pearlstone 1966) given the appropriate retrieval environment. In this sense the outer memories 'screened' the inner core of traumatic memories. Part of the purpose of therapy was to dismantle the layers of resistance, constituted by the progressive inaccessibility of the surrounding 'screen' memories, and establish access to the memories of trauma.

A central feature of Freud's reasoning was that traumatic memories, if retrieved, would lead to intensely dysfunctional emotions and behaviour and, therefore, they were represented in long-term memory in such a way as to virtually eliminate their accessibility. However, Freud reasoned that a defensive form of organization of knowledge structures in long-term memory was not in itself sufficient to fully ensure the irretrievability of traumatic memories. In addition, some form of central control was required. In Freud's (1900) later model of memory, which is surprisingly modern (see Erdelyi and Goldberg 1979), memories are stored in many different formats, i.e. verbal, imaginal, sensory, affective, etc., and are activated non-consciously. These different records retain different types of information with some retaining information of temporal co-occurrences of attributes of experiences while in others 'the same perceptual material will be arranged . . . in respect of other kinds of coincidence, so that one of these . . ., for instance, will record relations of similarity, and so on with others' (Freud 1900, p.539). Once activated, however, the route to consciousness is then determined by two broad classes of control processes. The first set of processes, which are unconscious, inhibit or even edit patterns of activation in long-term memory. The second set of preconscious processes act like a selective attention device and determine what specific knowledge enters consciousness. Freud (1900) says of representation in the preconscious that 'the excitatory processes occurring in it can enter consciousness without further impediment provided certain other conditions are fulfilled; for instance, that they reach a certain degree of intensity, that the function which can only be described as "attention" is distributed in a particular way . . . and so on' (Freud 1900, p.541).

Freud's account of AM and the cognitive model are surprisingly compatible. The proposals concerning the representation of autobiographical knowledge are similar to those developed from laboratory-based studies, although they differ in that for Freud memories appear to be more integrated, 'holistic', representations rather than patterns of activation distributed over a set of knowledge structures and bound up with a transitory retrieval model. His account of control processes is, if anything, even more compatible with current suggestions concerning how these operate in modulating patterns of activation in long-term memory. The comparison with, for example, Norman and Shallice (1980) who also focus on inhibition, selection, and attention, is striking for its similarity. Although, as Erdelyi and Goldberg (1979) point out, Freud did not have the computer metaphor available to him[4] and, consequently, was unable to develop his proposals concerning memory into a more detailed account. As we have already seen, control processes in memory construction must feature current goals and plans of the self which in active attempts to generate memories influence the retrieval processes and in the case of the automatic construction of a stable pattern of activation also determine whether or not that pattern enters into current processing sequences and, ultimately, conscious awareness. The psychoanalyst Ernst Kris (1975) placed a much stronger emphasis on the role of the self in preconscious processing and upon the relation of memories to the self. Kris (1956) proposed the concept of the *personal myth*, an extension of Freud's earlier notion of 'screen memories', in which the whole of a person's autobiography acted as a 'screen' or way in which memory access was constrained. Kris first identified the personal myth in those of his patients who presented with unusually well organized autobiographies, distinguished by a high degree of clarity. He observed that such patients often held the strong conviction that things could not have been otherwise and were resistent to placing multiple interpretations upon individual memories or sets of memories. Sometimes the personal myth would encompass a person's entire life history, whereas on other occasions for other individuals only a particular portion of their personal history would have a high degree of organization and clarity. Kris noted that individuals with this type of (defensive) personal myth were often secretive about their autobiography. During the process of therapy Kris discovered that often these personal myths were in fact incorrect, and contained carefully edited sections in which whole lifetime periods had been omitted. For instance, for one of his patients who claimed to have left home aged sixteen years it later transpired that he had in fact left when he was eighteen; the 'missing' two years representing a period during which traumatic events from childhood were repeated. Thus, the personal myth acted to screen or repress a lifetime period. Interestingly, Treadway *et al.* (1992) have recently reported two case studies of amnesics with lifetime period impairments similar to those described by Kris. The two patients studied by Treadway *et al.* were virtually totally amnesic for all memories and skills acquired during a lengthy period in adulthood and in both cases there was some indication of traumatic events occurring around the time to which the amnesias dated back, and there appeared to be no other reasons, such as neurological injury, for the onset of the memory loss. Treadway *et al.* interpret these deficits in terms of loss of what they call 'life contexts' and these appear to approximate to the notion of lifetime periods outlined earlier and to Kris's proposal of a protective, 'edited', personal myth.

The concept of a personal myth proved to be a useful construct in psychotherapy, but Kris considered that all individuals, not just patients

4 It is interesting to note that Freud was probably aware that he did not have the appropriate metaphor within which he could develop and expand his ideas concerning AM, and his paper (Freud 1925) 'A note on the mystic writing-pad' indicates a continuing search for an explanatory conceptual framework.

with psychogenic disorders, had personal myths. In the normal individual the personal myth was, according to Kris, constantly revised and restructured, such that it represented a dynamic life narrative in which the current plans, goals, and understandings, of the individual were enacted. Personal myths did not, however, only feature memories, they also included fantasies, beliefs, alternative models of the self (cf. Marrus and Nurius 1986), and expectations of contingencies likely to arise from goal attainment or failure to achieve goals. For Kris, then, individual memories were not in themselves particularly significant mental representations. Instead, memories were largely of interest only in the context of a current and dynamic personal myth. One interesting corollary of this view of AM is that the veracity of memories is not of major significance. As all memories will be part of a myth which itself contains fantasies, beliefs, hopes, and fears, it is the *meaning* of a memory, or set of memories, within this self-context which is of significance to the analyst and to the individual, (see BMI Ross (1991) for further discussion of Kris and the views of memory put forward by later analysts, especially, the Kris Discussion Group, (Fine *et al.* 1971). Not surprisingly, Kris himself was pessimistic about the possibility of accurately judging the veracity of memories and clearly felt that all memories, as part of a personal myth, were in important respects inaccurate. Kris's views, both on the dynamic nature of the personal myth, which operated at a preconscious level in the construction of memories, and on the truth content of AMs, are high compatible with the cognitive model of AM that also postulates the influence of the self in memory construction via the non-conscious operations of control processes and which conceptualizes memories as transitory constructions consisting of patterns of activation in long-term memory conjoined with a retrieval model.

MEMORY INACCESSIBILITY AND MEMORY RECOVERY

The notion that memories can be recovered necessarily implies that memories can become inaccessible for some period of time, in some way. In addition to this a further implication of memory recovery, and one which has not been greatly remarked upon, is that 'memories' are *objects*, mental objects, that can be forgotten or lost just like actual objects[5] (see Roediger (1980) for further discussion of the 'spatial' metaphor of memory, and also Roediger et al., Chapter 6 and Conway, Chapter 1, this volume). But the evidence reviewed here that emerges from many converging lines of AM research is not compatible

---

5 Neither Freud nor Kris held this view and, consequently, their models of AM are much closer to the constructivist view. More recent approaches to therapy, particularly in CSA area, do, however, apparently subscribe to the view that memories are like 'objects'. Loftus and Ketcham (1994, pp.49–53) in their critical review of repression touch upon this and Terr (1994) in her interpretation of a number of cases studies also seems to hold to the 'memories-are-objects' position.

with the notion that memories are stored in long-term memory as discrete, holistic units. Instead, a memory is a temporary compilation of knowledge from different sources effortfully constructed and briefly maintained.[6] Thus, the simple 'library' or 'storehouse' metaphor which proposes that memories can be 'lost', 'misplaced', 'hidden', or made inaccessible by some other means, is not tenable: there are no 'memories' (discrete, holistic, mental objects held in a long-term store) to which this could happen. In contrast, the constructivist account of autobiographical remembering, which is not based on a simple spatial metaphor and which conceptualizes AMs more as a *process* than a static mental object, suggests a number of ways in which construction could be attenuated or interrupted and later restored. This section then considers how the constructivist approach to autobiographical remembering can account for inaccessibility and later recovery. But first a number of illustrative case studies are briefly outlined.

The phenomenon of memory recovery has been somewhat reified in recent debates concerning recovered memories of CSA (for review see Lindsay and Read, 1994, 1995) where it has often been associated with the more debatable issues of repression and dissociation (cf. Holmes 1990). But memory 'recovery' is a fact of everyday remembering and there can be few individuals who have not been surprised by recalling memories of 'forgotten' experiences. On some occasions this may apparently occur 'spontaneously' and the rememberer has little comprehension of what prompted the construction of the memory or why it came to mind. On other occasions naturally occurring memory recovery may take place when an individual dwells on some period from their past, when they enter into discussions of some period from their past, or even when simply exposed to cues such as family photographs.

Indeed, Schank (1982) (see also Ross 1984) outlined a type of autobiographical remembering, that he referred to as *remindings*, in which memory recovery probably features fairly frequently. Remindings occur when an individual recalls a memory that is conceptually related to a current problem. In the well known 'steak and haircut' example Schank describes how one colleague's complaint that he could never get his steak cooked as rare as he liked it, reminded another colleague of how he had been unable to get his hair cut as short as he preferred when visiting England. Schank (1982) provides many other examples of remindings and it seems probable that at least some of these remindings consist in the construction of memories which, prior to the reminding, would have been classed by the individual as 'forgotten'.

Salaman (1970) too gives a number of examples of the *involuntary* recovery of memories documented it works of literature. For instance, Chateaubriand in *Memoires d'outre-tombe* recounts how when walking alone one evening 'I was drawn from my reflections by the warbling of a thrush perched upon the

---

6 The constructivist model of AM proposes that the representation of certain unique experiences may be more integrated and unified than the representation of other types of memories. Conway (1995a) discusses how this might apply to flashbulb memories and memories for trauma.

highest branch of a birch tree. At that instant the magical sound brought my paternal estate before my eyes: I forgot the catastrophes of which I had been a witness and, transported suddenly into the past, I saw again that country where I had so often heard the thrush sing.' Another example from an unfinished autobiographical novel (*Jean Santeuil*) by Proust describes how the protagonist, in a depressed state, started on a walk to the nearby Lake Geneva. The sight of the lake suddenly brought back to him memories of Begmeil and his depression lifted. He had tried many times to bring back his memories of Brittany but they had seemed 'dead'. Whereas, now, 'In a flash that life in Brittany, which he had thought useless and unusable, appeared before his eyes in all its charm and beauty, and his heart swelled within him as he thought of his walks at Begmeil when the sun was setting and the sea stretched out before him.' Salaman (1970) gives many more examples of memory recovery from De Quincey and other autobiographical writers as well as from her own autobiographical memory, the latter which she treats as a case study of involuntary remembering. Salaman's (1970) thesis is that memories of events, and what she calls *fragments* of events, are retained because at the time of experience these were associated with a 'shock' or 'disturbance'. Memories, or fragments, can be misremembered in that they may be located in the 'wrong' setting, although the relations between the objects in the memory fragment do not change and it is these which carry with them strong personal meanings: meanings which must often be discovered, or (re)constructed, by the rememberer in, what appears to be, fairly intense and lengthy sessions of reprocessing memories.

Salaman's (1970) suggestions are highly compatible with the account of memory construction developed earlier and her focus on the personal meanings of memories and fragmentary memories consonant with an emphasis on the role of the personal goals and plans in the construction of memories. There is, however, a noteworthy difference between Salaman's concept of involuntary memories and Schank's notion of remindings. Involuntary memories become more frequent and apparent when an individual actively attempts to construct memories. All Salaman's examples are from writers who invested great effort in recalling their pasts and the examples from her own memory are drawn from systematic attempts to recall, in detail, whole parts of her life whereas in Schank (1982, 1986) involuntary memories or remindings occur 'spontaneously' during the course of problem solving. Nevertheless, in both cases, memories arise in response to specific cues either externally presented or internally generated, and these can take many forms sometimes being sensory-perceptual details, conceptual structure of a problem, or affective states. Some especially clear cases of this have been reported by Terr (1994) in studies of recovered memories of childhood trauma.[7] In the much discussed and disputed case of Eileen Lipsker (cf. Loftus and Ketcham 1994), Lipsker unexpectedly and suddenly recalled

7 Recall that here we *not* concerned with the accuracy of recovered memories but rather with possible mechanisms that might support the type of memory constructions often observed in 'memory recovery'.

that as a child she had witnessed her father murder her childhood friend Susan Nason. A murder which, at the time, had remained unsolved for 20 years, and of which Lispker had apparently no memory during that period. Recovery of the memory took place in the following setting. Lipsker's own daughter, who apparently bore a close resemblance to Nason, was drawing with some friends on the floor in the Lipsker home while close by Lipsker herself sat on a couch. It was a warm and sunny afternoon and sunlight fell on the children as they played. At some point her daughter turned towards her and tried to catch her eye and at that point Lipsker had a vivid image of Susan Nason. In the image Lipsker was standing and Nason was turning her face towards her desperately trying to catch her attention. Also in the image Lipsker's father stood over the seated Nason about to strike the blow that would kill her (but see Loftus and Ketcham (1994, pp. 40–9) for a rather different account of how this memory was recovered). At the time this emotive image came to mind Lipsker was in a distracted state. Terr (1994) reports that Lipsker stated she was 'for all practical purposes, spaced out. I was thinking of nothing. It's – you know – the afternoon, and the kids are at home, and it's almost time to start dinner. Just boring, mundane, things. And the light is coming in through the slats of the Levolors, and it's warm. Who Knows? The temperature? The light? Sometimes something just happens.' Recovery of memories of trauma are not limited to CSA, and Christianson and Nilsson (1989) describe a single case study of a rape victim (referred to as CM) who developed a dense retrograde amnesia both for the assault and for her previous life. CM was, in fact, able to recall a few extremely detailed aspects of the event without apparently being able to comprehend how these related to the assault or why they had come to mind. The attack had taken place while CM was out jogging and a distinctive pattern of brickwork close by where the rape took place was remembered with extreme clarity. Some months after the incident CM was again out jogging at a different location when a similar pattern of brickwork unexpectedly cued full retrieval of memories for the rape; at the same time CM's retrograde amnesia lifted. Presumably at the time of the resolution of her retrograde amnesia CM too was in a distracted state and not focused on what she could in any case not remember, the details of the rape incident (the chapters by (Engelberg and Christianson, Chapter 10, and Schooler *et al.*, Chapter 11 this volume describe further findings relating to memory recovery to highly specific cues).

Specific cues can then initiate the construction of memories which were previously inaccessible and, on at least some occasions, this may take place when the rememberer is in an unfocused or distracted state. And this, perhaps, suggests that when the inhibitory function of central control processes is temporarily attenuated, stable patterns of activation can be constructed in the autobiographical base and enter into conscious awareness. In certain disorders, such as post-traumatic stress disorder (PTSD), strategies may be developed to consciously minimize the 'spontaneous' construction of memories and cues which might have this effect are actively avoided (APA 1986). The 'flashbacks' characteristic of PTSD, and the emergence of memory coping strategies, further demonstrate the hypersensitivity of AM to ESK cues. In a similar vein, consider recent reports of recovery from global retrograde amnesia following brain injury. In these cases confirmed neurological damage resulted in complete disruption of AM access, rendering more general and previously potent cues to memory construction wholly ineffective (cf. Conway (1993, 1995*b*) for reviews of impairments of autobiographical memory). Lucchelli *et al.* (1995) report two striking cases of recovery of *whole* autobiographies to specific cues following brain injury and protracted periods of global retrograde amnesia. Patient GR was a 67-year-old artist who suffered a stroke causing a lesion in the left anterior thalamus leading to dense anterograde and retrograde amnesia and some lesser impairment of frontal lobe function. His anterograde amnesia was mostly confined to verbal items, consistent with the left-side damage to the thalamus. His retrograde amnesia was so dense that in the days following the stroke he experienced uncertainty about his identity. He failed to recognize his own paintings, could not recall topics on which he had been writing books, and in response to a variety of cues was unable to recall anything about family members, friends, or associates. Tested two months later GR was able to relate some basic personal knowledge but described this as 'relearned' rather than 'true remembrance'. This is a common feature of patients suffering from retrograde amnesia who often are able to relearn basic autobiographical knowledge, usually from family members. One year after his stroke GR underwent a minor operation under local anaesthetic to fit a pacemaker. Lucchelli *et al.* comment:

... while he was lying awake on the operating table, a little discomforted by the surgeon working on his chest for the insertion of the cable ... he suddenly felt a change: he had a vivid memory of an almost identical situation he had experienced for a previous hernia operation some 25 years before (lying down, awake, local anaesthesia, a little discomfort, a little anxiety, the soothing voice of the surgeon). Then all his other 'medical' AMs came back and immediately afterwards, in a matter of minutes, countless events of his past life 'filled his head' one after the other, like a disorderly and overwhelming crowd. GR describe his experience 'as a catharsis'. He felt the urge to talk about his past life and did so almost continuously for two days ... In the following 3–4 days his memories 'rearranged' themselves in time and GR was 'himself again'.

GR's recovered autobiographical memory remained stable, although interestingly his verbal anterograde amnesia did not change and he continued to show impairments on tests of frontal lobe functions.

Patient MM, a 24-year-old man experienced a road traffic accident in which he incurred only minor injuries including a deep cut to the lower lip. Approximately three hours later MM, after showing no neurological symptoms, suddenly became confused and disoriented and 'could not remember anything'. Subsequent cognitive neuropsychological testing revealed that MM had no anterograde amnesia, he showed an excellent capacity for learning and retaining new information, and he had no signs of other cognitive impairment. MM's only impairment was a very dense global amnesia encompassing all his life. In the period immediately following the onset of his amnesia MM recovered some memories of events from childhood and relearnt basic personal knowledge from his family and friends, who he was totally unable to recognize. He remembered virtually no events from other parts of his life, and although able to recognize a friend's house from his hospital window could recall no events relating to the friend. His girlfriend, with whom he had been living for over two years, was unrecognized and he was unable to pick her out from a 'line-up' of nursing staff. Interestingly, however, he quickly came to relate and behave interpersonally with his family friends in much the same way as he had prior to his accident, but remained unable to recognize them or to recall any events in which they had been jointly involved. He claimed, during this period of global amnesia, to feel an 'emotional' familiarity building between himself and his family and friends. In contrast to these potential signs of recovery he was surprised by what he regraded as new and unfamiliar everyday objects such as phonecards and touch-tone public phones, apparently remembering only the round dial type of phone.

MM had been an enthusiastic and accomplished tennis player, and his memory returned one month after the accident while playing tennis. Lucchelli *et al.* state that:

. . . at some point during the match, he was struck by the awareness that he was making the same mistake he had made in another match, years before. This triggered the recall of all the details of that last tournament and, subsequently, of other tournaments; then, from that, in a matter of minutes, all his memories came flooding back, 'as if I had turned a tap on and let the water run'. Memories from his past life were now vivid and clearly loaded with emotional attributes, reflecting direct experience rather than passive relearning of reported events.

MM was able to resume his job without any difficulty and his AM remained stable and fully accessible after this point.

Memory recovery to specific cues does not, however, always take the form of the sudden and spontaneous emergence of highly detailed and emotive images. For instance, Harvey and Herman (1994) describe cases in which memories slowly returned. In one case a woman who relocated to an area where she had lived as a child began to feel anxious when in conversation with an older sister about various negative aspects of their childhood. Later, she experienced horrific dreams followed by the recovery of many memories of CSA. Similarly, Schooler (1994) cites a case first reported by Christenson *et al.* (1981) in which a war veteran working in a hospital was asked to clean up a boy in the emergency room. He was not aware that the boy was dead and the discovery horrified him. He then suffered extreme anxiety, depression, and nightmares, relating to his war experiences. He eventually revealed a 35-year-old memory of having to shoot a young boy during a particular incident during the war. As Schooler (1994) points out there was no evidence that this individual had suddenly recovered this memory, but his experience in the hospital clearly rendered the memory more accessible to consciousness. Terr (1994) too describes cases in which specific cues eventually, rather than immediately, led to the construction of highly detailed memories of trauma. As with the previous two examples, the specific cues rather than leading to memory construction when first coming to mind, evoked only a non-specific emotional response. For instance, a male victim of repeated sexual and physical abuse by his mother, became a outstanding scuba diver. By his own account he had always feared water, and in taking up the sport, in which he was to become expert, he attempted to come to terms with his fear. He described his first dive and the great sense of dread he felt when looking up at the silver surface of the water. This cue, the silver at the surface of the water, became particularly potent for this patient. He later recalled various memories of abuse and eventually recalled the first time he had seen the underside of water, in a terrifying episode in which his mother had tried to drown him. These memories, rather like those described by Salaman (1971), emerged suddenly; in fact in one episode the patient recovered three memories of abuse while driving his car which he then crashed as he blacked out at the emotional intensity of the memories. But memory recovery only began in earnest once the rememberer attempted to actively, consciously, persistently recall his childhood – this patient wanted to know what had happened in his childhood. In yet another case, which featured no single highly specific cue, a former beauty queen recalled how her father had systematically abused her over many years throughout infancy and adolescence (Terr 1994). The victim had adapted to the abuse by developing two versions of her autobiography, one for the 'day child' and one for the 'night child'. The two sets of memories did not intersect, although it seems from Terr's account that her patient was aware of the 'night child' but chose not to access knowledge available in this AM knowledge structure. When questioned by a trusted friend some years after the abuse had ceased she was able to disclose many of the abusive events.

Recovery of memories of experiences that were traumatic and of experiences which were not traumatic, indeed which were everyday experiences, frequently occurs to highly specific cues often when the rememberer is in a 'distracted' state. Memory recovery can also occur, again for memories of both traumatic and non-traumatic experiences, when the rememberer consciously and actively attempts to recall 'forgotten' events (see Erdelyi and Goldberg (1979) for a review of related research). Alternatively, and more frequently, memories may not have been forgotten but, rather, represented in the autobiographical knowledge base in such a way as to minimize access, as when memories of abuse are organized around a 'night child' structure. In this case the victim is aware, perhaps only in the most general of senses, that they have a history of abuse and can access specific knowledge about the abuse experiences if they so choose. Schooler *et al.* (Chapter 11 this volume) provide several very clear cases of this pattern of general awareness without access to specific memories prior to memory recovery. More generally, Harvey and Herman (1994, p. 297) observed that of the childhood abuse patients treated in their clinic 'Virtually all bring with them into psychotherapy a combination of long-remembered and more recently recalled material'.

According to the cognitive account there are two central factors that determine memory recovery: the organization of autobiographical knowledge and the retrieval process (as Freud (1900) recognized). Consider, first, the organization of autobiographical knowledge. Experiences will be represented in memory by lifetime periods, general events, and ESK. If the experiences are sufficiently coherent, i.e. thematically and conceptual related, then they may even be represented in the form of a 'mini-history' (Robinson 1992). The initial representation of these experiences in the AM knowledge base will be influenced by the self and its discrepancies, goals, and plans. In the case of repeated trauma, such as CSA, knowledge structures will be developed that represent this set of experiences. Given the dysfunctional nature of CSA experiences, the threat to self, feelings of powerlessness, physical pain, and negative affect, which they generate, then it would seem reasonable to assume that the resulting knowledge is represented in some interlinked way. Moreover, the cues which form indices between the different layers of knowledge will be specific in their content to the whole set of interrelated experiences and, in addition, may be marked by unique affect. The self-discrepancies which arise from the experience of trauma, and the plans and goals which they generate will determine what is retained and how. Although, as the model postulates, discrepancies and associated plans and goals will not necessarily be directly or explicitly represented in memory (cf. Conway 1996; Strauman 1990). Rather, the AM knowledge structures, the creation of which was modulated by the self, *reflect* in their organization and content the discrepancies, plans, and goals, of the traumatized self. By this view, representation in AM of repeated traumatic experiences does not differ from the representation of *any* other type of repeated experience, except in ways in which all AM knowledge structures differ from each other, i.e. in content and specific details of organisation.[8]

This view does not deny that AM records of trauma can take a primary role in promoting or supporting dysfunctional cognition, i.e. the creation and maintenance of negative self-schema. And in those individuals who continuously and effortfully expend resources avoiding or inhibiting the activation of potentially disruptive AM knowledge structures there must also be concomitant dysfunction due to resource depletion. Indeed, in this latter case it is the organization of the AM knowledge base which acts to facilitate the efficient

---

8 A potential exception to this is when the traumatic experiences are of events which occurred prior to the emergence of autobiographical memory. Autobiographical memories have been studied in children below the age of five years and even identified in preverbal children below the age of two years (see Fivush (1994) for a collection of recent studies and Fivush *et al.*, Chapter 3 this volume), suggesting that even at these very early ages memories of trauma may not differ in their principles of representation and organization from memories of non-traumatic experiences.

functioning of control processes. This is achieved by allowing access to different layers of AM knowledge which vary in their specificity. The construction of AMs is an effortful process and in everyday cognition the generation of highly specific memories is most probably not required or desirable (because of the costs on central resources). Organization of AM knowledge then intrinsically lends itself to 'surface' access, i.e. shallow activation of lifetime periods and general events. When a knowledge structures contains information relating to traumatic experiences – or indeed *any* experiences – then the system supports, by design, access to only the higher, more general, layers of knowledge. If in addition to this it is postulated that central processes modulate activation, then ways in which AM knowledge can be systematically 'forgotten' or 'suppressed' can be readily envisaged. For example, a CSA victim who experienced repeated trauma would encode their experiences into an interlinked set of AM knowledge structures. Encoding would be influenced by current self-discrepancies and associated plans and goals. Given the emotive and destabilizing nature of the encoded knowledge, structures which channelled initial access to more abstract layers of knowledge would be particularly beneficial as these would allow control processes to inhibit or enhance further activation of more specific knowledge according to the goals of active processing sequences and the discrepancies of the current configuration of the self. In this way access to a region of the AM knowledge base indexed by cues held in a lifetime period, such as *When I was abused*[9] (see Fig. 7.1) could be limited to only the lifetime period itself and further construction of full AMs prevented by inhibitory central control processing.

Alternatively, or additionally, the indexing cues of the lifetime period could be encoded in such a way as to impair access to general events and ESK. One possibility occurs when an the abused individual experiences disturbed states of consciousness during episodes of abuse. Dissociative states in which attention is narrowed to very specific aspects of the environment or internally generated cognitions, not conceptually related to the traumatic experience, may lead to AM knowledge representations in which the main cues facilitating access to specific knowledge are largely unusable by retrieval processes. That is to say that when these cues, held at some more abstract level of AM, are activated by retrieval processes, the activation which spreads from them makes available knowledge which the evaluation phase of the retrieval cycle cannot interpret, elaborate, or integrate with the retrieval model used to initiate access in the first place. Similarly, indexing cues created during traumatic experiences featuring disrupted consciousness, i.e. out-of-the-body perspective, may simply not be usable in later attempts to construct memories. Moreover, these restrictive indices formed during traumatic experiences may circumvent access by way other cues held in associated regions of the knowledge base. For instance, the

9 It is not suggested that such a lifetime period could seriously represent repeated experiences of abuse. The example is only for illustrative purposes.

cue *father* be will represented in many different AM knowledge structures and, according to our earlier reasoning, activation from this cue could spread at the level of general events into general events representing traumatic experiences. However, in order for activation to then spread to an indexing lifetime period there would have to be an association between the representation of *father* and knowledge held in the lifetime period. But if the knowledge in the lifetime period is dominated by a restrictive cue created during a period of abnormal consciousness then an appropriate index is unlikely to exist and, consequently, a stable pattern of activation cannot be formed across the knowledge structure.

The typical and normal organization of AM knowledge may then readily lend itself to the creation of knowledge structures which prevent or make difficult later access. At the same time, however, if a cue can activate ESK then a stable pattern of activation may be automatically generated within a AM knowledge structure or across an associated set of structures. When this occurs the probability of a memory being constructed is considerably raised. A major function of central control processes is to inhibit such patterns of activation entering into currently active processing sequences (Norman and Shallice 1980; see also Burgess and Shallice 1995), where typically they would have a disruptive effect; and this is the case regardless of the content of the activated knowledge. It is notable that many of Salaman's (1971) examples, and some of those described by Terr (1994), come from rememberers who were in distracted states when a memory was suddenly recovered. In distracted states, when the capacity of central control processes is fully used in a current processing task then the ability to inhibit the continuously arising patterns of activation in long-term memory may be reduced, with the consequence that some of these enter into the current processing sequence and 'spontaneous' or 'involuntary' memory construction occurs. In the more unusual case of recovery of the whole of the knowledge base following a period of global retrograde amnesia the effects of recovery of a single memory may be more wide-reaching. As a stable pattern is established by activation spreading from a single item of ESK, indices in the knowledge base become activated that can be used to access many other knowledge structures. For instance, once a lifetime period is activated, as activation spreads in a relatively unidirectional way from ESK through general event to lifetime period, then knowledge pertaining to significant others, locations, actions, goals, and plans characterizing that period become available to the retrieval process. These cues, which have many-to-many mappings to other lifetime periods and numerous general events, effectively provide (re)access to the whole of the knowledge base. It is particularly instructive to note that both GR and MM reported first retrieving memories of experiences closely associated with the initial memory that broke their retrograde amnesia. This suggests that indices activated in the initial memory construction accessed closely associated knowledge structures supporting the construction of related memories, i.e. of medical experiences and tennis matches respectively. This may reflect organization at the general event level and, conceivably, indicate mini-histories of associated experiences, for example *My medical history* and *My tennis career* (see Fig. 7.1), indexed, perhaps, by multiple lifetime periods. This whole phenomenon of re-establishing access to knowledge that can generate large sets of memories is, however, not limited solely to these (rare) neuropsychological cases. Virtually, all accounts of memory recovery in therapeutic settings outline a similar process: once a single memory is constructed then the construction of many other memories rapidly follows. The key feature of this, in both cases, appears to be reaccess of the indices that channel activation either through the whole knowledge base or through some subset of AM knowledge structures.

Memory recovery is an intrinsic feature of autobiographical remembering, and our current understanding of AM suggests a number of ways in which the process of recovery can occur. The underlying organization of knowledge may attenuate knowledge access simply because the indices binding together different types of knowledge are not usable by retrieval processes. It seems likely that this is the way in which most AM knowledge becomes inaccessible (Conway 1996). In cases of trauma the cues in the experiences which come to form indices in memory are unusual and unique to circumstances in which the self was threatened and conscious awareness was abnormal: because of this they restrict access to otherwise available knowledge. Recovery takes place when access to the indices is restored and this appears to be frequently effective when a single memory is constructed. The effect of constructing a single memory from knowledge in the attenuated region is to activate associated indices and this supports the construction of progressively more memories. Importantly, this account of memory inaccessibility (or constructability) and subsequent recovery is based on a cognitive account of AM and applies equally to all memories regardless of the content of any specific memory.

ERRONEOUS AND FALSE MEMORIES

Memories can be recovered, but are recovered memories 'accurate'? This question is at the heart of the recent recovered memories/false memories debate (for example Lindsey and Read 1994; Loftus 1993; Loftus and Ketcham 1994; Schooler 1994; Terr 1994), and in order to answer the question we must have some idea of what 'accuracy' might mean in the context of AM. The cognitive model conceives of AMs as transitory mental events in which stable patterns of activation in long-term memory enter into the operation of current control processes. Depending upon the nature of the temporarily instantiated memory certain states of conscious awareness may then follow (Conway *et al.* 1996; Dewhurst and Conway 1994; Gardiner 1988; Gardiner and Java 1993; Tulving 1985). But, because a memory is a combination of current and pre-stored knowledge it can never *only* be a record of past occurrence.

Furthermore, as a memory is always an incomplete record of an experience and as retrieval of the knowledge potentially available in an AM is limited by the cues that entered into the retrieval process, such that it is highly unlikely that all available knowledge could be retrieved in an single episode of construction, then any AM is necessarily a temporary and fragmentary record of a past experience. In addition to this, what is originally encoded into long-term memory is determined by control processes prevalent at the time and is, therefore, more an interpretation or comprehension of an experience rather than a veridical record of the external attributes of an experience.

If memories are fragmentary, transitory representations of the personal meanings of experiences, then the question 'Is this memory accurate?' is redundant. Instead we should ask 'In what ways could this memory be considered to be accurate?', 'Why and to what extent does the remember believe the memory to be accurate?', and 'What does this memory mean for the rememberer'?. One important way in which memories can be accurate is that they faithfully represent knowledge in long-term memory. For this to occur the influence of current control processes in memory construction would have to be minimal – as it perhaps is in the 'spontaneous' recovery of memories in distracted states. This variety of accuracy, based on internal consistency or correspondence, in which the retrieval environment is *integrated* with pre-stored knowledge (Conway *et al.* 1996), is certainly not what is usually meant when the term 'accuracy' is used in reference to memories. Nevertheless, it may be the primary and perhaps the only way in which AMs can be said to be 'accurate'. Of course, even in the case of a construction that was not directly or strongly influenced by current plans and goals of the self the knowledge in the AM knowledge base that constitutes the memory was, in turn, originally encoded in terms of past goals, plans, and comprehension of the experience. As a consequence, even when knowledge held in long-term memory becomes fully available this by no means leads to the construction of an accurate memory – for the AM knowledge may have been inaccurate in the first place. Thus, autobiographical memory might be said to be accurate to the extent that it faithfully reconstructs past interpretations of experiences, but past interpretations may themselves have been inaccurate representations of reality.

It does not follow from this that the veridicality of AM is minimal or non-existent – as we shall see it can be – but it does not have to be, and contrary to some views (for example, 1932; Loftus and Ketcham 1994; Neisser 1967, 1982, 1986), the veridicality of most AMs is probably high. The reason for this is straightforward; people comprehend effectively and respond adaptively to current experience. Given that events and the elemental actions and objects of which they are comprised as well as the socio-cultural context in which they are located are processed efficiently, any resulting memories must contain at least some, if not many, accurate details. Exactly which (accurate) details are retained in memory will depend on the dynamic cognitive model which determined processing at the time of experience (cf. Kahneman and Miller 1986). This same model will also determine the retention of inaccurate details. These could be as minor as retaining inferences which automatically arose during the processing of the experience but which were not themselves directly experienced (see Roediger and McDermott (1995) for a recent demonstration of this; Roediger *et al.* (Chapter 6) and Schacter *et al.* (Chapter 4) this volume and Johnson *et al.* (1993) for a review of source monitoring; Lindsay and Reed (1994) for a review of the substantial body of research into context effects, and Schacter (1995) for a wide-ranging review of memory distortions). Alternatively, erroneous details could be considerably more substantive and consist of major misinterpretations of an event and, in some cases, even encompass elaborate fantasies along with accurate details. Consider the following example from Johnson (1985):

My family was driving through the San Joaquin Valley in California when we had a flat tire. We didn't have a spare, so my father took the tire off the car and hitchhiked up the road to a gas station to get the tire patched. My mother, brother, sister, and I waited in the car. The temperature was over 100 degrees, extremely uncomfortable, and we got very thirsty. Finally, my sister took a couple of empty pop bottles and walked up the road to a farmhouse. The woman who lived there explained to her that the valley was suffering from a drought and she only had a little bottled-water left. She set aside a glass of water for her little boy, who would be home from school soon, and filled up my sister's pop bottles with the rest. My sister brought the water back to the car and we drank it. I also remembered feeling guilty that we didn't save any for my father, who would probably be thirsty when he got back with the repaired tire. (Johnson 1985, p. 1).

The error in Johnson's memory was pointed out by her parents who observed that although the car trip and breakdown had both occurred the water incident had not. Johnson (1985) suggests that as she waited in the hot car she may have fantasized the water incident and that this fantasy became integrated with her memory of the actual event with the consequence that the fantasy and the event could not be distinguished in her memory (see Conway 1995*a*, Chapter 2, for a review of similar memory errors). It follows, then, that if an event is misapprehended at the time of experience then later memories, although internally consistent and 'accurate' in the sense discussed previously, will contain erroneous details as well as accurate details. The frequency of such 'source monitoring errors' in everyday experience, when a rememberer fails to distinguish between what was actually experienced and what was internally generated, is unknown. However, the extensive work of Johnson and her colleagues (Johnson *et al.* 1993) has established that such errors can occur very frequently in even the simplest of laboratory experiments. A reasonable view is that in AM generally, minor source monitoring errors, in which an automatic inference is retained in memory as a detail of an event, are probably highly frequent. More gross errors in which whole fantasies become entangled in an AM knowledge structure are probably less frequent, but none the less do occur (Conway and Tacchi 1996). Any AM, whether recovered or not, whether of traumatic or everyday events, will then be likely to contain errors – errors that arise at encoding. These errors may often be minor and are represented along with many accurate details from which they are indistinguishable, and it is in in this sense that most AMs can be said to to be *basically* accurate. On the other hand external and internal experience may be encoded in such a way that any memory constructed from that knowledge will be grossly inaccurate or even false. Thus, paradoxically, AMs can be accurate in that they faithfully re-present long-term knowledge, at the same time as being strikingly inaccurate with respect to actual occurrence – as was the case for Johnson's (1985) memory.

One issue of particular interest in memory for traumatic events is the nature of the conditions which might predispose an individual to jointly encode both accurate and strikingly inaccurate details. A highly relevant set of proposals can be found in Gilbert's (1991) discussion of the creation of false beliefs. Gilbert considers Descartes (1644) account of how a proposition must be *comprehended* before a truth value can be assigned to it. According to the Cartesian view propositions are, as part of the comprehension process, assessed and marked for their truth or falsity prior to their integration in long-term memory. In contrast, Spinoza (1677) proposed that propositions were first represented (or 'accepted') in long-term memory and only later, if ever, evaluated for their truth value. In the Spinozan model a proposition (or experience) assessed as 'false' was marked in some way. However, propositions assessed as 'true' were left unmarked. In the Spinozan system it is not possible therefore to distinguish between propositions which have not been assessed (for their truth value) and propositions which have been assessed as true. In other words Spinoza's view was that the default assignment for long-term knowledge was that it was true unless judged false. Gilbert (1991) in his subsequent review of the psychological literature concluded that the evidence very strongly favoured the Spinozan over the Cartesian view. Of particular relevance to present concerns are Gilbert's discussion of the developmental emergence of doubt and the creation of false beliefs under conditions of stress. As Gilbert points out, theorists from the philosopher Thomas Reid (1895) through William James (1890) to Piaget (1962), and more recent commentators, have observed that doubt is less quickly acquired than belief, much as the Spinozan, but not the Cartesian, view would predict. The ability to reject propositions in a truth-functional negation is developmentally late (Bloom 1970; Pea 1980) and children who have yet to develop this form of negation are suggestible and biased towards accepting propositions as true (Ceci *et al.* 1987; Ceci and Bruck 1993). The implications of this for childhood memories are far reaching, and suggest that memories of events dating to before the period of the emergence of doubt are highly unlikely to contain any knowledge which might allow a rememberer to distinguish what is accurate in a memory construction from what is inaccurate, even when a memory is a fully coherent structure that accurately represents information originally formed at encoding.

Assessing the truth value of a proposition or a memory, or indeed some other mental representation, is a function of central control processes. The assessment process may be initiated by externally presented information, i.e. someone who was there tells you memory is wrong, or by internally generated information such as noticing an inconsistency or impossibility in a memory (cf. Neisser (1982) for an account of an 'impossibility' in a memory; Thomas and Cowan (1986) for particularly interesting modification of the noted 'impossibility'; and Neisser (1986) for a discussion of the role of a past self in bringing about his 'impossible' memory; Conway (1995) also reviews this debate). If, however, the capacity of central control processes is taken up by some other processing sequence then assessment cannot take place. But representation in memory can and by the Spinozan view (and by the available evidence – see Gilbert, 1991) this leads to long-term knowledge that by default is 'true'. Consider then a child or adult who experiences (repeated) trauma. Inevitably each experience must draw heavily upon the capacity of control process and in so doing create the conditions for the encoding of a memory in which inference and comprehension cannot be distinguished from experience. For an individual who has yet to develop truth functional negation and who experiences extreme stress at the time of encoding then the creation of long-term memory representations which mix externally acquired with internally generated knowledge will be maximized.

Errors in the knowledge base from which memories will later be constructed, established at or close in time to actual experiences, can give rise to memories which are basically accurate but contain minor errors or to memories that are grossly incorrect but which, none the less, contain some accurate details. Erroneous memories can also arise during retrieval. Schacter (1995) provides a thorough review of the main research areas in which such errors have been persistently observed. Here the discussion is confined to a few illustrative lines of research (see Schacter (1995) or Lindsay and Read (1994) for more comprehensive coverage). Neisser and Harsch (1992) in their recent study of flashbulb memories for the space shuttle *Challenger* disaster uncovered a particularly interesting form of retrieval-based error. In their study students gave an account, within 24 hours, of the personal circumstances under which they had first learned the news and then gave a second account over two years later. If the students had flashbulb memories then the two accounts should be highly similar even at the level of minutiae (Brown and Kulik 1977; Conway 1995a; Conway *et al.* 1994). In fact, Neisser and Harsch found that very few of their subjects gave similar accounts at retest. Most strikingly, many of the students gave *completely different* accounts and stood by these even when confronted with their first (handwritten), presumably correct, accounts. When this occurred the second account to be given very often had a 'TV-focus'. It seems that as the students would have been exposed to the news on a number of different occasions, i.e. were originally informed by a friend and then watched coverage of the explosion on the evening news, then when recalling (after a delay) the occasion when they first heard the news they select an incorrect memory.

These 'wrong-time-slice' errors (Brewer 1988) are particularly interesting for two reasons. First, they suggest that when recalling a specific event from a list of repeated events the retrieval process is driven by beliefs that are centrally generated. Essentially the rememberer elaborates a memory description which contains cues as to when they would have been *most likely* to have experienced the target event. Second, once retrieved it appears, at least in the case of Neisser and Harsch's student subjects, that the memory constructed on the basis of the belief-generated cues blocks access to other memories and to the original target memory – which is why the students denied that their original accounts were correct.

When retrieval is driven by a probabilistic set of cues selected for their likelihood of accessing sought-for-knowledge there is an additional potential for the creation of false memories rather than or in addition to wrong-time-slice memories. Consider the case of recovery from a false memory which came to light in our recent studies of flashbulb memories (Cohen *et al.* 1994; Conway *et al.* 1994) for the unexpected resignation of the British Prime Minister Margaret Thatcher. In the Cohen *et al.* (1995) study a very active 74-year-old man (this subject's data were not used in the study) originally described, in some detail, how he first learned the news of the resignation lying in bed listening to the 6.30 a.m. radio news. (Note that this could not have been on the actual day of the resignation as the news was announced at about 9.30 in the morning.) He appended a letter to his memory questionnaire (subjects were sampled by post) describing how after completing the questionnaire he began to doubt that he had accurately remembered his personal circumstances and commented that it was only after completing the questionnaire that he realized that he did not remember how he had learned the news. He was both disturbed and disappointed by this as he had very much wanted to retain this memory which for him, as a strong supporter of Mrs Thatcher, was a personally significant if sad event. After apparently many failed attempts to retrieve the memory he eventually asked his wife who was not taking part in the study to read his questionnaire responses. She was surprised at the wholly inaccurate responses he had made and reminded him that he had in fact first learned the news carrying out charity work at a local hospital bazaar. While at his stall selling plants the treasurer of their charity had announced the news of the resignation. Once reminded he commented 'Then I remembered it all' and provided a minutely detailed account of exactly how he had learned the news including his exact activity and the names and activities of others present. One year later, when retested, he provided virtually the same description including consistent accounts of minutiae of the event.

This case illustrates how a false memory might be created. The subject first generates a plausible memory description with which to search memory. For this person and this event the description consists of a representation of where he would typically be when catching the early morning news – drinking tea in bed. Let us assume that this description itself is based on knowledge activated in long-term memory which could conceivably be a personal script for his daily routine. The description is accurate, in the sense that it represents a habitually true state of the world, but it fails to lead to the retrieval of knowledge of any single event. There now arise two possibilities: the rememberer might simply respond by relating the memory description in the full knowledge that the 'memory' may be incorrect or the response may be made because the rememberer (mistakenly) believes the memory description to be an actual memory. The latter of these possibilities corresponded to the memories described by the elderly group sampled in the Cohen *et al.* 1994 study. Of the 60 per cent of older subjects who gave strikingly inconsistent memory descriptions over the two test sessions, with a retention interval of 11 months, virtually all showed a shift from a description of a specific event to a description of an event that was clearly schematized and which was often completely disjunct with the original description. The schema-driven erroneous description frequently had a 'bedroom focus' or 'kitchen focus', i.e. places the rememberer would most probably have first heard the news of the resignation. It is interesting to note that in the example cited above, intervention by the rememberer's wife appears to have 'innoculated' his memory against this error as 12 months later he was able to give a highly consistent and detailed account.

The emergence of schema-driven false memories has been examined in other studies which sampled a wider range of everyday events. For example, in studies by Barclay and his colleagues (Barclay 1986; Barclay and DeCooke 1988; Barclay and Subramaniam 1987; Barclay and Wellman 1986) subjects recorded everyday events in specially designed diaries over a period of a few weeks. The experimenters then created various foils by changing critical details of the diary entries. After a delay the diarists took a recognition test in which they discriminated between true and altered diary records. The main finding was that alterations which did not violate the meaning of the original records were not discriminable from unaltered records. Barclay and Wellman (1986) concluded that when a description of a purportedly experienced event corresponded closely to self-schema and AM knowledge structures then the probability of that description being accepted as a true description was increased. In a recent paper following on from Barclay's studies, (Conway *et al.* 1996) diarists recorded events over a six-month period. One innovation in the Conway *et al.* study was that each day the diarists recorded actual events as well as false events. False events were events which could plausibly have occurred on the day of recording but had not. The diarists also recorded naturally occurring thoughts and thoughts that were plausible but which had been contrived for the purposes of the study. For each record the diarists gave ratings of importance, consequentiality, affect, and distinctiveness of the event or thought and predicted what these ratings would have been had the event actually occurred.

In recognition tests taken some months later the diarists discriminated between true and false diary entries, and true and contrived thoughts.[10] False descriptions of events and contrived thoughts were incorrectly recognized as true and the false memory rate was found to be reliably higher for thoughts than for events. In a structural equation analysis of ratings collected at encoding and of further ratings collected at retrieval it was found that for true events the encoding and retrieval measures were closely integrated. For false memories of events and true and false memories of thoughts, no integration between the various measures was present. Conway *et al.* (1996) conclude that the *integration* between knowledge in the retrieval environment with AM knowledge is critical in promoting accurate memory. When this integration or embeddedness (Johnson and Raye 1981) of the retrieval environment with AM knowledge diminishes but a cue none the less remains highly plausible, then the false memory rate rises. One further notable finding was that contrived thoughts falsely recognized as spontaneously occurring everyday thoughts were often associated with imagery at retrieval. It appeared that imagery played a disproportionate role in the creation of false memories of thoughts. Imagery at retrieval may be one of the factors that act to convince a rememberer that their memory is true.

The influential roles of integration and imagery in false memories has also been observed in young children (Ceci *et al.* 1994*a*). In these studies children were presented with a list of events some of which they had experienced and some of which they had not. In the following 7 to 10 days after presentation the children repeatedly studied the events on the list, and for each event they were instructed to 'think real hard if it happened'. About one-third of the children came to believe in the false events and, importantly, developed memories to them. These memories were well embedded in the child's own AM and featured others, actions, and locations, not suggested by the experimenters but drawn from the child's own autobiographical knowledge. Thus, the false memories became integrated with AM and in a later study Ceci *et al.* (1994*b*) found that asking children to repeatedly recall (rather than judge the truth of) fictitious events produced an even higher false memory rate. It seems that in this later manipulation those children who developed false memories repeatedly rehearsed images of the false event. In a similar vein, Loftus (1993) described a number of naturally occurring cases of false memories and reported a study in which a small group of subjects, including two children and a teenager, came to believe in a childhood memory of being lost in a shopping mall. As in the other studies this fictitious story became integrated with long-term memory and elaborated into a memory replete with images and specific details (see Hyman and Billings (1996) and Hyman *et al.* (1995) for recent demonstrations of the same phenomenon of false memories in adults). In all these studies, many of the children who developed false memories were resistant to counter information and would not relinquish belief in the veracity of their memories even when confronted by various authority figures who explained how the memories had come about.

10 A further set of foils were generated by the experimenter, based on the diary records and corresponding to the foils used by Barclay and Wellman (1986); see Conway *et al.* (1996) for details.

In this respect, the children in the studies of Ceci and his colleagues are similar to the college students in Neisser and Harsch's (1992) flashbulb memory study who also resisted counter evidence to their mistaken memories. In both cases it seems likely that the false memories were a type of *source monitoring* error (Johnson *et al.* 1993) in which the rememberer becomes unable to distinguish the source of knowledge in long-term memory, i.e. imagined or thought about knowledge cannot be discriminated from knowledge arising from direct experience.

Source monitoring failures probably also account for the false memory rate in the Conway *et al.* (1996) diary study, However, a critical point considered by Conway *et al.* is how the rememberer comes to accept a mental construction as a memory of an experienced event. Conway *et al.* argued that when a cue, or description, maps onto pre-stored autobiographical knowledge and leads to an integration between the retrieval environment and long-term knowledge and no contradictory knowledge is accessed or 'impossibilities' generated, then there is nothing in the construction process or the resulting mental representation that can inform the rememberer as to whether or not the memory is true. Under these conditions, the rememberer must rely upon other aspects of the construction process in order to arrive at a judgment of the validity of the memory. Fluency of integration and imagery are two important sources of information that might sway a rememberer to accept the transitory representation as true. So when a memory comes quickly and effortlessly to mind accompanied by imagery then the probability of accepting the memory as being of an actual experience is raised. However, an additional source of information about the veracity of a memory is the nature of conscious awareness that accompanies the instantiation of the memory.

Tulving (1985, 1990) drew a distinction between two different types of memory awareness characteristic of accurate or true memories. One type of memory awareness – autonoetic consciousness – is characterized by *recollective experience* (cf. Dewhurst and Conway 1994; Gardiner 1988; Rajaram 1993; Tulving 1985) and features the conscious recollection of the occurrence of a previously studied item or experience, recall of details such as thoughts, feelings, sensory-perceptual experiences associated with the encoding event, and a sense of 'pastness'. The other type of memory awareness – noetic consciousness – does not feature recollective experience and is associated only with feelings of familiarity. In noetic states of consciousness a detail of an event or the event itself when recalled or recognized gives rise to a feeling of familiarity but does not give rise to other features of phenomenal experience such as sensory-perceptual experience and a sense of 'pastness' or of the self in the past. The diarists in the Conway *et al.* (1996) study indicated their state of memory awareness, recollective experience or familiarity, for each diary record judged to be 'old' or accurate. A key question here was whether false memories would be accompanied by recollective experience or by familiarity. False memories were found to be much more strongly associated with familiarity than recollective experience and this was especially evident in false memories for thoughts. Nevertheless, recollective experience for some false memories to both events and thoughts was observed. Conway *et al.* concluded that when AM knowledge is activated and a memory representation created, and in the absence of any other disconfirming knowledge, then a feeling of familiarity may be sufficient to convince a rememberer that a false description is a description of a true experience. When this occurs and a memory is recollectively experienced then confidence in the veracity of a false memory is extremely strong. Thus, state of conscious awareness at retrieval can be an influential factor in erroneously accepting a memory as true or accurate.

Different states of consciousness associated with the construction of AMs must be modulated by a central control process which responds to knowledge that becomes available during the retrieval cycle (cf. Dewhurst and Conway 1994; Jacoby *et al.* 1989). If this is the case, then patients with neurological damage to brain areas associated with control processes, i.e. the frontal lobes, should shown unusual patterns of autonoetic and noetic consciousness during remembering. Recent evidence indicates that this is the case. Schacter and Curran (1996), for example, described the recognition memory performance of their patient BG, who had sustained an infarction of the right frontal lobe but who did not confabulate. Nevertheless, BG had an abnormally high false positive rate in standard recognition tests and often claimed to have recollective experience for foils he incorrectly identified as 'old' (cf. Roediger and McDermott (1995) for related findings with intact subjects). In subsequent studies it was found that BG did not make these errors when the to-be-recognized items were from various categories and the foils from a different set of categories. Schacter and Curran argued that this pattern of findings reflected an impairment of strategic encoding mediated by a dysfunction of central control processes. Essentially, BG encoded the unstructured word list simply as '*a list of words*', when later presented with the recognition test all the words he was able to link to the knowledge structure '*a list of words*' led to recollective experience. In the categorized list only words he was able to associate with the categories were recollectively experienced. Thus, Schacter and Curran's findings further indicate that the integration of knowledge in the retrieval environment with pre-stored knowledge can be sufficient to bring about recollective experience: although, of course, this is abnormal due to the frontal injuries. Similarly, Dalla Barba's (1993) patient MB who, following brain injury to the frontal lobes, produced persistent and consistent confabulations featuring people, locations, and actions, from his own autobiographical knowledge. These memories were configured in events that had not occurred or in events that had occurred but not as described (and were, therefore, formally equivalent to the false events created by Barclay and Wellman (1986) and Conway *et al.* (1996)). For example, MB frequently and persistently described visiting his wife the day previously (in fact his wife was dead), visiting his mother in hospital who had died just before he arrived, or recounting long stories of shopping trips and being lost in Paris, none of which had actually occurred. As Dalla Barba (1993) points out, it would be difficult for an uninformed observer to detect that these were confabulations as, in principle at least, these and other events could plausibly have occurred. MB's confabulations were solely limited to his autobiographical knowledge and he was unaware that his 'memories' constructed from this knowledge were confabulations. He was unable to distinguish between confabulated and non-confabulated memories, and both types of memories were recollectively experienced (see Conway and Tacchi (1996) for a related case of motivated confabulations).

Memories which contain either minor or major errors and memories which are wholly false arise in number of different ways. The source of some incorrect memories can be traced to the intermingling of knowledge arising from external experiences with knowledge arising from co-occurring internal processes. When these two types of knowledge are stored together in an AM knowledge structure then it is difficult, if not impossible, for the rememberer to discriminate the source of different types of knowledge in a memory construction. Memory errors and false memories also emerge in retrieval when cues map onto to pre-stored AM knowledge and lead to representations which are at least partly integrated with the AM knowledge base. Often these types of memory construction will be associated with feelings of familiarity. Because of the dynamic and interactive nature of encoding and memory construction it is simply not possible, in the absence of other independent information, for a rememberer or an observer to accurately distinguish true from false memories and, consequently, the veracity of recovered memories cannot be established. Despite this, true memories have certain characteristics which can increase the confidence of a rememberer and of an observer that a memory construction is of an actual past experience. Typically, true memories are constructed fluently, they are tightly integrated with the AM knowledge base, they feature strong imagery, and lead to recollective experience. The evidence indicates that memories which have these qualities are far more likely to be true (in the sense that the recalled event actually occurred but not necessarily true in that all the recalled details are correct) than they are to be false. For memories which do not feature, or which are lower in, these qualities, i.e. which are difficult to construct, poorly integrated with the AM knowledge base, associated with weak or vague images, and which lead to feelings of familiarity rather than recollective experience, then the incidence of false memories (memories of experiences which never occurred) increases. Memories with these latter qualities need close scrutiny and claims concerning their truth content should be treated with scepticism.

CONCLUDING COMMENT: MEMORIES AND FANTASIES

A central purpose of this chapter has been to demonstrate that a cognitive model of autobiographical memory can be profitably used to understand both memory recovery and the generation of false memories. Claims that certain types of AMs, i.e. memories of CSA, fall outside the scope of the constructivist account of AM, and therefore should be treated separately, are simply wrong. It is a remarkable fact that Freud's prescient writing on AM in the *Studies of hysteria* (Breuer and Freud) and in *The interpretation of dreams* (1900) seems to have been so completely forgotten. The cognitive model of AM outlined earlier, which was developed independently of Freud's work and which is based on laboratory research, is highly compatible with Freud's original account of memory. Possibly Freud's sophisticated thinking about AM has been overshadowed by his later rejection of the 'seduction theory' in favour of the view that the 'memories' he encountered in his clinical work were largely fantasies representing unexpressible emotions and motivations from early childhood. Indeed, much has been made of this (i.e. Masson 1984) but it is by no means clear that Freud did in fact fully repudiate the seduction theory. Later psychoanalysts such as Kris (1956) considered that Freud never came to terms with the question of whether memories recovered in therapy were of actual events or fantasies or some mixture of both. Kris himself regarded the issue as unresolvable and instead proposed understanding 'memories' in the context of an individual's whole autobiography. For Kris it was the personal meanings of such memories that were important, and critical to the goal of therapy. The study of AM by cognitive psychologists bears many similarities to Kris's project and can be thought of as a development of both Freud's and Kris's proposals concerning AM. As Erdelyi and Goldberg (1979) point out, Freud's thinking on AM was held back by lack of an appropriate model with which to communicate his theory, and much the same can be said for Kris. The cognitive model with its emphasis on representation (the organization of knowledge) and the functions of control processes in coordinating memory construction suggests specific mechanisms that support variable knowledge access and the creation of both true and false memories. In this, the cognitive model demonstrates ways in which memories can be recovered, without postulating different mechanisms for different types of experiences, and it shows that *all* memories are mental constructions which encompass the present as well as the past.

REFERENCES

APA (American Psychiatric Association) (1986). *Diagnostic and statistical manual of mental disorders (3rd ed.) (DSM-IIr)*. APA, Washington DC.

Anderson, S.J. (1993). *Organization of specific autobiographical memories*. Doctoral dissertation, Lancaster University.

Anderson, M.C. and Bjork, R.A. (1996). Mechanisms of inhibition in long-term memory: a new taxonomy. In *Inhibition in attention, memory, and language*, (ed. D. Dagenbach and T. Carr). Academic, New York.

Anderson, S.A. and Conway, M.A. (1993). Investigating the structure of autobiographical memories. *Journal of Experimental Psychology: Learning, Memory, and Cognition*, **19**, 1178–96.

Baddeley, A.D. (1986), *Working memory*. Clarendon, Oxford.

Baddeley, A.D. and Wilson, B. (1986). Amnesia, autobiographical memory, confabulation. In *Autobiographical memory*, (ed. D.C. Rubin), pp. 225–52. Cambridge University Press.

Barclay, C.R. (1986). Schematization of autobiographical memory. In *Autobiographical memory* (ed. D.C. Rubin), pp. 82–99. Cambridge University Press.

Barclay, C.R. and DeCooke, P.A. (1988). Ordinary everyday memories: some of the things of which selves are made. In *Remembering reconsidered: ecological and traditional approaches to the study of memory*, (ed. U. Neisser and E. Winograd), pp. 91–125. Cambridge University Press, New York.

Barclay, C.R. and Subramaniam, G. (1987). Autobiographical memories and self-schemata. *Applied Cognitive Psychology*, **1**, 169–82.

Barclay, C.R. and Wellman, H.M. (1986). Accuracies and inaccuracies in autobiographical memories. *Journal of Memory and Language*, **25**, 93–103.

Barsalou, L.W. (1988). The content and organization of autobiographical memories. In *Remembering reconsidered: ecological and traditional approaches to the study of memory*, (ed. U. Neisser and E. Winograd), pp. 193–243. Cambridge University Press.

Bartlett, F.C. (1932). *Remembering: a study in experimental and social psychology*. Cambridge University Press.

Bloom, L. (1970). *Language development: form and function in emerging grammars*. MIT Press, Cambridge, MA.

Breuer, J. and Freud, S. (1895). Studies on hysteria. In *The standard edition of the complete psychological works of Sigmund Freud*, Vol. 2, (ed. J. Strachey). Hogarth, London.

Brewer, W.F. (1988). Memory for randomly sampled autobiographical events. In *Remembering reconsidered: ecological and traditional approaches to the study of memory*, (ed. U. Neisser and E. Winograd), pp. 21–90. Cambridge University Press, New York.

Brewin, C.R., (1989). Cognitive change processes in psychotherapy. *Psychological Review*, **96**, 379–94.

Brewin, C.R., Dalgleish, T., and Joseph, S. (1995). A dual representation theory of post-traumatic stress disorder. (In preparation.)

Brown, R. and Kulik, J. (1977). Flashbulb memories. *Cognition*, **5**, 73–99.

Brown, N.R., Shevell, S.K., and Rips L.J. (1986). Public memories and their personal context. In *Autobiographical Memory*, (ed. D.C. Rubin), pp. 137–58. Cambridge University Press.

Burgess, P.W. and Shallice, T. (1995). Confabulation and the control of normal memory. *Memory*. (In press.)

Ceci, S.J. and Bruck, M. (1993). The suggestibility of the child witness: a historical review and synthesis. *Psychological Bulletin*, **113**, 403–39.

Ceci, S.J., Ross, D.F., and Toglia, M.P. (1987). Suggestibility of children's memory: psycholegal implications. *Journal of Experimental Psychology: General*, **116**, 38–49.

Ceci, S.J., Huffman, M.L., Smith, E., and Loftus, E.F. (1994a). Repeatedly thinking about a non-event: source misattributions among preschoolers. *Consciousness and Cognition*, **3**, 388–407.

Ceci, S.J., Loftus, E.F., Leichtman, M.D., and Bruck, M. (1994b). The possible role of source misattributions in the creation of false beliefs among preschoolers. *The International Journal of Clinical and Experimental Hypnosis*, **17**, 304–20.

Ceci, S.J., Leichtman, M., and White, T. (1995). Interviewing pre-schoolers: remembrance of things planted. In *The child witness: cognitive, social, and legal issues*, (ed. D.P. Peters). Kluwer, Dordrecht. (In press.)

Christenson, R.M., Walker, J.I., Ross, D.R., and Maltbie, A. (1981). Reactivation of traumatic conflicts. *American Journal of Psychiatry*, **138**, 984–5.

Christianson, S-A. and Nilsson, L-G (1989). Hysterical amnesia: a case of aversively motivated isolation of memory. In *Aversion, avoidance, and anxiety: perspectives on aversively motivated behaviour*, (ed. T. Archer and L-G. Nilsson), pp. 289–310. Erlbanm, Hillsdale, NJ.

Cohen, G., Conway, M.A., and Maylor, E. (1994). Flashbulb memories in older adults. *Psychology and Aging*, **9**, 454–63.

Conway, M.A. (1990*a*). *Autobiographical memory: an introduction*. Open University Press, Buckingham.

Conway, M.A. (1990*b*). Autobiographical memory and conceptual representation. *Journal of Experimental Psychology: Learning, Memory, and Cognition*, **16**, 799–812.

Conway, M.A. (1991). In defense of everyday memory. *American Psychologist*, **46**, 19–26.

Conway, M.A. (1992). A structural model of autobiographical memory. In *Theoretical perspectives on autobiographical memory*, (ed. M.A. Conway, D.C. Rubin, H. Spinnler and W.A. Wagenaar), pp. 167–94. Kluwer, Dordrecht.

Conway, M.A. (1993). Impairments of autobiographical memory. In *Handbook of neuropsychology*, (8th edn), (ed. H. Spinnler and F. Boller), pp. 175–92. Elsevier, Amsterdam.

Conway, M.A. (1995*a*). *Flashbulb memories*. Erlbaum, Hove.

Conway, M.A. (1995*b*). Failures of autobiographical remembering. In *Basic and applied memory: theory in context* (ed. D. Herrmann, M. Johnson, C. McEvoy, C. Hertzog, and P. Hertel). Erlbaum, Hillsdale, NJ.

Conway, M.A. (1996). Autobiographical knowledge and autobiographical memories. In *Remembering our past: studies in autobiographical memory*, (ed. D.C. Rubin), pp. 76–105. Cambridge University Press.

Conway, M.A. and Bekerian, D.A. (1987). Organization in autobiographical memory. *Memory & Cognition*, **15**, 119–32.

Conway, M.A. and Rubin, D.C. (1993). The structure of autobiographical memory. In *Theories of memory*, (ed. A.E. Collins, S.E. Gathercole, M.A. Conway, and P.E.M. Morris) pp. 103–37. Erlbaum, Hove.

Conway, M.A. and Tacchi, P.C. (1996). Motivated confabulation. *Neurocase*. (In press.)

Conway, M.A., Anderson, S.J., Larsen, S.F., Donnelly, C.M., McDaniel, M.A., McClelland, A.G.R., Rawles, R.E., and Logie, R.H. (1994). The formation of flashbulb memories. *Memory & Cognition*, **22**, 326–43.

Conway, M.A., Collins, A.F., Gathercole, S.E., and Anderson, S.J. (1996). Recollections of true and false autobiographical memories. *Journal of Experimental Psychology: General*, **125(1)**, 69–95.

Crowder, R.G. (1993). Systems and principles in memory theory: Another critique of pure memory. In *Theories of memory*, (ed. A.E. Collins, S.E. Gathercole, M.A. Conway, and P.E.M. Morris), pp. 139–61. Erlbaum, Hove.

Dalla Barba, G. (1993). Confabulation: knowledge and recollective experience. *Cognitive Neuropsychology*, **10**, 1–20.

Descartes, R. (1984). Fourth meditation. In *The Philosophical writings of Descartes* Vol.2, (ed. and trans. J. Cottingham, R. Stoothoff and D. Murdoch), pp. 37–43. Cambridge University Press. (Original work published 1641).

Dewhurst, S.A. and Conway, M.A. (1994). Pictures, images, and recollective experience. *Journal of Experimental Psychology: Learning, Memory, and Cognition*, **20**, 1088–98.

Ericsson, K.A. and Kintsch, W. (1995). Long-term working memory. *Psychological Review*, **102**, 211–45.

Erdelyi, M.H. (1985). *Psychoanalysis: Freud's cognitive psychology*. Freeman, New York.

Erdelyi, M.H. and Goldberg, B. (1979). Let's not sweep repression under the rug: toward a cognitive psychology of repression. In *Functional disorders of memory*, (ed. J.F. Kihlstrom and F.J. Evans), pp. 355–402. Erlbaum, Hillsdale, NJ.

Fine, B.D., Joseph, E.D., and Waldhorn, H.F. (ed.) (1971). *Recollection and reconstruction* and *Reconstruction in psychoanalysis*, Monongraph IV: The Kris Study Group of the New York Psychoanalytic Insititute. International Universities Press, New York.

Fivush, R. (1994). Long-term retention of infant memories. *Memory*, **4**, 337–475.

Freud, S. (1900). The interpretation of dreams. In *The standard edition of the complete psychological works of Sigmund Freud*, Vols. 4–5, (ed. J. Strachey). Hogarth, London.

Freud, S. (1925). A note on the mystic writing pad. In *The standard edition of the complete psychological works of Sigmund Freud*, Vol. 19, (ed. J. Strachey). Hogarth, London.

Gardiner, J.M. (1988). Functional aspects of recollective experience. *Memory & Cognition*, **16**, 309–13.

Gardiner, J.M. and Java, R.I. (1993). Recognizing and remembering. In *Theories of memory*, (ed. A.E. Collins, S.E. Gathercole, M.A. Conway and P.E.M. Morris), pp. 163–88. Erlbaum, Hove.

Gilbert, D.T. (1991). How mental systems believe. *American Psychologist*, **46**, 107–19.

Harvey, M.R. and Herman, J.L. (1994). Amnesia, partial amnesia, and delayed recall among adult survivors of childhood trauma. *Consciousness and Cognition*, **3**, 295–306.

Higgins, E.T. (1987). Self-discrepancy: a theory relating self and affect. *Psychological Review*, **94**, 319–40.

Holmes, D. (1990). Th evidence for repression: an examination of sixty years of research. In *Repression and dissociation: Implications for personality, theory, psychopathology, and health*, (ed. J. Singer), pp. 85–102. University of Chicago Press.

Hyman, I.E., Jr. and Billings, J.F. (1995). Individual differences and the creation of false childhood memories. *Memory*. (In press.)

Hyman, I.E., Jr., Husband, T.H., and Billings, J.F. (1995). False memories of childhood experiences. *Applied Cognitive Psychology*, **9**, 181–97.

James, W. (1890). *The principles of psychology*, Vol. 2. Holt, New York.

Jacoby, L.L., Kelley, C.M., and Dywan, J. (1989). Memory attributions. In *Varieties of memory and consciousness. Essays in honour of Endel Tulving*, (ed. H.L. Roediger and F.I.M. Craile), pp. 391–421. Erlbaum, Hillsdale, NJ.

Johnson, M.K. (1985). The origin of memories. In *Advances in cognitive-behavioural research and therapy*, Vol. 4, (ed. P.C. Kendall), pp. 1–27. Academic, New York.

Johnson, M.K. (1988). Reality monitoring: an experimental phenomenological approach. *Journal of Experimental Psychology: General*, **117**, 390–4.

Johnson, M.K. and Raye, C.L. (1981). Reality monitoring. *Psychological Review*, **88**, 67–85.

Johnson, M.K., Foley, M.A., Suengas, A.G., and Raye, C.L. (1988). Phenomenal characteristics of memories for perceived and imagined autobiographical events. *Journal of Experimental Psychology: General*, **117**, 371–6.

Johnson, M.K., Hashtroudi, S., and Lindsay, D.S. (1993). Source monitoring. *Psychological Bulletin*, **114**, 3–28.

Johnson-Laird, P.N. (1983). *Mental models*. Harvard University Press, Cambridge, MA.

Kahneman, D. and Miller, D.T. (1986). Norm theory: comparing reality to its alternatives. *Psychological Review*, **93**, 136–53.

Kolers, P.A. (1973). Remembering operations. *Memory & Cognition*, **1**, 347–55.

Kolers, P.A. and Roediger, H.L. III (1984). Procedures of mind. *Journal of Verbal Learning and Verbal Behaviour*, **23**, 425–49.

Kris, E. (1956). The personal myth: a problem in psychoanalytic technique. In *The selected papers of Ernst Kris*. Yale University Press, New Haven, CT. (Collection published 1975.)

Kris, E. (1975). *The selected papers of Ernst Kris*. Yale University Press, New Haven, CT.

Lindsay, D.S. and Johnson, M.K. (1989). The eyewitness suggestibility effect and memory for source. *Memory & Cognition*, **17**, 349–58.

Lindsay, D.S. and Reed, J.D. (1994). Psychotherapy and memories of childhood sexual abuse: a cognitive perspective. *Applied Cognitive Psychology*, **8**, 281–337.

Lindsay, D.S. and Reed, J.D. (1995). 'Memory Work' and recovered memories of childhood sexual abuse: scientific evidence and public, professional, and personal issues. *Psychology, Public Policy and Law*. (In press.)

Linton, M. (1975). Memory for real-world events. In *Explorations in cognition*, (ed. D.A. Norman and D.E. Rumelhart), pp. 376–404. Freeman, San Francisco.

Linton, M. (1986). Ways of searching and the contents of memory. In *Autobiographical Memory* (ed. D.C. Rubin), pp. 50–67. Cambridge University Press.

Loftus, E.F. (1993). The reality of repressed memories. *American Psychologist*, **48**, 518–37.

Loftus, E.F. and Ketcham, K. (1994). *The myth of repressed memory*. St Martin's Press, New York.

Lucchelli, F., Muggia, S., and Spinnler, H. (1995). The 'Petites Madeleines' phenomenon in two amnesic patients. Sudden recovery of forgotten memories. *Brain*. **118**, 167–83.

Markus, H. and Nurius, P. (1986). Possible selves. *American Psychologist*, **41**, 954–69.

Moscovitch, M. (1992). A neuropsychological model of memory and consciousness. In *Neuropsychology of memory*, (2nd edn), (ed. L.R. Squire and N. Butters), pp. 5–22. Guilford Press, New York.

Mullin, P.A., Herrmann, D.J., and Searleman, A. (1993). Forgotten variables in memory theory and research. *Memory*, **1**, 43–64.

Neisser, U. (1967). *Cognitive psychology*. Appleton-Century-Crofts, New York.

Neisser, U. (1982). Snapshots or benchmarks? In *Memory observed: remembering in natural contexts* (ed. U. Neisser), pp. 43–8. W.H. Freeman, San Francisco.

Neisser, U. (1986). Remembering Pearl Habor: reply to Thompson and Cowan. *Cognition*, **23**, 285–6.

Neisser, U. and Harsch, N. (1992). Phantom flashbulbs: false recollections of hearing the news about *Challenger*. In *Affect and accuracy in recall: studies of flashbuld memories'*, (ed. E. Winograd and U. Neisser), pp. 9–31. Cambridge University Press.

Norman, D.A. and Bobrow, D.G. (1979). Descriptions and intermediate stage in memory retrieval. *Cognitive Psychology*, **11**, 107–23.

Norman, D.A and Shallice, T. (1980). Attention to action: willed and automatic control of behaviour. *Technical report No. 99*. University of California, San Diego.

Oatley, K. (1992). *The best laid schemes. The psychology of emotions*. Cambridge University Press.

Oatley, K. and Johnson-Laird, P.N. (1987). Towards a cognitive theory of emotions. *Cognition and Emotion* **1**, 29–50.

Ofshe, R. and Watters, E. (1994). *Making monsters: false memories, psychotherapy, and sexual hysteria*. Scribner's, New York.

Pea, R.D. (1980). The development of negation in early child language. *The social foundations of language and thought*, (ed. D.R. Olson), pp. 156–86. Norton, New York.

Pendergrast, M. (1995). *Victims of memory: incest accusations and shattered lives*. Upper Access, Hinesburg, VT.

Piaget, J. (1962). *Play, dreams, and imitation in childhood*. Norton, New York.

Rajaram, S. (1993), Remembering and knowing: two means of access to the personal past. *Memory & Cognition*, **21**, 89–102.

Reid, T. (1895). Inquiry into human mind. In *The philosophical works of Thomas Reid*, Vol. 1, (8th end), (ed. W. Hamilton), pp. 95–214. Longman, Green, London. (Originally published 1769.)

Reiser, B.J., Black, J.B., and Kalamarides, P. (1986). Strategic memory search processes. In *Autobiographical memory* (ed. D.C. Rubin) pp. 100–21. Cambridge University Press.

Ribot, T. (1882). *Diseases of memory: an essay in the positive psychology* (transl. W.H. Smith). Appelton, New York.

Robinson, J.A. (1992). First experience memories: contexts and function in personal histories. In *Theoretical perspectives on autobiographical memory*, (ed. M.A. Conway, D.C. Rubin, H. Spinnler, and W. Wagenaar, pp. 223–39. Kluwer, Dordrecht.

Roediger, H.L. III (1980). Memory metaphors in cogntive psychology. *Memory Cognition*. **8**, 231–46.

Roediger, H.L., III and McDermott, K.B. (1993). Implicit memory in normal human subjects. In *Handbook of neuropsychology*, Vol. 8, (ed. F. Boller and Grafman), pp. 63–132. Elsevier, Amsterdam.

Roediger, H.L. III and McDermott, K.B. (1995). Creating false memories: remembering words not presented in lists. *Journal of Experimental Psychology: Learning, Memory, and Cognition*. (In press.)

Ross, B.H. (1984). Remindings and their effects in learning a cognitive skill. *Cognitive Psychology*, **6**, 371–416.

Ross, B.M. (1991). *Remembering the personal past*. Oxford University Press, New York.

Salaman, E. (1970). *A collection of moments: a study of involuntary memories*. Longman, London.

Schacter, D.L. (1987). Implicit memory: history and current status. *Journal of Experimental Psychology: Learning, Memory, and Cognition*, **13**, 501–18.

Schacter, D.L. (1995). Memory distortion: history and current status. In *Memory distortion* (ed. D.L. Schacter, J.T. Coyle, G.D. Fischbach, M.M. Mesulam, and L.E. Sullivan). Havard Univeristy Press, Cambridge, MA. (In press.)

Schacter, D.L. and Curran, T (1996). The cognitive neuroscience of false memories. *Psychiatric Annals*, in press.

Schank, R.C. (1982). *Dynamic memory*. Cambridge University Press, New York.

Schank, R.C. (1986). *Explanation patterns: understanding mechanically and creatively*. Erlbaum, Hillsdale, NJ.

Schank, R.C. and Abelson, R.P. (1977). *Scripts, plans, goals, and understanding*. Erlbaum Hillsdale, NJ.

Schooler, J.W. (1994). Seeking the core: the issues and evidence surrounding recovered accounts of sexual trauma. *Consciousness and Cognition*, **3**, 452–69.

Schooler, J.W. and Herrmann, D.J. (1992). There is more to episodic memory than just episodes. In *Theoretical perspectives on autobiographical memory*, (ed. M.A. Conway, D.C. Rubin, H.Spinnler, and W.A. Wagenaar), pp. 241–62. Kluwer, Dordrecht.

Shallice, T. (1988). *From neuropsychology to mental structure* Cambridge University Press, New York.

Spinoza, B. (1982). *The ethics and selected letters*, (ed. S. Feldman and trans. S. Shirley). Hackett, Indianapolis, IN. (Original work published 1677).

Strauman, T.J. (1990). Self-guides and emotionally significant childhood memories: a study of retrieval efficiency and incidental negative emotional content. *Journal of Personality and Social Psychology*, **59**, 869–80.

Terr, L. (1994). *Unchained memories*. Basic Books, New York.

Thompson, C.P. and Cowan, T. (1986). Flashbulb memories: a nicer interpretation of a Neisser recollection. *Cognition*, **22**, 199–200.

Treadway, M, McCloskey, M., Gordon, B., and Cohen, N.J. (1992). Landmark life events and the organization of memory: evidence from functional retrograde amnesia. In *The handock of emotion and memory: research and theory*, (ed. S. Christianson), pp. 389–410. Erlbaum, Hillsdale, NJ.

Tulving, E. (1972). Episodic and semantic memory. In *Organization of memory*, (ed. E. Tulving and W. Donaldson). Academic, New York.

Tulving, E. (1983). *Elements of episodic memory*. Oxford University Press, New York.

Tulving, E. (1985) Memory and consciousness. *Canadian Psychologist*, **26**, 1–12.

Tulving, E. and Pearlstone, Z. (1966). Availablity versus accessibility of information in memory for words. *Journal of Verbal Learning and Verbal Behaviour*, **5**, 381–91.

Tulving, E. and Schacter, D.L. (1990). Priming and human memory systems. *Science,*, **247**, 301–5.

Tulving, E. and Thomson, D.M. (1973). Encoding specificity and retrieval processes in episodic memory. *Psychological Review*, **80**, 353–73.

Weiskrantz, L. (1995). Comments on the report of the working party of the British Psychological Society on 'Recovered Memories'. *The Therapist*, winter issue.

Williams, D.M. and Hollan, J.D. (1981). The process of retieval from very long-term memory. *Cognitive Science*, **5**, 87–119.

Williams, J.M.G. (1994). Overgeneral memories. In *Remembering our past: studies in autobiographical memory*, (ed. D.C. Rubin). Cambridge University Press.

Williams, J.M.G. (1996). Depression and the specificity of autobiographical memory. In *Remembering our past. Studies in autobiographical memory* (ed. D.C. Rubin), pp. 244–70. Cambridge University Press.

Williams, J.M.G. and Broadbent, K. (1986). Autobiographical memory in attempted suicide patients. *Journal of Abnormal Psychology*, **95**, 144–9.

Williams, J.M.G. and Dritschel, B.H. (1992). Categoric and extended autobiographical memories. In *Theoretical perspectives on autobiographical memory* (ed. M.A. Conway, D.C. Rubin, H. Spinnler and W.A. Wagenaar), pp. 391–412. Kluwer, Dordrecht.

Williams, J.M.G. and Scott, J. (1988). Autobiographical memories in depression. *Psychological Medicine*, **18**, 689–95.

EIGHT

*R*easoning about repression: inferences from clinical and experimental data

CHRIS R. BREWIN AND BERNICE ANDREWS

Repression has been one of the most contentious topics in psychology for the last hundred years. The recent resurgence in interest in repression, largely fuelled by the increasing attention being paid to treating the long-term sequelae of child abuse, has shown that it has lost none of its power to generate controversy. Clinicians treating and studying the effects of trauma, such as Herman (1992), Briere (1992), Courtois (1988), and Terr (1994), have all testified to the prevalence of repression as a means of coping with memories of overwhelmingly stressful events. Other clinicians (for example Kihlstrom 1995; Pope and Hudson 1995), cognitive psychologists (for example Ceci and Loftus 1994; Loftus and Ketcham 1994), and social scientists (for example Ofshe and Watters 1994), have questioned the existence of repression and offered alternative explanations of apparent memory recovery in the clinic, for example proposing that some if not all of these 'memories' are created by inappropriate therapeutic behaviours.

In this chapter we argue that in order to understand the intensity of the recovered memories debate it is necessary to discuss three aspects of psychological reasoning: views concerning what are appropriate explanations for human behaviour, the data available to both sides, and criteria for what constitutes an acceptable 'theory'. Without a more fundamental examination of the protagonists' assumptions, there is a danger that, instead of leading to new insights, the debate will remain bogged down in mutual incomprehension.

EXPLANATIONS FOR HUMAN BEHAVIOUR

In many ways the current debate is reminiscent of the arguments between behavioural and cognitive therapists that raged in the 1970s. In the period from 1950 to the mid-1970s behaviour therapists developed clearly defined procedures such as desensitization and response prevention that could be readily described and taught. These techniques required little investigation of the individual, only a careful description of the problematic behaviour and of the events that preceded and followed it. However, their usefulness tended to be restricted to the treatment of fairly circumscribed disorders such as specific phobias and compulsions. When behaviour therapists came to address depression and more generalized anxiety disorders, the significance of individual cognitive processes assumed a much greater importance. The assessment and modification of the individual's thoughts and assumptions, as recommended by Ellis, Beck, Bandura, and others, became the cornerstone of the new cognitive –behavioural treatments.

These new techniques were not embraced, however, without a prolonged period of soul-searching by behaviour therapists. There was great anxiety that investigating individual cognitions was not as 'scientific' or methodologically rigorous as purely behavioural approaches. The new methods were eventually adopted because they worked, but many expressed unease. The fear was frequently expressed that in taking this step behaviour therapy could no longer be so clearly differentiated from psychoanalysis, and that the project of creating a truly 'scientific' type of therapy was being abandoned for ever.

Intentional and non-intentional explanations

Bolton and Hill (1996) illuminate this debate by distinguishing the causality inherent in physics and chemistry from the causality inherent in biological systems that have inbuilt goals and are constantly working towards more or less well specified objectives. As they point out, explanations that are couched in terms of meaning or intention are extremely powerful in biology and psychology. They also show convincingly that these explanations work just as well for many examples of abnormal behaviour as they do for normal behaviour that follows predictable rules. According to intentional explanations (for example that a person wishes to forget a traumatic memory), symptoms arise because normally functioning biological and psychological systems are attempting to deal with information that is either internally inconsistent or is inconsistent with the person's goals. According to non-intentional explanations, the biological or psychological systems are themselves malfunctioning, probably as a result of some disease process. Both types of explanation may apply at different times, and both are equally 'scientific'.

Corresponding to these different types of explanation, numerous authors have distinguished psychological enquiry based on the effect of experimental manipulations of behaviour in the laboratory from the collection of experiential data either from subjects themselves or from participant observation. From the non-intentional standpoint, the prime objectives are to manipulate the external variables of interest while holding extraneous sources of variance constant. Introspective data are typically regarded as inadequate because of the difficulty in verifying them, and conscious thought processes as irrelevant to the explanation of behaviour. From the intentional standpoint, however, laboratory studies are a weak source of evidence because they create artificial constraints that reduce external validity. Introspective data, on the other hand, are a uniquely valuable source of information about the subject's goals and intentions, although they may not necessarily be taken at face value, particularly if there is evidence of inconsistency. The existence of both types of explanation and the value of both types of enquiry have been repeatedly noted, not just in clinical but also in social and cognitive psychology (for example Harré and Secord 1972; Neisser 1976).

Recently, Oatley (1992) distinguished between natural (mechanistic, non-intentional) science and human science, involving goals, intentions, and plans, arguing that psychology is unique among academic disciplines in including both approaches. As he noted, Freud developed a psychology of intention that recognized human actions as having multiple causal intents, of whose existence people have varying levels of awareness. For Oatley, Freud's concerns converge with those of cognitive psychologists studying the understanding of narrative. In evaluating intentional explanations, various kinds of criteria are available. For example, we can ask whether, within our culture, an explanation is generally considered adequate to explain an action, i.e. is there consensus? We can also ask whether the explanation satisfactorily accounts for consistencies and inconsistencies within the narrative. These criteria admit more ambiguity that those of natural science but, as Oatley again points out, exactly the same issues arise for anybody, whether historian, literary critic, therapist, or cognitive scientist, attempting to understand complex human behaviour.

Supporters of the concept of repression within this human science tradition regard it as either a conscious or an unconscious strategy to protect the individual from the recognition of a painful reality or of unacceptable impulses, that is, as an intentional behaviour to be inferred from introspective exploration of the person's thoughts and feelings. However, when this kind of reasoning is based not on explicitly stated intentions or descriptions of mental states but on the therapist's beliefs and interpretations, the problem of ambiguity noted above becomes acute. As demonstrated by Grünbaum (1993), Freud's claims of scientific legitimacy for his observations, and his belief that it was possible to infer repression as a universal cause of neurosis, rested on extremely shaky foundations. Similarly, attempts by experts to infer repression from clinical case material have not always yielded high levels of agreement (Holmes 1990).

Freud of course was well aware of the alternative interpretations of his data, and his view of memory as reconstructive and selective has been generally accepted by psychoanalysts, for example in work on people's earliest memories (Mayman 1968). Recently, however, investigations of repression have increasingly focused on a different kind of evidence, reports of the recovery of episodic memories of traumatic events that had previously been forgotten. Here, assumptions concerning a repressive process have been buttressed by clinical observations of the high frequency with which individuals attempt to block out and deny such memories. Trauma therapists, many of whom are not psychoanalytically trained, have on the whole been more struck by the reproductive than by the reconstructive aspects of traumatic memories. Like traditional psychoanalysts, however, they find the concept of repression to be consistent with their clinical observations and hypotheses about clients' intentions.

In contrast, other authors are strong believers in the pre-eminence of the experimental methods of natural science. Frequently cited is Holmes (1990, pp.96–7), who concluded 'At the present time there is no controlled laboratory evidence supporting the concept of repression . . . the evidence they (clinicians) offer consists only of impressionistic case studies and . . . those observations cannot be counted as anything more than unconfirmed clinical speculations'. Pope and Hudson (1995) excluded from consideration clinical observations of recovered memories on the grounds that they were 'unsystematic anecdotal reports' (p.121) and argued 'Laboratory studies over the past 60 years have failed to demonstrate that individuals can "repress" memories. Clinical studies, which extrapolate from the laboratory to the study of real-life traumas, must consequently start with the null hypothesis: namely, that repression does not occur' (p.125).

Wakefield and Underwager (1992, p.487) commented along similar lines, 'Claims of repressed memories of childhood abuse recovered in the course of therapy are not supported by credible scientific data. The scientific and popular literature in this area seems dominated by believing therapists who simply repeat clinical anecdotes, state subjective speculation, and make unsupported assertions about repressed abuse'. More recently, Kihlstrom (1995, p.66) wrote 'there is nothing in the available evidence that would permit us to have any confidence in any exhumed memory, in the absence of independent confirmation, or to have any confidence that there are causal links among trauma, amnesia, and psychopathology. To demur in this way . . . is to hold clinical theory and practice up to established standards of scientific knowledge'.

In these quotations scientific 'method' or 'standards' are contrasted favourably with the activities of clinicians, who are portrayed as, at best, biased judges or, at worst, active creators of the phenomena that they report. However, it is not clear that there is anything inherently more "scientific" in the methods advocated by these investigators or in their assumptions, which we briefly review below.

Data from the laboratory are more valuable than data from the clinic

This is a frequently voiced assertion. Data from the laboratory have a number of advantages, including the opportunity for enhanced experimenter control and verification. They also have a number of disadvantages, including reduced ecological validity, the omission of consideration of individual intentions, and the induction of often unrecorded expectations and demand characteristics. In addition, it is hard to see how traumas of the severity now thought to be associated with repressed memories could ever be simulated and therefore studied in a laboratory.

Clinically derived data, on the other hand, are often dismissed as subjective and biased 'impressions' or 'speculations'. However, this argument fails to distinguish between factual clinical observations, for example of the context or content associated with the recovery of an idea, and clinical beliefs, for example concerned with the truth or falsity of a supposed recovered memory. Whereas beliefs may be prone to error, there is little reason to reject the independent observations of clinical facts made by large numbers of trained clinicians and the systematic observations made by clinical researchers. Indeed, such observations, formalized in diagnostic systems developed by the American Psychiatric Association and the World Health Organization, form the basis for the practice of clinical psychology and psychiatry.

Although useful for descriptive purposes, these observations cannot on their own support causal inferences. They are not inherently less 'scientific', however: careful and systematic description of a phenomenon is often a prerequisite to designing appropriate experimental research.

Conclusions about the effects of trauma cannot safely be based on retrospective reports

Kihlstrom (1995) has argued that a particular type of introspective data, retrospective reports of childhood trauma, are inherently unreliable, and may be biased by the clinical state of the patient or by the preconceptions of the interviewer. For this reason, he believes, the entire corpus of research on trauma and memory is suspect and should not be accepted as scientifically proven. These claims, although widely accepted, have little empirical justification. Researchers (for example Baddeley 1990) are agreed that there is a basic integrity to autobiographical memory, even though there may be individual errors and biases of a minor nature. No data suggest that this integrity does not extend to reports of childhood trauma. Thus there is no reason to question the overall validity of a study that compares one group of subjects who report having had a particular childhood experience with another group who do not – any errors in recall will simply weaken the signal-to-noise ratio. It would in fact be contrary to what we know about memory to reject the findings of such a study *a priori*.

Similarly, claims of systematic biases have not been supported. The trauma–psychopathology relationship is present whether subjects are interviewed or complete self-report instruments, and thus cannot be an artefact of interviewer bias. And changes in clinical state have repeatedly been shown to have no effect on recall of childhood experience (Brewin *et al.* 1993), thus making less likely another potential source of bias.

Recovered memories must be assumed to be false in the first instance

Pope and Hudson (1995) are explicit about the assumptions contained in their review of the literature. Like Kihlstrom (1995), they propose that on scientific grounds it should be proven that recovered memories may actually correspond to historical events before accepting the validity of the concept of repression.

They then review four studies and conclude that none matches the standard of evidence they require, namely the existence of independent documentary support for events claimed to have been forgotten and then remembered. Given our knowledge of the integrity of autobiographical memory referred to above, and of the various strengths and weaknesses of experimental data, we may question why recovered memories have to be assumed to be false and proven to be true. It would seem strange to assume that ordinary memories were false unless proven otherwise, and there is no statement of the grounds on which recovered memories are believed to be different from ordinary memories. However, once the hypothesis is set up in this way, the available data can then be shown to fail a variety of stringent 'tests' set by the authors. In contrast, the adequacy of alternative explanations (for example that therapists are implanting false memories) is never examined. Once again, there does not on close inspection appear to be anything inherently 'scientific' about this reasoning.

Systematic studies providing independent documentary evidence are necessary to substantiate the concept of repression

Pope and Hudson (1995) suggested that at the time of their review no systematic study of repressed memory had provided convincing evidence for the actual occurrence of the remembered childhood trauma, such as contemporaneous medical evidence, photographs, or reports from reliable and unbiased witnesses. On this basis, in conjunction with their argument that repressed memories should be assumed to be false unless proven otherwise, they concluded that there were no data that confirmed the existence of repression or other forgetting of significant childhood trauma. Similar conclusions have been arrived at by Wakefield and Underwager (1992) and Kihlstrom (1995).

There are several issues to consider here. First, why were individual case studies not accepted as valid sources of evidence, as they are in neuropsychology for instance? Only one substantiated case would be required to confirm the possibility of forgetting and subsequently remembering childhood trauma, but all such material was rejected as being 'anecdotal' and hence unreliable. Second, what standard of corroboration should be considered appropriate, given that child abuse often occurs in a situation of extreme secrecy? It is important to be explicit about what level of corroboration is feasible given the circumstances, rather than insisting on absolute standards of documentary proof.

In fact there are reports of individual cases where documentary corroboration of forgotten trauma has been reported (Schooler 1994; Schooler, Bendiksen, and Ambadar, this volume). Moreover, recent systematic studies have also uncovered corroboration for forgotten abuse. Feldman-Summers and Pope (1994) found that, of their sample of therapists reporting amnesia for childhood trauma, approximately half had found corroborating evidence in the form of admissions by the perpetrator, reports from others who had known about the abuse or who had themselves been abused, diaries, or medical records. Williams (1995) was able to compare the accounts given by women who had forgotten their abuse for some period of time with original medical records describing the abuse, and found that their recall was no less accurate than that of women who had always remembered their abuse.

In the face of this converging evidence, much of which is relatively new, it would appear no longer plausible to dismiss the evidence on the grounds that no single study meets acceptable standards of scientific rigour. Many commentators have now been sufficiently impressed by the converging evidence for corroboration of forgotten memories to accept that forgetting of trauma does sometimes occur (for example Lindsay and Read 1995; Loftus *et al.* 1994; Toglia 1995).

Conclusions

We have tried to show that appeals to what is 'scientific' may reflect an overly narrow view of scientific enquiry and may involve assumptions that have little empirical support. Nevertheless, such claims may play a crucial role within an adversarial setting in which two versions of the truth are disputed. If clinical data are rejected as unsystematic and anecdotal, retrospective reports are criticized on grounds of unreliability, and recovered memories are assumed to be false in the absence of evidence to the contrary, the burden of proof on those who seek to establish the validity of a recovered memory is much greater. If recovered memories are accepted to be often, or even sometimes, veridical, the burden of proof reduces.

AVAILABILITY OF DATA

As we have seen, reasoning about repression as a way of explaining human behaviour will be influenced by the individual's knowledge base. Specifically, knowledge will affect what is regarded as a culturally sanctioned explanation, and will influence judgements of consistency. The plausibility of repression as an explanation in any individual case, and the plausibility of expert data and commentary, are likely to depend on personal and professional experience, and here once again the differences between protagonists in the recovered memories debate may be very marked. Pursuing the parallel with other debates within clinical psychology, it is striking how the extension of routine therapeutic practice to include clients with primarily interpersonal problems or severe problems such as personality disorder has led to a rapprochement between cognitive–behavioural and psychodynamic theory. A number of psychoanalytic concepts such as transference, unconscious knowledge, and defence, are now much more readily accepted by cognitive therapists, albeit translated into different terminology. In large part this rapprochement has happened because the type of clients seen by both types of therapist are more similar than ever before, i.e. there has been a convergence in the data available to both groups.

The clinical perspective

A recent survey of over 4000 qualified British psychologists (Andrews *et al.* 1995) showed that having a client recover a traumatic memory from total amnesia was not an uncommon experience – of the 27 per cent who responded, almost half had had at least one client of this kind. From the clinical perspective, then, memory recovery is likely to be consistent with at least some independent observations of other clients made by colleagues, supervisors, or by therapists themselves. Increasingly, these observations are being made, not just by psychodynamically trained clinicians, but by clinicians with a cognitive–behavioural training working with clients traumatized by recent or childhood experiences. Their evaluation of laboratory research on memory is likely to be influenced by the extent to which the phenomena described are consistent with clinical observations.

The clinical experience of traumatic memories is typified by the syndrome of post-traumatic stress disorder (PTSD). PTSD, defined in the American Psychiatric Association's Diagnostic and Statistical Manuals and based in part on observations of veterans from the Vietnam war, is characterized by intrusive memories or nightmares, attempts to avoid these intrusions, and high levels of arousal. A particularly common form of intrusive memory are called 'flashbacks', which tend to differ from ordinary memories in two main respects (Brewin *et al.* in press; van der Kolk and Fisler 1995). The first is that people experiencing a flashback often feel as though they are reliving the original event. They experience in an intense and detailed way the sensory, motor, and emotional components of the memory, and these details remain remarkably constant with repetition of the flashbacks. During the flashback the subjective sense of time changes so that the event appears to be happening now rather than belonging to the past.

The second way in which these memories differ is that they cannot be deliberately accessed through a normal search of autobiographical memory. Rather, people learn which internal or external cues are likely to trigger them, and develop strategies to increase or decrease the probability of accessing the memories by manipulating their exposure to the relevant cues.

Other phenomena regularly encountered by the trauma therapist include: dissociative states, in which clients temporarily lose contact with their surroundings and may become unaware of the therapist's presence; memory lapses, frequently occurring in conjunction with dissociative states, in which clients cannot remember what was said minutes or seconds before; and reversible amnesia for aspects of the traumatic experience. It is extremely common to find that, once clients focus on the content of flashbacks rather than trying to avoid them or distract themselves, they recall numerous details that were hitherto inaccessible. Avoidance is a pervasive problem in the treatment of post-traumatic stress disorder, and clients often display a variety of deliberate and not-so-deliberate strategies for protecting themselves against the recall of horrific or otherwise distressing experiences. The recall of previously forgotten material often only occurs with great reluctance, and it can be a punishing experience for all concerned. In this context the idea of motivated forgetting, or of repression following a period of deliberate avoidance, is consistent with the available data.

These phenomena, although common enough in clinical practice, have been almost completely ignored by cognitive psychologists. The recent *Handbook of emotion and memory* (Christianson 1992a), for instance, had no entry for flashbacks in its subject index. And until recently (for example Conway 1995), studies of flashbulb memory have not been directly compared with traumatic memories seen in clinical practice. For clinicians involved in treating trauma survivors, therefore, the experimental literature on emotion and memory often appears to have numerous important gaps, and claims of expertise by cognitive psychologists may sometimes appear less than convincing.

The kind of data that the therapist is most interested in generally concern why the client still has intense emotions attached to an event in the past. In pursuing the idea that symptoms may be explicable from the intentional stance, the therapist will want to know to what extent the event has been thought about, discussed, or forgotten, whether there are aspects of the event that are particularly difficult to think about, whether the event is related to previous experiences, and what implications the event has currently. Also relevant are the situations that trigger intrusive memories, and the degree of control the client can exercise over them.

Clinicians' advantages in constructing causal hypotheses are that they have ready access to a client's experiences, which may validate or invalidate clinical hunches and act as a source of unexpected information generating new hypotheses. There are also numerous opportunities for checking the consistency of the account and for detecting inconsistent facts. On the other hand, clinicians' lack of access to external verification may lead them to overestimate the accuracy of clients' memories and to base their hypotheses on unreliable or incomplete data.

The experimental perspective

For the experimental cognitive psychologist, conclusions about emotion and memory have until recently been based largely on laboratory studies of recall for emotional material, or on naturalistic investigations of observers of traumatic events, rather than on studies of people who have experienced trauma at first hand. Although in some ways limited, this research has demonstrated some very important phenomena. For example, in the recall of stressful events, central features of the event tend to be well preserved while at the same time recall of peripheral details may be impaired (Christianson 1992b). The focus on the details of remembering, and the use of standard stimuli, has made cognitive psychologists far more aware than many of their clinical colleagues of how common it is to misremember details of events.

Other relevant phenomena reviewed by Lindsay and Read (1994) include the ease with which subjects may be misled by subsequent suggestions, even to the extent of sometimes believing an event to have occurred that in fact had no basis in reality (for example, Loftus 1993). What is particularly striking is that subjects may develop strong beliefs in the veridicality of some aspects of a memory that are in fact false. As noted by Lindsay and Read, memory suggestibility appears to increase with the delay between the event and the attempt to remember, with the authority of the source of the suggestions, with repetition of suggestions, with plausible suggestions, and with instructions leading people not to monitor carefully the source of their 'memories'. Moreover, some individuals are markedly more susceptible to suggestion than others.

Experimental cognitive psychologists thus have available an enormous quantity of data on the fallibility of memory, and this undoubtedly alerts them to dangers that clinicians may be less aware of. At the same time, it is fair to say that the high levels of interest in memory failings may have tended to obscure the fact that autobiographical memory is more often right than wrong, providing individuals do not go beyond what they can readily recall and attempt to fill in the gaps (Baddeley 1990). The greater availability of these data does not guarantee that experimental psychologists' concerns are well founded, although they may be.

For the vast majority of experimental psychologists, therefore, the idea of repression is inconsistent both with their own experience and with the other information available to them and to their colleagues. Moreover, we believe that repression has little explanatory value for someone who is not aware of the ways in which early trauma may pose a threat to a child's sense of identity and confidence in their own continued existence. It is dangerous to make assumptions about what kinds of experience are equally traumatic, or to assume that physical and sexual abuse are similar in their emotional or affective nature, as do Hembrooke and Ceci (1995). There are many features of child abuse, including sadism, threats of violence or rejection, denial and disbelief by others, lack of any form of escape, and simultaneous needs to be cared for, that may create quite unimaginable conflicts and disturbances in the child's sense of reality. Unless these are fully appreciated, there is likely to be little agreement on appropriate intentional explanations.

CRITERIA FOR AN ACCEPTABLE THEORY

We have already noted that whereas evidential criteria in the natural sciences are relatively clear-cut, criteria in the human sciences are more ambiguous, as befits attempts to understand multiple and possibly conflicting intentions. In addition, however, there may be other criteria that divide protagonists on either side of the recovered memories debate.

The clinical perspective

While certainly being concerned with the authenticity or otherwise of recovered memories, the clinician's main aim is to construct a plausible hypothesis that makes sense of the facts and to negotiate this with the client. What is plausible will depend on the internal consistency of the client's story, the availability of corroborating evidence, the therapist's previous experience, and the experience of other therapists acting as advisors or supervisors. The pressure for therapeutic progress makes additional demands, in that the purpose of data collection is to make an informed decision as quickly as possible about which therapeutic direction to take. Therapists have an ethical obligation not to prolong treatment unnecessarily and not to imperil the therapeutic relationship by challenging the client where this is in their own interests rather than those of the client.

Clinical psychology, like medicine, has a long history of developing effective treatments whose theoretical base is poorly understood. In their turn, both behaviour therapy and cognitive therapy have had or are having their underlying theories completely revised by new clinical research, despite having enjoyed considerable practical success. For the clinician, then, adopting an effective treatment strategy may be more important than understanding the nature of the problem or even the nature of the treatment. This pragmatic orientation inevitably influences how data are collected and what hypotheses are tested.

The experimental perspective

Unlike the clinician, the experimental psychologist can readily countenance delay in putting forward a plausible theory, and may be content simply to report data. From the point of view of natural science, the best theories should be open to falsification but resist challenges from the current data. The other important criterion is parsimony. All things being equal, the best theory is the simplest one, or the one that makes fewest additional assumptions.

In the recovered memories debate, experimental psychologists have been very concerned with parsimony. Once it was accepted that traumas could be forgotten, it has been argued that this can be accounted for by ordinary forgetting (Loftus *et al.* 1994) or by motivated forgetting (Hembrooke and Ceci 1995), and that no additional special mechanism ('repression') is required. Similarly, there has been relatively little interest in offering alternative theoretical accounts of repression, despite recent evidence about inhibitory mechanisms in attention and memory (Dagenbach and Carr 1994).

CONCLUSIONS

To sum up, we have argued that the recovered memories debate can be best understood in terms of differing models of psychological enquiry. Whereas the clinical perspective represents a human science that is concerned with intentions and goals, the experimental perspective represents a natural science that is concerned with non-intentional mechanisms and processes. The two approaches also differ in the availability of different sorts of data, and in their attitudes to alternative explanations and corroboration, reflecting a concern with plausibility and parsimony respectively. Clinical data collection tends to be driven by the guiding principles of utility and plausibility, attempting to arrive at an idiographic formulation that gives meaning to the symptoms. The experimenter has the advantages and disadvantages of greater distance from the data, being relatively free from pressure to arrive at a premature conclusion but less able to revise hypotheses in response to new and unexpected information. There is less need to adopt a working hypothesis until all other possibilities have been rejected, and less need to have a convincing alternative explanation.

In our view it is unfortunate that these two groups are competing with one another in their claims for possession of the most relevant expertise. Each is able to answer questions that the other cannot, and neither on its own is in a position to put forward a convincing account of repression. We would like to see far more collaboration between the two groups, with experimental tests being made of hypotheses rooted in clinical observations. There is an urgent need for systematic clinical studies of repressive phenomena, based on interviews with therapists and clients. There is an equally urgent need for experimental studies of inhibitory processes in memory that may throw light on these phenomena. It appears, for example, that there are individuals with bad childhoods who have an impaired ability to process negative information (Myers and Brewin 1994, 1995). Experimental research can help to determine whether difficulties in retrieving negative memories or in processing negative information are best explained by inhibitory or non-inhibitory mechanisms (Anderson and Bjork 1994), but both types of psychological enquiry are necessary to discover whether the clinical concept of repression can be firmly rooted in a cognitive science that recognizes the central role of individual intentions and goals.

REFERENCES

Anderson, M.C. and Bjork, R.A. (1994). Mechanisms of inhibition in long-term memory: a new taxonomy. In *Inhibitory processes in attention, memory and language*, (ed. D. Dagenbach and T.H. Carr), pp. 265–325. Academic, San Diego, CA.

Andrews, B., Morton, J., Bekerian, D., Brewin, C.R., Davies, G.M., and Mollon, P. (1995). The recovery of memories in clinical practice. *The Psychologist*, **8**, 209–14.

Baddeley, A.D. (1990). *Human memory: theory and practice*. Erlbaum, Hove.

Bolton, D. and Hill, J. (1996). *Mind, meaning, and mental disorder: causal explanation in psychology and psychiatry*. Oxford University Press.

Brewin, C.R., Andrews, B., and Gotlib, I.H. (1993). Psychopathology and early experience: a reappraisal of retrospective reports. *Psychological Bulletin*, **113**, 82–98.

Brewin, C.R., Dalgleish, T., and Joseph, S.J. A dual representation theory of post-traumatic stress disorder. *Psychological Review*. (In press.)

Briere, J. (1992). *Child abuse trauma*. Sage Newbury Park, CA.

Ceci, S.J. and Loftus, E.F. (1994). 'Memory work': a royal road to false memories? *Applied Cognitive Psychology*, **8**, 351–64.

Christianson, S.-Å. (1992a). *Handbook of emotion and memory*. Erlbaum, Hillsdale, NJ.

Christianson, S.-Å. (1992b). Emotional stress and eyewitness memory: a critical review. *Psychological Bulletin*, **112**, 284–309.

Conway, M.A. (1995). *Flashbulb memory*. Erlbaum, Hove.

Courtois, C.A. (1988). *Healing the incest wound: adult survivors in therapy*. Norton, New York.

Dagenbach, D. and Carr, T.H. (ed.) (1994). *Inhibitory processes in attention, memory and language*. Academic, San Diego, CA.

Feldman-Summers, S. and Pope, K.S. (1994). The experience of 'forgetting' childhood abuse: a national survey of psychologists. *Journal of Consulting and Clinical Psychology*, **62**, 636–9.

Grünbaum, A. (1993). *Validation in the clinical theory of psychoanalysis*. International Universities Press, Madison, CT.

Harré, R. and Secord, P.F. (1972). *The explanation of social behavior*. Rowman & Littlefield, Totowa, NJ.

Hembrooke, H. and Ceci, S.J. (1995). Traumatic memories: do we need to invoke special mechanisms? *Consciousness and Cognition*, **4**, 75–82.

Herman, J.L. (1992). *Trauma and recovery*. Basic Books, New York.

Holmes, D.S. (1990). The evidence for repression: an examination of sixty years of research. In *Repression and dissociation*, (ed. J.L. Singer), pp.85–102. University of Chicago Press.

Kihlstrom, J.F. (1995). The trauma-memory argument. *Consciousness and Cognition*, **4**, 63–7.

Lindsay, D.S. and Read, J.D. (1994). Psychotherapy and memories of childhood sexual abuse. *Applied Cognitive Psychology*, **8**, 281–338.

Lindsay, D.S. and Read, J.D. (1995). 'Memory work' and recovered memories of childhood sexual abuse: scientific evidence and public, professional and personal issues. *Psychology, Public Policy and the Law*, **1**, 846–908.

Loftus, E.F. (1993). The reality of repressed memories. *American Psychologist*, **48**, 518–37.

Loftus, E.F. and Ketcham, K. (1994). *The myth of repressed memory: false memories and allegations of sexual abuse*. St Martin's Press, New York.

Loftus, E.F., Garry, M., and Feldman, J. (1994). Forgetting sexual trauma: what does it mean when 38% forget? *Journal of Consulting and Clinical Psychology*, **62**, 1177–81.

Mayman, M. (1968). Early memories and character structure. *Journal of Projective Techniques and Personality Assessment*, **32**, 303–16.

Myers, L.B. and Brewin, C.R. (1994). Recall of early experience and the repressive coping style. *Journal of Abnormal Psychology*, **103**, 288–92.

Myers, L.B. and Brewin, C.R. (1995). Repressive coping and the recall of emotional material. *Cognition and Emotion*, **9**, 637–42.

Neisser, U. (1976). *Cognition and reality*. W.H. Freeman, San Francisco.

Oatley, K. (1992). *Best laid schemes: the psychology of emotions*. Cambridge University Press.

Ofshe, R.J. and Watters, E. (1994). *Making monsters: false memories, psychotherapy, and sexual hysteria*. Scribner, New York.

Pope, H.G. and Hudson, J.I. (1995). Can memories of childhood abuse be repressed? *Psychological Medicine*, **25**, 121–6.

Schooler, J.W. (1994). Seeking the core: the issues and evidence surrounding recovered accounts of sexual trauma. *Consciousness and Cognition*, **3**, 452–69.

Terr, L.C. (1994). *Unchained memories: true stories of traumatic memories lost and found*. Basic Books, New York.

Toglia, M.P. (1995). Repressed memories: the way we were? *Consciousness and Cognition*, **4**, 111–15.

van der Kolk, B.A. and Fisler, R. (1995). Dissociation and the fragmentary nature of traumatic memories: overview and exploratory study. *Journal of Traumatic Stress*, **8**, 505–25.

Wakefield, H. and Underwager, R. (1992). Recovered memories of alleged sexual abuse: lawsuits against parents. *Behavioral Sciences and the Law*, **10**, 483–507.

Williams, L.M. (1995). Recovered memories of abuse in women with documented child sexual victimization histories. *Journal of Traumatic Stress*, **8**, 649–73.

NINE

Delayed memories of child sexual abuse: critique of the controversy and clinical guidelines

CHRISTINE A. COURTOIS

The controversy that has surrounded delayed and recovered memories of child sexual abuse is entering its fifth year. It has spawned considerable public debate and has had a profound effect on the mental health professions and the practice of psychotherapy. The positions taken in the controversy have often been extreme, overdrawn, and caustic. A rational middle ground that incorporates the legitimate issues of each side is lacking and is much needed to ensure that a newly emerging field of inquiry and practice is not suppressed and that previously abused individuals can continue to receive psychotherapeutic services. This chapter begins with a summary of several of the most common points made by the critics followed by counter arguments to some of them, and a call for a more temperate, balanced, and accurate position. It then moves to an articulation of the current consensus among experts as well as guidelines for clinical practice with traumatized individuals, especially as concerns repressed/delayed memory issues.

The gist of the argument made by proponents of the false memory position is as follows: therapists (especially those who are young, female, inadequately trained, and who are uninformed about the nature of human memory and misinformed about memory for trauma) routinely suggest or even implant memories of sexual abuse in gullible (usually female) clients who enter treatment for some other problem(s) not having any outward relation to abuse. The presenting problem is treated as the manifestation of repressed memory of child sexual abuse by therapists who further believe it is their responsibility to ferret out the abuse. They do so by inadvertently or intentionally planting false memories through direct suggestion, pressure to recall abuse, and the use of what the critics have determined to be non-traditional and suggestive methods such as hypnosis, guided imagery, sodium amytal, and a variety of expressive therapies. Furthermore, these suggestive therapeutic strategies are used with little or no regard to the client's level of suggestibility in general and more specifically as it pertains to therapeutic influence. The end result is the development of what has been termed 'false memory syndrome' in the client (False Memory Syndrome Foundation, 1992; Loftus 1993; Loftus and Ketcham 1994; Ofshe and Watters 1993).

In line with this therapeutic focus on repressed memories, clients are encouraged to see all of their problems as related to abuse and to actively pursue hidden abuse memories. They are further encouraged to repeatedly remember and to relive the trauma with great emotional intensity in order to recover from its effects. Therapists naively and foolishly believe anything and everything their clients recall, no matter how improbable – this even includes multi-generational Satanic ritual abuse involving human and animal sacrifice and other depravities and sexual abuse in the context of alien abductions and past lives. Therapists then use this information to encourage their clients, in the guise of protecting them or helping them gain revenge or restitution, to confront parents and other family members with their new-found memories. Subsequently, clients are told to limit or sever contact with these same individuals and/or initiate ill-advised civil lawsuits against them. Families are thus falsely accused and familial relationships destroyed. Last but not least, this approach has the effect of fostering therapists' personal and economic agenda: clients become very dependent and engage in treatment of long duration – lasting as long as insurance coverage holds out – a personal as well as financial boon to the therapist.

The repressed memory theory on which this therapeutic approach is founded is held to be faulty by the memory critics. Their position is that repression is not scientifically proven and memory that is repressed for long periods of time (later to emerge in pristine or not so pristine form) violates what is currently known about human memory processes (Ornstein *et al.* 1996). They are also not swayed by the alternative theory put forth by trauma researchers and therapists that post-traumatic responses and particularly the defence mechanism of dissociation account for variable access to memory in previously abused adults. The critics hold to the position that, since data are not available to demonstrate otherwise, the accumulated knowledge about memory for ordinary events is applicable to memory for traumatic events. Repressed memory and what has been labelled by the critics as 'Recovered Memory Therapy' used to unearth long-buried memories of past abuse are considered bogus. Therapists who believe in the possibility of repressed memory for past trauma are ill-informed; if they use techniques deemed to be suggestive that fall under the rubric of 'Recovered Memory Therapy' (even when their use is within accepted standards of practice and not used in a way that is suggestive) they are practising quackery and should be charged with fraud and have their licenses revoked.

Just how accurate are the points of this critique? In the opinion of this author and many others who specialize in researching human traumatization and treating adult survivors of abuse, they are overstated, overgeneralized, and unnecessarily adversarial (Alpert 1995; Alpert *et al.* 1996; Briere 1995; Brown 1995; Courtois 1995*a*, *b*; Herman 1994). No doubt, the delayed/recovered memory controversy has revealed some problematic and harmful therapy and flawed therapeutic beliefs and practices along with some therapeutic excesses among credentialed professionals (see Yapko 1994*b* and Chapter 2 this volume) and that many individuals without adequate training or appropriate licensing offer 'treatment' for adult survivors that is clearly counter-therapeutic, beyond the scope of their abilities, and that needs regulation; nevertheless, the critique has been made in ways that are highly inflammatory, that exceed the available data, and that are quite harmful to clinicians, their patients, and the general public.

ASSUMPTIONS MADE BY THE CRITICS: ARE THEY SUPPORTABLE?

In this section, I address two main concerns each with a number of sub-points. The first involves the scope of the problem including such issues as the number of individuals who have total repression of past events, the number of therapists utilizing so-called 'Recovered Memory Therapy' strategies, and the method for determining false versus true memories of abuse. The second concern includes issues of a more ideological and political nature: the backlash against the newfound recognition of the prevalence and seriousness of sexual abuse, the misunderstanding of the characteristics and cultural context of sexual abuse that could cause memory disturbance and, in a related vein, depreciation of available (largely clinical and observational) information on pathologies of memory in post-traumatic and dissociative conditions by academic memory researchers.

The scope of the problem

The scope of the problem of delayed recall of memories of childhood abuse is different from that implied or assumed by many of the commentaries on the controversy. The memory scenario that evokes the greatest debate and scepticism has to do with the apparent *total* loss of memory for an extended period of time and *delayed and detailed retrieval years later*. From the available research, this appears to be the least common scenario. Instead, data suggest that the majority of traumatized individuals (including those sexually or otherwise abused as children) retain conscious memory (complete, partial, and/or with variable accessibility over time) whether or not they fully understand it or disclose it and that the minority of traumatized people have total memory loss and possible later delayed recall (Alpert *et al.* 1996; British Psychological Society 1995; Elliott and Briere 1994, 1995; Gold and Hughes unpublished; Gold *et al.* 1994; van der Kolk *et al.* 1994; van der Kolk and Fisler 1995).

The implication is, of course, that the scenario generating the greatest amount of debate is significantly smaller than the critics imply. The therapeutic situation is far different when the client enters therapy reporting abuse that was never forgotten or reporting partial or fluctuating recall or motivated forgetting (the much more common occurrence) than when knowledge of past abuse is totally absent and unavailable (the much less common occurrence). The misrepresentation of the scope of the problem has had numerous repercussions, perhaps the most serious of which is the scepticism and even hostility greeting adults who report variable memory accessibility over time and later recall for past abuse. This situation seems to be occurring ever more often, especially in the legal arena where the repressed memory controversy is being used quite routinely (and many believe prematurely and without adequate substantiation) to rebut the claims of those who report abuse (even in cases where no allegations of memory loss have been made).

In contrast, a number of reports and guidelines recently issued by professional organizations have underscored that total repression is possible, although the mechanisms underlying the process are not understood at present, and that it is a relatively uncommon scenario yet should not be used to disqualify an individual's account (American Psychiatric Association, 1993; American Psychological Association 1994, 1996; British Psychological Society 1995; Hammond *et al.* 1995).

A similar problem is evident in the depictions of psychotherapy practices. The false memory critics charge that large numbers of therapists are practising a form of therapy they have chosen to label 'Recovered Memory Therapy'. (Note: this is not a term that is found anywhere in the literature produced by clinicians and researchers of sexual abuse trauma and treatment.) Some critics have even gone so far as to call the problem epidemic. But is this an accurate depiction of what happens in psychotherapy and what large numbers of therapists are doing?

Thus far, several surveys have been conducted on beliefs held by therapists and on their clinical practices. In aggregate, they do not support these contentions, especially those that are the most extreme. Yapko (1993, 1994) surveyed a non-random convenience sample of therapists as to their beliefs about memory and hypnosis. He reported that a significant number of this sample held erroneous beliefs that *could lead* to misapplications of hypnosis and result in the inadvertent suggestion rather than recovery of memories of abuse. While this survey is important and serves as a caution to therapists, it is not clear how often beliefs actually convert to practice. Poole and Lindsay (unpublished) surveyed a random sample of licensed doctoral therapists and found that a minority responded in ways that suggested a strong focus on recovering suspected repressed memories of child sexual abuse. In a follow-up survey of US and British licensed doctoral psychotherapists, Poole *et al.* (1995) reported the same finding, but cautioned that a minority still translates to a possibly large number of practitioners. Yet, they further noted that their results are inconsistent with the idea that a large percentage of psychotherapists have a single-minded focus on getting their clients to remember child sexual abuse.

In another survey of therapists with findings consistent with those of the Poole *et al.* surveys, Waltz (1994) reported that approximately 20 per cent of respondents reported using those techniques most in question to assist adult clients to remember sexual abuse; however, these same authors emphasized that the majority of their respondents reported a focus on sexual abuse with none or a small percentage of their clients. The findings of a national survey of 1000 psychologists sampled from practice-oriented divisions of the American Psychological Association reported by Follette and Polusny (1995) support those of the Waltz study in terms of the percentage of therapists who report using the techniques in question and a low focus on sexual abuse with their clients. A limitation of this study is its 22 per cent response rate. Additionally, in a vignette study of 269 members of the Illinois Psychological Association, participants expressed no strong opinions about past child sexual abuse and did not endorse controversial treatments or suggestive statements (Sullins 1995). The author concluded that the overall results counter the allegations made about therapists' assumptions about child sexual abuse.

Although these studies are preliminary and do not provide data endorsing the critics' positions, they do offer other information that strongly suggests the need for additional research on the efficacy of recommended treatment for sexual abuse trauma and empirically based training of practitioners. Cognitive and clinical psychologists have the opportunity to collaborate on studies of memory processes in traumatized versus non-traumatized individuals to determine whether differences exist and to make direct application of findings to clinical practice (American Psychological Association 1996).

A related concern regarding the scope of the problem is the critics' portrayal of psychotherapy and therapists as the major sources of influence and the most likely triggers for the retrieval of previously absent memory. They do so without enough data to support this perspective – one research study and a small number of anecdotal accounts do not constitute adequate substantiation – and they ignore other possible sources of influence. Two recent studies support clinical observations about an alternative explanation: that the most potent memory cues come not from psychotherapists but from other sources – some form of media, experiencing something similar to the original trauma, and a sexual experience (Elliott 1994; van der Kolk *et al.* 1994; van der Kolk and Fisler 1995), associational cueing of the sort that is recognized in the memory literature.

Another concern within the scope of the problem has to do with how memories are determined to be false. Proponents of the false memory theory are quick to point out that, in the absence of evidence or corroboration, a memory cannot be determined to be historically true. What they do not mention as readily, and in fact downplay, is how a memory is determined to be historically false when no corroboration is available for that position. These individuals allege memories to be false without hard evidence; they accept the denial of the accused abuser(s) as more accurate and truthful than the allegation of the aggrieved party. Undoubtedly, some accusations of abuse are inaccurate and lead to false accusations of innocent people, a tragedy that needs to be avoided whenever possible. What is not clear is how the determination is made that a delayed report of abuse is false and what data are available to support that position. False negatives can also be tragic.

The false memory perspective is one that unfortunately favours real abusers and bolsters their denials. Ironically, the possibility of alleged offenders having false memories is not discussed as a possibility. The critics, by and large, are not trained in the assessment of sexual abuse allegations and theirs is certainly a risky position since real abuse perpetrators are notoriously dishonest about reporting or disclosing their offences (Prendergast 1993; Salter 1988, 1995). A very real consequence of the false memory defence is to make true abusers less responsible for their actions and to put more children at risk of abuse. A more reasonable position for the critics to take is to call for the individual assessment of each allegation of abuse rather than routinely labelling such an allegation false (especially if the individual with recollections of abuse is in therapy or has delayed recall). The defence of the accused can go to the extreme as can belief in the accuser. Both sides need assessment of the particulars of each individual case as well as a weighing of whatever evidence is available.

Ideological and political aspects of the controversy

The current controversy encompasses many ideological and political issues, several of which are discussed below. As mentioned just previously, one involves the rather automatic assumption that false memory pertains only to those who allege abuse and does not apply to the accused, this despite research and clinical evidence to the contrary (Prendergast 1993; Salter 1988, 1995). This assumption has historically been made on the basis of gender and on presumptions deriving from gender stereotypes: hysterical girls and women are not credible and their reports of abuse are not to be believed especially when made against upstanding men who deny the allegations. In the current formulation, as noted earlier, it is young female therapists who are identified as most at fault for suggesting abuse to their female clients to meet their own needs or to work out their own unresolved abuse issues. Concerning female therapists, one false memory commentator wrote: 'What better way to wreak vengeance on men than to become a therapist and use one's patients to act out one's morbid hostility?' (Gardner 1992, p. 654). This emphasis is but a new variation on the old theme that women (now women therapists) are less credible and trustworthy than their male counterparts and, further, that they have unbridled aggressive impulses towards men; therefore, their work with abuse is automatically suspect, a sign of their mental instability and/or need for retaliation or revenge.

Other ideological/political issues concern the challenging or disregard of some of the most important advances in the study and recognition of child sexual abuse, namely its prevalence and its most common dynamics and characteristics, along with a skewed interpretation of the changed social context in which child abuse has emerged as a social issue. The modern-day study of child sexual abuse/incest began in earnest in the 1970s in conjunction with the focus on stranger rape and domestic violence generated by the Women's Movement. As these two social problems began to be systematically investigated, researchers made a surprising and unexpected discovery: a significant number of women subjects who described experiences of rape and domestic violence in adulthood also reported sexual assault experiences in childhood perpetrated by acquaintances and, most surprisingly, by family members.

The social significance of this research finding has been enormous. Incest has long been the most forbidden of human sexual contacts, with societal disapproval and approbation directed at both perpetrators and victims. Researchers began to discover that the taboo did not seem to prevent its occurrence but rather kept its victims in silence, forbidden from disclosing due to their shame and the social prohibition (Meiselman 1978; Russell 1986; Rush 1980). This, in turn, supported the secrecy encouraged and needed by perpetrators. A cultural change of major proportions has taken place as the taboo on disclosure has been breached: previously hidden child sexual abuse has been acknowledged and discussed as never before in human history, due largely to the widespread dissemination of research information about sexual abuse/incest in the mass media. This public exposure has had the side effect of encouraging additional disclosure and, in the process, of uncovering previously unacknowledged forms of incest and sexual abuse (i.e. sibling incest, sexual abuse of boys, abuse by clergy and other professionals, to name but a few).

Research undertaken in the past 20 years, based on both retrospective reports of abuse by adults (in small sample and large random survey form) and on yearly compilations of reports of contemporaneous abuse, document with great consistency a high prevalence of sexual abuse across all major demographic strata and cultural groups. Current estimates are that up to 1 in 5 adult women and between 1 in 7 to 1 in 11 men in North America have been sexually abused as children (Finkelhor 1994; Russell 1983). Despite the consistency between the various studies and the belief of experts in the study of child maltreatment that the statistics are likely *underestimates*, false memory advocates charge that the documented high prevalence and the increase in reports in recent years is due not to real abuse but false reporting (often fanned by media reports).

Clearly, media attention has been extensive and increasingly sensationalized over the years. This has had numerous repercussions, perhaps the most common and controversial being the permission it has given individuals to reflect on their personal histories and to consider abuse. In some cases, the recollection and/or disclosure of previously hidden abuse experiences has been cued or triggered by the media. In others, it has not. In still others, the question of creating illusory or false memories of abuse has been raised. The whole area of media, social, and therapeutic influence on recall of past events, especially events that were previously taboo and *verboten*, remains to be investigated as does the iatrogenic creation of memories. Additionally, the issues of false and/or unfounded reports of abuse remain open and in need of more research. The currently available data suggest that false reporting occurs at a rate that is fairly constant but low and that unfounded reports do not necessarily mean that abuse did not occur, only that sufficient evidence is not available. These reporting and investigation issues are very important and require additional study; nevertheless, they should not be used prematurely to deny sexual abuse as a significant and prevalent social problem.

In a related vein, the critics seem to dismiss or ignore the identified characteristics and dynamics of sexual abuse, especially incest, that provide possible explanation and rationale for inconsistent memory in adult survivors. Incest has been the topic of psychiatric and psychological investigation since the late 1880s. Clinical case studies documenting its characteristics, family dynamics and roles, and initial and long-term aftereffects have appeared sporadically since the 1920s, becoming somewhat more regular in the 1940s, 50s and 60s (Butler 1978; Courtois 1979; Herman and Hirschman 1977; Meiselman 1978). These studies consistently documented characteristics of occurrence within the family: skewed role relationships, role reversals, and boundary blurring between family members; situational versus chronic occurrences; single versus multiple perpetrators; patterns of risk due to children's birth order and gender (the oldest female child the most at risk for paternal incest) and single versus multiple victims (the abuse of the oldest female child often repeated with the younger female – and sometimes male – siblings); patterns of occurrence in conjunction with other forms of domestic violence and parental illness including alcoholism and drug use; and, patterns of secrecy and non-intervention even with disclosure and observation. These studies did not identify sexual abuse as particularly traumatic. Rather, it was viewed as stigmatizing and damaging but not as overly disturbing to the individual.

Research conducted in the last 20 years has substantiated some of the early findings, particularly those concerning family roles, dynamics, and characteristics of the abuse, and has underscored those that, on average, pose the greatest hazard to victims. A more sophisticated understanding about initial and long-term aftereffects and the developmental impact of sexual abuse/incest has also been generated. A series of group studies and analyses conducted in the 1950s, 60s and 70s (for example Benward and Densen-Gerber 1975; Berry 1975; Cormier *et al.* 1962; Landis 1956; Lester 1972; Peters 1976) began the elaboration of what was then known about abuse aftereffects. Sexual abuse/incest emerged as a significant stressor for a child with high potential for psychological and relational damage at the time of its occurrence and/or across the lifespan. Researchers Burgess and Holmstrom were among the first to identify sexual abuse as traumatic in their seminal article 'Sexual trauma of children and adolescents: pressure, sex and secrecy' (Burgess and Holmstrom 1974). The inclusion of the diagnosis of post-traumatic stress disorder in the *DSM-III* (American Psychiatric Association 1980), largely the result of the study of war trauma in returning Vietnam veterans, further spurred this development. Clinicians and researchers alike began to identify sexual abuse as meeting the criteria of a traumatic stressor as described in the diagnosis and the aftereffects as post-traumatic (Donaldson and Gardner 1985; Goodwin 1985; Green 1983; Herman 1981; Lindberg and Distad 1985).

Many characteristics of sexual abuse were found to be traumatic for the victim, beginning with the fact that it was most often perpetrated by a family member or by someone known to the child. Abuse that occurs within an ongoing relationship is more likely to be repeated than is abuse perpetrated by a stranger – a family context in particular or any relationship that allows ongoing contact with or accessibility to the child creates a higher risk for recurrence. All things being equal, the closer the degree of relatedness, the greater the betrayal of the relationship, and the higher the potential for damage. Parent–child incest is the most damaging by far, followed by the other type within the nuclear family, that between siblings (Courtois 1988; Russell 1986). Additionally, the more atypical and therefore the more taboo the incest, the more damaging its potential. For example, mother–son, mother–daughter, and father–son incest is believed to be much less common than the father–daughter type; it thus carries additional stigma and shame for the victim. It is also possible that abuse variables such as these affect a child's remembering patterns – victims of abuse involving massive degrees of betrayal and associated shame and stigma would likely result in increased use of dissociation, memory suppression, and motivated forgetting (Freyd 1994).

The usual pattern of incestuous abuse is for it to begin when the child is prepubertal, often in early childhood, and to involve repeated and progressively intrusive and severe sexual activity over its duration, the average of which is four years. In contrast, abuse outside of the family is likely to be of shorter duration, without the same degree of physical or emotional entrapment of the child or the same progression of sexual acts. Although most sexual abuse does not involve physical violence *per se*, it may involve physical force and inevitably involves some sort of coercion and misrepresentation of the relationship and the sexual activity. The child is manipulated in a number of ways: by what the abuser tells him/her about what is happening between them (this often involves gross misrepresentation, blame, shame, and outright threats and blackmail), by the child's immaturity (physical, emotional, sexual), by the unequal power and status in the relationship, and by the child's dependence on family members and other adults for attachment, safety, and nurturance. Another aspect of the coercion is the perpetrator's need for secrecy, necessary to minimize outside interference and intervention while allowing for repetition of the behaviour. Obviously, all of these contextual elements of incest/sexual abuse can have an effect on recall. Preliminary findings from a rather new body of memory research that investigates memory for unpleasant (if not traumatic) events suggest how developmental issues, source monitoring, the effect of social discourse and support on remembering can contribute to an understanding of how memory loss might occur (Fivush 1994; Goodman *et al.* 1994; Hewitt 1994; Tessler and Nelson 1994).

Perhaps the most damaging dimension of abuse is the fact that it is perpetrated not on an adult whose psychosexual development is relatively complete and whose personality is largely formed but instead involves a child who is 'in process', whose body and personality are immature and developing. Thus, the child's growth and maturation are at risk, impacted by protracted abuse by a primary caretaker with little or no possibility of escape without outside assistance. Children caught in such an isolated situation cope as best they can – behaviorally, emotionally, and socially – according to their age, developmental stage, and degree of maturation. They usually develop strong defences and have been found to have patterns of both stunted and accelerated psychosexual development as well as physical maturation (Trickett and Putnam 1995). Although some are or appear asymptomatic (Beitchman *et al.* 1991) many develop symptomatology associated with post-traumatic stress disorder (acute at the time of the abuse and/or in chronic or delayed form over time). Patterns of post-traumatic coping and adaptation consequent to exposure to various forms of prolonged domestic trauma often become intertwined with ongoing personality development (Browne and Finkelhor 1986; Herman 1992*a*, *b*), to result in a personality disturbance or disorder, the most common being borderline personality (now often identified as PTSD/Borderline) or a personality disorder with mixed features (Briere 1989; Herman *et al.* 1989; Kroll 1993; Ross 1989).

Another line of research, the study of clinical dissociation, has contributed to increased understanding of the complexity of abuse aftereffects and memory variability. Dissociation, described generally as defensive disruption in the normally occurring connection among feelings, thoughts, behaviours, and memories that is consciously or unconsciously invoked to reduce psychological distress during and after traumatic episodes (Briere 1992), has been identified as a quite common and adaptive response to traumatization. In fact, psychogenic or dissociative amnesia is recognized as the most common of the dissociative disorders. A number of researchers have proposed that PTSD is inherently dissociative in terms of its two signature phases, the phase of re-experiencing/remembering of the trauma alternating with the phase of avoidance/numbing/forgetting of the same (Horowitz 1986; Putnam 1989; Ross 1989). Patterns of remembering and forgetting are thus characteristic of the post-traumatic response, posited by some researchers as a mechanism that allows for the gradual assimilation of the traumatic material over time or, alternatively, that blocks assimilation in post-traumatic reactions that become pathological (Horowitz 1986; McCann and Pearlman 1990). Studies of traumatized children have identified PTSD as a common aftermath, and the routine use of dissociation and other strong defences especially when the trauma is ongoing or otherwise extreme (Putnam 1989; Terr 1988, 1991).

Dissociation is currently understood as perhaps the most likely defensive operation available to the chronically traumatized and entrapped child and as another post-traumatic adaptation that interweaves with and interferes with personality development. Some clinical researchers have speculated that a new diagnosis, encompassing these common adaptations and their developmental impact and variously referred to as Complex PTSD or Disorders of Extreme Stress, Not Otherwise Specified (DESNOS) (Herman 1992*a,b*), Trauma Disorders, Acute and Chronic, Dissociative or Nondissociative (Ross 1989) or Complex Dissociative PTSD (Herman 1992*a,b*; Kluft 1990) be given consideration in future editions of the *DSM*.

Furthermore, current thinking is that dissociation, alone or in interaction with some of the most salient developmental and contextual aspects of abuse trauma, may account for the variability of memory in former abuse victims as reported by clinicians and researchers (Briere 1989; Briere and Conte 1993; Courtois 1988; Elliott and Briere 1994, 1995; Feldman-Summers and Pope 1994; Gold and Hughes unpublished; Gold *et al.* 1994; Harvey and Herman 1994; Herman and Schatzow 1987; Loftus *et al.* 1994; van der Kolk *et al.* 1994; van der Kolk and Fisler 1995; Williams 1994, 1995). The issues of memory processes and memory disruption in trauma are highly complex and multiply determined and require intensive investigation by both researchers in traumatology and in human memory processes. Clinical observations and field studies can and should be used to inform future research on the nature of traumatic memories as suggested by Alpert *et al.* (1996), Harvey and Herman (1994), and Terr (1988, 1991).

One final ideological/political issue deserves mention: the difficulty in achieving such a rapprochement and collaboration between academic memory researchers and practising clinicians. The polarization of the current debate is attributable, in part, to the vastly different traditions between the two. As noted recently by Alpert (1995, pp. 3–4):

In general, those engaged in scientific memory research are cognitive psychologists who have no clinical training or experience, while those engaged in the scholarly literature on trauma and child sexual abuse are practitioners or scientist-practitioners who treat victims of trauma and may also be engaged in the scientific study and research of traumatology. Until recently the experimental writings have been published in journals and books that are not oriented to clinicians. Similarly, the more clinical writings have been published in journals and books that are not oriented to scientists. Consequently, there has been little consolidation. What has been incorporated from one literature to the other has often been misinformation. While this schism does not do justice to the existence of some heterogeneity, it is telling.

Parallel work by trauma and memory experts and wholesale depreciation of the methods of one by the other do not contribute to science, practice, and to the public at large. What is needed is a trauma-focused clinical paradigm that attends to the reconstructive nature of memory as well as a memory research paradigm that attends to traumatic events and their possible impact on memory (Alpert *et al.* 1996). Such cross-fertilization of scholarship will ultimately advance research, theory, and practice.

IMPLICATIONS FOR THERAPISTS: THE EVOLVING
STANDARD OF CARE AND GUIDELINES FOR PRACTICE

Therapists are at 'ground zero' and at substantial risk in this controversy. Not only have the critics mounted an extremely effective media campaign undermining the work and credibility of therapists (across the board and not only concerning repressed memory issues – see Butler (1995) for a discussion of the crisis of confidence in psychotherapy in general) but they have also mounted a legislative initiative that would tightly regulate the practice of psychotherapy. It would dismantle some standard and accepted techniques of psychotherapy, not only those deemed to be suggestive (The Truth and Responsibility in Mental Health Practices Act also known as The Mental Health Consumer Protection Act) (Barden 1994). The American Psychological Association went on record as being against this legislation in February 1995 with a resolution stating in part that: '. . . while seeming to protect the consumer, [the bill] actually creates a bureaucracy and unnecessary barriers that interfere with consumer access to mental health services and fails to protect the consumer' (American Psychological Association 1995).

Additionally, some former patients who complain of the use of suggestive techniques and individuals who claim to be falsely accused by someone whose memories emerged in therapy are being encouraged to bring ethics or licensing board charges against the treating clinician or to initiate a lawsuit as plaintiff or as aggrieved third party. Although lawsuits are certainly an avenue of redress in all sorts of alleged injuries and malpractice, the zeal which they have been encouraged in some repressed memory cases is remarkable. Workshops are currently being offered across the country on how to successfully sue therapists and, to paraphrase one attorney prominent in this undertaking, such lawsuits are 'the up and coming area of litigation of the late 90's'.

The authority to determine psychotherapeutic practice belongs, by professional credentialing and by law, to those who have specialized advanced training and a licence to practice psychotherapy. As I have written elsewhere, 'A peculiar and rather novel part of the current controversy is that researchers in the cognitive sciences are challenging practice without having been trained in providing therapy and their opinions are holding sway in a way that suggest that clinicians have no specialized training or expertise (Courtois 1995*a*, p. xiii). This is contrary to and in violation of Principle A (Competence) and Ethical Standard 1.04 (Boundaries of Competence) of *The ethical principles of psychologists and the code of conduct* that specifically caution psychologists about the limitations of expertise and urge them to work within the boundaries and training of particular competencies (American Psychological Association 1992).

It is obvious that therapists must take action to challenge and correct what has so rapidly become the *status guo*. They must become pro-active, both to ensure the continued development of this important area of practice and to furthermore protect themselves and the professional practice of psychotherapy.

Therapists can undertake many different initiatives, including but not limited to challenging and correcting the misinformation being conveyed about them; requesting data in support of claims continuing to generate research data about the dynamics of family violence in general and child sexual abuse in particular with emphasis on the initial and long-term effects on victims and on the characteristics and dynamics of offenders; developing specialized empirically based treatment and training for post-abuse reactions with particular attention to the issue of memory; developing specialized empirically based treatment and training for offenders with particular attention to the issue of memory; working collegially and collaboratively with cognitive scientists who specialize in memory processes and incorporating their suggestions about practice where appropriate; working through professional organizations to encourage state legislatures to more tightly regulate the practice of psychotherapy to prevent untrained or minimally trained laypersons from advertising and practising as psychotherapists; developing treatment guidelines to assist therapists in their work with child victims and adult survivors of sexual abuse, especially as pertains to memory processes; and, confronting, educating, and, where necessary, disciplining peers who have practiced outside of the evolving standard of care and who, for whatever reason, have engaged in malpractice.

To date, a number of professional organizations have made attempts to respond to the controversy both to guide practitioners and to educate the public and the consumer. In 1993, the American Medical Association issued a report, the American Psychiatric Association issued guidelines, and the American Psychological Association empaneled a six-member Working Group made up of three cognitive scientists specializing in memory and three scientist-practitioners specializing in trauma and adult survivors of child sexual abuse. The latter group issued an interim report in 1994, the Board of Directors of the American Psychological Association issued a pamphlet on delayed memory in 1995, and the full report of the Working Group has recently been released. The British Psychological Society empaneled a Working Party that issued a report in 1994, The American Society of Clinical Hypnosis (Hammond *et al.* 1995) issued guidelines for clinicians and for forensic hypnosis on the topic of clinical hypnosis and memory, and other professional groups such as the American Professional Society on the Abuse of Children and the National Organization of Social Workers are currently reviewing the issues and drafting guidelines for practice. Many suggestions from these various reports are incorporated into the following two sections on the evolving standard of care and guidelines for practice.

THE EVOLVING STANDARD OF CARE

The standard of care for sexual abuse treatment as presented here is in agreement with the general definition offered recently by Brown (1995, p. 16):

'evolving professional peer definitions of a standard established by expert testimony, by authoritative clinical-scientific literature, and also by regulatory and ethics guidelines. The standard of care for trauma treatment is defined by the evolving literature on diagnosis, as defined by *DSM-IV* (American Psychiatric Association 1994), and on trauma treatment written by trauma experts'. Therapists working with traumatized or possibly traumatized individuals have a professional responsibility to stay informed about treatment recommendations from both trauma and memory experts and to incorporate them in their work as warranted. They must pay particular attention to social influence and risk factors that might lead to false beliefs, reports, and memories, monitor their own beliefs and countertransference as might influence the application of problematic strategies and techniques, and further monitor issues of ethics and boundaries, role strain, and self-care (Enns *et al.*, 1995).

The available treatment models for the long-term effects of sexual abuse (Briere 1989, 1991, 1992; Brown and Fromm 1986; Courtois 1988; Davies and Frawley 1994; Gil 1988; Herman 1981, 1992*b*; Jehu 1988; Kepner 1995; Kirschner *et al.*. 1993; Kluft 1990; Kluft and Fine 1993; McCann and Pearlman 1990; Meiselman 1978, 1990; Putnam 1989; Ross 1989; Salter 1995) differ from more generic therapy by virtue of a post-traumatic perspective as articulated in Herman (1992), Horowitz (1986), Janet, (1889), Ochberg (1988), and Meichenbaum (1994) among others. This perspective acknowledges rather than dismisses the impact of exogenous trauma on the individual and, in particular, its possible aetiological role in the individual's symptoms. In the case of chronic traumatization (especially occurring in childhood), it posits enduring implication in the individual's personality development. Much of what is later considered maladaptive and even pathological may have originated as the child's attempts to cope with ongoing abuse and lack of protection. Therapeutic gain is achieved by normalizing rather than pathologizing these responses as the 'normal reactions of a healthy child to an unhealthy situation' and by educating the client as a preliminary step in the change process.

Although abuse receives direct attention in this treatment, it is not the sole point of therapeutic attention and intervention. Numerous other life events and personal characteristics/resiliency factors are taken into account, and the treatment is geared towards the client's strengths and towards change and resolution, not towards ongoing dependency. A comprehensive assessment at the outset of treatment is always recommended as a baseline, with subsequent assessments undertaken as needed (Courtois 1995*a,b*). As noted by Briere (1989), Courtois (1988, 1995*a*), and Jehu (1988), the emergence of previously unrecognized issues may only occur after the resolution of other issues and/or only as the therapeutic relationship deepens enough to support additional disclosure.

In this therapy, it is assumed that the majority of clients retain full or partial memory for the abuse and that a small minority have totally absent memory and later recall; however, it is also assumed that partial or fragmentary memory as well as delayed disclosure is normal in traumatized individuals and that the abuse material may emerge in response to a wide array of cues or triggers, some of which might occur in therapy. The treatment is directed towards the exploration of the individual's subjective experience and hence is a primary place for the emergence or disclosure of forbidden or split-off material. Therapist and client work together with the material to allow reconstruction, understanding, and the resolution of symptoms. In the case of absent or hazy memory (with or without constellations of symptoms that might have association to an abuse history) the reality of abuse may never be known; both therapist and client must be able to tolerate ambiguity and uncertainty. The therapist's job is to create and maintain an environment conducive to exploration, an atmosphere that is neutral in position yet supportive in stance that neither errs in the direction of overbelief and suggestion or of under-belief and suppression. The therapy *is not* driven either by memory retrieval or memory retrieval techniques. Rather, it is oriented towards a number of treatment goals and is theoretically and strategically eclectic, using a broad array of theoretical perspectives and techniques to understand and work with the client's particular issues (Briere 1989; Courtois 1988).

Sequenced treatment oriented around phases and healing tasks

A strong consensus exists among trauma experts regarding the format and sequence of treatment for post-traumatic conditions. These experts caution clinicians regarding the complexity and difficulty of this treatment population which presents a broad array of life problems, characterological issues, and traumatic process and content, along with intense and shifting relational demands. They stress the utility of an overall strategy by which to organize what are usually a multitude of serious treatment issues and targets. They also recommend the study of transference and countertransference phenomena in the treatment of traumatized individuals because this therapy poses especially difficult and rather unique problems and risks (Chu 1988; Pearlman and Saakvitne 1995). Whenever possible, this treatment should be undertaken by the experienced rather than the novice therapist, especially when supervision or consultation is not readily available to the novice. As noted earlier, it is likely that some of the controversy has been generated in response to errors made by inexperienced, naive, uninformed, or overwhelmed therapists who practice without adequate supports. Training programs are beginning to give this issue consideration by incorporating information on post-traumatic conditions and their treatment into the training curriculum and by providing supervision attuned to the particular issues that are likely to arise in this therapy (Enns *et al.* 1995; Hotelling 1995; Payne 1995).

As opposed to a treatment strategy that is oriented around a full remembering and/or re-experiencing of trauma (commonly identified as an abreactive therapy), the model currently espoused is oriented towards what Kepner

(1995) has labelled 'healing tasks' or what Liebowitz *et al.* (1993) have called 'stage by dimension' treatment. Treatment goals or tasks are organized sequentially, progressively, and hierarchically in several main treatment stages. Within each stage the goals (or healing tasks or dimensions) are organized according to the client's capacities and tolerance, the content and affect titrated accordingly. Although the model appears to be linear, in practice it is spiral and recursive. Clients move back and forth between phases and tasks as needed, repeatedly reworking in more depth and sophistication issues initially addressed during the crucial first phase. The duration of treatment thus varies markedly according to the client's needs and functioning. Some move through therapy in a straightforward way while majority have more lengthy treatment requiring close monitoring and titration.

Any attention to trauma/abuse issues early in treatment are in the cognitive domain and educational in nature. Direct attention to or exploration of any abuse or trauma – likely to evoke strong emotional reactions – is undertaken only when the client has achieved enough stability, skills, and ego strength to handle the emotions. Because of this, some clients who do not have the personal resources or motivation to do so never directly address the trauma. Their therapy is focused on stability and functioning only.

The available treatment models are generally encompassed by the following three general phases:

1. *Stability and safety with an emphasis on client education, daily functioning, self-management of symptoms and development of the therapeutic relationship.* Typical issues given attention in this phase include assessment and treatment planning; the development of coping skills, ego defences, self-capacities, and self-protection/personal safety; the stabilization of mood and personality disturbances and disorders; the management of any intrusive/re-experiencing and numbing symptoms associated with PTSD and dissociative disorders; the development of relationship skills and the building of a support system outside of therapy; and, the resolution of current life crises and difficulties, the most common of which involve abusive relationships, revictimizations, addictions and compulsions, eating disorders, suicidality, and self-injurious behaviours. As can be seen from this brief listing, the goals of this phase are ambitious and comprehensive. Although they resemble those of non-trauma-oriented therapy, they also differ and are compounded due to post-traumatic influence. For example, the development of a therapeutic relationship may be extremely difficult due to the mistrust that many abuse survivors hold towards authority figures. Previously traumatized clients often return to maladaptive coping strategies when stressed and might do so repeatedly, especially during this phase. Some clients never move beyond the work of this stage and some choose to end treatment at this point after having made substantial progress.

2. *Systematic, prepared and titrated work with the abuse/trauma.* This phase is also organized according to the client's needs, defences, and capacities. The

client is assisted to gradually face and integrate the traumatic material and its associated emotions at a pace that is safe and manageable. This work is done not to foster regression or dependence within the therapy in a morass of more and more serious (and implausible) trauma and certainly not to create traumatic memories; rather, the purpose is to allow personal reconstruction of trauma and the ventilation and assimilation of associated emotion in the interest of resolution and healing. While such trauma work is not always indicated, its utility in many cases is demonstrated by outcome research that has demonstrated that exposure to traumatic memories, along with their cognitive and emotional desensitization and processing, is related to symptom relief in the behavioural treatment of PTSD.

3. *Reconsolidation and reconnection.* This phase involves continued and more in-depth work on self-development (including attention to personality issues, mood disturbances, coping strategies, the capacity to be intimate and sexual), relations with others (including intimate relationships and parenting), and major life decisions, all less encumbered by post-traumatic effects. This phase often includes a great deal of personal, relational, and even vocational reassessment and change. Many of the issues are those addressed throughout the therapy but it is only after trauma resolution that additional resolution and refocus are possible.

Therapy issues pertaining to delayed/repressed memory

Throughout the course of treatment, the therapist must 'walk a fine line' to be neutrally supportive of the client, especially when clear memory of past abuse is not available, when abuse is suspected, and/or when the client is confused, or pressuring, or suggestible. This approach calls for the therapist to not prematurely either suggest or dismiss the possibility of abuse in the client's past and to carefully manage risk factors in both client and therapist that could encourage the production of false beliefs or reports. It is advisable for the therapist to adopt a scientific attitude regarding treatment in general and traumatic recall in particular and to teach the client to do the same (Brown 1995; Hammond *et al.* 1995). In a similar vein, the therapist should correct any misinformation held by the client about memory processes and should provide information (verbally and in writing) about how the therapy is to proceed, especially as concerns memory-related material. Specifically, this calls for education about the reconstructive nature of memory, developmental issues, memory for emotional events, and narrative versus historical accuracy.

Clients must additionally be advised that the therapist cannot confirm or disconfirm the historical truth or accuracy of a client's recollections especially in the absence of outside corroboration or evidence. A search for outside corroboration is sometimes pursued by the client, a process that the therapist can support but that should not be expected to always result in conclusive evidence. As discussed above, when cognitive memory is absent and evidence or corroboration are not found, therapist and client are left with uncertainty and ambiguity, something they must both be able to tolerate. Clients must be advised that such a circumstance is not a roadblock; rather, the therapy's overall orientation toward other aspects of the client's life and functioning has the benefit of not emphasizing the retrieval of absent memories to the exclusion of other life issues.

Therapists must also not overemphasize sexual abuse as the sole type of trauma or developmental/family events that could account for the client's symptoms. As discussed by Alpert *et al.* (1996) in their literature review of the effects of sexual abuse, no one symptom is pathognomic of sexual abuse and many symptoms are not exclusive to sexual abuse. Although the therapist must not make assumptions, fill in the blanks, or jump to conclusions (especially when memory is spotty or some symptoms or behaviours that are in evidence are suggestive), he or she must assist in exploration and remain open to the emergence of abuse and trauma issues over time.

Additionally, client psychodynamics, family relations, outside influences, and sources of secondary gain must be assessed and monitored. The therapist must resist any pressure to become the client's rescuer or surrogate parent and must work against overdependence. Clients should be actively discouraged from drawing insupportable conclusions and particularly from taking premature and ill-advised action against family members or others. This would include the confrontation of family members (alleged perpetrators and others) about abuse, severing ties with family members, reporting abuse to the authorities, and initiating civil lawsuits when cognitive memory is absent or uncertain. (This must be distinguished from those circumstances of actual or threatened violence to a client where the therapist is obligated, in the interest of the client's immediate safety and protection, to suggest courses of action such as no contact, a restraining order, a move to a shelter.) Therapists must assist clients to understand the radical difference between exploring or speculating about (or even becoming absolutely convinced about the reality of something in the absence of concrete evidence) in therapy and using it as the basis for serious and sometimes irreversible actions outside of the therapy setting, especially in the legal arena.

Finally, the treatment of this population holds singular demands and challenges, now more than ever before. Therapists must constantly attend to themselves – their beliefs that might lead to biases, their knowledge base and continuing education, their countertransference reactions and their management, and their own mental health and self-care – to guard against burn-out and unhelpful enactments with their clients or others. It is strongly recommended that therapists doing this work (especially those in solo practices) have a source of outside support, whether formal supervision or ongoing consultation. By engaging in self-monitoring and self-care and by working in an informed way within the evolving standard, therapists can and will continue to treat this formerly underserved population.

CONCLUSION

This chapter has reviewed some of the main critiques of the recovered/delayed memory controversy. Among other things, therapists as a group have been accused of professional irresponsibility for misunderstanding human memory, particularly memory for traumatic events, and for using overly suggestive techniques to implant false memories of sexual abuse in their clients. Many of the critiques are speculative, overgeneralized, and driven by political and ideological issues; however, they raise a host of questions and issues for investigation and have contributed to the articulation of an evolving standard of care for practice. This standard, informed by studies of trauma and child sexual abuse and by observation in clinical settings, is outlined and discussed in this chapter. A treatment strategy is presented that is progressive and hierarchical, organized around symptom stabilization and personal and interpersonal functioning rather than memory recall *per se*, except as clinically necessary. Preliminary suggestions for work with delayed/repressed memory are also presented.

REFERENCES

Alpert, J. (ed.) (1995). *Sexual abuse recalled: treating trauma in the era of the recovered memory debate*. Aronson, Northvale, NJ.

Alpert, J., Brown, L., and Courtois, C. (1996). *Symptomatic clients and memories of childhood abuse: what the trauma and child sexual abuse literature tells us*. American Psychological Association, Washington, DC.

American Psychiatric Association (1980). *Diagnostic and statistical manual of mental disorders*, (3rd edn.). Washington, DC.

American Psychiatric Association (1993). *Statement on delayed memories of sexual abuse*. Washington, DC.

American Psychiatric Association (1994). Diagnostic and statistical manual of mental disorders, (4th edn.). Washington, DC.

American Psychological Association (1992). Ethical principles of psychologists and code of conduct. *American Psychologist*.

American Psychological Association (1994). *Interim report of the working group on investigation of memories of childhood abuse*. Washington, DC.

American Psychological Association (1995). *Council of Representatives Resolution Concerning 'Mental Health Consumer Protection Acts'*. Washington, DC.

American Psychological Association. (1996). *Final report of the working group on investigation of memories of childhood abuse*. Washington, DC.

Barden, R.C. (1994). A proposal to finance preparation of model legislation titled *Mental Health Consumer Protection Act*. Unpublished.

Beitchman, J., Zucker, K., Hood, J., daCosta, G., and Ackman, D. (1991). A review of the short-term effects of childhood sexual abuse. *Child Abuse and Neglect*, **5**, 537–56.

Benward, J. and Densen-Gerber, J. (1975). Incest as a causative factor in anti-social behavior: an exploratory study. *Contemporary Drug Problems*, **4**, 323–40.

Berry, G.W. (1975). Incest: some clinical variations on a classical theme. *Journal of the American Academy of Psychoanalysis*, **3**, 151–61.

Braun, B.G. (ed.).(1986). Treatment of multiple personality disorder. American Psychiatric Press, Washington, DC.

Briere, J. (1989). *Therapy for adults molested as children*. Springer, New York.

Briere, J. (ed.). (1991). *Treating victims of child sexual abuse*. Josey-Bass, San Francisco.

Briere, J. (1992). *Child abuse trauma: theory and treatment of the lasting effects*. Sage, Newbury Park, CA.

Briere, J. (1995). Science versus politics in the delayed memory debate: a commentary. *The Counseling Psychologist*, **23**, 280–9.

Briere, J. and Conte, J. (1993). Self-reported amnesia for abuse in adults molested as children. *Journal of Traumatic Stress*, **6**, 21–31.

British Psychological Society (1995). *Report of the Working Party on recovered memories*. Leicester, UK.

Brown, D. (1995). Pseudomemories: the standard of science and the standard of care in trauma treatment. *American Journal of Clinical Hypnosis*, **37**, 1–24.

Brown, D.P. and Fromm, E. (1986). *Hypnotherapy and hypnoanalysis*. Erlbaum, Hillsdale, NJ.

Browne, A. and Finkelhor, D. (1986). Impact of child sexual abuse: a review of the research. *Psychological Bulletin*, **99**, 66–77.

Burgess, A. and Holmstrom, L.L. (1974). Sexual assault of children and adolescents: pressure, sex and secrecy. *Nursing Clinics of North America*, **10**, 554–63.

Butler, K. (1995). Caught in the cross fire: therapy under the glass. *The Family Therapy Networker*, March/April, 25–39, 80.

Butler, S. (1978). *Conspiracy of silence: The trauma of incest*. Bantam, New York.

Chu, J. (1988). Ten traps for therapists in the treatment of trauma survivors. *Dissociation*, **1**, 24–32.

Cormier, B.M., Kennedy, M., and Sangowicz, J. (1962). Psychodynamics of father–daughter incest. *Canadian Psychiatric Association Journal*, **7**, 203–17.

Courtois, C.A. (1979). Characteristics of a volunteer sample of adult women who experienced incest in childhood and adolescence. *Dissertation Abstracts International*, **40A**, Nov./Dec., 3194–A.

Courtois, C.A. (1988). *Healing the incest wound: adult survivors in therapy*. Norton, New York.

Courtois, C.A. (1991). Theory, sequencing, and strategy in treating adult survivors. In *Treating victims of child sexual abuse*, (ed. J. Briere), pp. 47–60). Jossey-Bass, San Francisco.

Courtois, C.A. (1995*a*). Recovery memory/false memory polarities: balance and collaboration needed. *Consciousness and Cognition*, **4**, 133–4.

Courtois, C.A. (1995*b*). Scientist-practitioners and the delayed memory controversy: scientific standards and the need for collaboration. *The Counseling Psychologist*, **23**, 294–9.

Davies, J.M. and Frawley M.G. (1994). *Treating the adult survivor of childhood sexual abuse: A psychoanalytic perspective*. Basic Books, New York.

Donaldson, M.A. and Gardner, R. (1985). Diagnosis and treatment of traumatic stress among women after childhood incest. In *Trauma and its wake: the study and treatment of post-traumatic stress disorder*, (ed. C.R. Figley), pp. 356–77. Brunner/Mazel, New York.

Elliott, D.M. (1994). Trauma and dissociated memory: prevalence across events. Paper presented at the annual meeting of the International Society for Traumatic Stress Studies, Chicago, IL.

Elliott, D.M. and Briere, J. (1994). Posttraumatic stress associated with delayed recall of sexual abuse: a general population study. Paper presented at the annual meeting of the International Society for Traumatic Stress Studies, Chicago, IL.

Elliott, D.M. and Briere, J. (1995). Posttraumatic stress associated with delayed recall of sexual abuse: a general population study. *Journal of Traumatic Stress*, **8**, 629–48.

Enns, C.Z., McNeilly, C.L., Corkery, J.M., and Gilbert, M.S. (1995). The debate about delayed memories of child sexual abuse: a feminist perspective. *The Counseling Psychologist*, **23**, 181–279.

Eth, S. and Pynoos, R.S. (ed.) (1985). *Post-traumatic stress disorder in children*. American Psychiatric Press, Washington, DC.

False Memory Syndrome Foundation (1992). *False memory syndrome* (brochure). Philadelphia.

Feldman-Summers, S. and Pope, K.S. (1994). The experience of 'forgetting' childhood abuse: A national survey of psychologists. *Journal of Consulting and Clinical Psychology*, **62**, 1–4.

Figley, C. (ed.) (1985). *Trauma and its wake: the study and treatment of post-traumatic stress disorder*. Brunner/Mazel, New York.

Finkelhor, D. (1994). Current information on the scope and nature of child sexual abuse. *The Future of Children*, **4**, 31–53.

Fivush, R. (1994). Young children's event recall: are memories constructed through discourse? *Consciousness and Cognition*, **3**, 356–73.

Follette, V.M. and Polusny, M.A. (1995). Psychologists' clinical practices, beliefs, and personal experiences related to childhood sexual abuse. Paper presented at the annual meeting of the International Society for Traumatic Stress Studies, Boston, MA.

Freyd, J. (1994). Betrayal-trauma: traumatic amnesia as an adaptive response to childhood abuse. *Ethics and behavior*, **4**, 304–9.

Gardner, M. (1992). *True and false accusations of child sex abuse*. Creative Therapeutics, Creskill, NJ.

Gil, E. (1988). *Treatment of adult survivors of childhood abuse*. Launch Press, Walnut Creek, CA.

Gold, S.N. and Hughes, D.M. Degrees of memory of childhood sexual abuse among female survivors in therapy. (Unpublished.)

Gold, S.N., Hughes, D., and Honecker (1994). Degrees of repression of sexual abuse memories. *American Psychologist*, **48**, 441–7.

Goodman, G.S., Quas, J.A., Batterman-Faunce, J. M., Riddlesberger, M.M., and Kuhn, J. (1994). Predictors of accurate and inaccurate memories of traumatic events experienced in childhood. *Consciousness and Cognition*, **3**, 269–94.

Goodwin, J. (1985). Post-traumatic symptoms in incest victims. In *Post-traumatic stress disorder in children*, (ed. S. Eth and R.S. Pynoos), pp. 155–68. American Psychiatric Press, Washington, DC.

Green, A.H. (1983). Dimensions of psychological trauma in abused children. *Journal of the American Academy of Child Psychiatry*, **22**, 231–7.

Hammond, D.C. *et al.* (1995). *Clinical hypnosis and memory: Guidelines for clinicians and for forensic hypnosis*. American Society of Clinical Hypnosis Press, Chicago.

Harvey, M. and Herman, J.L. (1994) Amnesia, partial amnesia and delayed recall among adult survivors of childhood trauma. *Cognition and Consciousness*, **3**, 295–306.

Herman, J.L. (1981). *Father–daughter incest*. Harvard University Press, Cambridge, MA.

Herman, J.L. (1992*a*). Complex PTSD: a syndrome in survivors of prolonged and repeated trauma. *Journal of Traumatic Stress Studies*, **5**, 377–91.

Herman, J.L. (1992*b*). *Trauma and recovery*. Basic Books, New York.

Herman, J.L. (1994). Presuming to know the truth: based on three questionable propositions, journalists treat memories of childhood abuse as 'hysteria'. *Neiman Reports*, Spring, 43–5.

Herman, J.L. and Hirschman, L. (1977). Father–daughter incest. *Signs: Journal of Women in Culture and Society*, **2**, 735–56.

Herman, J.L. and Schatzow, E. (1987). Recovery and verification of memories of childhood sexual trauma. *Psychoanalytic Psychology*, **4**, 1–14.

Herman, J.L., Perry, J.C., and van der Kolk, B.A. (1989). Childhood trauma in borderline personality disorder. *American Journal of Psychiatry*, **146**, 490–5.

Hewitt, S.A. (1994). Preverbal sexual abuse: what two children report in later years. *Child Abuse & Neglect*, **18**, 821–6.

Horowitz, M. (1986). *Stress response syndromes*. Aronson, New York.

Hotelling, K. (1995). Ethical issues in the recovery of sexual abuse memories. Paper presented at the Annual Meeting of the American Psychological Association, New York City.

Janet, P. (1889). *L'automatisme psychologique*. Alcan, Paris.

Jehu, D. (1988). *Beyond sexual abuse: therapy with women who were childhood victims*. Wiley, New York.

Kepner, J.I. (1995). *Healing tasks: psychotherapy with adult survivors of childhood abuse*. Jossey-Bass, San Francisco.

Kirschner, S., Kirschner, D.A., and Rappaport, R.L. (1993). *Working with adult incest survivors: the healing journey*. Brunner/Mazel, New York.

Kluft, R.P. (ed.) (1990). *Incest-related syndromes of adult psychopathology*. American Psychiatric Press, Washington, DC.

Kluft, R.P. and Fine, C.G. (eds.) (1993). *Clinical perspectives on multiple personality disorder*. American Psychiatric Press, Washington, DC.

Kroll, J. (1993). *PTSD/Borderlines in therapy: finding the balance*. Norton, New York.

Landis, J.T. (1956). Experiences of 500 children with adult sexual deviation. *Psychiatric Quarterly* (supplement), **30**, 91–109.

Lester, D. (1968). Incest. *Journal of Sex Research*. **8**, 268–85.

Liebowitz, L., Harvey, M., and Herman, J. (1993). A stage-by-dimension model of recovery from sexual trauma. *Journal of Interpersonal violence*, **8**, 378–92.

Lindberg, F.H. and Distad, L.J. (1985). Post-traumatic stress disorder in women who experienced childhood incest. *Child Abuse and Neglect*, **9**, 329–34.

Loftus, E.F. (1993). The reality of repressed memories. *American Psychologist*, **48**, 518–37.

Loftus, E.F. and Ketcham, K. (1994). *The myth of repressed memory: false memories and allegations of abuse*. Martin's Press, New York.

Loftus, E.F., Polonsky, S., and Fullilove, M.T. (1994). Memories of childhood sexual abuse: Remembering and repressing. *Psychology of Women Quarterly*, **18**, 67–84.

McCann, I.L. and Pearlman, L.A. (1990). *Psychological trauma and the adult survivor*. Brunner/Mazel, New York.

Meichenbaum, D. (1994). *A clinical handbook/practical therapist manual for assessing and treating adults with Post-traumatic Stress Disorder (PTSD)*. Author, Waterloo, Ontario.

Meiselman, K.C. (1978). *Incest: a psychological study of cause and effects with treatment recommendations*. Jossey-Bass, San Francisco.

Meiselman, K.C. (1990). *Resolving the trauma of incest*. Jossey-Bass, San Francisco.

Ochberg, F.M. (ed.) (1988). *Post-traumatic therapy and victims of violence*. Brunner/Mazel, New York.

Ofshe, R. and Watters, E (1993). Making monsters. *Society*, **30**, March/April, 4–16.

Ornstein, P., Ceci, S., and Loftus, E. (1996). *Adult recollections of childhood abuse: Cognitive and developmental perspectives*. American Psychological Association, Washington, DC.

Payne, A.B. (1995). Training and supervision issues regarding trauma and recovery of memories. Paper presented at the annual meeting of the American Psychological Association, New York City, NY.

Pearlman, L.A. and Saakvitne, K. (1995). *Trauma and the therapist: Countertransference and vicarious traumatization in psychotherapy with incest survivors*. Norton, New York.

Peters, J.J. (1976). Children who are victims of sexual assault and the psychology of offenders. *American Journal of Psychotherapy*, **30**, 398–421.

Poole, D.A. and Lindsay, D.S. Psychotherapy and the recovery of memories of childhood sexual abuse: doctoral-level therapists' beliefs, practices and experiences. (Unpublished.)

Poole, D.A., Lindsay, D.S., Memon, A., and Bull, R. (1995). Psychotherapy and the recovery of memories of childhood sexual abuse: U.S. and British practitioners' opinions, practices, and experiences. *Journal of Consulting and Clinical Psychology*, **63**, 3, 426–37.

Prendergast, W.E. (1993). *The merry-go-round of sexual abuse: identifying and treating survivors*. Haworth Press, New York.

Putnam, F. (1989). *Diagnosis and treatment of multiple personality disorder*. Guilford, New York.

Ross, C. A. (1989). *Multiple personality disorder: diagnosis, clinical features, and treatment*. Wiley, New York.

Rush, F. (1980). *The best kept secret: sexual abuse of children*. McGraw-Hill, New York.

Russell, D. E. H. (1986). *The secret trauma: incest in the lives of girls and women. Basic Books, New York.*

Russell, D. E. H. (1983). The incidence and prevalence of intra-familial and extra-familial sexual abuse of female children. *Child Abuse & Neglect*, **7**, 133–46.

Salter, A. (1988). *Treating child sex offenders and victims: A practical guide*. Sage, Newbury Park, CA.

Salter, A. (1995). *The transformation of trauma*. Sage, Newbury Park, CA.

Sullins, C.D. (1995). *Repressed childhood sexual abuse: Gender effects on diagnosis and treatment*. Paper presented at the annual convention of the American Psychological Association, New York City, NY.

Terr, L. (1988). What happens to early memories of trauma? A study of twenty children under age five at the time of documented traumatic events. *American Journal of Child and Adolescent Psychiatry*, **27**, 96–104.

Terr, L. (1991). Childhood traumas: an outline and overview. *American Journal of Psychiatry*, **148**, 10–20.

Tessler, M. and Nelson, K. (1994). Making memories: the influence of joint encoding on later recall by young children. *Consciousness and Cognition*, **3**, 307–26.

Trickett, P. and Putnam, F. (1995). Impact of child sexual abuse on females: toward a developmental, psychobiological integration. *Psychological Science*, **4**, 81–7.

van der Kolk, B.A. (1987). *Psychological trauma*. American Psychiatric Press, Washington, DC.

van der Kolk, B.A. and Fisler, R.E. (1995). Dissociation and the fragmentary nature of traumatic memories: overview and exploratory study. *Journal of Traumatic Stress*, **8**, 505–26.

van der Kolk, B.A., Fisler, R.E., Vardi, D.J., Herron, N., Hostetler, A., Kenny, G., Moore, R., Rodriguez, J., and Zakai, A. (1994). *Trauma and memory*. Presentation made at the Harvard Medical School Consolidated Department of Psychiatry, Cambridge, MA.

Waltz, J. (1994). Treatment and memory recall. Paper presented at the annual meeting of the International Society for Traumatic Stress Studies, Chicago, IL.

Williams, L. (1994). Recall of childhood trauma: a prospective study of women's memories of child sexual abuse. *Journal of Consulting and Clinical Psychology*, **62**, 1167–76.

Williams, L. (1995). Recovered memories of abuse in women with documented child sexual victimization histories. *Journal of Traumatic Stress*, **8**, 649–74.

Yapko, M. (1993). Suggestibility and repressed memories of abuse: a survey of psychotherapists' beliefs. *American Journal of Clinical Hypnosis*, **36**, (3), 163–71.

Yapko, M. (1994). *Suggestions of abuse: true and false memories of childhood sexual trauma*. Simon & Schuster, New York.

TEN

Remembering and forgetting traumatic experiences: a matter of survival

SVEN-ÅKE CHRISTIANSON
AND ELISABETH ENGELBERG

Numerous laboratory and real-life studies indicate that highly emotional, traumatic events tend to be remembered differently over time from non-emotional events (for example Christianson 1992*a*). A major finding obtained in studies on both children and adults is that traumatic memories tend to be accurate and persistent with respect to the traumatic event itself and the central, critical detail information about the emotion-laden event, that is, the information that elicits the emotional reaction (Christianson 1992*b*; Heuer and Reisberg 1992; Rudy and Goodman 1991; Terr 1990). This is not to say that traumatic memories are always fully accurate. For example, it is often found that emotional events are less accurately recalled with respect to peripheral or more irrelevant details within an emotional scenario or information preceding and following traumatic events (Christianson and Loftus 1990; Christianson and Nilsson 1984; Loftus and Burns 1982).

Another major finding is that traumatic memories might be available, but not always accessible to conscious retrieval. There is extensive documentation showing that memories can be lost through trauma, for example victims of rape, torture, sexual abuse, and war may show an initial psychogenic amnesia, but these memories may be successfully retrieved later on. This chapter aims at discussing the two seemingly contradictory findings that traumatic memories are persistent in memory but sometimes not accessible. In providing an interpretation of these phenomena in terms of a survival function, we suggest that there are two opposing mechanisms at work when we are exposed to and try to remember emotional events. From the workings of the first mechanism we can infer that it is important to identify and recognize threatening situations. We doubt that mankind would have survived and developed in the way it has without this memory function. From the workings of the second mechanism we can infer that it is important to 'forget' unpleasant experiences. Life would be unbearable if we were forced to always carry unpleasant memories with us in our conscious awareness. Thus, to the same extent that we need mechanisms to identify and recognize unpleasant events, we also need mechanisms to 'forget' unpleasant experiences.

From an evolutionary perspective it is essential to recognize and remember emotional events and, in particular, unpleasant situations in order to ensure appropriate responses in maintaining protective, withdrawing, or defensive behaviour. Thus, survival has, to a great extent, hinged on some sort of emotional system that is fast enough to alert us to threatening or disturbing stimuli. Results of experimental research strongly seem to support the existence of this sort of emotional system. Christianson *et al.* (1991) showed that the level of memory performance for subjects presented with emotional stimuli, for example involving blood, at very short exposures (180 ms) was almost the same as that found for subjects presented with the same emotional stimuli at longer exposures. In a study by Christianson and Fällman (1990) it was further found that very unpleasant stimuli (pictures of victims of traffic accidents, war, malady, famine, etc.) shown for very brief durations (50 ms followed by a mask slide) were recognized better than neutral scenes (pictures of people in everyday situations), or very positive stimuli (for example sexual pictures of nudes in very sensual summer scenes).

The ability to quickly recognize and respond to environments and circumstances that are dangerous and upsetting is in some way also illustrated by so-called 'flashbulb' memories (Brown and Kulik 1977). That is, the phenomenon that people tend to remember in great detail the circumstances at hand when they received shocking news events (for example the assassination of a president). Although 'flashbulb' memories are not immune to deterioration with regard to the specific circumstances of the flashbulb event, a number of studies have shown an impressive concordance and consistency in subject's remembering of the core information (i.e. the informant, the location, the time, people present, any ongoing activity, the subject's own affect, etc.) (Winograd and Neisser 1992).

These memory findings suggest that certain characteristics of negative emotional events are perceived and retained in an automatic fashion by specific mechanisms, which may not involve consciously controlled memory processes, either during acquisition or retrieval (cf. evolutionary early perceptual subsystems (Johnson and Multhaup 1992), perceptual representation system (Tulving and Schacter 1990), and pre-attentive mechanisms (Öhman and Dimberg 1984).

Thus, we seem predisposed to quickly identify and recognize stimuli indicative of threatening situations for the purpose of survival. With evolution, we also seem to have developed other types of mechanisms which help us to cope with more modern-day situations in life. These mechanisms exclude from conscious awareness negative types of experiences that would impede efficient functioning in everyday life. They involve denial, active inhibition, suppression, and repression, and would, in the words of Briere (Denton 1993), represent a 'continuum of cognitive avoidance' proportional to the psychological pain tolerated by the individual. These types of Freudian defence mechanisms, or 'ego controls', are considered to be activated in order to regulate emotional stress. The ideas of Freud have been translated by Horowitz (1979) into an information processing theory postulating an interaction between stressful information, pre-existent cognitive schemata, and so-called 'control operations'. Total inhibition of a memory occurs when the individual is unable to integrate the experience with existing schemata pertaining to self-image and life in general. A partial inhibition is achieved through 'control operations' selecting certain trains of thought, which restrain threatening ideas or emotions associated with the unpleasant experience (see discussion of control operations below).

An example of active inhibition or suppression of memories is given in the following statement from a child who had once been sexually abused: 'When I remember it, I keep trying to think about good things like Christmas and it goes away' (McCahill *et al.* 1979, p. 44). Another example is provided by a Swedish serial killer (Case 5 below), who was interviewed by the senior author of this chapter and asked about handling memories of the murders he had committed. When memories of the victims and the killings were evoked, he took a bottle of washing-up liquid or a package of food (it had to be something boring) and started to read the label of contents over and over again until anxiety-provoking memories of the victims and killings vanished.

Blocking out traumatic experiences by means of dissociative mechanisms has been clinically observed in a wide range of traumatic situations, and not seldom in victims of rape and acts of violence. For example, a former rape victim temporarily dissociated during sexual contact with her partner in order to avoid the sensation to trigger any memories of the rape experience. She began to think intensely until 'she felt she only had her head, an enormous head and no longer a body' (van Wageningen 1994). Examples of more severe stages of inaccessible memories of trauma are provided by the following two case studies.

Case 1: Two couples are sitting on a bench outside a restaurant. One of the women sees three men coming towards them. She gets a sense of their hostility, primarily directed towards the men in her company. The next thing she can remember is kneeling beside her husband who has just been stabbed to death.

Case 2: One summer evening, a woman is bicycling home from work. Twenty-four hours later she is found naked in the forest with severe head injuries. The woman undergoes surgery and regains consciousness about two weeks after she was found. She remembers her identity and previous life history, but cannot recall what happened to her that particular evening.

The woman in Case 1 was not under the influence of alcohol or other types of drugs at the time of the event. Two years after the traumatic event, she still could not remember approaching the perpertrators in an attempt to ward them off, being thrown to the ground, having a knife held against her throat and then watching her husband being killed. This sequence of events was observed by witnesses who did not dare to intervene. The amnesic condition of this woman for this specific incident is of course a psychological reaction to a very stressful and emotional experience. The overall pattern for such psychogenic amnesia shares many of the characteristics of organic amnesia, which was eventually diagnosed in Case 2. The typical pattern for both types of amnesia is the inability to recall events prior and subsequent to the eliciting trauma, but also the trauma *per se*. There are, however, major differences, which will be clarified in a more throughout discussion of Case 2.

In Case 2, the woman's (EA) life was saved through several neurosurgical operations on the right frontal lobe. Two weeks after the assault she regained consciousness and was well aware of her identity and previous life history, but was unable to recall the time period of approximately one week prior to the assault and her awakening. In addition to the amnesic condition, EA was not very well oriented in time and answered simple questions at a slight delay. Her health nevertheless improved steadily and after almost three months she was released from the hospital. There was some recovery of her retrograde amnesia with a lasting loss of the three days prior to the attack. There was, however, no recovery of memories related to the assault. EA was questioned by the police at regular intervals, but had not been able to retrieve any information about the perpetrator or the assault.

It had been seven months since the assault, when the senior author met EA for the first time. The hospital had requested a more thorough examination with regard to her memory ability and the persistent amnesia for the assault. EA herself thought that her memory capacity had improved rapidly. She described how, after her awakening, it had been very difficult to remember things. As far as the assault itself was concerned, she had absolutely no memory at all. She also exhibited a retrograde amnesia for a period of three days prior to the assault, and an anterograde amnesia covering the two weeks after the assault. There were, however, a few isolated memory fragments, scattered details pertaining to the time both prior and subsequent to the assault.

Emotionally EA could be described as being indifferent toward dealing with questions about the assault. Her general demeanor indicated a certain emotional numbness, which had also been noted in previous evaluations by the hospital staff. There are three plausible interpretations for this lack of emotional reactions. First, EA was, from a psychological point of view, an exceptionally stable person before the assault. All of her relatives, friends, and collegues at work described EA as a very secure person, mainly due to close family ties. Second, some of the injuries to her head may have hampered her ability to perceive and express emotions. These injuries comprised the right frontal lobe, which plays an important role in governing emotional behaviour and personality. Third, neither being brought back to the scene of crime nor being exposed to the perpertrator triggered any emotional reactions in EA, which indicates that she truly does not harbour any memory of the assault. EA may, however, suppress emotions associated with learning about the assault. The author asked EA whether she had any desire to remember what had happened to her, and she answered with a plain 'no'. Her detachment to having learnt about the extreme violation of her integrity may nevertheless reveal a desire to have remained ignorant of this fact, and thus avoid feelings of humiliation or outrage.

Results from testing of EA's memory functions revealed a normal short-term memory function, but an impaired long-term memory function with regard to both verbal and visuo-spatial information. Test results also showed a decreased ability to access information in memory. When the memory testing was repeated one year later, EA still showed an impaired ability to encode episodic information and a great dependency on cues to remember information from the tests and autobiographical events. Another six months after the follow-up test, EA was able to remember personal events that had occurred during the past several months. In spite of this, she had difficulty in correctly recalling their chronological order, which is commonly seen in patients with frontal lobe damage (Anderson *et al.* 1993; Milner 1971; Milner *et al.* 1991).

In studying the pattern of the retrograde amnesia and evaluating the ability to encode and recall new information after a trauma, the type of amnesia may with great certainty be diagnosed as either organic or psychogenic. In cases of injury to the head and unconsciousness, the likelihood of recovering memory of the trauma itself is very small. In contrast to organic amnesia, psychogenic amnesia is mostly characterized by a complete, but temporary, retrograde amnesia, including the traumatic event. The anterograde amnesia effects usually cover very short time periods, unless dissociative reactions have given rise to a changed personality (psychogenic fugue, multiple personality (see Putnam 1989). In such cases, a gradual process of recovery from the retrograde amnesia normally includes previously forgotten information as well as the eliciting event. The role of retrograde amnesia in developing psychogenic memory disturbances will be discussed in Case 3 below.

Case 3: A woman (CM) is out jogging in a wooded area in a suburb when she is suddenly attacked. She ferociously tries to escape, but the man beats and rapes her. Badly shocked, she is later found by another jogger who helps her gain consciousness. But she cannot account for what has happened to her, who she is and where she lives.

Because CM had obviously been assaulted, she underwent a neurological examination at the Karolinska Hospital in Stockholm and a diagnosis of organic amnesia was ruled out. For the next few days, she exhibited a total retrograde amnesia and a limited anterograde amnesia up to the moment she was found by the other jogger. A week and a half later, she was released from the hospital. Her physical injuries were almost healed, but apart from two relatives, she was still amnesic about her past prior to being found by the other jogger. Three weeks after the trauma, her retrograde amnesia began to recede, but very few personal memories were recovered. At this time, CM was escorted by the police through the area where she had been found. She reacted with great anxiety to specific places and spontaneously uttered: 'and then there is the brick'. She could not explain why these details crossed her mind, only respond: 'the brick and the path'. In guiding her onto a path, she got very distressed at the sight of crumbled bricks spread over the path and into the wooded environment. Even though she did not, at that point in time, have any conscious memory of the rape, she expressed a definite feeling that something had happened to her at that particular spot. As the rapist had confessed a few days earlier, the police knew that this was the place where she had been assaulted and forced out onto a meadow where she was raped. Forcing herself to once again be exposed to the location of the assault, she began to cry, perspire profusely and feel very nauseous upon reaching the meadow. Shortly afterwards she had to be brought away from the area.

To begin with, CM's memory disturbance could be explained in terms of the theoretical interpretation of hysterical phenomena (see Breuer and Freud, 1895; Freud 1915; see Singer 1990 for an overview). According to this view, excessive stimulation is seen as the primary cause for triggering repressive mechanisms. In this case, such excessive stimulation would consist of the physical exhaustion, emotional stress, and fear that were paramount in the consciousness of CM during the assault and rape. Freud described such an effort to master an extremely evocative event as 'motivated forgetting), and a few experimental studies of the repression hypothesis have produced results that seem to corroborate the ideas of Freud (see for example Erdelyi 1970; Flavell 1955; Glucksberg and King 1967; Holmes 1972; Jung 1906; Levinger and Clark 1961; Zeller 1950). In terms of Horowitz's, translation of the repression hypothesis, one might say that the excessive emotional strain evoked during the attack and the act of rape produced a defensive shift in the woman's inner models of reality. Horowitz argues that in order to cope with a trauma, some people will remember only fragments of the event, obscuring images and details to avoid emotional stress. This control process of selecting certain information is exemplified in our case study by CM's fragmented memory of some isolated details, i.e. 'the brick and the path'. Such control operations also work through selecting possible self-images, resulting in various progressions or regressions of identity that commonly occur after a traumatic experience. A control failure in choice of available self-images, or the stabilizing of a self-image, can lead to a chaotic lapse of identity as was seen to occur with CM.

The CM's memory disturbance could, however, also be explained in terms of the notion that highly emotional situations entail attentional selectivity, which in turn would produce amnesic effects. The cornerstone of this argument is Easterbrook's (1959) hypothesis of cue-utilization. According to this theory, there is a progressive restriction of the range of cues utilized or attended to as a function of an increase in emotional arousal. A very large increase in emotional arousal, as in states of high stress or anxiety, implies a reduction of relevant and critical cues attended to and would therefore impair cognitive efficiency (see also Bacon 1974; Baddely 1972; Korchin 1964; Wachtel 1967, 1968). Easterbrook's (1959) hypothesis was extended by Mandler (1975) who suggested that it is the perception of activity of the autonomic nervous system that interferes with ongoing conscious processing. Attention allocated to physiological responses concomitant with stressful situations is therefore the critical component that relates emotional arousal to restricted cue-utilization. This theoretical point of view was in turn developed by Eysenck (1982). Eysenck suggested that high arousal leads to a reduced ability to engage in parallel processing, the reason being that attentional capacity diminishes to such a degree that task processing cannot run its proper course.

A similar line of reasoning has been put forth in experimental research by Christianson and collegues. That is, coping activities and preservative tendencies used when focusing on critical aspects of an emotional event expend considerable resources of conscious attention. Further processing of other, more peripheral information will therefore be severely restricted. In a study by Christianson (1984), it was shown that subjects who watched an emotional version of a thematic sequence of pictures, remembered the story immediately after presentation as accurately as subjects presented with a neutral version of the slide sequence. In a delayed recall test, however, the emotionally aroused subjects were more accurate and persistent in remembering the central features of the emotional slides than subjects presented non-emotional slides. Further support for the persistence in remembering emotional events was provided by Christianson and Loftus (1987). In this study, subjects showed a higher recall performance for central features of the emotional pictures (for example 'blood', 'eye injury') than did subjects presented with non-emotional pictures. Moreover, research by Burke *et al.* (1992) and Heuer and Reisberg (1990) has shown that subjects presented with an emotional version of a story remembered more of the information associated with the central characters in the slides and the gist of the event than subjects in a neutral condition.

In Case 3, we believe that hightened emotional arousal led to a redistribution of attentional resources such that only limited information about the environmental context was processed. The fact that CM's attention was restricted with respect to the external information probably made her focus upon the most central and critical details in the environmental context. It seems as though this information centred on the pieces of bricks which were spread out along the path that the woman chose as her escape route. Although CM did not specifically recognize relevant places in the area where she had been assaulted and raped, she revealed an implicit memory of associated details through her mentioning of the bricks and the path and her intense distress at the sight of these. Thus, these isolated memory fragments could be considered as a central detail in the sequence of events experienced by CM and hence will have the strongest cue validity to the traumatic event. A complication in amnesic cases such as CM's is that the heightened level of emotion and intrusive thoughts concerning her apparent lack of any real knowledge about what had happened to her, make the victim unable to focus her attention on the most crucial aspects of the retrieval information provided. During recovery (see below) CM understood that she had perceived crumbled bricks spread over the path on which she was running to escape from the attacker. Similarly, the woman in Case 1, who after two years is still unable to remember the sequence of events pertaining to the stabbing of her husband, also harbours some isolated fragments of the trauma, such as the memory of a blue glove and her head and neck being pushed backwards.

The retention of isolated memory fragments of certain critical details or cues related to a trauma is in conformity with other clinical cases of psychogenic amnesia. This general observation has been interpreted as a type of non-conscious indirect recall of aspects that are central to the repressed emotional trauma. The repressed event may not be recalled until associations or ideas make contact with the emotional response relevant to the repressed memory (see Breuer and Freud 1895; Erdelyi and Goldberg 1979; Janet 1965). The implication of this interpretation is that amnesic effects produced by emotionally stressful situations are a matter of accessibility of information rather than availability. A major factor to consider is thus the type of retrieval support present in remembering traumatic experiences.

Experimental results do show that memory improves with an increase in retrieval support for stressful events, compared with non-stressful events. In a study by Christianson and Nilsson (1984) subjects were shown a series of ordinary human faces at the beginning and end of an experimental session. In the middle of this series, however, grotesque forensic pathology photographs of facial injuries were presented. Control subjects were shown a whole series of ordinary looking faces. Each face was presented along with biographical information, such as a name, an occupation, a hobby, etc. Using this design, the effects of the traumatic pictures were studied for memory of associated verbal material, and also for memory of the ordinary faces and associated verbal material. Results showed memory impairment during free recall for words associated with the traumatic pictures as well as for the to-be-remembered information presented before and after these grotesque pictures (i.e. demonstrating retrograde and anterograde amnesia effects). The retrograde and anterograde amnesia effects, however, receded completely in a subsequent recognition test, in which there were four alternatives presented for names, occupations, hobbies, etc. with each face. During free recall, subjects reported that vivid images of and thoughts about the faces came to mind. This made it difficult to recollect associated verbal information. During recognition, on the other hand, access to the verbal information was presumably facilitated due to strong retrieval support provided by the different alternatives.

It is commonly found in situations involving strong emotions that the individual is preoccupied with intrusive thoughts or images about the stressful stimulus. It may, therefore, be the process of 'tunnel memory' that is responsible for the way certain emotionally stressful aspects are processed (Safer *et al.* 1994). The term 'tunnel memory' is given in reference to the process of narrowed attention and heightened psychological focus on certain details of the traumatic event, which engages conceptual mechanisms (cf. 'post-stimulus elaboration' (Christianson 1992*a*) allocated to the emotion-provoking stimulus. That is, a concern to come to terms with the emotional impact of stressful events, such as accidents or crime, prompts a cognitive processing which will be focused upon critical details of such events. This mode of processing would promote memory of central detail information and the gist of the emotional event due to elaborative rehearsal, but actively inhibit processing of details that are irrelevant and/or spatially peripheral to the emotion-eliciting event. Heuer (1987) argues along similar lines in that the recall pattern for emotional memories, as opposed to non-emotional memories, centres around central elements in the experience that evoked certain feelings, thoughts, and reactions in the subject. If involvement in stressful events has major implications for sense of self, conceptual processing may be inadequate and result in a failure to cope with the trauma. As discussed at the beginning of the chapter, failure to cope with a traumatic experience may be seen to constitute a failure to assimilate the trauma with schemata of self-image. Dissociative reactions would then be triggered and produce psychogenic amnesia, psychogenic fugue, or multiple personality disorder.

A series of experiments using different emotional stimuli, such as accidents or violent crimes, as well as different methods of testing recognition, has provided support for the hypothesis of tunnel memory (see Safer, *et al.* 1994). That is, subjects tend to remember a traumatic scene as more focused than the actual stimulus, and they remember a traumatic scenario as more focused than a matched neutral scene. Effects of tunnel memory, as shown in experiments by Safer *et al.* (1994), tend to decrease over time. Thus, the focusing involved in effects of tunnel memory most likely occurs in memory, and not in vision or perception. Such a change in memory representation of an emotional event may additionally imply that greater access to peripheral information will be allowed with time.

Studies on hypermnesia (net gain in memory when memory of certain information is tested repeatedly (see Payne 1987, for a review)) similarly point to a prime problem of accessibility and not availability of information. For example, in a study by Scrivner and Safer (1988), subjects were presented with a videotape portraying a burglary in which three people are shot to death. Subjects were then tested for detail memory in four consecutive recall tests within 48 hours. Results showed that details that had been presented before, during and after watching the videotape were more accurately recalled with repeated testing. On the basis of similar findings of hypermnesia effects, Davis (1990) concludes that the difficulty in remembering certain kinds of negative emotional experiences does not reflect a problem of availability, but limited access to these experiences. Our next case of a traumatized individual is an example of such limited accessibility requiring an appropriate cue to gain some strength in the retrieval process.

Case 4: A woman in her early twenties is watching a TV programme about incest. To her own surprise, she suddenly finds herself arduously exclaiming: 'It really happened to me!' The confession of her stepfather eventually verifies that she was sexually abused for six years starting at the age of eight. Watching the programme has triggered a retrieval process of different abuse-related memories which would no longer yield to suppression.

Details presented in the programme apparently provided strong enough retrieval cues to trigger a recollection through her emotional reaction. This is consistent with often cited clinical observations (for example Bagby 1928; Janet 1893) as well as with CM (Case 3). That is, an emotional response to some stimulus reveals the experience of a previous event that may not be explicitly recalled. The revival of the emotional reaction, as originally experienced in some of these cases, may act as a cue to trigger access to the emotion-provoking event.

Another factor to consider in gaining access to repressed event memory is that of context effects. An interesting demonstration of context-dependent memory was provided by Godden and Baddeley (1975). They gave divers the task of learning 40 unrelated words either on land or under water. Memory performance turned out be better when encoding and recall took place in the same environment. This effect was, however, not obtained when the divers were provided with recognition alternatives. Similarly, Eich (1980) found that better recall during intoxication induced by drugs in the same manner as during encoding was inhibited at the presentation of recognition alternatives.

Studies on mood-state-dependent memory have shown that ability to remember a certain event is enhanced if the individual experiences the same emotional state as during the original event (Blaney 1986; Bower 1981; Kuiken 1989). Other studies more specifically indicate that effects of mood-state dependency appear only in situations where the specific mood or emotion emanates from the information or event that is to be recalled (Bower 1987; Bower and Mayer 1985; Eich and Metcalfe 1989 Gage and Safer 1985; 1989). Although Bower focused upon mood as prime factor, he also specified other inherent characteristics of a situation that could act as critical context cues: 'posture, temperature, room and apparatus cues, and stray noises, as well as internal physiological stimuli such as a dry throat, pounding heartbeat, stomach gurgles, nausea, and boredom (Bower 1972, p. 93). Effects of internal and external context were also evident in Case 3 (CM), and were also the major turning point in her recovery almost 12 weeks after the trauma.

CM spent the weekend at a cottage in the countryside. She felt restless, nervous and went jogging for the first time since the trauma. She was running along a road where cavities were filled with gravel mixed with crushed pieces of brick. She experienced a growing feeling of discomfort and the sight of crushed brick suddenly blended into a memory of the assault. She became dizzy, desoriented, and had to stop by a big pile of bricks. Memory fragments of the traumatic experience got very intense and slowly started to fall into place. Along with these memories, those of another incident in childhood began to surface. The first thing she remembered was the smell of beer from the rapist, and this is something that triggered the memory of a sexual abuse she had experienced as a nine-year-old girl. The abuser in childhood had also smelled of beer. Within two to three months after this breakthrough in her recovery, CM was able to recall most of the repressed memories which were corroborated by the confession of the rapist.

Internal context was most likely reinstated by muscle movements required for jogging during both occasions, and by the heightened body temperature, hyperventilation, and cardiac activity from the physical exercise. The external environment was also similar, the wooded area, the occurrence of crumbled brick and a pile of bricks. (Her earlier memory of 'bricks and path', isolated from its initial context, suggests that this detail information was focused upon during the attack and hence high in cueing validity to the specific traumatic event.) The combination of these internal and external cues probably provided a reasonably similar context that aided CM in recollecting aspects of the situation just preceding the actual rape.

The phenomenon of isolated memories of specific details pertaining to traumatic events may to some extent be explained in light of results obtained in studies on hypnosis. When coming out of hypnosis, people have initially had difficulties in remembering events that they experienced during the hypnotic state. If provided with retrieval cues, however, they have been able to remember this type of information. Kihlstrom and Evans (1979) have shown that hypnotized people do not remember events in the same logical order as they do in a normal, non-hypnotized state. This suggests that it is not only event information that is affected in amnesia, but also memory for temporal order which in itself is a very important aspect for reconstructing a sequence of events (see also Treadway *et al.* 1992). Encoding and retrieval of pieces of information that are causally connected to each other normally takes place on a sequence by sequence basis. It may be that information is not encoded in this organized fashion in traumatic situations. The fragmented encoding and isolation of the event in memory therefore makes it more difficult to access and reconstruct the original traumatic event.

Another example of an isolated type of detail in memory that may provide efficient context-dependent cues at retrieval is olfactory sensations. Apart from CM, another example of this phenomenon is described by the rape victim and American actress Kelly McGillis, who got nauseated in the subway because the smell reminded her of the rapists (McMurran 1988). The significance of smells in retrieving emotional memories, and especially those related to sexual situations, may be explained by the close connections running between the olfactory bulbs and different limbic structures (see Cain 1974;

Sieck 1972). Traumatic experiences in general are normally represented as memories of feelings and bodily sensations. It may be argued that this sort of emotionally monitored memory response is a rudiment of earlier stages in evolution, i.e. a type of 'hard-wired' mechanism that ensures automatic and non-conscious retention of distinct emotional information from stressful events. They constitute the kind of memories that may be difficult to express verbally, but that are, nevertheless, expressed through different symptoms. This is, for example, seen with the woman in Case 4 who frequently had been forced to perform oral sex on her stepfather. She was very reluctant to drink milk or brush her teeth until the toothpaste became foamy. In those instances, she could recall feelings of great disgust, but not specific episodes of sexual abuse, as an urge to block out this part of her reality presumably prevailed. This is in sharp contrast to CM's restless state of mind on the day she went jogging for the first time since the assault. In that situation, she experienced a tolerable level of stress and personal safety, and her restlessness most probably indicated a readiness to confront details of the trauma. Yet another example of the reinstatement of internal and external context as retrieval support is provided by Case 5 below.

Case 5: A man is receiving therapeutic treatment at a psychiatric ward. After some time, he begins to tell about one murder after the other that he has committed. Murders committed during a time span of 25 years, and which he had been very reluctant to consciously access before going into therapy.

Not until this serial killer was sentenced to psychiatric treatment for a series of minor crimes and found himself in the relatively safe environment surrounding therapeutic treatment, did he begin to slowly recover memories for the sexual-sadistic murders that he had committed on young boys. Memories of the killings caused overwhelming anxiety, due to the fact that they were in part a re-enactment of the sexual-sadistic abuse that the serial killer himself had been subjected to as a child. It was therefore difficult for him to tell about the murders during interrogations by the police. During the murder investigation, the reinstatement of internal and external context information was found to be surprisingly effective for retrieval, for example at a site where he had dissected a boy 14 years earlier. Before specific questions were asked about the killing, the senior author assisted in reinstating both the internal and external context that he had experienced at the time. A method similar to the cognitive interview technique (see Fisher and Geiselman 1992) was used, in which memories of smells, body positions, various sounds, and emotions were triggered. After the reinstatement of his internal context, he showed strong emotions and could describe vivid memories of the killing. He was able to give specific details, which he had not had access to in previous interrogations. The accuracy of the detailed information provided by the serial killer was confirmed by the parents of the victim, as well as by physical evidence observed by the forensic pathologist.

As seen in the cases of the serial killer and of CM, information about the traumatic events was difficult to retrieve due to different states of mind, different physical conditions, and different environments when questioned by the police. Whereas emotional stress at encoding enhances long-term remembering of a specific event, stress at retrieval impairs access to the same event, especially if the source of stress experienced is unrelated to the event to be remembered.

Inability to recall and report details about traumatic experiences in both adults and children may therefore partly be explained by stress induced during interrogations about very personal matters by unfamiliar people. Loftus (1980) provides several examples of effects of emotional stress on memory where the source of stress is dissociated from the to-be-remembered event. Loftus refers for instance to a study by Baddeley (1972) in which servicemen were tricked into believing that an emergency situation had arisen. In evaluating the results of the simulated emergency situation, an impaired ability to remember detailed instructions was revealed. In her own research, Loftus (1980) showed a complex event to people who greatly feared snakes. Those who had a snake in the vicinity of where the event was shown, performed less well on a subsequent recall test in comparison with subjects who had a teddy bear nearby. This experimental situation is, however, slightly different from the study by Baddeley in that the subjects were aroused during encoding, and that the to-be-remembered information was not at all associated with the stressor. It nevertheless points to the necessity of being aware of general memory performance at states of high emotional arousal or stress elicited by an extraneous source that is dissociated from the to-be-remembered event, and not to confuse this with a lack of memory retention.

Memories of very unpleasant or traumatic experiences are difficult to retrieve, especially if these events occurred during early childhood. Thus we will review a few points raised in the debate on infantile amnesia. One view claims that memories of childhood events are stored intact (see Nash 1987). However, as older children or adults attempt to retrieve this sort of event information, there is a clear discrepancy between the internal and external context prevailing during these very different periods in life. This discrepancy at encoding and retrieval makes it difficult to access memories of events in early childhood. One aspect of critical importance for this incongruence is the linguistic development of children. Researchers such as Pillemer and White (1989) argue that we are born with a primitive memory system which is only capable of retaining fragmentary information, conditioned responses, emotion-laden associations, and very general experience. Before the child has started to develop a linguistic ability, memory retention is accessed through emotional cues or cues specific to certain situations, and is expressed through behaviour rather than verbally. The child develops a more sophisticated memory system once she has developed an adequate speech ability. She is then able to share her experience with others verbally.

The argument put forth by Pillemer and White seems to be corroborated by results obtained in two different studies. One of these, a study by Myers *et al.* (1987), suggests that very young children do retain memories implicitly through behaviour. Infants aged around six to 40 weeks were taken to a room used in examining the hearing ability amongst infants. About two years later, these children revisited the room. It was then observed that they looked more at sound sources used at both occasions, such as a rattle and a drum, and that they played more as compared with children of the same age who visited the room for the first time. In another study by Sheingold and Tenney (1982), a set of questions were put to groups of four-, eight-and-twelve-year-olds concerning their memory of the birth of a sibling when they all had been between three and four years old. The questions were specific and could be answered with a few words, such as: 'Who told you that your mom was going to the hospital?', 'At what time during the day did your mom go to the hospital?' etc. Results showed that four-year-olds could answer most of these questions and that their memory retention was nearly as good as the eight- and twelve-year-olds.

There is generally a certain scepticism towards the accuracy or even veracity of childhood memories. Recent research has, however, shown that such scepticism is unwarranted. Brewin, Andrews and Gotlieb (1993) argue that most childhood memories are relatively accurate, specifically memories of events that were unique, unexpected, and entailed personal consequences (cf. Rubin and Kozin 1984). Such unique memories are typical in the flashbulb memory literature. Children's flashbulb memories have been observed to be similar to adults'. That is, children show an impressive concordance and consistency in remembering shocking news events over time (see above). Warren and Swartwood (1992) found that children who reported higher emotional responses to the flashbulb event of the Space Shuttle 'Challenger' explosion, were more consistent over a two-year period than those who reported lower emotional responses.

The fact that even younger children can accurately recall and describe stressful experiences has been reported by Merrit, *et al.* (1993, cited by Ornstein *et al.* in press). Three- to seven-year-olds were interviewed after being subjected to a voiding cystourethrogram (an aversive and stressful radiological procedure involving urinary catheterization). Open-ended recall immediately after the medical procedure and after a delay of six weeks revealed impressive levels of recall with relatively little forgetting observed over the six week delay interval. The overall recall performance dropped from 88 per cent to 83 per cent. Importantly, the level of recall of this stressful experience was found to be higher in comparison with combined data from studies on routine visits to the doctor. Initial recall was further only marginally correlated with age, and forgetting over time was not associated with age in contrast to the other studies on recall of visits to the doctor. The performance among three-year-olds was, in other words, equal to that among seven-year-olds.

Terr (1988) has found that traumatic experiences in childhood, in particular single events of trauma, seem to be very well preserved in memory over several years. Repression of childhood memories thus occurs as a reaction to experiences of repeated trauma and is a relatively rare phenomenon. Children who have witnessed traumatic events outside of the home, for instance accidents, catastrophes or people dying, usually have the possibility of talking about the memory of such an experience with their parents. In such cases, they have the security and safety of their parents and can deal with and mourn the experience. A child is not in the same position if her parents are responsible for inflicting the trauma. This is, for example, illustrated by the woman who had been sexually abused as a child in case study 4: 'I mostly remember I was afraid of him (the stepfather who abused her). Sometimes he would come in to the bedroom for me . . . I tried to hide from him. But there was nowhere to go.' A child who is threatened with physical punishment, who is told she will be abandoned if she tells about the abuse, may prevent herself from thinking of any experiences that these threats relate to. Children may also feel shame and guilt for what has happened to them, that they are not worth loving, and that they have given their consent to the abuse. Threats and feelings of guilt may be decisive for triggering a repressive reaction, which may be a way for the child to acquire a sense of relief and of being more in control.

The existence of repressed traumatic experiences in adults has been shown in some of the cases discussed in this chapter, but there is also a large amount of data showing traumatic amnesia for childhood experiences. Besides research by Terr and others, police investigations of child pornography films reveal an extensive suppression or repression of the experiences among the children when they are interviewed about their experiences several years later or when contacted as adults; some of them have no recollection of the abuses which have been documented on film. As noted by the American Society of Clinical Hypnosis regarding guidelines for clinicians and forensic hypnosis, 'Thus, the weight of available evidence strongly supports the existence of traumatic amnesia and delayed recall, but what still remains at issue is whether the genuine base rate of repressed memory in an abuse population might be something closer to 19% (Loftus *et al.* 1994), 38% (Williams 1992), 40% (Feldman-Summers and Pope 1994), or 59% (Briere and Conte 1993).' (Hammond *et al.* 1994, p. 8).

Retrieval of repressed memories may take place when the individual for instance no longer resides in the environment where she was traumatized, enjoys a sufficient feeling of personal security, or finds herself in situations where strong retrieval cues prevail (for example internal and external context of the trauma is reinstated as discussed above). Memory retrieval may also occur during hypnosis (although at times no recovery is achieved) and clinical interviews. The vast majority of cases of memory recovery occur before entering therapy, and the purpose of psycho-therapeutic treatment is therefore to further uncover blocked memories. A proper interviewing technique to promote retrieval of emotional or traumatic events is to ask for central details (i.e. details that arouse emotions), emotions *per se*, thoughts, bodily memories, or olfactory sensations (see Fisher and Geiselman 1992; Raskin 1989). Some researchers, however, point to certain problems with childhood memories that are recovered during therapy. Memories could be contrived as a result of implicit demands that may prevail in a therapeutic situation, expectations of the psychotherapist, suggestions, and so on. Some of these apprehensions are justified in cases such as the one described in a book by a Swedish author (Kali 1993). A woman describes how memories of childhood are recovered during hypnosis and writes for instance: 'The first day I remember that the instructor mentioned something briefly about incest . . . but (I) forgot until the next day when she briefly mentioned that people can repress experiences of incest, but can come back to them during hypnosis and that afterwards one can feel a whole lot better . . . From the instructor I got the phone number to . . . and I had a long conversation which she wrapped up by saying that she thought I had been abused and perhaps quite badly . . . There was however a small possibility that the abuse had been psychological, not sexual . . . that I, after a little more than a year in therapy, for the first time had dared to express a thought, a feeling, that I might have been sexually abused . . . What had come out of hypnosis, Rosentherapy – it all pointed exclusively in one direction: I had been abused, both by my father and my grandfather . . . I think this is the way it was – I was abused by my father and my grandmother . . . Lena (the hypnotherapist) asked me if I could feel the fingers of my grandmother anywhere on my body. After a few signs I thought I could feel them on my neck . . . Lena's questions may possibly, possibly have been a bit leading (however not about grandmother? or what happened to grandfather?) . . . It sounds perfectly clear, as if it happened yesterday, says Annika (the rosentherapist). Yes, but I may be making it all up, I answer . . . Well, that sounded like a memory to me! (the hypnotherapist).' This account, regardless of the authenticity of these memories, points to the extent to which the therapist's way of dealing with her client creates difficulties in determining the reliability of what this woman claims to remember of childhood sexual abuse.

There are studies showing that we can erroneously remember whole sequences of events due to an inappropriate interviewing technique. One of these studies by Hyman *et al.* (1993) demonstrated that a few subjects could recognize and 'remember' certain aspects of a fictional 'birthday party with pizza and a clown' or a 'visit to the hospital because of an ear infection'. A very relevant point illustrated by these studies is the importance of the interview process and the necessity of being alert as to how one asks for information. These studies do not, however, tell us anything about the authenticity of memories recovered from childhood, or whether or not they have been implanted by therapists, the police, or other types of investigative personnel.

As pointed out by Loftus (Reichenbach 1991), other studies have shown that unrelated information may exert substantial influence on memory at recall, even to the extent that subjects claim to remember events that have never actually taken place. It should, however, be noted that these studies are based on samples consisting of university students, who were tested for retention of details in a series of pictures and short stories. In this type of situation, memory is very susceptible to the influence of unrelated sources of information. Such studies cannot therefore be considered comparable with situations in which individuals are manipulated to forget sequences of events actually experienced, and particularly of repeated events of traumatic character.

Do we have any reliable criteria for determining the validity of recovered memories of trauma? One criterion may be based on observations of the way recovery normally runs its course. There is an initial phase in which a memory is very suddenly brought to consciousness, and then there is a subsequent phase in which recovery of early experiences occurs gradually. Strong emotions are exhibited along with the recovery of this type of memory. Sometimes there are even very strong physical reactions like pain. Another criterion may be based on the fact that valid memories of experience usually contain very personal details. The individual may have focused on specific emotions (for example, feelings of disgust from drinking milk or foamy toothpaste as in Case 4), or auditory, visual, or other sensory impressions like smells (for example smell of beer as in Case 3), or details that are of no direct relevance to the event itself (as for example observed in Case 4: 'Once in bed, we had taken a bath, and he wanted me to perform oral sex on him. I remember I was so disgusted . . . The bathrobe was white, I think . . . the bathroom . . . I don't recall what the room looked like . . . striped curtains. There were stripes on the wall from the sun . . . which was shining through the curtains . . . I remember we both stepped out of the bathroom, I can't recall whether I had also taken a bath . . .'). False memories usually contain general descriptions with few details and are not associated with strong emotional reactions. An example of this, provided by Terr, is illustrated by a girl who accused a therapist of forcing her to perform sexual acts. When asked to describe the type of sex, the girl looked puzzled and said: 'Just sex.' (Franklin and Wright 1991; Terr 1990).

Empirical findings from both real-life studies and laboratory experiments reviewed in this chapter suggest that certain critical detail information in emotionally arousing events is less susceptible to forgetting than similar information in non-emotional events. Amnesic effects of highly emotional events and spare retention of memory fragments may be explained by an attentional narrowing during states of high emotional arousal. This would in turn explain that associated information prior and subsequent to emotional events, as well as peripheral, background information, tends to be less accurately retained. This relative decrement in memory has been seen to recede with strong retrieval support (for example recognition cues, internal and external contextual cues), at delayed testing or after repeated memory testing. In sum, emotional stress may inhibit retrieval of certain detail information, or the whole event as seen in traumatic amnesia, but helps long-term remembering of emotionally stressful events. On the basis of this, we conclude that when detailed and personal memories are described – memories associated with strong emotional reactions – and when symptoms and related accounts from other people concur, then it is highly probable that memories of very emotional or traumatic events reflect authentic experiences.

ACKNOWLEDGEMENTS

The preparation of this chapter was an equal collaborative effort and was supported by Grant F 793/95 from the Swedish Council for Research in the Humanities and Social Sciences to Sven-Åke Christianson.

REFERENCES

Anderson, S.W., Damasio, H., and Tranel, D. (1993). Impaired memory for temporal order (recency) following ventromedial frontal lobe damage. *Society of Neuroscience Abstracts*, **19**, 791.

Bacon, S.J. (1974). Arousal and the range of cue utilization. *Journal of Experimental Psychology*, **102**, 81–7.

Baddeley, A.D. (1972). Selective attention and performance in dangerous environments. *British Journal of Psychology*, **63**, 537–46.

Bagby, E. (1928). *The psychology of personality*. Holt, New York.

Blaney, P.H. (1986). Affect and memory: a review. *Psychological Bulletin*, **99**, 229–46.

Bower, G.H. (1972). Stimulus-sampling theory of encoding variability. In A.W. Melton & E. Martin. In *Coding processes in human memory*, (ed. A.W. Melton and E. Martin), pp.85–124. Winston, Washington, DC.

Bower, G.H. (1981). Mood and memory. *American Psychologist*, **36**, 129–48.

Bower, G.H. (1987). Invited essay: commentary on mood and memory. *Behavioral Research and Therapy*, **25**, 443–55.

Bower, G.H. and Mayer, J.D. (1985). Failure to replicate mood-dependent retrieval. *Bulletin of Psychonomic Society*, 39–42.

Breuer, J. and Freud, S. (1895). Studies on hysteria. In *The standard edition of the complete psychological works of Sigmund Freud*, Vol. 2, (ed. J. Strachey). Hogarth Press, London.

Brewin, C.R., Andrews, B., and Gotlieb, I.H. (1993). Psychopathology and early experience: a reappraisal of retrospective reports. *Psychological Bulletin*, **113**, 82–98.

Brown, R. and Kulik, J. (1977). Flashbulb memories. *Cognition*, **5**, 73–99.

Burke, A., Heuer, F., and Reisberg, D. (1992). Remembering emotional events. *Memory & Cognition*, **20**, 277–90.

Cain, D.P. (1974). The role of the olfactory bulb in limbic mechanisms. *Psychological Bulletin*, **18**, 654–71.

Christianson, S.-Å. (1984). The relationship between induced emotional arousal and amnesia. *Scandinavian Journal of Psychology*, **25**, 147–60.

Christianson, S.-Å. (1989). Flashbulb memories: special, but not so special. *Memory & Cognition*, **17**, 435–43.

Christianson, S.-Å. (1992*a*). Remembering emotional events: potential mechanisms. In *The handbook of emotion and memory: research and theory*, (ed. S.-Å. Christianson), pp. 307–42. Erlbaum, Hillsdale, NJ.

Christianson, S.-Å. (1992*b*). Emotional stress and eyewitness memory: a critical review. *Psychological Bulletin*, **112**, 284–309.

Christianson, S.-Å. and Fällman, L. (1990). The role of age on reactivity and memory for emotional pictures. *Scandinavian Journal of Psychology*, **31**, 291–301.

Christianson, S.-Å. and Loftus, E.F. (1987). Memory for traumatic events. *Applied Cognitive Psychology*, **1**, 225–39.

Christianson, S.-Å. and Loftus, E.F. (1990). Memory for traumatic events. *Applied Cognitive Psychology*, **1**, 225–39.

Christianson, S.-Å. and Nilsson, L.-G. (1984). Functional amnesia as induced by a psychological trauma. *Memory & Cognition*, **12**, 142–55.

Christianson, S.-<., Loftus, E.F., Hoffman, H., and Loftus, G.R. (1991). Eye fixations and memory for emotional events. *Journal of Experimental Psychology: Learning, Memory, and Cognition*, **17**, 693–701.

Davis, P.J. (1990). Repression and the inaccessibility of emotional memories. In *Repression and dissociation: Implications for personality theory, psychopathology, and health*, (ed. J.L. Singer), pp. 387–403. The University of Chicago Press.

Denton, L. (1993). Loftus, Brière draw a crowd to repressed memory debate. *Monitor*, November.

Easterbrook, J.A. (1959). The effect of emotion on cue utilization and the organization of behavior. *Psychological Review*, **66**, 183–201.

Eich, E. (1980). The cue-dependent nature of state-dependent retrieval. *Memory & Cognition*, **8**, 157–73.

Eich, E. and Metcalfe, J. (1989). Mood dependent memory for internal versus external events. *Journal of Experimental Psychology: Learing, Memory, and Cognition*, **15**, 443–56.

Erdelyi, M.H. (1970). Recovery of unavailable perceptual input. *Cognitive Psychology*, **1**, 99–113.

Erdelyi, M.H. and Goldberg, B. (1979). Let's not sweep repression under the rug: toward a cognitive psychology of repression. In *Functional disorders of memory*, (ed. J.F. Kihlstrom and F.J. Evans), pp. 355–402. Erlbaum, Hillsdale, NJ.

Eysenck, M.W. (1982). *Attention and arousal: cognition and performance*. Springer, Berlin.

Fisher, R.P. and Geiselman, R.E. (1992). *Memory-enhancing techniques for investigative interviewing*. Thomas, Springfield, IL.

Flavell, J.H. (1955). Repression and the 'return of the repressed'. *Journal of Consulting Psychology*, **19**, 441–3.

Franklin, E. and Wright, W. (1991). *Sins of the father*. Fawcett Press, New York.

Freud, S. (1915). Repression. In *The standard edition of the complete psychological works of Sigmund Freud*, Vol. 14, (ed. J. Strachey), pp. 146–58. Hogarth Press, London.

Gage, D.F. and Safer, M.A. (1985). Hemisphere differences in the mood state-dependent effect for recognition of emotional faces. *Journal of Experimental Psychology: Learning, Memory, and Cognition*, **11**, 752–63.

Glucksberg, S. and King, L.J. (1967). Motivated forgetting mediated by implicit verbal chaining: a laboratory analogue of repression. *Science*, **158**, 517–19.

Gooden, D.R. and Baddeley, A.D. (1975). Context-dependent memory in two natural environments: on land and underwater. *British Journal of Psychology*, **66**, 325–31.

Hammond, D.C., Garver, R.B., Mutter, C.B., Crasilneck, H.B., Frischholz, E., Melvin, A.G., Hibler, N.S., Olson, J., Scheflin, J.D., Spiegel, H., and Wester, W. (1995). *Clinical hypnosis and memory: guidelines for clinicians and for forensic hypnosis*. American Society of Clinical Hypnosis Press.

Heuer, F. (1987). Remembering detail: the role of emotion in long-term memory. Unpublished dissertation. New School for Social Research, New York.

Heuer, F. and Reisberg, D. (1990). Vivid memories of emotional events: the accuracy of remembered minutiae. *Memory & Cognition*, **18**, 496–506.

Heuer, F. and Reisberg, D. (1992). Emotion, arousal, and memory for detail. In *Handbook of emotion and memory: research and theory*, (ed. S.-Å. Christianson), pp. 151–75. Erlbaum, Hillsdale, NJ.

Holmes, D.S. (1972). Repression and interference? A further investigation. *Journal of Personality and Social Psychology*, **22**, 163–70.

Horowitz, M.J. (1979). Psychological response to serious life events. In *Human stress and cognition*, (ed. V. Hamilton and D.M. Warburton), pp. 235–63. Wiley, New York.

Hyman, I.E. Jr., Billings, F.J., Husband, S.G., Husband, T.H., and Smith, D.B. (1993). Memories and false memories of childhood experience. Poster presented at The Annual Meeting of The Psychonomic Society, Washington, DC.

Janet, P. (1893). Continuous amnesia. *Revue Generale des Sciences*, **4**, 167–79.

Janet, P. (1965). *The major symptoms of hysteria*, (2nd edn). Hafner, New York.

Johnson, M.K. and Multhaup, K.S. (1992). Emotion and MEM. In *The handbook of emotion and memory: research and theory*, (ed. S.-Å. Christianson), pp. 33–60. Erlbaum, Hillsdale, NJ.

Jung, C.G. (1906). Experimental researches. In *Collected works*. Routledge, London. (Collection published 1972.)

Kali, A. (1993). *Det kan inte vara sant*. Bonnier Alba.

Kihlstrom, J.F. and Evans, F.J. (ed.) (1979). *Functional disorders of memory*. Erlbaum, Hillsdale, NJ.

Korchin, S.J. (1964). Anxiety and cognition. In *Cognition: theory, research, promise*, (ed. C. Scheerer), pp. 58–78. Harper & Row, New York.

Kuiken, D. (ed.) (1989). Mood and memory: theory, research, and applications. *Journal of Social Behavior and Personality*, **4**, (2), special issue.

Levinger, G. and Clark, J. (1961). Emotional factors in the forgetting of word associations. *Journal of Abnormal and Social Psychology*, **62**, 99–105.

Loftus, E.F. (1980). *Memory*. Addison-Wesley, New York.

Loftus, E.F. and Burns, T. (1982). Mental shock can produce retrograde amnesia. *Memory and Cognition*, **10**, 241–63.

Mandler, G. (1975). *Mind and emotion*. Wiley, New York.

McCahill, T.A., Meyer, L.C., and Fischman, A. (1979). *The aftermath of rape*. Lexington Books, Lexington, MA.

McMurran, K. (1988). Memoir of a brief time in hell. *People Weekly*, 14 November, 154–60.

Milner, B. (1971). Interhemispheric differences in the localisation of psychological processes in man. *British Medical Bulletin*, **27**, 272–7.

Milner, B., Corsi, P., and Leonard, G. (1991). Frontal-lobe contribution to recency judgments. *Neuropsychologia*, **29**, 601–18.

Myers, N.A., Clifton, R.K., and Clarkson, M.G. (1987). When they were young – almost-threes remember two years ago. *Infant Behaviour and Development*, **10**, 123–32.

Nash, M. (1987). What, if anything, is regressed about hypnotic age regression? A review of the empirical literature. *Psychological Bulletin*, **102**, 345–66.

Öhman, A. and Dimberg, U. (1984). An evolutionary perspective on human social behavior. In *Sociophysiology*, (ed. W.M. Waid), pp. 47–86. Springer, New York.

Ornstein, P.A., Gordon, B.N., Baker-Ward, L.E., and Merrit, K.A. In *The child witness in context: cognitive, social, and legal perspectives*, (ed. D.P. Peters). Kluwer, Dordrecht. (In press.)

Payne, D.G. (1987). Hypermnesia and reminiscence in recall: a historical and empirical review. *Psychological Bulletin*, **101**, 5–27.

Pillemer, D.B. and White, S.H. (1989). Childhood events recalled by children and adults. In *Advances in child development and behavior*, (ed. H.W. Reese), pp. 297–340. Academic, San Diego, CA.

Putnam, F.W. (1989). *Diagnosis and treatment of multiple personality disorder*. Guilford Press, New York.

Raskin, D.C. (1989). *Psychological methods in criminal investigation and evidence*. Springer, New York.

Reichenbach, J. (1991). 'Buried memories' *Columns*, September.

Rubin, D.C. and Kozin, M. (1984). Vivid memories. *Cognition*. **16**, 81–95.

Rudy, L. and Goodman, G.S. (1991). Effects of participation on children's reports: implications for children's testimony. *Developmental Psychology* **27**, 527–38.

Safer, M.A., Christianson, S.-Å., Autry, M., and Österlund, K. (1994). *Tunnel memory for traumatic events*. (Submitted.)

Scrivner, E and Safer, M.A. (1988). Eyewitnesses show hypermnesia for details about a violent event. *Journal of Applied Psychology*, **73**, 371–7.

Sheingold, K. and Tenney, Y.J. (1982). Memory for a salient childhood event. In *Memory observed: remembering in natural contexts,* (ed. U. Neisser), pp. 201–12. Freeman, New York.

Sieck, M.H. (1972). The role of olfactory system in avoidance learning and activity. *Physiology and Behavior*, **8** 705–10.

Singer, J.L. (ed.) (1990). *Repression and dissociation: implications for personality theory, psychopathology, and health*. The University of Chicago Press.

Terr, L. (1988). What happens to early memories of trauma? A study of twenty children under age five at the time of documented traumatic events. *Journal of the American Academy of Child and Adolescent Psychiatry*, **27**, 96–104.

Terr, L. (1990). *Too scared to cry: Psychic trauma in childhood*. Harper & Row, New York.

Treadway, M., Cohen, N.J., McCloskey, M., and Gordon, B. (1992). Landmark life events and the organization of memory: evidence from functional retrograde amnetesia. In *The handbook of emotion and memory*, (ed. S.A. Christianson), pp. 389–401. Erlbaum, Hillsade, NJ.

Tulving, E and Schacter, D.L. (1990). Priming and human memory systems. *Science*. **247**, 301–6.

van Wageningen, A. (1994). *Sexual abuse, body awareness and sexuality*. Paper presented at the Second Congress of the European Federation of Sexology, Copenhagen, Denmark.

Wachtel, P.L. (1967). Conceptions of broad and narrow attention. *Psychological Bulletin*, **68** 417–29.

Wachtel, P.L. (1968). Anxiety, attention, and coping with threat. *Journal of Abnormal Psychology*, **73** 137–143.

Warren, A.R. and Swartwood, J.N. (1992). Developmental issues in flashbulb memory research: children recall the Challenger event. *Affect and accuracy in recall: studies of flashbulb memories,* (ed. E. Winograd and U. Neisser), Cambridge University Press, New York.

Winograd, E. & Neisser, U. (1992). *Affect and accuracy in recall: studies of flashbulb memories*. Cambridge University Press, New York:

Zeller, A.F. (1950). An experimental analogue of repression. Historical summary. *Psychologcal Bulletin*, **47**, 39–51.

ELEVEN

*T*aking the middle line: can we accommodate both fabricated and recovered memories of sexual abuse?

JONATHAN W. SCHOOLER, MIRIAM BENDIKSEN, AND ZARA AMBADAR

Psychology is currently in the midst of a fundamental paradigm clash between clinical and experimental views regarding the status of recovered memories of sexual abuse. Many practising clinicians, relying on their own personal experiences, have come to the conclusion that recovered memories of seemingly long-forgotten sexual abuse should generally be considered valid (for example Bass and Davis 1988; Blume 1990; Harvey and Herman 1994; Olio 1994). At the same time, many experimental psychologists have argued, on the basis of the extensive empirical research on memory distortions, that these so-called recovered memories may often be the product of therapists' suggestions (for example Ceci *et al.* 1994a; Dawes 1994; Holmes 1990; Lindsay and Read 1994; Loftus and Ketcham 1994). The discrepancy between these two perspectives is rather extreme and exacerbated because each side of this debate is anchored in a particular epistemological view of what constitutes meaningful evidence, with each discounting the evidence promoted by the other side. For example, clinicians are frequently wary of the applicability of the findings of laboratory studies to their own clinical practices. On the basis of such reasoning, Harvey and Herman (1994, p. 4) argued 'there is no evidence to suggest that psychotherapists have the degree of power and influence that would be required to produce this [fabricated memories] effect'. In contrast, experimental researchers are trained to rely on solid experimental evidence in order to support psychological claims. From this perspective, Holmes (1990, p. 97) recently dismissed the notion of repression observing that 'there is no controlled laboratory evidence for repression'. Holmes (1990, p. 97) further discounts clinical observations suggesting that they 'cannot be counted as anything more than unconfirmed clinical speculations, certainly not as evidence for repression'. Although Holmes's dismissal of the clinical evidence for repression does not necessarily rule out the possibility that recovered memories of sexual abuse might be authentic, it has certainly been used as a strong argument for questioning their validity (cf. Loftus and Ketcham 1994).

In reviewing the evidence on this debate it is difficult to avoid being biased by one's training and professional experience. It is understandable that clinicians, many of whom have encountered individuals who they believe to have recovered actual memories, would be sceptical of the applicability of laboratory research in discounting their professional conclusions. On the other hand, experimental researchers are understandably wary of the biasing influence of various judgement heuristics (for example confirmation bias (Dawes 1989)) that can confound conclusions not founded in controlled experimentation. Such biases could readily influence the judgements of clinicians, thereby bringing their conclusions regarding the validity of recovered memories into doubt (Dawes 1994; Lindsay and Read 1994). Moreover, the vast scientific documentation of the extent of memory distortions, further fuels researchers' views that recovered memories may simply be the product of suggestion.

Admittedly, the two camps are perhaps not quite as clearly delineated as the above discussion might imply. For example, there are a few experimental researchers who have taken more sympathetic views of the likelihood of authentic recovered memories (cf. Mandler 1995; Morton 1994; Lindsay and Read, 1995; Schacter 1995), including some whose position more closely approximates that of the clinicians (for example Freyd 1994; Pezdek and Roe 1994). There are also some clinicians who have emphasized the dangers and sources of memory fabrication (for example Brown 1995; Haaken and Schlaps 1991; Yapko 1994). Moreover, many discussants from both 'camps' take less extreme positions than those quoted above. Nevertheless, even when writers on the topic attempt to take a more balanced view, their discussions typically take the form of a forceful argument for one alternative, only slightly tempered by conceding the possibility of the other. How should we proceed to reconcile this debate? The magnitude of the rift is sufficiently great that it is tempting to throw up our hands, ignore the other side, and simply continue to communicate with that population of the field with whom we identify. It was, arguably, this belief that 'we will never see eye to eye' that led researchers, disenfranchised with the increasing clinical orientation of the American Psychological Association, to establish a new organization the American Psychological Society, specifically dedicated to the values and orientations of the psychological research community. More recently, this oil and water quality of the two sides of psychology was revealed by the failure of an APA panel to reach consensus on the recovered memory debate. Instead of presenting a general conclusion, this committee has had to settle for two disparate sets of conclusions: one by the researchers on the committee, the other by the practioners (American Psychological Association 1996).

Unfortunately, the field cannot afford to just agree to disagree. There is simply too much at stake. Our credibility as a scientific discipline is jeopardized if we cannot determined a way to progress in deciding the status of a phenomenon that has been engendering widespread public attention. There are also major legal decisions that need to be reconciled. At the moment many states have introduced laws that make exemptions to the statute of limitations for recovered memories of sexual abuse. Finally, and perhaps most important of all, are the personal tragedies of individuals who may have authentic 'recovered' memories, as well as accused parents etc whose lives may have been torn apart as the result of a mere fiction.[1]

In short, the status of recovered memories of sexual abuse is an issue that demands that we consider all available evidence, whatever form it may take. We must avoid behaving like the proverbial drunk who, upon losing his keys in a dark area, looks for them under a lamp post because 'the light is better'. We cannot afford to only look at that side of the issue that best suits our own professional training. We need to look everywhere, even if it requires adopting new methodologies and sources of evidence. In this chapter we attempt some first steps toward developing a line of analysis that may open a meaningful dialogue between researchers and practioners. Although we have no illusions that this chapter will completely bridge the gap between the two views, we hope to begin to establish a foundation upon which such a bridge may some day be built. Toward this end, we first review the substantial scientific evidence suggesting the powerful role that memory suggestions have in planting fictitious memories of sexual abuse. In this section, we hope to impress on researchers that we are sensitive to the important implications of this literature (indeed the first author has spent most of his career inducing memory distortions). We also hope to at least begin to persuade practioners that there is a real risk that therapists may unknowingly plant suggestions that can lead to the subsequent flourishing of fabricated memories of abuse. We then turn to the existing evidence for recovered memories of abuse. Our conclusion from this section is that although the documented evidence for the factual basis of such memories may be scant, this absence of support may be more a reflection of the quality and extent of prior investigations rather than of the existence of the phenomenon itself. In support of this view, we introduce four cases of recovered memories of sexual abuse for which we personally were able to find corroborating evidence. We consider these cases in light of the various mechanisms that might contribute to the production of recovered memory experiences. This analysis suggests that recovered memories may involve a disparate set of mechanisms, some of which are well established in standard memory findings, some of which require new twists to old findings, and some of which may require the discovery of processes potentially more unique to this situation. We take on this discussion with some trepidation, as we know from experience that this is an explosive topic, laden with emotional mines and conceptual pitfalls. None the less, the seriousness of this topic demands that we find some common ground, even if it requires charting unfamiliar territory.

1 It is important to emphasize here that no one is questioning the validity of the memories of individuals who have maintained intact memories of their abuse throughout their lives. Rather the question involves the status of recovered memories of events believed to have been long forgotten and then suddenly remembered.

EVIDENCE FOR FABRICATED MEMORIES OF SEXUAL ABUSE

We begin our discussion by exploring the various sources of evidence that recovered memories of sexual abuse might, at least sometimes, be entirely fabricated. The malleability of memory represents one of the fundamental findings of cognitive psychology over the last 50 years. From early research on the impact of schemas (for example Allport and Postman 1947; Bartlett 1932) and retroactive memory interference (Barnes and Underwood 1959; McGeoch 1942), to more recent research on misinformation (Ceci *et al.* 1994*b*; Loftus *et al.* 1989*a*) and source monitoring (Johnson and Raye 1981; Johnson *et al.* 1993), the converging finding is that memory is highly susceptible to change. This absolutely fundamental aspect of memory has enabled experimental cognitive researchers to readily appreciate the possibility that recovered memories might be fabricated. Indeed, memory malleability is so ingrained in cognitive psychology's basic conception of memory that it has come as somewhat of a surprise to many of us that anyone would doubt that such processes could apply in clinical settings.

Our case for the likely role of fabrication in some recovered memory cases draws on several distinct strands of evidence. First, there is the research from cognitive psychology labs indicating that the mind is capable of confusing fact with fantasy. Second, there is the frequent usage in therapy of practices, such as suggestion and hypnosis, known to produce memory fabrications. Third, there are the various clinical cases of memory recoveries of incredible events, such as alien abductions, that seem best explained in terms of memory fabrication. Fourth, there is the testimony of retractors who believe that they were led to fabricate memories of abuse. And finally, there is the powerful lessons from history on the dangers of discounting individuals' susceptibility to persuasion. We briefly consider each of these sources of evidence in turn.

Cognitive evidence for memory fabrications

There is now a substantial body of research documenting the degree to which individuals' memories can be distorted by the suggestions of others (for a recent review see Garry *et al.* 1995). The resulting memories can be held with as much confidence as real memories (Loftus *et al.* 1989*a*), can be described in marked detail (Schooler *et al.* 1986, 1988) and are as likely as real memories to be maintained in the face of contradictory information (Loftus *et al.* 1989*b*). Although much of the research on the impact of misleading suggestion on memory has focused on the altering of relatively minor aspects of individuals' memories, recent research has documented more extensive memory distortions. For example, as a result of suggestions, individuals have come to remember entire childhood events such as being lost in a shopping mall (Loftus and

Ketcham 1994), spilling punch on the bride at a wedding (Hyman 1995), and going to the hospital after getting a finger caught in a mouse trap (Ceci *et al.* 1994*b*). In a recent particularly compelling example, Kelley and Lindsay (described by Lindsay 1994) found that an experimenter's suggestion caused many right-handed subjects to falsely remember that they had once been left handed! Like their more modest counterparts, these extensive fabricated memories can be described in great detail and maintained in the face of contradiction (Ceci *et al.* 1994*b*).

In addition to external sources, memory distortions can also arise from individuals' own beliefs, expectations, and motives. When we recall information, we are constantly attempting to fit it into a coherent life narrative (Nelson 1993; Ross 1989). In order to make sense of and fill in the details of their life experiences, individuals often unwittingly introduce memory distortions of their own. One important source of such distortions is general knowledge of different types of generic situations ('scripts') and the events that such situations typically involve (for example Schank and Abelson 1977). Such scripts can enable individuals to supplement their memories with non-factual details (for example Bower 1990) and can even provide the fodder for generating recollections of entire events that never actually occurred (for example Neisser 1981).

The above memory distortion processes can be exacerbated by a variety of individual and situational variables. Suggestions are particularly likely to be incorporated into memory, when introduced: after a significant delay (Loftus *et al.* 1978) by a credible authority (for example Dodd and Bradshaw 1980), or under hypnosis (Orne 1979). Individuals with high trust in authorities, vivid imagery skills, or who score particularly highly on suggestibility or dissociative experience scales are also particularly likely to incorporate suggestions into memory (see Gudjonsson 1992; Hyman and Billings 1995; Schooler and Loftus 1993).

In short, the cognitive literature suggests that people are extremely vulnerable to memory distortion processes, and further helps to indicate what some situations are that are most likely to elicit memory distortions. Particularly critical factors appear to be: the occurrence of leading suggestions from a credible source, the significant passage of time since the original experience occurred, a script for the experience, and a propensity for suggestion either as result of personality factors or through hypnosis. Alarmingly, all of these factors appear to be present in at least some clinical settings, a topic that we turn to next.

Therapy practices

Recently there have been several surveys of licensed clinicians to determine extent of usage of therapeutic techniques that the cognitive literature suggests may be capable of inducing false memories of abuse (for example Polusny and Follette 1996; Poole *et al.* 1995; Yapko 1994). In a random survey of licensed clinicians from both the US and Britain, Poole *et al.* found a majority of therapists (71 per cent) reported using at least one memory recovery technique to help patients recover memories of abuse. Techniques used in the service of recovering abuse memories included hypnosis (29 per cent), dream interpretations (44 per cent), and the presentation of family photographs as memory cues (47 per cent). Most alarmingly, Poole *et al.* found that 25 per cent used a combination of these techniques as well as endorsing a variety of sentiments suggesting a focus on memory recovery (for example recovery is important for therapy effectiveness, they were sometimes fairly certain about non-reported sexual abuse after one session). These therapists estimated that on average 60 per cent of patients who initially denied any memory of abuse eventually recovered them during the course of therapy (as compared to 35 per cent for therapists who did not show this constellation of beliefs and practices).

One possible criticism of the Poole *et al.* study is that they did not clearly distinguish in their questionnaire between using memory recovery techniques with patients who had no memory of abuse versus patients who may have had some memories of abuse. A number of therapists have pointed out to us that while they are reluctant to use memory techniques on patients denying any abuse, they still feel it is appropriate to use such techniques on patients who already possess abuse memories. However, a more recent survey of licensed clinicians by Polusny and Follette (1996) suggests that a substantial minority of clinicians still reported using a variety of techniques when explicitly asked to indicate 'the MEMORY RECOVERY TECHNIQUES you use with adult clients *who have no specific memory of childhood sexual abuse but who you strongly suspected were sexually abused*'. Using this more strident criterion, this survey still found substantial usage of a variety of potentially suggestive techniques including recommending books on sexual abuse (33 per cent), guided imagery (27 per cent), hypnosis (20 per cent), and even referral to sexual abuse survivor groups (29 per cent).

In light of the cognitive literature reviewed earlier, the use of memory recovery techniques for the specific purpose of recovering memories of sexual abuse that are unbeknownst to the patient seems quite dangerous indeed! Recommending sexual abuse literature or participation in survivor group clearly communicates to patients that the therapists suspects abuse occurred, i.e. it plants a powerful suggestion from a trusted authority. Techniques such as guided imagery and hypnosis greatly enhance suggestibility. Actual participation in a survivor group or reading books about sexual abuse provide patients with the necessary knowledge regarding the 'scripts' of sexual abuse. In short, while such suggestive techniques might sometimes aid in the recovery of long-lost memories, they represent the very type of procedure that cognitive psychologists would likely recommend if one explicitly wanted to plant a false memory of abuse.

Memories of the incredible

Although there is compelling evidence that individuals can readily distort their memories, and although evidence suggests that the necessary ingredients for the planting of such memories occur in therapy, it still might be questioned whether such processes could lead to the fabrication of memories as significant as being sexually abused (cf. Harvey and Herman 1994). However, consideration of the incredible things that individuals have come to falsely remember suggests that there is no limit to the magnitude of events that can be fabricated in memory. For example, individuals have been known to report recovering memories of having been visited or abducted by space aliens (Persinger 1992) and being stuck in the fallopian tube (Loftus and Ketcham 1994).

Perhaps of all the implausible memories that individuals have been encouraged to remember, the most frightening are the recovered memories of satanic rituals (Ofshe & Waters 1994). Countless patients have been diagnosed as victims of satanic ritual and caused to recall their experiences of abuse. (For a particularly alarming example of this process see *Frontline*, November 1995.) Such recollections have caused patients to be committed to institutions for extensive treatments for years on end. Although the recollections of such abuse are widespread, the evidence for it is scant at best. Indeed, a recent seven year FBI investigation of more than 300 alleged cases of satanic abuse failed to find any substantive evidence of satanic ritual abuse (Lanning 1989). While it is possible that the absence of evidence for such abuse is the consequence of the remarkable cunning of satanic groups, it seems far more likely to be the result of the over-zealous imaginations of certain therapists (see Bottoms *et al.* in press).

Recoveries of memories of the implausible often resemble, in a variety of significant ways, recoveries of memories of sexual abuse. For example, Persinger (1992) found that recovered memories of having been visited or abducted by space aliens were similar to some recovered memories of sexual abuse occurring in survivor support groups, in that they were (1) elicited following the suggestions of the leader of a group, (2) 'remembered' suddenly, (3) associated with a reduction of anxiety and panic attacks, and (4) accompanied by subsequent recollections of additional 'memories'. Others have also noted that recovered memories of implausible experiences such as alien abductions, intrauterine trauma, or satanic cult sacrifices, like recovered memories of sexual abuse, often involve great distress (cf. Lindsay and Read 1995). Our point in making the comparison between recovered memories of the incredible and recovered memories of sexual abuse is not to argue that they invariably involve the same mechanisms. Indeed, as we will demonstrate shortly, in contrast to the other types of memories described here, at least some recovered memories of sexual abuse have been shown to correspond to actual incidents. Our point is simply that if individuals can come to (presumably falsely) remember being stuck in the fallopian tube or abducted by aliens, then there is no principled reason to believe that they should not be equally capable of falsely remembering childhood sexual abuse.

Retractors

If therapists were in fact planting false memories of abuse in patients then one would expect that some patients might eventually come to realize that their memories were false. Recently, there have been a growing number of cases in which individuals come to the conclusion that a recovered memory was nothing more than a collaboration between their imaginations and the suggestions of a therapist. Goldstein and Farmer (1993) provide a number of examples of such retractors including the account of Pasley (1993) who sought treatment for bulimia. Following repeated suggestions by her therapist, often while under hypnosis, Pasley began having bizarre dreams and flashbacks of group sexual abuse and being sexually abused by animals, all of which Pasley's therapist insisted really happened. After four years in therapy, Pasley came to the conclusion that these alleged memories were the product of her therapist's suggestions, a conclusion with which a jury agreed.

Pasley's case is not an isolated instance but rather reflects the sentiment of a growing number of individuals who have come to doubt the veracity of their recovered memories of abuse. It is of course possible that such individuals are merely entering a denial stage (for example Gleaves 1994). However, there is simply no principled reason why we should believe individuals when they recover memories but then disbelieve them when they retract them. Nor, for that matter, can we disbelieve recoveries and use retractions as evidence of memory fabrication. Ultimately, the fact that individuals can shift between believing and disbelieving their recovered memories illustrates the fundamental uncertainty that surrounds such memories. As we will argue, without independent corroboration, any recovered memory might be real, might be fabricated, or might be some complex combination of the two.

Lessons from history

For those stalwart readers who still remain unpersuaded (and we hope you are among the minority) we offer a few final observations. A common error of the twentieth century has been the failure to appreciate just how susceptible individuals can be to the suggestions of individuals in positions of authority. Prior to World War II, few believed that people could be persuaded to carry out the atrocities that are known to have occurred. Prior to Milgram's (1963) classic experiments, nobody anticipated the frequency with which normal subjects could be induced to apply what they believed to be lethal shocks to an innocent volunteer. From the reactions to Orson Welles' broadcast of the Martian invasion to the drinking of Jonestown punch, and from the readers of sensational tabloids to the misguided youth that follow Aryan Nation propaganda, we see just how persuadable people can be. It seems there will always be people who can be convinced to believe just about anything. Why then should suggestions of prior sexual abuse be any different?

Another important lesson from history is that great damage can be done by well meaning health practioners. From the leaching of past centuries to the all too recent debacle of lobotomies, members of the healing arts/sciences have all too often harmed those they seeked to help because they were unaware of the full impact of their procedures. The errors of the past have led the medical establishment to use great caution in the application of new treatments. If several independent lines of evidence implicate a drug as being dangerous, it typically is used with great caution, or not all, even if it has not been directly shown to be harmful. So too it seems that the evidence for the possibility of inducing fabricated memories of abuse is sufficiently strong that practioners should exercise great caution so as to avoid inadvertently contaminating their patients' memories.

We hope to have at least begun to persuade practioners of the real dangers of planting memories of abuse, and experimentalist that we are deeply aware of the potential sources of false memories of abuse. Before discussing the other side of this issue, however, we feel it is important to make one final admonition. Even those who are persuaded of the dangers of planting false memories, may still continue activities that promote such memories. In other words, practioners may simply fail to recognize the dangerous practices that they are using. This point is well illustrated by Polusny and Follette's (1996) finding that whereas 89 per cent of their sampled clinicians reported that 'repressed memory therapy' was not appropriate for patients who had no memories of abuse, nevertheless 25 per cent reported that they used retrieval techniques such as guided imagery, assigning books on sexual abuse treatment, and referring patients to sexual abuse survivor groups, in order to help clients remember childhood sexual abuse for which they currently report no memory. This disparity may arise because practitioners, like the rest of us, are susceptible to the belief that practices that are dangerous when in the hands of others, may be safely used by oneself (cf. Wilson and Brekke 1995). It thus seems that increasing awareness of the dangers of false memories of sexual abuse is only the first step. The second, and perhaps even more challenging task, will be to change the specific practices that may lead to such memories.

EVIDENCE FOR RECOVERED MEMORIES

Although often treated as an either/or debate, the claim that some recovered memories of sexual abuse may be the product of suggestion does not necessitate that they all are. Indeed, it seems quite likely that whereas some recovered memories are the product of suggestion, others may correspond to actual incidents of abuse. However, before considering such evidence it is critical that we precisely define the construct of recovered memories so as to avoid confouding the alleged phenomenon with possible explanations for it (for example repression).

In disentangling the complex evidence surrounding this controversial topic, it is important to note that the construct of recovered memories actually entails several distinct claims, each of which may be associated with different sources of validation. First there is the *reality of the event*, that is, whether the recollection corresponds, in at least a general sense, to an actual event or set of events. Second, there is the *reality of the forgetting*, that is whether the individual was in fact unaware of the existence of the memory prior to the recollection experience. Third, there is the *reality of the recovery experience*, that is, whether the individual had a phenomenological experience of remembering incidents of sexual abuse of which they believe they were previously unaware. In conceptualizing the recovered memory phenomenon it is critical to recognize that these three elements are quite distinct. For example, as already discussed, it is possible that the recovery experience could be sincere, and yet not actually correspond to a real event. It is also possible that the event occurred, but that both the recovery experience and the forgetting were simply contrived in order to enable the individual to begin to discuss the experience. Yet another possibility is that both the memory and the recovery experience actually occurred, and yet the degree of prior forgetting is misconstrued, that is the event is believed to have been previously inaccessible, when in fact the individual had previously revealed knowledge of it.

The existence of multiple components to recovered memory claims highlights the fact that these experiences cannot be simply classified into black and white categories of factual or false. Rather, each case needs to be considered from the context of all three of these elements. We now briefly review the existing evidence for recovered memories and then consider the evidence that we ourselves have gathered.

Existing evidence for recovered memories

Although substantial effort has been given to determining the factors that might cause individuals to fabricate recovered memories of sexual abuse, surprisingly little research has been directly devoted to determining the validity of actual reported cases of recovered memories. Moreover, the limited available evidence is subject to criticisms of one sort or another. Nevertheless, given the dearth of investigation on this issue, it is important to consider the available evidence even if it may not be of the quality that we might like. The existing evidence for recovered memories can be divided into two general categories: public cases that have been discussed in the media, and clinical cases that have been investigated by psychologists.

Public cases

We are aware of two public cases for which there appeared to be reasonable corroborative evidence that a recovered memory corresponded to an actual incident of abuse. One case, reported in *U.S. News and World Report* (Horn 1993), describes the recovered memory experience of Ross Cheit.[2] According to this source, several months after learning that his nephew had joined a boys' choir, Cheit awoke one night to images of his former choir camp administrator, Bill Farmer, hovering over him. The following day he recovered memories of being sexually abused by Farmer. The *U.S. News and World Report* article describes multiple sources of indirect corroboration of the event. Specifically, the author of this article was able to find other individuals who had independently recorded instances of Farmer's sexual improprieties, both before and after Cheit's recovered memory experience. Although these sources of evidence do not conclusively demonstrate that Cheit himself was the victim of abuse, their implication of Farmer as a sexual abuser clearly supports the possibility that he may have abused Cheit as well.

A second publicly discussed recovered memory claim that has received some corroboration in the public forum is the court case of Commonwealth of Massachusetts versus Porter in 1993. In this case, Frank Fitzpatrick reported that he had been lying in bed with unexplainable anguish when he recalled being sexually molested many years earlier by Father James Porter. Indirect corroboration of this case came from multiple sources. Church officials conceded that they had observed or heard of Porter's sexual improprieties. In addition, after Fitzpatrick made his charges public, nearly 100 people reported having been sexually abused by Porter.

Although these public cases provide some evidence for the claim that recovered memories can correspond to actual events, they have some significant limitations. First, since there are only two of them, researchers could reasonably question their generalizability. Second, while they may help to substantiate the reality of the reported event, they provide no evidence regarding the validity of either the recovery experience, nor the prior forgetting of the memory. Finally, these public cases were not directly investigated by psychologists, making them difficult to compare to more traditional sources of psychological evidence.

Cases investigated by psychologists

The case for recovered memories of sexual abuse would be more compelling if it could be documented by psychological investigators. Such an analysis would help to ensure that the criteria for evidence as applied in other domains of psychological inquiry was as compatible as possible in this domain. Unfortunately, the psychological documentation of recovered memories is

2 It should be noted that the reporter who investigated this case was a friend of Cheit's. While such an affiliation need not invalidate the evidence provided, it is possible that the evidence was not collected in a completely unbiased manner.

rather modest. Several studies have elicited retrospective reports of patients reporting prior history of sexual abuse (for example Briere and Conte 1993; Gold *et al.* 1994; Loftus *et al.* 1994*b*). These studies have found some evidence that patients reporting sexual abuse believe that their memory of the abuse had once been previously forgotten. There are, however, some significant difficulties with these studies. First, it is not clear in these cases that patients absolutely understood what they were being asked; i.e. whether they believe they absolutely forgot the memory or whether they may simply have failed to think about it for some period of time (cf. Ceci *et al.* 1994*a*). Additionally, these studies did not attempt to corroborate the abuse. Thus, given the evidence already reviewed, it is possible that the patients reporting that they remembered completely forgotten episodes of abuse may have been the victims of memory fabrication. Surprisingly, given the centrality of the question of the validity of recovered memories, there have been very few explicit attempts to corroborate abuse associated with individuals' reports of having forgotten and then recovered memories of abuse. We briefly review the two published efforts to corroborate recovered reports of sexual abuse of which we are aware.

Herman and Schatzow (1987) described their efforts to corroborate the memories of a sample of patients who reported recovered accounts of childhood trauma. Of 53 patients participating in group therapy for childhood abuse, they found that 64 per cent reported severe or moderate forgetting of childhood abuse and 74 per cent were able to provide what the authors viewed as strong corroboration (for example pornographic photos, diaries, confessions from the perpetrator). While this study provides suggestive evidence in support of memory recoveries, it is not as well documented as it might be. For example, although the authors gave some examples of corroborative evidence, they did not give a complete characterization of the sources of evidence that they considered as corroborative. Thus there is the possibility that they were relying on evidence that other members of the psychological community might not find compelling. Moreover, these authors made no attempt to independently verify the claims of their patients, but instead relied on the corroborative efforts of the patients themselves. Given that the patients were likely to be motivated to demonstrate the veracity of their experiences, their construal of the corroborative evidence may have been biased. The analysis of this study is further complicated because the authors provided no independent analysis of the group of greatest interest, the 26 per cent who reported completely forgetting their abuse. On the basis of the published manuscript it could be speculated that the corroborated memories were limited to the 74 per cent of the patient population who had full or partial recall. In a personal communication, Herman (June 1994) indicated that there was no relationship in this study between patients' reports of forgetting and their likelihood of providing corroborating evidence. However, the absence of a published analysis of the relationship between corroboration and forgetting makes assessment of this issue difficult. In short, while Herman and Schatzow's study hints at the possibility that recovered memories can correspond to actual incidents of abuse, there are a sufficient number of flaws in the study that anyone with a sceptical predisposition could readily dismiss it.

The final source of published evidence for recovered accounts of sexual abuse was provided by the first author in a recent paper on the topic (Schooler 1994). This article described the first author's efforts to corroborate a case of an individual who recovered a memory of being sexually abused by a priest. We will defer discussion of the details of this case, so that we can consider it together with three new cases that we have investigated. However, there are several aspects of this case that are important to note here. On the positive side, this case represents to our knowledge the only published analysis in which a psychological researcher provided detailed analysis of both the recovered memory case and the researcher's independent efforts to corroborate that case. The case also differs from prior cases in that there was some, albeit modest, evidence not only for the veracity of the event, but also for the forgetting of the event. Nevertheless, the article only described a single case, thus again bringing its generalizability into question. More compelling evidence would be provided if this case were complimented by additional cases with comparable corroboration. Moreover, systematic analysis of the similarities and differences of the cases might begin to provide a window on the various mechanisms that may be involved in this elusive phenomenon. Towards this end, we review the prior case described by Schooler (1994) along with three[3] new cases for which we were able to generate independent corroborative evidence that the recovered memories did in fact correspond to real events.

A corroborated case study approach

Recently we have become acquainted with several cases of recovered memories of sexual abuse for which corroborative evidence was available. These cases were not deliberately sought out: three were discovered by the first author in the course of discussing this issue with colleagues, and one was brought to the attention of the second author in the context of her private practice. Our approach to assessing these cases has been relatively straightforward. We first queried the individuals regarding (1) the recovery experience, (2) their perceptions regarding the prior extent of forgetting, (3) the existence of any sources of corroboration for the event, and (4) the existence of any sources of corroboration of the forgetting. Following our interviews, we attempted to contact other individuals who could corroborate the event and/or the prior extent of forgetting. With respect to the event, corroboration took one of

---

3 Since the completion of this chapter we have found two additional cases of recovered memories of (single incidents) of childhood abuse that we were personally able to corroborate. These cases share many similarities with the present cases and will be described in subsequent writings on this topic.

two forms. In three of the cases the corroboration involved reports of others who knew of the abuse prior to the recovery experience. In one case, the corroboration involved the report of another individual who was abused by the accused. Corroboration of the prior forgetting was a bit more complex, as it is typically quite difficult to assess whether the absence of discussing an event reflects actual forgetting. Nevertheless, in all of the cases we were able to find some evidence pertinent to the claims of forgetting. For example, in one case the individual in question had actually been interviewed prior to the recovery experience about her sexual abuse history and had disclosed other incidents of abuse, but not the one in question. In other cases, the corroborative evidence suggests that the individuals may have actually been aware of the memory during a period in which they believed themselves to have completely forgotten it.

Ideally, in addition to assessing the validity of the memory and the prior forgetting, it would also be helpful to determine the veracity of individuals' reports of their recovered memory experiences. However, we simply cannot get inside our subjects' heads to see whether their recovered memory experiences really were as they claim. Nevertheless, in each case we provide our reasons for believing that our subjects are accurately describing their recovery experiences, at least to the best of their abilities. Our confidence in our subjects' efforts to accurately recount their phenomenological experience of the memory recovery is ultimately a critical element for understanding the recovered memory phenomenon. If the status of individuals' memory states prior to the recovery experience is often in question, then it may be the phenomenological experience of the memory recovery itself, with its concomitant emotion and surprise, that ultimately distinguishes recovered memories from more conventional recollections.

After we review each of the cases and the corroborative evidence we will then turn to a discussion of the possible mechanisms that may be involved in each of these cases. To foreshadow this section just a bit, consideration of the characteristics of these cases suggests that although there are some notable commonalities to these various cases, there are also some significant differences, suggesting that a complex set of mechanisms that may be differentially involved in the various cases. We will highlight what we consider to be some particularly promising mechanisms, wary of the real possibility that other, yet-to-be determined, mechanisms may also be involved.

Case 1

Subject

Case 1 (previously described in part in Schooler (1994)) involves a 39-year-old male, here after called JR. His case was brought to our attention by a colleague of the first author. JR was interviewed approximately nine years after the recovery experience occurred.

Recovery Experience

JR provided the following characterization of his recovery experience. One night JR went to see a movie where the main character grapples with memories of sexual molestations. As the movie went on, JR found himself more and more agitated without understanding why. Hours later, when he was in bed, he remembered the experience of being abused (genital fondling) by a parish priest on a camping trip when he was 12 years old (18 years previously). The memory came 'fairly suddenly' with great vividness. As JR described it: 'I was stunned, I was somewhat confused you know, the memory was very vivid and yet . . . I didn't know one word about repressed memory.' Over the following six to ten months after the first memory was recovered, JR remembered at least ten other incidents of abuse by the same individual that he estimated occurred over the next several years, all of which were recalled as occurring while the two were on trips to different places.

Characterization of the forgetting

Prior to the recovery experience, JR believes that he had no recollection whatsoever about this history of sexual abuse. As he put it: 'If you had done a survey of people walking into the movie theater when I saw the movie . . . asking people about child and sexual abuse "have you ever been, or do you know anybody who has ever been", I would have absolutely, flatly, unhesitatingly, said no!' JR further believed that he forgot the memory of each episode of sexual abuse right after it happened so that when he woke up the next morning he did not have any sense of what had occurred the night before. JR suggested that his immediate forgetting of the incidents accounts for why he continued to willingly go on subsequent trips with the priest.

Corroboration of the abuse

Corroborative evidence in support of JR's claim that he was abused comes from several sources. First, there is JR's account of his attempts to corroborate his memory. JR reported that he directly confronted the priest regarding the prior molestation. According to JR, during confrontation, the priest acknowledged the molestation and tried to assuage him by indicating that he had sought treatment for sexually abusive clergy following an incident with another individual. JR also reported that several of his brothers also indicated that they had been approached by the priest.

In addition to JR's accounts of his corroborative efforts, there is also indirect corroborating accounts of other individuals. First there are the reports of the colleague of the first author (a well respected university professor here after called ND) who introduced us to this case. Although ND only learned of the events of this case indirectly, he maintained regular contact with JR throughout this ordeal. Thus, ND can, at a minimum, corroborate the temporal order in which the reported corroborating events took place. ND also knows JR quite well and it is therefore of some interest that ND strongly discounts the possibility that JR could have invented all of the corroborating evidence that he reported in their numerous conversations. In addition, subsequent to JR's memory recovery and attempted law suit, another individual reported that he too had been sexually approached by the priest. In a separate telephone interview, this individual described how at age 18 he went to the priest for counselling about homosexuality, whereupon the priest made sexual advances towards him. This individual indicated that he had maintained an intact memory of the abuse all of his life, but had previously failed to discuss the memory due to his embarrassment.

Corroboration of the forgetting

Although it is quite difficult to assess the full extent of JR's forgetting throughout the entire period during which he claims to have forgotten his history of abuse, there is some evidence suggesting that this memory may not have been accessible to him during some periods in his life. Specifically, several years prior to his recovery experience, JR was in therapy with ND regarding an entirely unrelated difficulty. Although the issue of sexual abuse was never raised in these sessions, ND indicated that JR discussed many other intimate aspects of his life, leading ND to conclude that JR was truly unaware of possessing the memories of abuse.

Corroboration of the recovery experience

As indicated earlier, it is also quite difficult to conclusively document the authenticity of a recovered memory account. One possible argument against the authenticity of this case is that JR did ultimately attempt to press charges. Thus, sceptics might argue that JR's recovered memory report was simply a ruse to get past statute of limitation laws. However, it is important to note that at the time of his recovery (1986) there were no cases in which memory repression had been successfully used as an argument for overturning statute of limitation laws, and indeed it was such laws that ultimately prevented the prosecution of this case. Thus, the recovery of this memory did not occur in an environment in which the possible legal advantages of characterizing it as having been 'recovered' would have been appreciated.

Further evidence for the authenticity of JR's recovered memory experience comes from the accounts of ND. According to ND, JR described his recovery experience to him soon after it occurred in a manner much the same as it was described to us. At that time, JR was very upset about the memory recollection and completely unaware of the phenomenon of recovered memories. As a good friend of JR, ND sees it as inconceivable that JR would have feigned this extremely emotional recovery experience.

Discussion of Case 1
Undoubtedly, readers who are sceptical of the recovered memory phenomenon will have found various ways to discount Case 1. Some readers may question whether the corroboration of the event is really as strong as we have suggested. Perhaps, they may argue, our independent source's recollection of abuse was the product of suggestion from having heard about JR's abuse. To this criticism we remind the reader that the corroborating source claimed never to have forgotten about having been sexually abused. Thus, if we are to question his claims, we must also question the claims of all other sexual abuse survivors who, for whatever reasons, have suffered silently about their experiences. And this is a line that, so far, few have been willing to cross (see footnote 1, p. 253). Others may question whether JR's forgetting was really as profound as he suggested. Indeed, we find it a bit difficult (although not impossible) to believe that every experience of sexual abuse was forgotten as soon as it occurred. However, as we will illustrate later, it appears that forgetting processes may not only influence individuals' recollection of the event but also of their prior knowledge of that event. Thus, we need not believe JR's complete assessment of his prior forgetting in order to believe that he had a real recovered memory experience. And this leads us to perhaps the most important aspect of JR's account: his characterization of the recovery experience. Again we concede that some readers may question its authenticity, perhaps suggesting that it was either a convenient way to disclose embarrassing information or a ploy to allow him to overcome statute of limitation laws. However, considering that he had been known to reveal other embarrassing aspects of his life, and at the time of the recovery the statute of limitation laws were still binding, strongly argues against the suggestion that he feigned the recovery experience.

We will defer a detailed discussion of the possible mechanisms that led to this recovery experience for the moment, although we alert the readers to some of the themes of this recovery which will be seen in other cases and which may help our understanding of this phenomenon. These themes include: (1) the correspondences between the cuing conditions and the original memory; (2) the suddenness of the recollection experience; (3) the extreme shock and emotion associated with the recovery; and (4) the possibility that the experience may have been interpreted differently at the time of recovery then it was when it actually occurred. We turn now to a consideration of three new cases.

Case 2

Subject
Case 2 involves a 40-year-old female hereafter called WB. WB came to the attention of the second author (a practising clinician) as a result of a referral

from a patient. WB sent the second author a letter describing her recovered memory experience one week after it was recovered. Although the second author subsequently treated WB, it is important to emphasize that the recovery experience occurred outside of and prior to therapy.

Recovery experience

In her initial letter, WB described her recovery experience which was triggered by a conversation with a male friend at a party. Apparently, WB commented to a male friend about his advances towards a young woman. He defended himself by saying 'She isn't exactly a virgin', which upset WB to such a degree that she left the party in a rage. The following night she had stormy nightmares and then awoke the next morning with the startling recollection of having been raped at knifepoint while hitchhiking when she was a teenager (20 years previously). As WB put it in her original letter: 'I awoke the next morning with a sudden and clear picture: "My God . . . I had been raped!! I was 16, just a kid! I couldn't defend myself.' In a subsequent interview, WB further characterized the recovery experience suggesting that it was 'complete chaos in my emotions'. Following her recollection, WB experienced a violent emotional reaction that lasted all day. She then experienced a 'kind of confused relief . . . everything seemed very far away . . . just sort of numb and paralyzed'. She even wondered whether she might have 'made the whole thing up'. However, several days later her emotions returned, and she realized she needed help.

Characterization of the forgetting

WB's characterization of her memory prior to the recovery reveals a marked sensitivity to the inherent difficulty of estimating a prior knowledge state from the vantage of a new state. When asked whether she was surprised, at the time of the memory recovery, by the existence of this memory, she observed that she was quite startled, noting 'I was overwhelmed, rather than surprised, surprised is too neutral a feeling for what I felt.' Although she indicated that she was shocked to recall that she had been raped, on several occasions she suggested that she might have possessed some prior memory for the event. For example, in her original letter WB observed:

In a way, I have managed to repress the *meaning* of what happened all of these years. I may have not completely forgotten the experience . . . but I have pushed it away, minimized it . . . It wasn't a real rape.

Later in an interview, when asked if there was ever a time in which she believes she was completely unaware that this event occurred, she suggested that it:

It is something like, you know, your first day at school or your 10th birthday. You know that the event occurred, but you don't think about it, or even remember how it was, but you know it was there.

Thus, on the one hand WB suggested that she was startled to recall that she had been raped, yet at the same time she recognizes the possibility that she may have had some knowledge about the experience all along. This ambiguity regarding her prior state of memory is further illustrated by her response to the question of whether she thinks there was ever a time in which she would have honestly believed that she had not been raped had she been asked directly. In response, she observed:

I actually think this is the case. When I wrote my story about rape (WB is a novelist) I can honestly say I had absolutely no connection to the fact that it had been a personal experience. I was writing it 'on behalf of others,' I thought this is what it must be like for those who experienced rape. I am really uncertain how I would have responded if someone had asked me directly.

Although it is difficult to fully resolve WB's perceptions of her prior memory state for the rape, two conclusions from this discussion seem clear. (1) Her marked shock at the recollection of this event suggests that it (or at least its emotional significance) was not entirely accessible to her prior to the recovery experience. (2) Individuals can have unambiguous memory recovery experiences even when their prior memory state is ambiguous, even to them.

Corroboration of the experience

WB indicated that following her rape experience she described it to several of her co-workers at the camp at which she was working at the time. One of those co-workers was an individual whom she later married. In a separate interview, WB's former husband recounted the day in which she had returned from her day off and reported having had a 'bad experience' in which she had sex 'involuntarily' but had not protested. A few days later she described it as 'something like rape'.

Corroboration of the forgetting

As described above, WB experienced real ambiguities regarding her prior awareness of the rape. Her ex-husband's recounting of her discussions of the rape during the marriage further highlight this ambiguity. In an independent interview, her ex-husband further disclosed that during the years that they were married, WB mentioned in passing several times that she had been raped, but totally without affect. Interestingly, WB has no recollection whatsoever of having mentioned her rape to her ex-husband during their marriage, and was quite startled to learn that she had done so.

Corroboration of the recovery experience

There are a number of reasons to believe WB's account of her recovery experience. First, there was absolutely nothing for her to gain by feigning the recovery. The individual who raped her was long gone, so there was no potential legal advantage of framing this recollection as a memory recovery. Second, WB contacted the second author barely a week after the experience occurred, thus reducing the possibility that the memory for the recovery would have been significantly forgotten. There was also partial corroboration of the recovery experience by the individual who was at the party where the precursors to the memory recollection were first planted. Specifically, the individual whose comments prompted WB was also a patient of the second author, and recounted WB's behavior at the party in a manner closely corresponded to WB's description.

Discussion of Case 2

Case 2 illustrates some of the complexities of the recovered memory experience. On the one hand, this case is quite compelling with respect to corroboration of the abuse event with independent verification by an individual who was present immediately after the event occurred. On the other hand, the nature of the forgetting that preceded the recovery is of real question. And indeed, it is clear that the subject was aware of the rape many years after it occurred. Despite these complications, several traits of this case fit into the emerging picture of the recovered memory process: (1) the memory was triggered by a cue that had some resemblance to the original abuse: the mentioning of the virginity of a young woman (WB was a virgin when the incident occurred); (2) the recovery experience involved a sudden startling recollection associated with great emotion (in this case contrasting prior seemingly non-affective recollections); (3) there is the possibility that the interpretation of the event may have changed: a brutal rape rather than an unpleasant sexual experience; (4) it is extremely difficult to remember the prior state of one's memory for an abuse event after a recovery experience.

Case 3

Subject

Case 3 involved a 51-year-old female (hereafter called TW). TW's case was brought to our attention through a colleague of the first author. TW was interviewed approximately 17 years after her recovery experience.

Recovery experience

In a telephone interview, TW described a memory recovery experience that took place in her office. One afternoon, TW's office mate asked her whether she wanted to go to a talk on child molestation. TW turned to her office mate to say either yes or no, when all of a sudden she had a very vivid and immediate memory about being molested when she was nine years old (16 years previously). TW recalled the recollection experience quite vividly noting:

I've never experienced [anything] like that before, it was like a . . . a package of some sort ... something there that's completely unwound instantly and not only the experience was available but the sequel of the experience ... telling my mother later when we returned to my house in Jamaica ... The whole thing was evident and immediate to me, simultaneously ... altogether ... so the package had been unwrapped or something. And it was very different from any memory I've ever had before or since.

As in the other cases, when TW recovered the memory she was quite startled. As TW describes it: 'When I first remembered it, I was surprised. Completely taken back by it. Then I . . . I don't even remember speaking . . . I was completely out of it.' In short, TW had what is now appearing to be the standard phenomenological experience of a recovered memory: marked surprise at the sudden unfolding of a powerfully emotional and vivid memory of seemingly forgotten sexual abuse.

Characterization of the forgetting

According to TW, prior to the recovery, she had no recollection whatsoever about the incident. As TW noted, in between the time she told her mother about the experience and the time she actually recovered it, she believed that 'the state of my memory in that period was none . . . Non-existent.' She was consequently quite astonished, when she learned later that she actually had told her former husband about it. According to TW, upon the encouragement of friends familiar with recovered memory controversy, she asked him whether or not she had told him about having had any bad experiences in Jamaica. He indicated that she had previously mentioned having been sexually abused. TW had no recollection whatsoever of such a discussion, or even of being aware of the memory at the time her husband indicated that she had mentioned it to him. As TW observed in describing her reaction to learning of this earlier conversation:

I felt like falling over. Absolutely shocked and floored that it happened. And I still am. . . . I can't remember telling him, I can't think of anything about the memory before [the recovery], and it's very disturbing, actually.

In short, TW was as startled at her forgetting that she once had remembered this memory as she was at having forgotten it in the first place.

Corroboration of the event

TW's former husband was interviewed to determine whether in fact TW had discussed the abuse with him. He reported that she talked about the abuse several times over the course of their marriage (which ended prior to the recovery). As in the previous case of WB, she apparently mentioned the abuse in a relatively matter of fact manner, with little expression of emotion and no reference to any memory difficulties associated with the recollection.

Corroboration of the forgetting

In the case of TW, there is suggestive evidence that her forgetting may have involved a failure to remember her prior knowledge of the event. Specifically, even though her original recollection was of not having spoken to anyone about the event, the corroborative interview with her husband clearly indicates that she was aware of the event during a period of time in which she believed herself to have forgotten it. Her ex-husband also corroborated her surprise at discovering that she had told him about the experience, further substantiating her claim that she had actually forgotten that this memory had once been intact.

Corroboration of the recovery experience

As in the other cases described here, there is no reason to believe that TW intentionally fabricated her recovery experience. She was not pursuing legal recourse regarding the accused individual and would have nothing that we can see to gain from deliberately misleading us. It might be noted that the recovery did occur quite some time ago and consequently her recollection of the recovery experience may have altered somewhat over the years. Indeed, one individual who spoke to her about her recollection several years ago, recalls that while she perceived this recollection as somewhat peculiar, he does remember her ascribing quite as much emotion or significance to it as she does today.

Discussion of Case 3

Case 3 illustrates a number of the characteristics seen in some of the earlier cases. As in the other case, her recovery experience was triggered by a related event which elicited a sudden emotional unravelling of a surprisingly extended memory of which she believed herself to be previously unaware. As in the prior case of WB, this powerfully emotional recollection strikingly contrasts with her earlier affectively flat recollections (of which she still does not recall). Case 3, thus, also provides the most compelling evidence yet that recovered memory experiences can be associated with a misrecollection of the prior knowledge state. At the time of her memory recovery, TW believed that she had not remembered this event since soon after its occurrence, when in fact there is clear evidence that she was talking about it years later. While this brings into question the extent of her forgetting of the event itself, it highlights the degree to which individuals can forget their prior knowledge about an event. It also illustrates once again that the critical element of memory recovery experiences may be the individual's perceptions of their memory at the time of the recovery, not their actual memory state prior to the recovery.

Case 4

Subject

Case 4 involves a 41-year-old female (hereafter called DN) who brought her case to the attention of the first author following a colloquium presentation that he gave on this topic. She was interviewed approximately six years after her recovery experience.

Recovery experience

DN had been in group therapy for victims of child abuse (a memory that she had kept intact all of her life). At one of the therapy sessions, the therapist mentioned that victims of child abuse often continue to be victimized as adults. On her drive home after the session, she thought about the therapist's remark and then all at once she remembered being raped by a stranger at age 22 (13 years previously). DN recounted her recovery experience as follows:

What she [her therapist] had said popped into my mind, and then all at once I remembered being a victim when I was like in my early twenties, when I was a nurse at a hospital. And it really kind of freaked me out because I remembered that not only had I been a victim but I had to go to court and prosecute the person who had attacked me. And he had been found guilty. And yet I had forgotten all of that.

The sudden memory of the incident elicited a very intense emotional state that required her to pull of the road. As DN put it:

I had to just sit there for a while because it was just this extreme emotion of fear and total disbelief. Disbelief that it happened, disbelief that I could have forgotten something that traumatic.

Characterization of the forgetting

DN was positive that she remembered the attack for the approximately two years after the rape that she continued working at the same hospital. She then moved to a different state and worked at a different hospital. At some point following her move, she believed that she completely forgot the whole incident including the trial. Indeed, it was her amazement at having forgotten the rape and the ensuing trial that contributed to the remarkable quality of her recovery experience. As DN put it: 'It's like how could I forget this. As horrible as it was having to go to court . . . and having to tell what happened and everything, how could I forget that? I had no idea when I did forget it but I really feel that it had been totally forgotten until that night.'

Corroboration of the event

Because DN's case was actually taken to trial, corroboration was relatively straightforward. In a telephone interview, her lawyer at the time (who is now a judge) verified that the case did in fact go to court, and that the accused was found guilty of rape. Thus we have incontrovertible evidence for one component of this traumatic experience (taking the rape case to court) and extremely compelling evidence for the other component of this trauma (the rape itself) as the individual was found guilty.

Corroboration of the forgetting

In this case we have what is perhaps the strongest evidence from any of the cases described here that true forgetting had occurred prior to the recovery.

When DN entered therapy for victims of sexual abuse, she was given an initial interview to assess her history of abuse. During this interview (as revealed in hospital records made available to the first author), DN described in detail her abuse as a child, but did not mention her rape experience. While it is possible that she simply failed to disclose the rape at this time this seems relatively unlikely for the following reasons: the fact that she previously took the case to trial clearly establishes her history of a willingness to talk about the rape; the incidents that she did disclose were comparably embarrassing; and as soon as she had the memory recovery experience she mentioned the rape at therapy. Of course, it is possible that she may not have thought about the rape in the same way that she thought about her early childhood abuse and so she may have failed to mention it at that time. However, together with her self-report of her shock at the recovery experience, her failure to mention her rape in the initial assessment interview is at least strongly suggestive that actual forgetting did in fact take place.

Corroboration of the recovery experience

As in the other cases, there is no reason that we are aware of to believe that DN intentionally fabricated her memory recovery experience. DN sought legal recourse prior to the memory recovery experience and there is no legal benefit that she would have gotten from construing her memory as a recovery. It is also of interest that the recovery experience is mentioned in her therapy records, further substantiating the validity of her report.

Discussion of Case 4

Case 4 has many of the characteristics that we found in the earlier cases. As in the prior cases, the memory was prompted by a cue corresponding to the original incident (in this case learning that childhood victims of sexual abuse are often abused as adults). The nature of the recovery experience was also quite similar, with a sudden emotional onrush in which the entire experience seemed to unfold all at once. In addition to these similarities, there were also some differences. Unlike several of the prior cases in which it is clear that memory was possessed at a time when it was believed to be forgotten, in this case there is at least suggestive evidence that DN may have had complete forgetting of the experience. DN's case is also particularly notable because it entailed forgetting of both the rape and of the subsequent trial, both of which were corroborated. It is sometimes suggested that while forgetting of a single incident is possible, forgetting of an entire period of abuse is not possible (Ofshe and Watters 1994). Arguably, being raped and then having to testify about it in court constitutes an extended period of abuse, consequently the fact that both elements of this recovered memory were corroborated suggests that recovered memories of extended incidents of abuse can be veridical.

MECHANISMS THAT MAY CONTRIBUTE TO PERCEIVED RECOVERIES OF AUTHENTIC MEMORIES

Our discussion so far has focused on attempting to delineate the characteristics of memory recovery experiences corresponding to authentic memories. We have intentionally avoided speculating about the mechanisms underlying these recovery experiences because all too often mechanisms and the phenomenon itself are hopelessly intertwined, thereby further confounding an already complex and controversial topic. For example, the construct of recovered memories is often treated synonymously with the construct of repression. However, as illustrated below, there are many other mechanisms that might, in principle, account for memory recovery experiences. In the following discussion we consider our four cases in light of such mechanisms. We first briefly review the possible applicability of standard factors typically associated with variations in the accessibility of normal memories. In keeping with standard discussions of memory processes we first consider encoding factors, then storage factors, and finally retrieval factors. This section is based on the premise that even though we cannot be certain whether the memories involved in these cases were ever entirely forgotten, it nevertheless seems quite likely that they fluctuated in accessibility, i.e. there were some points in time in which the individuals were more aware of these memories than others. Thus, an understanding of the possible mechanisms that could have contributed to changes in the accessibility of these memories is likely to be helpful, even if the memories were never entirely unavailable. Indeed, in our subsequent discussion of possible non-standard cognitive mechanisms that may be involved, we specifically argue that the access of these powerful emotional memories may (at least sometimes) cause a misconstrual of the degree to which the memories were previously unavailable.

We must emphasize that this analysis is meant to be illustrative not definitive. We are not claiming that these mechanisms entirely account for all recovered memory cases, nor even necessarily for the four that we have documented here. Moreover, as we illustrate below, it is quite likely that these experiences may draw on an interacting assortment of processes, with potentially different combinations of mechanisms contributing to each case. Nevertheless, we believe these mechanisms provide a useful starting point for a discussion of how basic cognitive processes might be integrated into an understanding of a phenomenon that basic cognitive psychologists have had considerable difficulty conceptualizing and therefore accepting.

Encoding factors

There are a number of characteristics of the encoding of these memories that could have reduced the initial accessibility of these memories, thereby causing their subsequent retrieval to be perceived as a memory 'recovery'. As will be seen, some apply better than others.

Salience

Generally speaking, the more salient an experience the more likely it is to be remembered (for example Wagenaar 1986). The salience of traumatic experiences has been used in the past to help to account why they are often remembered quite well (for example Brown and Kulik 1977; Femina *et al.* 1990; Malmquist 1986), and indeed, the fact that salient negative experiences are often remembered all too well has been used as a powerful argument to question the pervasiveness of recovered memories of abuse (Loftus 1993; Lindsay and Read 1995). Given the role of salience in enhancing memory performance, one possible interpretation of the initial reduced accessibility of the experiences described above is that they were not interpreted as being that important at the time. Changes in the perceived importance of these experiences may well have contributed to the reduced accessibility in some of the above cases. For example, as will be discussed in the reinterpretation section below, it is possible that WB may not have fully interpreted her experience as a rape at the time that it occurred. Similarly, TW, being only nine when the alleged fondling took place, may not have viewed it as significant an experience as she does today. Although low salience may partially account for these two cases, we should be cautious in assuming that low salience was responsible for the reduced accessibility of these memories. The individual who spoke to WB the day after she was raped, indicated that she was quite upset about the experience at the time. Similarly, TW's recalls of having expressed marked concern about the experience to her mother, were sufficient, she claims, to cause the family to never return to their favourite vacation place. Thus, while these experiences may not have been as salient at the time as they are today, they were still probably pretty significant, and likely more significant than other memories that these individuals never believe they forgot. Furthermore, the issue of salience seems inapplicable to the accessibility of the experiences reported by both JR and DN. Admittedly, JR might not have perceived the priest's advances as negatively as he does today (see reinterpretation section) nevertheless it is hard to imagine that a 12- to 15-year-old boy would not find a long-term sexual relationship with a priest quite memorable. Finally, DN clearly found her abuse quite salient as it was sufficient to cause her to press charges. In short, although salience may have played a role in some of these cases, it does not appear to offer a full account for the fluctuations in the accessibility of these experiences.

Duration

Another encoding factor known to influence subsequent memory performance is whether the memory corresponds to a single isolated event or is repeated over a duration of time. Although repetition may cause individuals to forget the details of specific incidents, it typically leads to excellent memory for the gist of the experience (Schank and Abelson 1977). Indeed, the issue of the duration of the abuse has been a critical dividing line for the types of abusive incidents that have been considered possible to be forgotten. For example, Ofshe and Watters (1994) suggest that the forgetting of extended durations of abuse would require 'robust repression', a phenomenon for which they claim there is no evidence. Similarly, although Lindsay and Read (1995) are more sympathetic to the notion of authentic recovered memories, they nevertheless conclude that forgetting of repeated incidents of abuse is likely to be especially rare. In this context, it should be noted that several of our cases involved memory recovery experiences corresponding to extended incidents. JR recalls incidents of abuse spanning several years. While we cannot confirm the specifics of these individual incidents, his report of having going on numerous overnight trips with the priest over a period of several years (a memory which he claims was always intact) is at the least very supportive of JR's current recollection of multiple incidents of abuse. DN provides another example of an individual whose abuse covered an extended duration. Although the rape itself was brief, the subsequent trial lasted for several months. During this time DN was subjected to all of the pain, stress, and embarrassment that accompanies trying to successfully prosecute someone for rape. While this may not be sexual abuse in the standard sense, it clearly represents an extremely disturbing situation that spanned an extended period of time. Indeed, DN's case highlights the fact that most traumatic sexual abuse incidents, even if they physically occurred at only one brief moment in time, would be expected to psychologically extend over a much greater duration as the individual attempts to grapple with the experience.

Storage factors

There are also a number of standard storage factors that could have influenced the accessibility of the memories in the previous cases. We briefly consider several such factors.

Rehearsal

Rehearsal is another factor long known to increase memory retention (for example Atkinson and Shiffrin 1969). Explicit rehearsal (recounting a memory to someone else) is particularly important because it can help individuals to integrate memories into their life narrative (Nelson 1993). It is thus of some note that in three of the four cases, documented incidents of explicit rehearsal occurred. WB discussed her hitchhiking rape with her co-workers/friends at the time and also mentioned the experience several times in passing to her husband. TW similarly discussed her sexual molestation in Jamaica with her mother after it happened, and later on with her husband. Finally, DN went through excruciating rehearsal processes in the context of testifying about the rape in court. JR does not appear to have engaged in any explicit rehearsal prior to his recovery. However, as mentioned before, he seems likely to have been the victim of multiple incidents of abuse, thereby providing an external source of rehearsal. Thus, an absence of rehearsal also does not seem to provide a full account of the reduced accessibility of the memories in these cases.

Interference

Another possible storage mechanism that could, in principle, have been responsible for the temporarily reduced accessibility of the memories in these cases is interference. Considerable evidence suggests that exposure to related similar events can cause confusion and reduced accessibility of individual experiences (for example Neisser 1981; Underwood 1967; Wagenaar 1986). Such interference has been suggested by several researchers (for example Loftus *et al.* 1994a; Schooler 1994) as a possible account for the recent observation that victims of sexual abuse can forget documented incidents of abuse (Williams in press). Accordingly, if individuals have been the victims of multiple incidents of sexual abuse (as most of the individuals in the Williams study were) then interference between the various incidents might cause them to confuse or forget individual incidents. However, an interference account does not seem to explain the forgetting reported here. In three of the four cases the subjects were aware of no other incidents of sexual abuse other than those associated with the memory recovery experiences. DN was aware of having been sexually abused by family members as a child. However, such childhood abuse seems markedly different from an adulthood rape by a stranger and thus seems unlikely to have been a source of interference.

Directed forgetting

Another potentially promising storage factor that may have played a role in several of these cases is directed forgetting. It is now well established that active attempts to forget information can result in reduced access to that information (for example Bjork 1989). In fact, there is evidence that directed forgetting may have been involved in at least one of the cases described here. When asked whether she could recall ever intentionally trying to put out of her mind the experience of being raped while hitchhiking, WB specifically replied in the affirmative noting: 'I tried not to think about it.' Interestingly, none of the other individuals recalled intentionally trying to put the memory out of their minds. For example, DN had no recollection of intentionally trying to forget being raped in the hospital noting 'I really don't remember putting it out of my mind, and I really don't know when I forgot it. I really didn't try to forget it, it was just like it never happened until all at once . . . it came back.' A similar absence of intentional forgetting were reported by JR and TW. It is possible that these individuals simply forgot that they engaged in directed forgetting. Alternatively, it may be that directed forgetting was important in some of the cases but not others.

Delay

A final potentially relevant storage factor long known to influence the accessibility of memories is the simple passage of time (for example Ebbinghaus 1913). In all of the cases, many years passed between the occurrence of the event and the subsequent recovery experience. Thus the simple passage of time may have contributed to our subjects' forgetting. As the saying goes 'Time heals all wounds.' Although decay may have contributed to the forgetting associated with these incidents, it should be noted that the experiences of the second and third decades of life (during which the majority of these abuse events occurred) are often the most memorable (Conway and Rubin 1993). Thus the passage of time, while potentially important, may not alone account for the reduced accessibility of the memories in these cases.

Retrieval factors

Standard memory mechanisms also suggest a number of retrieval factors that might in principle help to account for the recovered memory experiences. Unlike encoding and storage factors, retrieval factors seem more contributive to the recovery experiences than to the forgetting experiences. However, as will be seen, one of the retrieval factors (encoding specificity) can account for both the forgetting and the recovery.

Reinterpretation

Changes in individuals' interpretations of events can sometimes result in their retrieval of previously inaccessible information (for example Anderson and Pitcher 1978). It is thus possible, that changes in the interpretation of the experiences could have been involved in at least some of the present recovered memory experiences. For example, WB specifically acknowledged that initially she had tried to frame the experience as not being as serious as she later concluded it was. It also might be noted that WB's experience occurred in the 1960's a time in which sexual encounters were perceived differently than they are today, thereby also potentially contributing to a shift in WB's interpretation of this experience. It is also possible that JR might have initially had some ambivalence about the priest's sexual advances, which later were recalled as a negative experience. Such changes in perspective on the events could well have led to the access of previously inaccessible information. Moreover, if the experiences were later recalled as worse than they were originally perceived, this could help to account for the severe emotional upset that was associated with the retrieval. At the same time, however, we must be cautious in pushing this reinterpretation explanation too far. DN, for example, unambiguously initially interpreted her experience as rape and pressed charges accordingly. And as already argued, all four cases were quite likely to have found these experiences to be extremely salient at the time.

Hypermnesia

Another retrieval factor that could, in principle, be involved in recovered memory experiences is hypermnesia; the increased recollection of information following multiple retrieval attempts (for example Erdelyi and Kleinbard 1978; Mandler 1994). In the context of recovered memories, hypermnesia might occur in situations in which individuals are repeatedly encouraged to attempt to recall memories of abuse during therapy. In such situations, hypermnesia processes might enable individuals to discover memories that they initially had failed to recall (cf. Bower 1990). (Of course, memory fabrication processes might equally well lead to the recovery of memories that never actually occurred.) In the present case, hypermnesia processes appear to be of no relevance to three of the cases where recollection occurred without even a single active attempt to recall an incident of abuse. Hypermnesia might, however, have played some roles in DN's recovery of being raped in the hospital. In DN's case, her recovery experience followed several prior attempts to remember earlier incidents of sexual abuse. Thus, hypermnesia represents yet another process that may be differentially involved in the various cases.

Encoding specificity

Of all of the standard memory mechanisms reviewed so far, encoding specificity (Tulving and Thompson 1973) seems to have the clearest role in every case. The encoding specificity principle states that the probability of retrieving a memory is maximized when the retrieval conditions correspond to the encoding conditions. A clear correspondence between the encoding and retrieval conditions is one of the striking similarities between all four of the cases described here. JR recalled his sexual abuse after seeing a movie in which the main character grappled with her experiences of abuse. WB recalled being raped as a virgin, when a friend made some disparaging remarks about the virginity of another woman. TW spontaneously remembered her childhood sexual abuse when the topic was raised in conversation by her office mate. DN recovered her memory after being prompted to think about adult sexual abuse by her therapist. In short, although these memories felt as if they occurred 'out of the blue', in fact, in each case there were appropriate retrieval conditions, which according to the principle of encoding specificity would have been useful cues for eliciting the memories.

Although the encoding specificity principle seems to apply quite well to each of these cases in the sense that there is a clear correspondence between the original experience and the retrieval conditions, encoding specificity also seems to pose somewhat of a puzzle. Specifically, it is hard, although perhaps not inconceivable, to believe that these individuals could have gone for the duration that they claimed to have without encountering other equally relevant conditions that should have, according to encoding specificity, prompted the retrieval of the memory. There are a number of possible resolutions to this puzzle. For example, it may be that retrieval following reinstatement of encoding conditions is a probabilistic process, such that on any given cueing situations there is some probability that the critical memory will be retrieved (cf. Raaijmakers and Shiffrin 1981). If this probability is sufficiently low, this could account for why prior potential cueing conditions failed to elicit the memory. Another possibility is that encoding specificity interacts with other mechanisms, so that even though the cue conditions may have been appropriate at prior times, these other mechanisms prevented access. Yet a third possibility is that these individuals may in fact have been cued and remembered the experiences previously, but simply forgot these prior remembering experiences; we will return to this possibility when we discuss the forgot-it-all-along effect.

Accounting for some of the unusual characteristics of recovered memories

Consideration of the possible standard memory mechanisms suggest that, some of these mechanisms (for example directed forgetting, reinterpretation, hypermnesia, encoding specificity) may play an important role in some memory recovery experiences. At the same time, however, it must be conceded that some of the characteristics of these experiences at least appear to differ from standard memory recollection experiences. We consider several of these distinctive characteristics, and then introduce a few new constructs that might help further clarify the phenomenon.

The phenomenology of the recovered memory experiences

Although the four cases that we described differed in a number of ways, there is one respect in which all four were strikingly similar: the manner in which they described the recovery experience. All of the recovery experiences were characterized as suddenly and vividly coming out of nowhere, followed by a great onrush of emotion. As WB put it 'like a flood, the locks were opened'. As TW put it 'like a . . . a package of some sort . . . something there that's completely unwound instantly.'

This startling emotional recovery of a seemingly intact memory is simply an aspect of autobiographical memory that has not been well documented in the past. We just do not know how often individuals are startled by the sudden recollection of significant memories. Do people ever have the experience of saying, for example, 'My God, I just suddenly remembered I had my tonsils out. I can't believe I forgot that!' Although full resolution of this issue awaits further research, there is a hint in the literature that such experiences may be rather commonplace. Read *et al.* (cited in Lindsay and Read 1995) found that 31 per cent of 204 undergraduates reported having experienced 'recovered' memories of long-forgotten autobiographical experiences. Although it is not clear whether these individuals also experienced the emotional 'rush' associated with recovered memories reported here, it seems quite plausible that many of them may have been quite surprised at the product of their recovery experiences. Clearly, systematic efforts (perhaps using diaries or health records as a source of corroboration) need to be conducted to determine how unique the recovered memory phenomenology is to the retrieval of memories of sexual abuse.

Although there is little parallel to the recovered memory experience in the autobiographical memory literature, there are other domains in which a somewhat similar phenomenology has been reported. One such domain is insight problem solving (cf. Schooler and Melcher 1995). Like recovered memories, insight solutions involve situations in which a coherent bit of knowledge startlingly pops into mind in a surprisingly intact form, followed by an onrush of emotion (Schooler *et al.*, 1995). Although the emotion associated with insight is often positive (Gick and Lockhart 1995), this is probably because the sudden solution is desirable; one might well imagine situations in which insights might be associated with equally strong negative emotions. For example, imagine what Einstein's experience might have been like if he suddenly had the insight that his formula could lead to the production of weapons of mass destruction! Thus, it seems that recovered memory experiences might well be conceived of as a type of memory insight, and processes previously examined in the context of insight (cf. Sternberg and Davidson 1995) might be useful for helping us to better conceptualize recovered memories as well.

Another domain in which a phenomenology comparable to the recovered memory experiences have been reported is the flashbacks of individuals suffering from post-traumatic stress disorder (PTSD) (McGee 1984; Williams 1983). Like the recovered memory experiences described here, such flashbacks often involve the extremely vivid recollection of a traumatic experience along with a great onrush of emotions. Although such flashbacks typically occur with individuals who are in the midst of grappling with their traumatic experiences, flashbacks can, like recovered memories, also occur after durations in which individuals experience relatively few symptoms (Christenson *et al.* 1981). Like recovered memories, traumatic flashbacks can also be prompted by cues corresponding to the encoding situations. These parallels suggest that recovered memory experiences may also share some mechanisms with traumatic memory flashbacks (Schooler 1994).

The forgot-it-all-along effect

The startling surprise and emotional onrush associated with recovered memories may be related to another remarkable characteristic of at least two of the cases described here: the capacity to forget about a period in which one was aware of the memory and discussed it with others. Both WB and TW were astounded to discover that they had told their husbands about the incidents at a time in which they thought the memory had been forgotten. To our knowledge, this profound *underestimation* of one's prior memory state has not been documented in the literature before. However, the *overestimation* of prior knowledge has been well documented. Research on the 'knew-it-all-along effect' has demonstrated that individuals who are told facts about a topic tend to misremember that they previously knew those facts, even when independent evidence suggests that they did not (Fischoff 1982). The basic explanation of this effect is that individuals use their current knowledge state to infer their earlier knowledge.

It seems quite possible that a process analogous to the knew-it-all-along effect may occur in the context of some recovered memories. As with the knew-it-all-along effect, recovered memory experiences can be associated with a misconstrual of one's prior knowledge state, except that the knowledge is *underestimated* rather than *overestimated*. This bias may also be the result of inferences stemming from one's knowledge state at the time of the memory recovery. The marked shock and onrush of emotion associated with the recovered memory experience may influence individuals' assessments of their prior knowledge. For example, 'If I am this shocked and surprised then I must have previously completely forgotten about the experience.' Although previous complete forgetting is one possible explanation for the recoverer's shock and emotion, it is not the only one. For example, at the time of retrieval the individual may reinterpret the experience in a more negative light then it was originally perceived. This shock at the severity of the abuse may then be misattributed as being a shock at the remembering itself. Alternatively, it may also be that if one does not access a very emotional memory for some period of time, one may be startled by how much emotional power the memory still has, particularly if the recollection is associated with the huge emotional onrush (mentioned above) that can sometimes co-occur with recollections of traumatic experiences. This shock at the emotional power of the memory may once again be misattributed as occurring because the memory was previously completely unavailable. In short, the emotional onrush associated with the recollection of traumatic memories may cause individuals to mistakenly believe that their memory must have been forgotten all along in order for it to pack that much punch.

It is clear that this 'forgot-it-all-along' account applies, at least to some degree, in several of our cases. Both WB and TW believed that they were unaware of the memory at a point in time in which corroborative evidence indicates that they were in fact aware of it. However, their reported recollections at that time were affectively quite flat, strongly contrasting with the subsequent emotional onrush that they experienced at the time of the memory recovery. Thus there is the real possibility that they may have erroneously attributed this difference in their emotional reaction to the memory to a difference in their actual awareness of the memory. Indeed, WB was cognizant of her difficulty in determining what exactly she was so startled about at the time of her memory recovery. Although the forgot-it-all-along effect appears to apply well in at least several of these cases, it should be noted that the fact that these individuals misremembered their memory state at certain points in time does not necessarily demonstrate that they have not actually forgotten the incident at some time prior to the recovery. Moreover, for JR and DN we have no evidence for memory misconstrual but we have at least suggestive evidence that the abuse incident was not readily accessible at points in time in which the memories might have been expected to have been retrieved. Thus, although this 'forgot-it-all-along' account is quite possibly an important element in some recovered memory experiences, it is unlikely to provide the whole story.

The forgetting of extremely salient experience

Understandably, researchers are wary of drawing on special mechanisms to account for a memory phenomenon that might be more parsimoniously accounted for by known mechanisms. We are sympathetic to this perspective, and as the above discussion illustrates have devoted considerable effort to developing conceptualizations of recovered memories that do not necessarily require any 'special mechanisms'. At the same time, however, we believe that it is premature to rule out the possibility that more unusual forgetting and remembering mechanisms may be at play. It is certainly the case that each of our four subjects perceived their recovered memory experiences as absolutely qualitatively different from any other forgetting/remembering experience that they had ever had. And indeed we must concede that the experience of suddenly remembering extremely salient life events that spanned extended durations (JR and DN) stretches the bounds of standard memory mechanisms. (Indeed it is the implausibility of such experiences from the perspective of standard memory models that has likely contributed to the scepticism of many cognitive psychologists toward these types of recovered memories). We therefore think it is important to at least keep the door open to the possibility that recovered memories may be the consequence of memory processes that are not readily observed under more standard memory conditions.

There are hints from the present cases that certain specialized mechanisms may be at work. For example, all four of our subjects reported deep shame about their experiences. It is possible that shameful memories may trigger self-defence mechanisms that enhance memory distortion and forgetting. Such mechanisms might bear some relationship to the general self-enhancement memory distortion processes occasionally included in discussions of standard memory processes (for example Greenwald 1980). However, the possible role of shame in causing disturbing memories to be reduced in accessibility would probably not represent a memory mechanism that occurs every day, and might well resemble those sometimes proposed to be involved in repression (Lewis 1990).[4]

We recognize that specialized processes that have been hypothesized to

---

4 It should be noted that there does not appear to be any clear consensus about what the construct of repression really means. For example, Freud originally defined repression as occurring when 'A hysterical subject seeks intentionally to forget an experience or forcibly repudiates, inhibits and suppresses an intention or idea' (Freud 1940, p.153). However, others have defined repression as an *involuntary* mechanism that automatically leads to the forgetting of unwanted memories (for example Erdelyi 1990; Holmes 1990). Still others defined repression in terms of a particular outcome, i.e. profound forgetting of traumatic life events (for example Ofshe and Watters 1994). In our view the field might be well served if the term repression were dropped altogether and replaced with less loaded and more precisely defined terms.

help account for recovered memories such as repression (for example Erdelyi 1990), dissociation (for example Spiegel and Cardena 1991), or trauma-induced physiological processes (Southwick *et al.* 1993; van der Kolk 1988) have not been well examined within the framework of cognitive psychology, making them difficult for cognitive psychologists to accept. However, cognitive psychology is not so advanced that we can assume that we understand all of the basic mechanisms involved in the complexities of autobiographical memory. Given the current limitations in our understanding of autobiographical memory, we should be most cautious in discounting possible mechanisms that go beyond the fray of our existing knowledge. This is not to say that the specialized mechanisms that have been proposed to date are necessarily the correct ones, merely that we should keep our minds open to the possibility that some, perhaps yet to be defined, mechanism(s) may be critically involved in this remarkable type of memory experience. After all, scientific advances are riddled with examples of instances in which the phenomenon preceded an understanding of the mechanisms underlying it.

CONCLUSION

Summary

In this chapter we have attempted to demonstrate that both fabricated and recovered memories are likely to correspond to real phenomena. With respect to fabricated memories, there is now a large body of research documenting the ease with which memory can be distorted and the extent to which individuals can come to remember fantastic events that are highly unlikely to have occurred. When these properties of memory are combined with the suggestive memory techniques known to be used in therapy, the possibility of the formation of memory fabrications becomes quite real.

With respect to recovered memories, we offered four case studies of recovered memory accounts for which we were able to provide independent corroborative evidence, suggesting that the memories did in fact correspond to actual incidents of abuse. We believe that these cases provide an existence proof for at least the phenomenological reality of recovered memory experience; i.e. that the experience of suddenly remembering an incident of sexual abuse that is believed to have been previously forgotten can in fact correspond to a real incident. A brief analysis of the possible mechanisms leading to such phenomenological experiences suggests that they may be the result of some standard, and some perhaps less standard, cognitive mechanisms. With respect to standard mechanisms, it seems quite clear that in all four cases recovery was initiated by cues sharing some significant similarities with the original experience, thus strongly implicating the possible role of encoding specificity. The startling quality of the recovered experiences and their emotional potency (also exhibited in all four cases) further suggests the possible role of processes akin to those leading to 'a-ha' insight experiences, and perhaps also associated with the emotional flooding of traumatic PTSD flashbacks.

Although we have provided what we believe to be compelling evidence for the validity of the phenomenological experience of recovered memories, our evidence for the extent of the prior forgetting was less clear cut. On the one hand, several of our cases provided at least suggestive evidence that actual forgetting may have occurred. On the other hand, other cases provided strong evidence that individuals can underestimate the extent of their prior memory leading to our suggestion of a 'forgot-it-all-along' effect analogous to the 'knew-it-all-along' effect, except that individuals underestimate rather than overestimate their prior knowledge state. We hope that this example of a likely role of a memory distortion processes in at least partially accounting for recovered memories may help cognitive psychologists to more readily conceptualize and ultimately accept recovered memories as a real phenomenon. Recovery experiences corresponding to authentic memories may well be viewed as yet another example of the distorting quality of memory that cognitive psychologists have so effectively documented over the years. In some cases, these distortions may not surround the original memory itself, but rather individuals' recollection of their subsequent self-knowledge of that experience. Other potential memory distortion factors may include, directed forgetting, reinterpretation, ego maintenance, and/or some other yet-to-be-discovered sources of memory impairment.

Two looming questions

Having argued that there is good reason to believe in *both* fabricated and authentic recovered memories, two difficult questions naturally arise:(1) Which is the more likely?, and(2) How can we distinguish between them? Determining the relative incidence of authentic and fabricated recovered memories will probably never be fully possible because we can never be certain about memories for which there is no corroboration. At the same time, future careful and systematic studies using well defined sampling techniques and independent corroboration of abuse could at least provide some bottom line estimates. Moreover, by comparing the frequency of memory corroboration for individuals drawn from different populations, such as patients of therapists using more and less suggestive memory techniques, we could begin to get a sense of the relative likelihood that recovered memories are the product of suggestion. Of course, even if it is possible to establish some approximate figures for the frequency with which recovered memories correspond to actual versus fabricated abuse, this still would be of only modest help for individuals who believe themselves to have recovered memories of abuse. If the above corroborative case analyses were conducted, we might begin to identify certain characteristics that tend to distinguish corroboratable versus non-corroboratable memories, for example whether or not they were induced in the context of suggestive therapy. In the present study, all four corroborated recovered memories occurred outside of therapy and were associated with marked surprise. It might well turn out that these attributes are particularly associated with corroboratable recovered memories, and hence might serve as possible indicators of a memory's likely authenticity. However, even if such associations are found they are unlikely to perfectly distinguish real from fabricated memories (cf. Schooler *et al.* 1986). Thus, in the absence of actual corroborative evidence, science may never be able to tell an individual for certain whether his/her memory is real or simply the product of fabrication. Such an individual, like the field as a whole, may have to come to accept the fundamental ontological uncertainty of many recovered memories.

Final remark

In this chapter we have tried to maintain a balanced perspective, to objectively document the evidence as we see it, to highlight what we consider the strengths and weaknesses of each source. Despite our efforts, we recognize that some will remain unpersuaded because 'remarkable claims require remarkable evidence' (Brewer personal communication). This basic epistemological observation gets right to the heart of this debate since the claims of each side might be seen by some as implausible. Some might find it difficult to conceive that vivid and detailed memories of sexual abuse could simply be fabricated, while others might find it harder to accept the notion that experiences of sexual abuse could be forgotten and then suddenly remembered. Which of these two views is seen as more remarkable may powerfully influence how one perceives the evidence and thus further fuel the polarization on this topic.

It is our hope that we have begun to illustrate how both sides of this issue become at least a little less remarkable when considered in the context of the well known fallibility of memory. If individuals can remember bizarre events such as being abducted by space aliens, why is it all that much more remarkable that individual might falsely remember being sexually abused? If memory for events is so vulnerable to distortion, then why shouldn't knowledge about what one remembers also be vulnerable to distortions. In the end, recovered memories of both fabricated and actual events may come to be understood as different examples of the many remarkable ways in which memory can misrepresent and obfuscate the past.

ACKNOWLEDGEMENTS

The writing of this chapter was supported by a grant to the first author from the National Institute of Mental Health. We thank Stephen Fiore, Stephen Lindsay,

Elizabeth Loftus, George Mandler, Tonya Schooler, and Joseph Melcher for their helpful comments on earlier drafts.

REFERENCES

Allport, G.W. and Postman, L.J. (1947). *The psychology of rumor*. Henry Holt, New York.

Anderson, R.C. and Pitcher, J.W. (1978). Recall of previously unrecallable information following a shift in perspective. *Journal of Verbal Learning and Verbal Behavior*, **17**, 1–12.

American Psychological Association. (1996). *Working Group on Investigation of Memories of Childhood Abuse*, final report. Washington, D.C.

Atkinson, R.C. and Shiffrin, R.M. (1968). Human memory: a proposed system and its control processes. In *The psychology of learning and motivation*, Vol. 2, (ed. K. Spence and J. Spence), pp. 89–195. Academic, New York.

Barnes, J.M. and Underwood, B.J. (1959). 'Fate' of first-list associations in transfer theory. *Journal of Experimental Psychology*, **58**, 97–105.

Bartlett, F.C. (1932). *Remembering*. Cambridge University Press.

Bass, E. and Davis, L. (1988). *The courage to heal: a guide for women survivors of child sexual abuse*. Harper and Row, New York.

Bjork, R.A. (1989). Retrieval inhibition as an adaptive mechanism in human memory. In *Varieties of memory and consciousness: essays in honour of Endel Tulving*, (ed. H.L. Roediger and F.I.M. Craik). pp. 309–30. Erlbaum, Hillsdale, NJ.

Blume, E.S. (1990). *Secret survivors: uncovering incest and its aftereffects in women*. Ballantine, New York.

Bottoms, B.L., Shaver, P.R., and Goodman, G.S. An analysis of ritualistic and religion related child abuse allegations. *Law and Human Behavior*. (In press.)

Bower, G.H. (1990). Awareness, the unconscious, and repression: an experimental psychologist's perspective. In *Repression and dissociation*, (ed. J.L. Singer), pp. 209–31. University of Chicago Press.

Briere, J. and Conte, J. (1993). Self-reported amnesia for abuse in adults molested as children. *Journal of Traumatic Stress*, **6**, 21–31.

Brown, D. (1995). Pseudomemories, the standard of science and the standard of care in trauma treatment. *American Journal of Clinical Hypnosis*, **37**, 3–29.

Brown, R. and Kulik, J. (1977). Flashbulb memories. *Cognition*, **5**, 73–99.

Ceci, S.J., Crotteau, M.L., Smith, E., and Loftus, E.F. (1994a). Repeatedly thinking about a nonevent: source misattributions among preschoolers. *Consciousness and Cognition*, **3**, 388–407.

Ceci, S.J., Loftus, E.F., Leichtman, M.D., and Bruck, M. (1994b). The possible role of source misattributions in the creation of false beliefs among preschoolers. *International Journal of Clinical and Experimental Hypnosis*, **42**, 304–20.

Christenson, R.M., Walker, J.I., Ross, D.R., and Maltbie, A. (1981). Reactivation of traumatic conflicts. *American Journal of Psychiatry*, **138**, 984–5.

Conway, M.A. and Rubin, D.C. (1993). The structure of autobiographical memory. In *Theories of memory*, (ed. A.F. Collins, S.E. Gathercole, M.A. Conway, and P.E. Morris), pp. 103–37. Erlbaum, Hove, East Sussex.

Dawes, R.M. (1989). Experience and the validity of clinical judgment: the illusory correlation. *Behavioral Sciences and the Law*, **7**, 457–67.

Dawes, R.M. (1994). *The house of cards*. Maxwell Macmillan Canada, Toronto.

Dodd, D.H. and Bradshaw, J.M. (1980). Leading questions and memory: pragmatic constraints. *Journal of Verbal Learning and Verbal Behavior*, **19**, 695–704.

Ebbinghaus, H. (1913). *Memory: a contribution to experimental psychology*. Columbia Teacher's College, New York.

Erdelyi, M.H. (1990). Repression, reconstruction, and defense: history and integration of the psychoanalytic and experimental frameworks. In *Repression and dissociation*, (ed. J.L. Singer), pp. 1–31. University of Chicago Press.

Erdelyi, M.H. and Kleinbard (1978). Has Ebbinghaus decayed with time? The growth of recall (hypermnesia) over days. *Journal of Experimental Psychology: Human Learning and Memory*, **4**, 275–89.

Femina, D.D., Yeager, C.A., and Lewis, D.O. (1990). Child abuse: adolescent records vs. adult recall. *Child Abuse and Neglect*, **14**, 227–31.

Fischoff, B. (1982). For those condemned to study the past: heuristics and biases in hindsight. In *Judgment under uncertainty: Heuristics and biases*, (ed. D. Kahneman, P. Slovic, and A. Tversky), pp. 335–51. Cambridge University Press, New York.

Freud, S. (1940). Sketches for the preliminary communication of 1893. In *The standard edition of the complete psychological works of Sigmund Freud*, (ed. J. Strachey), **1**, 145–54. Hogarth Press, London.

Freyd, J.J. (1994). Betrayal trauma: traumatic amnesia as an adaptive response to childhood abuse. *Ethics and Behavior*, **4**, 307–29.

Garry, M., Loftus, E.F., and Brown, S.W. (1995). Memory: a river runs through it. Special issue: the recovered memory/false memory debate. *Consciousness & Cognition: An International Journal*, **3**, 438–51.

Gick, M.L. and Lockhart, R.S. (1995). Cognitive and affective components of insight. *In the nature of insight*, (ed. R.J. Sternberg and J.E. Davidson), pp. 197–228. MIT Press, Cambridge, MA.

Gleaves, D.H. (1994). On 'The reality of repressed memories'. *American Psychologist*, **49**, 440–1.

Gold, S.N., Hughes, D., and Hohnecker, L. (1994). Degrees of repression of sexual abuse memories. *American Psychologist*, **49**, 441–2.

Goldstein, E. and Farmer, K. (ed.). (1993). *True stories of false memories*. Sirs Publishing, Boca Raton, FL.

Greenwald, A.G. (1980). The totalitarian ego: fabrication and revision of personal history. *American Psychologist*, **35**, 603–18.

Gudjonsson, G.H. (1992). *The psychology of interrogations, confessions and testimony*. Wiley, New York.

Haaken, J. and Schlaps, A. (1991). Incest resolution therapy and the objectification of sexual abuse. *Psychotherapy*, **28**, 39–47.

Harvey, M.R. and Herman, J.L. (1994). Amnesia, partial amnesia and delayed recall among adult survivors of childhood trauma. *Consciousness and Cognition*, **3**, 295–306.

Herman, J.L. and Schatzow, E. (1987). Recovery and verification of memories of childhood sexual trauma. *Psychoanalytic Psychology*, **4**, 1–14.

Holmes, D. (1990). The evidence for repression: an examination of sixty years of research. In *Repression and dissociation: implications for personality theory, psychotherapy, and health*, (ed. J. Singer), pp. 85–102. The University of Chicago Press.

Horn, M. (1993). Memories lost and found. *U.S. News and World Report*, November 29, 53–63.

Hyman, I.E. (1995). False memories of childhood experiences. *Applied Cognitive Psychology*, **9**, 181–97.

Hyman, I.E., Jr. and Billings, F.J. (1995). Individual differences and the creation of false childhood memories. (Submitted).

Johnson, M.K., Hashtroudi, S., and Lindsay, D.S. (1993). Source monitoring. *Psychological Bulletin*, **114**, 3–28.

Johnson, M.K. and Raye, C.L. (1981). Reality monitoring. *Psychological Review*, **85**, 67–85.

Lanning, K.V. (1989). Satanic, occult, ritualistic crime: a law enforcement perspective. *The Police Chief*, October, 62–83.

Lewis, H.B. (1990). Shame, repression, field dependence, and psychopathology. In *Repression and dissociation*, (ed. J.L. Singer), pp. 233–57. University of Chicago Press.

Lindsay, D.S. (1994). Contextualizing and clarifying criticisms of memory work. Special issue: the recovered memory/false memory debate. *Consciousness & Cognition: An International Journal*, **3**, 426–37.

Lindsay, D.S. and Read, J.D. (1994). Psychotherapy and memories of child sexual abuse: a cognitive perspective. *Applied Cognitive Psychology*, **8**, 281–338.

Lindsay, D.S. and Read, J.D. (1995). 'Memory work' and recovered memories of childhood sexual abuse: scientific evidence and public, professional, and personal issues. *Psychology, Public Policy, and Law*, **1**, 846–908.

Loftus, E.F. (1993). The reality of repressed memories. *American Psychologist*, **48**, 518–37.

Loftus, E. and Ketcham, K. (1994). *The myth of repressed memory: false memories and allegations of sexual abuse*. St Martin's Press, New York.

Loftus, E.F., Miller, D.G., and Burns, H.J. (1978). Semantic integration of verbal information into visual memory. *Journal of Experimental Psychology: Human Learning and Memory*, **4**, 19–31.

Loftus, E.F., Donders, K., Hoffmann, H.G., and Schooler, J.W. (1989a). Creating new memories that are quickly accessed and confidently held. *Memory and Cognition*, **17**, 607–16.

Loftus, E.F., Korf, N., and Schooler, J.W. (1989b). Misguided memories: sincere distortions of reality. In *Credibility assessment: a theoretical and research perspective*, (ed. J. Yuille), pp. 155–74. Klumer, Boston.

Loftus, E.F., Garry, M., and Feldman, J. (1994a). Forgetting sexual trauma: what does it mean when 38% forget? *Journal of Consulting and Clinical Psychology*, **62**, (6), 117–81.

Loftus, E.F., Polonsky, S., and Fullilove, M.T. (1994b). Memories of childhood sexual abuse: remembering and repressing. *Psychology of Women Quarterly*, **18**, (1), 67–84.

Malmquist, C.P. (1986). Children who witness parental murder: post traumatic aspects. *Journal of the American Academy of Child Psychiatry*, **25**, 320–5.

Mandler, G. (1995). The abuse of repression. *Applied Cognitive Psychology*, **9**, 539–41.

McGee, R. (1984). Flashbacks and memory phenomena. *Journal of Nervous and Mental Disease*, **174**, 4–14.

McGeoch, J.H. (1942). *The psychology of human learning*. Longmans, Green, New York.

Milgram, S. (1963). Behavioral study of obedience. *Journal of Abnormal and Social Psychology*, **67**, 371–8.

Morton, J. (1994). Cognitive perspectives on memory recovery. *Applied Cognitive Psychology*, **8**, 389–98.

Neisser, U. (1981). John Dean's Memory: a case study. *Cognition*, **9**, 1–22.

Nelson, K. (1993). The psychological and social origins of autobiographical memory. *Psychological Science*, **4**, 1–8.

Ofshe, R. and Watters, E. (1994). *Making monsters: false memories, psychotherapy, and sexual hysteria*. Scribners, New York.

Olio, K.A. (1994). Truth in memory. *American Psychologist*, **49**, 442–3.

Orne, M.T. (1979). The use and misuse of hypnosis in court. *International Journal of Clinical and Experimental Hypnosis*, **27**, 311–41.

Pasley, L.E. (1993). Misplaced trust. In *True stories of false memories*, (ed. E. Goldstein and K. Farmer), pp. 347–65. Sirs Publishing, Boca Raton, FL.

Persinger, M.A. (1992). Neuropsychological profiles of adults who report 'Sudden remembering' of early childhood memories: implications for claims of sex abuse and alien visitation/abduction experiences. *Perceptual and Motor Skills*, **75**, 259–66.

Pezdek, K. and Roe, C. (1994). Memory of childhood events: how suggestible is it? *Consciousness and Cognition*, **3**, 374–87.

Polusny, M.A. and Follette, V.M. (1996). Remembering childhood sexual abuse: a national survey of psychologists' clinical practices, beliefs, and personal experiences. *Professional Psychology: Research and Practice*, **27**,(1), 41–52.

Poole, D.A., Lindsay, D.S., Memon, A., and Bull, R. (1995). Psychotherapy and the recovery of memories of childhood sexual abuse: U.S. and British practitioners beliefs, practices, and experiences. *Journal of Consulting and Clinical Psychology*, **63**, 426–37.

Raaijmakers, J.G. and Shiffrin, R.M. (1981). Search of associative memory. *Psychological Review*, **88**, 93–134.

Ross, M. (1989). Relation of implicit theories to the construction of personal histories. *Psychological Review*, **96**, (2), 341–57.

Schachter, D. L. (1995). Memory wars. *Scientific American*, April, 134–9.

Schank, R.C. and Abelson, R. (1977). *Scripts, plans, goals, and understanding*. Erlbaum, Hillsdale, NJ.

Schooler, J. (1994). Seeking the core: issues and evidence surrounding recovered accounts of sexual trauma. *Consciousness and Cognition*, **3**, 452–69.

Schooler, J.W. and Loftus, E.F. (1993) Multiple mechanisms mediate individual differences in eyewitness accuracy and suggestibility. In *Mechanisms of everyday cognition* (ed. J.M. Puckett and H.W. Reese), pp. 177–203. Erlbaum, Hillsdale, NJ.

Schooler, J.W. and Melcher, J.M. (1995). The ineffability of insight. In *The creative cognition, approach*, (ed. S.M. Smith, T.B. Ward, and R.A. Rinke), p. 351. MIT Press, Cambridge, MA.

Schooler, J.W., Gerhard, D., and Loftus, E.F. (1986). Qualities of the unreal. *Journal of Experimental Psychology: Learning, Memory, and Cognition*, **12**, 71–181.

Schooler, J.W., Clark, C.A., and Loftus, E.F. (1988). Knowing when memory is real. In *Practical aspects of memory*, (ed. M. Grueneberg, P. Morris, and R. N. Sykes), pp. 83–8. Wiley, New York.

Schooler, J.W., Fallshore, M.F., and Fiore, S.M. (1995). Epilogue: putting insight into perspective. In *The nature of insight*, (ed. R.J. Sternberg and J.E. Davidson), pp. 559–87. MIT Press, Cambridge, MA.

Southwick, S., Krystal, S.M., Morgan, J.H., Andrew, C., and Johnson, D. (1993). Abnormal noradrenergic function in posttraumatic stress disorder. *Archives of General Psychiatry*, **50**, (4), 266–74.

Spiegel, D. and Cardena, E. (1991). Disintegrated experience: the dissociative disorders revisited. *Journal of Abnormal Psychology*, **100**, 366–78.

Sternberg, R.J. and Davidson, J.E. (ed.). (1995). *The nature of insight*. MIT Press, Cambridge, MA.

Tulving, E. and Thompson, D.M. (1973). Encoding specificity and retrieval processes in episodic memory. *Psychological Review*, **80**, 352–73.

Underwood, B.J. (1967). Interference and forgetting. In *Human learning and memory: selected readings*, (ed. N.J. Slamecka), pp. 3–13. Oxford University Press, New York.

van der Kolk, B. (1988). The trauma spectrum: the interaction of biological and social events in the genesis of trauma response. *Journal of Traumatic Stress*, **1**, 273–90.

Wagenaar, W.A. (1986). My memory: a study of autobiographical memory over six years. *Cognitive Psychology*, **18**, 225–52.

Williams, C.C. (1983). The mental foxhole: the Vietnam veteran's search for meaning. *American Journal of Orthopsychiatry*, **53**, 1, 4–17.

Williams, L.M. Recall of childhood trauma: a prospective study of womens' memories of child sexual abuse. *Journal of Consulting and Clinical Psychology*. (In press.)

Wilson, T.D. and Brekke, N. (1995). Mental contamination and mental correction. unwanted influences on judgments and evaluations. *Psychological Bulletin*, **116**, (1), 117–42.

Yapko, M. (1994). *Suggestions of abuse: real and imagined memories*. Simon & Schuster, New York.

Index

WARNER MEMORIAL LIBRARY
EASTERN COLLEGE
ST. DAVIDS, PA. 19087